MEDIA AND IDENTITY IN AFRICA

INTERNATIONAL AFRICAN SEMINARS

New Series

MEDIA AND IDENTITY IN AFRICA

EDITED BY
Kimani Njogu and **John Middleton**

Edinburgh University Press
for the
INTERNATIONAL AFRICAN INSTITUTE

Edinburgh University Press Ltd
22 George Square, Edinburgh

Distributed in East Africa by
Twaweza Communications Ltd
P.O. Box 66872-00800 Westlands
Twaweza House, Parklands Road
Mpesi Lane, Nairobi, Kenya

Typeset in Plantin 10/12 pt
by Servis Filmsetting Ltd, Stockport, Cheshire, and
printed and bound in Great Britain by
CPI Antony Rowe, Chippenham and Eastbourne

The publication of this book was made possible
by a grant from the Ford Foundation, Office
of Eastern Africa.

A CIP record for this book is available from the British Library

ISBN 978 0 7486 3522 1 (hardback)

CONTENTS

CONTRIBUTORS

Abdalla Uba Adamu, Centre for Hausa Cultural Studies, Kano, Nigeria

Eric Masinde Aseka, Department of History, Archaeology and Political Studies, Kenyatta University, Nairobi, Kenya

Kelly Askew, Department of Anthropology, University of Michigan, Ann Arbor, USA

Karin Barber, Centre of West African Studies, University of Birmingham, UK

Heike Behrend, Institut für Afrikanistik, Universität Köln, Cologne, Germany

Walter Bgoya, Mkuki na Nyota Publishers, Dar es Salaam, Tanzania

Ann Biersteker, Center of African Studies, Yale University, New Haven, USA

Diane M. Ciekawy, Associate Professor of Anthropology and African Studies, Ohio University, USA

John Collins, Department of Music, University of Ghana, Legon, Accra, Ghana

Patrick Gathara, General Secretary, Association of East African Cartoonists, Nairobi, Kenya

Michelle Gilbert, Trinity College, Hartford, USA

Cecilia Kimani, Programme Officer with the Legal Resources Foundation, Nairobi, Kenya

Alamin Mazrui, Department of African American and African Studies, College of Humanities, Ohio State University, USA

Birgit Meyer, Department of Anthropology, University of Amsterdam, The Netherlands

John Middleton, Departments of Anthropology and Religious Studies, Yale University, New Haven, USA

Valentin Y. Mudimbe, Duke University, Durham, USA

Macharia Munene, Department of History and International Politics, US International University, Nairobi, Kenya

Mbugua wa Mungai, Department of Literature, Kenyatta University, Nairobi, Kenya

Bantu Mwaura, Department of Performance Studies, New York State University, USA

Goretti Linda Nassanga, Mass Communications Department, Makerere University, Kampala, Uganda

Charles Ngome, Department of Educational Foundations, Kenyatta University, Nairobi, Kenya

Kimani Njogu, Director, Twaweza Communications, Nairobi. Formerly, Associate Professor of African languages, Kenyatta University, Nairobi, Kenya

Francis Nyamnjoh, Head of Publications and Communications, CODESRIA, Dakar, Senegal

Simiyu Wandibba, Institute of African Studies, University of Nairobi, Nairobi, Kenya

Mary Kabura Wanjau, Programme Officer, Africa Health and Development International (AHADI), Nairobi, Kenya

John Kiarie Wa'Njogu, Center for African Studies, Yale University, New Haven, USA

Paul Tiyambe Zeleza, Departments of African Studies and History, Pennsylvania State University, University Park, Pennsylvania, USA

PROLOGUE

This brief Prologue is to introduce a collection of papers given at a seminar held in Nairobi, Kenya, from 3 to 7 August 2004, on the topic 'Media and the Construction of Identity in Africa'. A wide view of the seminar is given by its Chairman, Professor Valentin Y. Mudimbe, in his Epilogue at the end of the book. Here we attempt to summarize some of the arguments put forward by the participants at the seminar itself and later put into writing by them (all have been slightly edited for presentation in book format).

The seminar was the most recent of a long series of meetings held in Africa by the International African Institute, London, and was funded by the Ford Foundation, Office of Eastern Africa. The Institute was founded in London in 1926, as a research and publishing organization independent of governmental, missionary, or commercial control. Its main aim has been to disseminate knowledge about an ever-changing Africa whose people have all too often been regarded in Europe and America as culturally, intellectually, and morally inferior; a view linked to colonialism, to the modern political, financial, and commercial dependence of most African countries on the West, and to sheer ignorance. The Institute has for three-quarters of a century combatted that view and has demonstrated the formerly unrecognized qualities and importance of African civilizations to the rest of the world. An important part of its programme has been to organize seminars at various universities in Africa and to publish the papers presented at them. The long-term aim has been to advance knowledge, that comes from within Africa, of African societies, their cultures, their languages, and the many problems that face them, and to bring together African and non-African scholars so as to construct a common understanding of these problems and to emphasize the commonality of Africans and non-Africans in the world.

This particular seminar was also planned to reflect postcolonial changes in academic scholarship and specialization. With an ever-increasing number of African scholars themselves working in various parts of Africa, it included more participants from the local region – in this case, eastern Africa – than had been usual in the past. Former seminars had included local observers, but they had been marginal. We decided to transform them into participants, and to include people working outside universities – in publishing, radio, government and other occupations. Finally, we opened the seminar to the public rather than to a solely academic audience. Several hundred local observers attended the formal panels, participated in discussions, and came to the informal meetings of the seminar held not in a local university but in a hotel where all could come. The proceedings were also reported in the local press and by radio and television stations. This seminar was a deliberate and pioneering effort to link 'academics', 'practitioners', and 'the public'.

THE 'NEW' AFRICA AND IDENTITY

Most previous International African Institute seminars had been on often rather limited and 'academic' subjects; here the emphasis was on a wider and more obviously contemporary and political topic. 'Media and the Construction of Identity' reflected both the growing importance of the process rather clumsily known as 'globalization', and also the widespread local concern in, hope for, and, often, fear of the so-called 'media' in a time of often rapid and unexpected construction of new social and cultural identities throughout Africa. These days there is nowhere in Africa whose local people are not affected by the 'media' in one form or another.

Discussions, books, and conferences on the media have become popular during the last few years, almost all concerned with the place of the media in American and European societies, but with little attention given to Africa. There have been discussions on the provision and promotion of the internet and computers in Africa, but few have considered the crucial role of African cultures and enterprises in this venture. Africa is seen primarily as a target for Northern technology and commerce but rarely as a continent largely lacking in the material means required for their use. There is a major focus on elites and their interests, but little concern with the mass of the people and their problems, most of which are linked to poverty. This reflects a bias in most 'development projects', which, whatever their ostensible purpose to help the underprivileged, in practice are usually controlled by powerful and wealthy urban elites. Few development strategies have been informed by the immediate needs of people in rural areas, or work through the various cultures of a region to address those needs. Development paradigms designed in the West are inappropriately transplanted to an Africa of which national and international understanding is typically woefully inadequate, and the same may be said of the media.

Today the various media bring about both the formation of new social systems and identities, the maintenance or reshaping of existing ones, and frequently the destruction of believed 'traditional' ones. Those outside Africa who initiate and control most media assume that their African recipients are essentially similar to those of Europe and America. In addition, their approach takes the elites – and the urban elites at that – as the norm, and ignores the nature of the majority of the varied and ever-changing social groups and networks in both urban and rural Africa. It is not merely a problem of the relationship between an intrusive global culture and a passively receiving local one. Many forms of media in eastern Africa have local origins, but their importance is rarely recognized. Many are based upon 'traditional' forms of cultural expression that are no longer purely local but are adaptations of wider African themes. Examples include commentaries of the Bible and the Qu'ran, traditional and new forms of literature, music, art, clothing, even foods. Therefore the seminar's emphasis was on the natures and needs of African societies and their cultures and on local societies' responses to media influences and saturation, rather than on media technologies.

Most of the companies that produce and control the media invent their own versions of both global and local cultures. They produce new worlds of experience and imagination, especially in representations of religious alienation and military violence. Whatever the overt aims of those who control the media, those who receive its communications use them for their own various purposes, political, social, religious, which are often opposed to and not even comprehended by the controllers. There are usually two levels of communication in media messages, and all messages from originators' to recipients' media have responses by the latter, some overt and others concealed. Most of the chapters that follow discuss these structures of messages of the various media that affect local African societies.

Many of the media, such as television, are usually considered as worldwide in their culture and impact, yet television is visible to only a small minority of those living in Africa. The internet reaches only a minute proportion of African urban dwellers and virtually none outside the elite of the larger cities. Radio reaches the majority, newspapers and films reach a fair part of the total population, and religious works also affect the majority. However, newspapers, radio, and television are today also initiated within Africa itself, frequently for very small, local audiences. The situation is far more complicated than has often been assumed, and the seminar participants were all involved in one way or another with this complexity.

The media, whether global or local, represent ways of living and provide models of how one might appropriately relate with others, as well as how recognition, status, honour, and prestige are given or withheld. Newspapers and magazines may, for example, ridicule or ignore certain sectors of society and promote – or occasionally attack – the ideas of the powerful economic or social classes. Information packaging may be skewed in order to pursue certain goals, and certain truths may be withheld. The media play an important role in the processes of entrenching public consent because media texts can construct definitions which are then presented as 'reality'. These constructions are guided mainly by the politically powerful as well as by commercial media owners. A consequence of this process is the emergence of alternative media which are distinct from the mainstream. As an example, media liberalization in Africa has led to the growth of privately owned FM stations, especially in the urban areas. FM radio stations are faster paced than the government stations, and more often than not target youth as well as the middle class. They play hip-hop music, composed locally or internationally, and they pay particular attention to sports. Because they play popular international music and are financially assisted by private advertisers, they link the youth of Africa with the youth of other nations and contribute to the growth of global youth identity and culture. In contrast, community radio stations, such as Bush Radio in South Africa, target rural populations or those in poor settlements. Their content, including news, music, advertisements and discussion programmes, is predominantly local and informational.

A major medium for the perpetuation of moral values is, of course, religion. Religious organizations have continued to expand their media outlets from the Bible and the Qu'ran to street preaching, outdoor rallies, video production, radio and television broadcasts, and religious magazines and newspapers with limited circulation. Different religions in Africa have distinct symbols and markers ranging from dress codes to greeting rituals.

In brief, the participants considered the impact of the media on everyday African social, cultural, political and religious life, and the identities both of those who control and also those who are directly and indirectly affected by them. The seminar was not on popular culture *per se* in modern African societies, but essentially on the impact of world capitalism upon African societies at the local level and the latter's responses. The media in this era of globalization may seek to challenge cultures and reframe identities: how does this happen and what is the impact of this configuration? The participants discussed the fluidity of identity formation and how local communities renegotiate their identities in the face of changing circumstances; and they examined how the media can accentuate or deny loyalty to ethnic identities and the implication of such accentuation and denial.

The Epilogue, by the Chairman of the International African Institute, Professor V. Y. Mudimbe, presents an original and deep analysis of what took place at the seminar. The author, a distinguished philosopher, is renowned for his many writings. Especially relevant to the seminar, of course, is his work on the images and the inventions of 'Africa', a concept too often taken for granted without any very clear understanding of what it has meant at different times and to different people. The author discusses the consequences of the activities of the media as experienced in Africa, and suggests the shallowness of the common view of the media bringing 'globalization', even 'civilization', from the 'North' to the 'South', essentially a continuing form of the invention of 'Africa', and an historical process of great complexity. It is a conflict between the global and the local that is not invariably won by the global interests – local interests always fight back.

THE MESSAGES: CONSTRUCTION AND CREATIVITY

At first glance the following chapters may appear too wide-ranging, even too disparate, to form a consistent body of discussion. More consideration shows that they present diverse ways of dealing with the problems of achieving identities based not on the periods of colonialism and immediate post-colonialism but on an unclearly defined 'Africa', of which various meanings have been invented by both non-Africans and Africans. The chapters that follow the Introduction are grouped into three sections. The first section includes chapters on 'the media, community, and identity'. They discuss the history of the media in Africa and the problems of defining new communities and their identities as affected by the media. The media can be used for social change, but in a world that is undergoing intense polarization, they can be used to alienate communities and deny them opportunities for their voices to be heard. The immediate problems discussed in these first chapters include the effects of colonial institutions and the establishment of forms of government over citizens whose wishes may be different from those of their rulers; the nature of social groups and institutions which have endured through colonialism and globalization; and the means of communication – the 'media' – necessary to be controlled by ordinary people rather than by outside commercial and other interests if new national and local groups and identities are to be linked to still persistent 'traditional' cultures. These chapters attempt to define or redefine the meanings of processes such as 'nationalism', 'tribalism' and 'tribalization', territorial, political and cultural boundaries, commercialization, and all the other aspects of 'identity'.

The other two sections are on the media themselves, the first on the global media and the second on the less familiar local media, not only as responses to the former but with histories and cultural meanings in their own right that show their complexity and vibrancy. We may conveniently distinguish global and local media, a distinction both between the nature and content of media and also between their originators and recipients, although the categories are hardly exact. First we may discern the global media: books, newspapers, world-made films, radio, television. Then we may discern local media at any given point in history: local literature, poetry, music, clothing, naming, local news reporting, advertisements, cartoons, bus painting, and so on.

The basic questions discussed by the authors of these chapters are 'what do the media do in Africa?' and 'how do they work?'. The answers are found by presenting ethnographic examples of a wide range of media, some literally coming from outside Africa, and others emerging from within it. During the seminar itself, the two means of communication were considered as leading to certain consequences, 'creativity' leading to 'construction'.

By 'creativity' we refer both to local responses to the global media and to the invention and control of media by local people. What is meant by the word 'construction'? Can identity be 'constructed' at all, and if so by whom? How deliberate or conscious a process is it? Can it be constructed by outsiders – the controllers of the media – or only by local people who receive, and pay for, the media initiated and controlled by others? The participants of the seminar generally assumed the meaning of 'identity' to be the sense of belonging to almost any kind of social group that has some form of self-identification: an ethnic, language or cultural group, a nation, member of a continent or local area, a category of people with a common cultural, political or religious aim. All are defined by their members and by outsiders. These outsiders were, at one time, the colonial rulers; today they are usually the controllers of a national government. Identity is shown to be a consequence of many factors and is continually shifting and under constant negotiation. Many writers on the effects of the Western-controlled media, as part of the process of globalization, maintain that the process of identity formation involves, even necessitates, the standardization or homogenization of all cultures and societies wherever they are. Many of the participants expressed doubts that this is necessary or even possible, and presented arguments for ongoing cultural diversity and divergence.

Yet all participants explicitly or implicitly argued that 'construction of identity' means making or retaining the sense of cohesion of the members of a moral community, whether a bounded group or merely a category of some kind. Such a community or category must have common interest and morality, and must be able to control conflict and disharmony. It seems impossible to do so altogether, but one seemingly universal way of doing so is to find culturally accepted means of expressing conflict and disagreement that obviate openly expressed violence and that do in fact form ties between latent enemies, the so-called 'peace in the feud'. One such way is, of course, the performance of ritual directed towards a deity or ancestor, as worship in a congregation, monastery or convent, or worship of a new deity held by a particular sect. Another way is to avoid open hostility by use of certain forms of communication in which words or other messages are understood by all involved but are expected not to lead to violence; examples include Swahili songs and the use of cloth and personal names in southern Ghana.

These and other examples described refer to the avoidance of personal violence in societies which are both literate and where literary competence is given high praise and is held as an essential quality of citizenship, usually based on 'correctness' of ancestry, of rank, and of 'good manners'. They are of communities and categories with an agreed-upon single history (even if mythical) and morality: they are already 'constructed' or are in the process of being so. They are aware of change and of threats from outside, and of the fact that some of their members welcome change or 'development' and others do not. 'Change' here was once called 'colonialization'; today it is called 'globalization'. In the former case those against it were called 'tribal', in the latter we prefer to speak of 'local'. The participants largely analyzed the nature, purpose and reception of the various media found in Africa in these terms.

A point made by many of the contributors is that of the dissolution of mainly formal 'Western' boundaries of behaviour, language, art, music and comedy, and their creative mingling to compose new forms and cultural ambivalences and ambiguities. Boundaries are broken, and newness and freshness are introduced. Nothing remains the same after it comes into contact with another. Although it is often held that globalization is cultur-ally and socially an overwhelmingly uniform process, this Euro- and Americo-centric view is neither correct nor illuminating. It is today occa-sionally fashionable to dismiss the social and cultural variety of African civ-ilizations as old-fashioned, linked to 'ethnographical exoticism' and the like. This viewpoint is held by those who, even now, find it difficult to see 'Africa' in terms other than of colonialization and decolonialization and who fail to see the strength of intra-African variation. It comes out very clearly from these chapters that to study 'globalization' we still need to study the local: if media help to construct identities, these are very local ones with an immense range of detail. The people of any region may have to accept 'Western' media, but they nonetheless are able to change its many modes and forms to suit themselves (often to the annoyance of the media con-trollers), and they also use their own 'traditional' media to carry 'global' messages. To participate in globalization, in 'modernity', by linkage to the 'media', may include divergence from a 'world uniformity'. Indeed, as Mudimbe suggests, divergence is not only possible or probable – it may well be inevitable.

To understand better the significance of the distinction between 'global' and 'local', the participants discussed the aims of those who control them and the responses of those who receive them. The former do not only trans-mit their own wishes and viewpoints but aim to manipulate the thoughts and behaviour of the recipients; the latter may refuse to be manipulated and themselves become originators and transmitters of their own wishes and viewpoints and argue back. Media are both conduits and barriers. We may perhaps define the conduits as those controlled by those who also break and so abolish boundaries, and the barriers as those who make and mark boundaries. In the latter case, the messages are the weapons of the weak that are often unforeseen by the powerful. The seminar participants asked, often by implication only, what are the wishes of those who are, at first sight, judged to be weak. They also asked why and how do these people use the media as weapons? There are other possible weapons, such as the ballot box and ultimately rebellion. The use of the media in this way has occurred less often, although they are often – in the end perhaps, usually – the more successful choice.

All these matters were discussed not only by those who gave papers but also by members of the audience, who played a crucial (and perhaps rather unexpected) role. Among the most widely mentioned by both the formal participants and the audience were the reasons why journalists, as well as other writers, portray Africa as a hungry, ailing, and poor continent prone to internal conflicts and wars; that the links between modern African societies and those of the diaspora and of other links outside Africa, such as to most Muslim countries, are rarely discussed; that within Africa, more information is needed on the roles of governments and commercial interests, including degrees of censorship and the roles of the proprietors of media of all kinds; that there are important problems to do with local creativity in the media representations of African cultural behaviours, of language policies and practices, of music and art, of public means of cultural expression in advertising, in public transport, in cartoons, in forms of humour and obscenity, and in representations of gender and sexuality. In general, questions were raised about the aims and control of the media, their roles in processes of globalization, in local and international commerce, in problems of health, education, party politics, in the expenses needed to establish and practise the media by small local groups in the constantly changing political systems of the day, where some sections of national populations, especially women, the rural and the poor, are scarcely represented.

Finally, the seminar reflected the growing concern of international foundations and of the International African Institute to place the centre of African studies and scholarship within Africa. Three bodies were concerned in its planning and execution: the International Council of the Institute, in London; the Ford Foundation, through its representatives in Nairobi; and in Nairobi a private company, Twaweza Communications, established by one of the organizers, Dr Kimani Njogu, formerly a member of the Kenyan university community. This sharing of responsibility was new and successful. We owe thanks to Professor Tade Aina, the representative of the Ford

Foundation, Office of Eastern Africa, and Rob Burnet, programme officer, Ford Foundation; to the chairman and the then administrative director of the International African Institute, Professors V. Y. Mudimbe and Paul Spencer, and others of the Institute's staff – Elizabeth Dunstan, Sue Kibble, and William Burgess; to the staff of Twaweza Communications in Nairobi; and to Nancy Gratton for her careful, patient and sensitive editing.

Kimani Njogu and John Middleton

Note
John Middleton passed away on 27 February 2009 at Yale-New Haven Hospital just as this volume was going to press. He maintained a vigorous research and publishing life until his death, playing a full and active editorial role in the preparation of this book for publication into what turned out to be the final stages of his life. The volume brings together work from the IAI's programme of international seminars, of which he was a key advocate. It represents his last major project on Africa and his final intellectual and institutional contribution to the work of the IAI. It is a valedictory to us all.

PART I

THE MEDIA, COMMUNITY AND IDENTITY

1 Karin Barber

ORALITY, THE MEDIA AND NEW POPULAR CULTURES IN AFRICA

Print and electronic media have had profound transformative effects in African culture. Nor is this a recent result of late twentieth-century global flows. For more than 100 years, virtually all new popular cultural forms in Africa have been shaped by techniques and conceptions drawn from the media; while older oral genres have been subtly but definitively recast as they have been drawn into new performance spaces on the airwaves or in print. Most of what is now regarded as 'popular' – as distinct from 'traditional' – in African culture (see Barber 1987, 1997) was forged in colonial and post-colonial contexts deeply entwined with print, film, radio and later television and video. Most of what is regarded as 'traditional' has been in one way or another touched by these media too.

The 'cultural imperialism' thesis posits that the impact of the media on non-Western countries has been baleful, swamping indigenous cultural production, wiping out cherished traditions and force-feeding entire populations with cheap, meretricious American consumer culture. This has certainly been a cause for deep concern among progressive African policy makers, and should not be underestimated. Nonetheless, it is important to recognize the extent to which African cultural innovators have seized upon the possibilities of the media to revitalize their traditions and generate new forms. Real loss has gone hand in hand with intriguing gain. The rush to condemn or deny the impact of imported media has stood in the way of an empirically informed understanding of what people have actually done with these media, in different regions and moments in Africa's history. In contrast to the cultural imperialism thesis is the attractive argument that imported media open windows on to alternative lives, expanding people's conceptions of the possible and enhancing the role of the imagination in social life (Appadurai 1996). But this too needs to be weighed against the empirical evidence of what people in Africa actually do with the media.

Live, oral, improvised popular culture with traditional roots (that is, in some sense handed down from previous generations) has retained its vitality in most of Africa. It is a matter for investigation – investigation which has not been done, and is unlikely to be done within the framework of either of the approaches mentioned above – to find out to what extent locally-originated popular culture flourishes, and where it is being swamped and displaced. The assumption that the media are always experienced as exogenous to Africa – whether as imperialist aggression or as opportunities to enter new imaginative realms – needs to be questioned. The effects of media technology and representations can only be understood in relation to live, home-grown popular traditions and the long history of local appropriations, invasions and adaptations of imported media genres. This history began with print – newspapers in African languages, written and in some cases owned by Africans, have existed since the mid-nineteenth century. Then followed film: Charlie Chaplin movies, beamed out from portable projectors soon after the beginning of the twentieth century, fed into new, live, improvised forms such as Ghanaian concert party. Records of dance-band music, and of local transformations of it, circulated from the 1920s onwards, and their effect was magnified by the advent of radio. Waltzes, foxtrots, ragtimes, Charlestons and cha-cha-cha galvanized local musicians and were catalysts in the generation of new popular musical genres – highlife, juju, Congolese jazz, marabi. From the late 1950s, television began to provide a space in which new, local genres of drama took shape. Cassette recordings in the 1970s, video in the 1980s, and most recently the internet have successively stimulated new local genres and been absorbed into local popular culture. In short, media in much of Africa are not experienced as a recent and external force, but as a constitutive element in the formation of African popular culture from the early twentieth century onwards. What we think of as live, local popular culture in Africa was often inspired by new media technologies. Examples include popular print fiction which combines the conventions of the thriller, the romance and the folktale; music shaped by the possibilities of electronic amplification; popular art shaped by film posters and book or magazine illustrations; new forms of popular theatre which were stimulated by a two-way relationship with radio, television, film and video.

MEDIA INTERACTING WITH ORAL TRADITIONS

Across Africa, a number of 'media interventions' can be pinpointed. First, even when existing oral genres are simply broadcast 'as is', without any intentional modification, the media frame subtly transforms them. The text becomes a sign of something else – 'our tradition', conceptualized perhaps for the first time as a boundaried entity that can be described, documented and exemplified by selected public demonstrations. When the media are controlled by a centralizing multi-ethnic nation state, such performances may be presented as tesserae in the national cultural mosaic – 'contributions' to a larger, plural cultural whole. Or they may be treated, metonymically, as representatives of the entire cultural repertoire of the nation, or even of a whole region, as has happened with the Sunjata epic in Mali and Guinea. Alternatively, they may be understood as claims to recognition by a specific, bounded ethnic group – affirmations of autonomy, or even assertions of superiority in an ethnic-nationalist contest. The same broadcast may be taken to stand for different things, depending on the interests of the listeners. But however it is taken, no oral performance broadcast on national media can be a simple continuation of the mode of local, face-to-face performances.

Second, the media provided new means of learning and retaining oral genres. The apprentice who formerly sat at his master's feet for a decade now holds his audio-cassette recorder to his master's lips and then goes off to learn the text at his leisure. This technique may be valued as a way of preserving texts for posterity, and it may be continuous with recording for other purposes – broadcasting, commercial dissemination or private enjoyment. But equally, the recording may simply function as an aide-mémoire, discarded once the text has been mastered. An example of the latter scenario is the *gurna* songs of the Tupuri people of northern Cameroon (Ignatowski 2006). These long, complex songs are composed annually by specialist poets, learned by heart by the members of the *gurna* society during their seclusion in the bush, and subsequently performed in mass gatherings, first exclusively among *gurna* members and later to wider village audiences. Each *gurna* society sends a representative to its chosen poet to learn that year's song from him; in the past, by painstaking memorization, nowadays by turning on a tape recorder. The emissary returns to his *gurna* gathering and teaches the song to them. Once they have mastered it, the recording has no further relevance. The following year, a new song will be composed and learned, and the previous one will be allowed to fall into desuetude, remembered in fragments by people who found it particularly interesting. One could hypothesize that the 'media', in the form of the tape recorder, is simply a shortcut in a wholly traditional, oral pathway. The *gurna* society indeed represents, to local people, the defence of tradition against the onslaught of 'modern ways'. What is interesting, however, is the extent to which the *gurna* society members conceptualize their practice in terms derived from modern print and electronic media. When they take the performance out from seclusion in the bush to a wider village audience, they refer to 'publishing' the poem. They pride themselves on the speed and distance with which a successful performance will 'travel' out to other communities as audiences are drawn in from far and wide and then return home to pass on what they have heard. 'Composers of *gurna* song (*siŋ gurna*) routinely drew upon images of modern technology – "telephone", "telegram", "mail", "car" – as metaphors for the communicative and institutional power of the *gurna* dance society' (Ignatowski 2006: 93).

Third, the electronic media opened spaces in which new categories of performer could come to the fore. Mamadou Diawara (1997) and Lucy Durán (1995) have shown how women griots in the Mande culture area were able to become soloists and superstars in the media, whereas formerly they had been accompanists to their husbands, the kora players and reciters of epic narratives. Because modern popular media favoured melodious sung lyrics over instrumental music and narrative, stars such as Ami Koita and Fanta Damba were born. Not only this, but categories of people who would formerly have been excluded from performance altogether now entered the new, mediatized sphere and made a success of it – the most obvious example being Salif Keita, who, as his patronymic shows, is a descendant of the founder of the Mali empire Sunjata Keita and as such should traditionally be a recipient rather than a disburser of praise songs. Because music purveyed by the electronic media is easily absorbed into global popular culture flows, these new categories of performer were able to gain international fame.

Fourth, the electronic media brought texts and performances to new audiences, within Africa as well as beyond the continent. Genres which had previously been the preserve of specific segments of society were exposed to all and sundry. In western Uganda, for example, aristocratic BaHima men had traditionally composed and performed *ebyevugo* poetry as an expansion of the self: each man composed his own, as part of the process of creating his own manhood. Allusions to his own cattle, and to memorable events he had personally participated in, consolidated and enhanced his social presence in appropriate circumstances – receiving honoured guests, competing with his peers for prestige. It was unthinkable that his *ebyevugo* should be performed by anyone else, or that it should be performed in front of people unversed in the genre's specialized, allusive poetic form. In the context of an ongoing transformation of social hierarchy in modern Uganda, however, those long-established relations between text, performer and audience were overturned. Traditional masters of the genre were horrified to see 'agriculturalists' – the peasant majority – tuning in to performances of *ebyevugo* on the radio as they cultivated their fields. Not only this, non-aristocratic enthusiasts could learn the poems themselves, and perform them at weddings, for money, to audiences 'from different walks of life', or play recordings of their performances in commercial centres in an ambience far removed from that of aristocratic pastoralists who had originally created and owned the poems (Kiguli 2004: 87–102).

Fifth, the electronic media brought disparate traditions into conjunction with each other, whether in the free-for-all of commercial dissemination or in the orchestrated mosaic promoted by national cultural policy. Performers became aware not only that other ethnic-cultural traditions existed, but also that they were parallel and comparable to their own – potential candidates for imitation, borrowing or synthesis. This accelerated tendencies already fostered by urbanization and the creation of new polyglot forms. When highly local poetic and dramatic performances are available on video in the same rental store as national film productions and imported football, sit-coms and feature films, a sense of alternatives and parallels is encouraged and cross-fertilization is assured. As Peter Manuel showed in the case of South Asia, some kinds of electronic technology can have the effect of pro-liferating and reviving local oral traditions rather than swamping them. Cas-sette recording, because it is small-scale, cheap and easy to operate, allowed small local recording companies in the 1970s to specialize in recording and disseminating very local oral performance genres, which had previously been eclipsed by the dissemination of large-scale, centrally-produced LPs and films (Manuel 1993). In Africa, Kimani Njogu has noted similar devel-opments in the case of Bedouin *ghinnawa* love poems (citing Abu-Lughod 1990) and Swahili dialogue poetry (Njogu 2004). Hand-held video record-ing technology in West Africa has also stimulated a proliferation of local cre-ative activity – innumerable small-scale local production companies now specialize in lifecycle celebrations (weddings and funerals particularly), and in local theatrical performances. While some of these are extremely parochial in orientation, they nonetheless occupy a notionally equivalent place on the shelf to *Rocky I, II, III, IV* and *V*, and thus participate at least vicariously in a global media culture. Local media entrepreneurs are often astute in using editing tricks that produce a superficial impression of glitzy international sophistication, even when the content of the video is a wobbly, interminable, hand-held record of an event of interest only to those who participated in it.

Finally and most broadly, the media supplied expanded publicity, unprecedented glamour and new genre conventions to live popular per-formance genres. Radio, television and other recording/ disseminating tech-nologies have helped to create a vast intermediate zone which is both live and mediatized, both local and trans-local, and which absorbs models and elements from the formal, official, literate sphere without being subjugated to it.

Consider the example of Yoruba popular theatre, which took off as a com-mercial, popular, travelling genre in the late 1940s (Jeyifo 1984; Barber 2000). One of the most prominent creators of this theatrical form, Oyin Adejobi, in his narration of the history of his company stressed the fact that his group started off in Lagos, around 1948, as a church choir singing Adejobi's own religious compositions. It was because Radio Nigeria, con-stantly questing for material, heard one of their performances and invited them to fill a regular radio slot, that Adejobi was able to convert the choir into a mixed group outside of the church, which he dubbed the 'Adejobi Singing Party'. He composed a repertoire of new songs on topical, satirical and philosophical topics as well as moral homilies for this group. It was their radio fame which enabled Adejobi to make the transition to musical Bible drama, a form which had been in existence since the turn of the century, but which was given a new lease of life and new creative development in the 1940s. Many church leaders, attracted by the group's performances on Radio Nigeria, invited Adejobi to work with their choirs to produce 'cantatas' or 'native air operas' on such themes as Adam and Eve in the Garden of Eden, and Hannah's Trial and Triumph. When in 1962 Adejobi decided to turn his group into a commercial, professional and secular travelling theatre company, he was immediately taken up by the fledgling Western Nigeria Television Service. The WNTS broadcast his first non-Biblical musical drama live, to audiences across the Yoruba-speaking Western Region and beyond. From the mid 1960s onwards, until the demise of the live popular theatre in the early 1990s, the Adejobi Theatre Company created and performed weekly instalments of several immensely popular radio and television sit-coms. From the beginning, television served as a form of amplification and advertising for the live popular theatre, greatly increasing the pulling power of the stage shows. Television and live theatre shaped each other. The demands of the television studio managers encouraged tight plotting, restrictions on length, smaller casts, realistic settings, and a preference for naturalistic dialogue over operatic sung text. These characteristics were gradually absorbed by the theatre as well as the made-for-media programmes. On the other hand, television was forced to accept the theatre companies' irreverent and sometimes chaotic improvisations, their approximate time-keeping and their exuberant populist morality, for the Yoruba-language dramas were by far the most popular items on TV and the only ones capable of drawing in large audiences from outside the TV-owning middle class.

When the live theatre eventually succumbed to the Nigerian economic collapse and pervasive social insecurity, the actors and actor-managers moved en masse into video drama, where they interacted with a new cadre of professional TV actors including those who performed in slightly more upmarket English-language serials. The techniques, plots and characters of the live Yoruba theatre were blended with those drawn from these TV serials and from Nigerian films, to create a vast new repertoire, a 'video boom' which has attracted much attention within and beyond Nigeria. This history shows how crucial the media were to the development and success of the improvised popular travelling theatre. Radio and television lay at the root of the live theatre's formation and efflorescence, but they in no way overshadowed it – they were always seen by the performers themselves merely as a useful adjunct to their main business of improvising in front of vast, noisy, live crowds in hotels and town halls around the whole Yoruba-speaking area. Only when live theatre was in decline for economic and social reasons did the media, in the shape of video cassettes, absorb and displace it. And

throughout this history, the emphasis was on the popularity of locally produced, Yoruba-language media productions. Both radio and TV were avid
for live Yoruba performance genres, partly on principle but partly because
these were so much more successful than imported programmes or national,
English-language productions. This may be an unusually strong case, but it
is not a weird exception. Everywhere in Africa, new genres grew up in the
twentieth century, dialogically intertwined with new media technologies,
partly stimulated, partly shaped by these technologies – but also significantly
affecting the way the media functioned.

MEDIA AND NEW PUBLICS

The media, then, are undoubtedly associated with profound changes in
African life, as they are with all life everywhere on the planet. But I would
not see these changes *primarily* as a late twentieth-century expansion of the
imagination, an imaginative identification with global counterparts; and I
would not see these changes as being *caused* by media flows. I would see the
development, importation, utilization and uptake of media as part of a much
broader and deeper shift in the nature of sociality – in what it means to
belong to society – a shift precipitated by wage labour, urbanization, literacy, the church, the school, dating back, in some parts of Africa, to the early
nineteenth century. These well documented and much discussed transformations of community and personal relations made possible the conceptualization of an audience as a 'public' – an indefinitely extensive collectivity
made up of equivalent, anonymous units with (in principle) equal access and
equal publicly available knowledge. Addressing the audience as a public
encouraged far-reaching transformations in form, style and the very conception of how performances and texts had meaning.

Traditional oral genres were, very widely in Africa, premised on the
assumption that society is segmented, that knowledge is by definition
unequally distributed (otherwise it would not be knowledge) and that the
interpretation of texts often requires knowledge of parallel, supplementary
oral traditions not contained within the texts themselves, and only known to
certain people.

Deliberate textual obscurity requiring specialized interpretative knowledge is characteristic of innumerable historical and eulogistic genres across
Africa. The *ajogan* songs of the kings of Porto Novo were 'deliberately allusive, even hermetic' (Rouget 1971: 32). Ila elders in Zambia will regard a
praise poem 'which is immediately self-evident and which lacks layers of
allusion as ipso facto uninteresting' (Rennie 1984: 530). The reciters of the
apae praises of Akan royalty and chiefs have a special vocabulary to 'conceal
the messages' (Arhin 1986: 167). All of these genres depend on specialized
ancillary traditions of narrative, or specialized techniques of decoding. In the

Yoruba town where I studied *oríkì* (praise poetry), the text and exegesis are transmitted as two separate traditions, the praise poetry usually performed by women, the narrative tradition on which exegesis rests by elderly men – who, in turn, were dependent on phrases of *oríkì* which they would quote as stepping stones or springboards to help their narrative along. When asked about the meaning of their texts, women performers would often direct the enquirer to the elderly males of the household; when the old men were asked for fuller texts of *oríkì*, they would summon their wives. Thus the meaning of the text was co-constituted by two categories of people, neither one having a definitive command of the 'whole'. The Gikuyu *gĩcandĩ* genre documented by Kimani Njogu is 'essentially a competitive, yet cooperative, riddle-like dialogue poem and poetic exchange' (Njogu 2004: 153). In this genre, what is put on display seems to be the act of exegesis itself – a staged contest between poets, each of whom takes it in turn to solve an enigma proposed by the other. The coded, riddle-like allusions not only demand extensive contextual knowledge of the objects or institutions they refer to, but also knowledge of strategies of deriddling.

The complex, plural mode of textual constitution of genres such as these evoked identity and subjectivity in ways that may appear, to a teleological eye, as an extraordinary 'anticipatory modernity', a kind of postmodernism *avant la lettre*. I have discussed elsewhere the polyvocality of Yoruba *oríkì*, the way that pronouns are unmoored and the speaking position shifts from moment to moment, dissolving any fixed authorial identity (Barber 1991, 2007). In the case of Gikuyu *gĩcandĩ*, the performer, Njogu says, 'dissolves the distinction between the singular and the plural and makes the self inter-individual' (Njogu 1997: 55).

This kind of collaborative allusiveness, where the constitution of textual meaning is distributed across several sites and agents, is only possible in communities with close, continuous interaction – communities where everyone knows everyone else's business, remembers their actions and sayings, and observes their foibles; where the transmission of text and narrative explanation is secure enough for composers and transmitters to expect that someone will be able to put them together; and where valuable knowledge is always withheld from some sections of the community, to the point where withholding knowledge may itself confer value on it. Transparent, perspicuous texts are felt to be dull, even worthless. Very obscure and allusive texts are prized, especially but not only by the privileged few who can expound them.

It does not require the advent of electronic media to broaden, dilute and generalize highly allusive local traditions. Paulette Galand-Pernet in her book on Berber literatures speaks of an oral poem from southern Morocco, 'The complaint of Amismiz', which tells of the tragic fate of a young woman who refuses to marry her cousin, chosen for her by her family. The family curses her; she robs her parents and flees with her lover to the city. Her lover then murders her and makes off with the booty. In the village in which it was created, according to Galand-Pernet, this narrative alluded to real current events known to all. But when the poem diffused gradually, by word of mouth, across the whole of Berber-speaking southern Morocco, it became 'stripped of detailed references to the real world' and became increasingly an abstract, moralizing scheme without the implied assumption of local knowledge (Galand-Pernet 1998: 37–9). One is reminded of H. M. Chadwick's suggestion that the heroic epic poem of early medieval northern Europe arose when allusive, context-bound praise poetry began to be carried beyond the local courts in which it was composed to audiences not informed about the events and personalities to which the poems alluded. The stories to which the praises obscurely alluded had to be brought into the text itself to make it comprehensible to those not already in the know (Chadwick 1926).

Though this kind of transformation can happen without print or electronic media, it is obvious that the media are likely to accelerate it and widen its range. In the shift to addressing an unknown, absent, dispersed public, old modes of textual constitution in Africa were abandoned and new forms were generated. Transparency became a positive value instead of the mark of a shallow, immature composer.

There are examples of this transformation taking place rapidly and dramatically within a single genre. One such case is the *nnwonkoro* genre, an informal women's recreational song, performed in Ghana (Anyidoho 1993). Traditionally, *nnwonkoro* songs are performed in a circle in the village arena by women for their own pleasure. They are packed with obscure allusions that can only be known to those participants with 'inside knowledge'. In the following verse, for example, no one who was not in the know could guess what meaning had been attached to the expression 'I ran after him, but I could not catch up with him':

> I depend on him for my sustenance
> The man, the leader of the club
> I depend on him for my sustenance
> > Alas! Yaw Baawua
> > Alas! Alas
> Mother, the tongue depends on the chin
> Once bitten, twice shy
> The tongue depends on the chin
> > Alas! Yaw Baawua
> > Alas! Alas
> Mother, I ran after him, I did not catch up with him
> Grandsire Osei, the leader of the club.
> I ran after him, but I could not catch up with him
> > Alas! Yaw Baawua
> (Anyidoho 1993: 221)

To the uninitiated, this might sound like an allusion to a relationship with a man, perhaps a husband, with the suggestion of some unhappy experience. It comes as a surprise to learn that MrYaw Baawua became the chairman of Asante Kotoko Soccer Club when this club's fortunes were at a low ebb, and poured money and effort into rebuilding it. Just as women depend on men for support, and the tongue depends on the jaw to hold it in place, so the club depends onYaw Baawua for its success.The final lament, 'Mother, I ran after him, I did not catch up with him', turns out to be the 'voice of rival clubs admitting defeat' (Anyidoho 1993: 221–2). The meaning thus attached cannot be guessed by the uninitiated, and the art and pleasure of the genre is to exercise your insider's knowledge to decipher the hidden meaning.

The genre was reinvented in 1944 when an enterprising individual – a man – heard that a radio station was looking for Akan traditions to include in a cultural programme. He convened a five-member *nnwonkoro* troupe of a new type, with a new style of song. The idea spread, and soon the mixed performing group offering entertainment to an audience became the norm. The new-style *nnwonkoro* groups were consciously oriented and responsive to modern values and institutions. They aimed to produce albums and audio-cassettes as well as performing live at public engagements such as funerals. They perform at state occasions like the memorial ceremonies for Nkrumah and Dubois, and state-sponsored cultural festivals, including *nnwonkoro* festivals where teams are brought in from all over the country to compete. At these events, the organizers prescribe topics, which tend to be educational or geared to public enlightenment about social problems such as AIDS, drug abuse, alcoholism and teenage pregnancy. The desire to appear on national television also 'motivated the composition of songs whose contents go beyond the traditional *nnwonkoro* to incorporate national issues' (Anyidoho 1993: 184).

Modern-style media *nnwonkoro* draw on imagery that is publicly available and does not rely on insider knowledge. Dr Nkrumah is praised posthumously in the following words:

The light he lit in Africa is still shining
The fire he lit is still burning
Today, we will praise him in song
One who does good deserves gratitude
We become ingrates if we do not express our gratitude to
    you
You did a great deal for this nation . . .

When you died [in exile]
Ghanaians realised that
A royal is never left in a foreign land
When a trap is disturbed it goes back to its original
    position . . .
(Anyidoho 1993: 287–8)

This text is not simplistic: it encapsulates a graceful apology on behalf of a nation which was slow to recognize Nkrumah's service to it, a discursive move to assimilate Nkrumah to the category of royalty, and a smooth deployment of a homespun saying or image, that of the trap snapping shut, to suggest the force and inevitability of the repatriation of Nkrumah's body. But the imagery contains no secrets. The beacon of light, and the burning flame, as symbols of enlightenment and hope are internationally recognized, thoroughly public symbols – the torch of learning was actually used as a street sign for schools in the UK until the 1960s, so standardized was its symbolism.

What we see here, then, is local individuals and groups grasping the possibilities and implications of new technologies of communication and mobilizing them in a conscious move to constitute a new kind of public – in the case of *nnwonkoro*, a national public, a public that needs to receive instruction, and which is assumed to be receptive to new styles of address.

The significance of new means of dissemination is thrown into sharp relief, and can be politically crucial, in situations where art forms are consciously deployed to raise consciousness, forge solidarity or mobilize a political constituency. A telling and well documented example is the worker poetry that became popular in Durban, South Africa in the mid-1980s at the height of the struggle against apartheid. When activists in Durban introduced drama to publicize the labour movement's political struggles, the 'worker actors decided something was missing from their dramatic performances' (Kromberg 1993: 149). One of them, Alfred T. Qabula, came up with the idea of adding *izibongo* (oral praise poetry) in praise of Fosatu, the general council of trade unions. This innovation was ecstatically received by the audience, and so, in Qabula's words, 'Another form of expression had been discovered' (Kromberg 1993: 149). The new genre drew on recognizable features of the older *izibongo* tradition, including performative elements such as style and speed of delivery, intonational contours, and costume. It continued the mode of affirmation and validation of identity – now the corporate identity of the unions rather than the identity of the chief and by extension his subjects – and it continued to excite and inspire individual listeners (Gunner 1989: 46). There were also continuities in the mode of composition. Though Qabula used writing as an instrument of composition, his method of collecting pieces of information and observations from a variety of sources (in his case, a number of different trade union members, meetings and branches) and stringing them together in a disjunctive and allusive mode was characteristic of *izibongo* (and indeed of praise poetry all over Africa) (Gunner 1989: 50–1).

However, performers had a delicate path to tread. On the one hand, part of the reason for the immediate enthusiasm for *izibongo*-like performances was that members of the audience associated the genre with their rural places of origin and with their older relatives. They responded to the recognizable features of the genre, while welcoming the new and more congenial subject-matter. The rousing, exhortatory, vividly metaphorical style of *izibongo* was well suited to the charged-up atmosphere of mass rallies. But on the other hand, cultural displays of 'Zulu tradition', and especially the performance of a genre associated with the glorification of the Zulu monarchy, risked giving wrong and potentially dangerous signals. Durban in the 1980s was criss-crossed with splits and antagonisms along racial, cultural-ethnic, class, religious, age, gender and community lines. The violent hostility between supporters of Inkatha and the ANC sometimes mutated into open warfare and infiltrated many aspects of community life. Inkatha controlled the local government, and supported a Zulu cultural nationalism focused on the Kwazulu homeland with its rickety royal establishment. Traditional *izibongo* were part of the insignia of this movement. The trade union movement, initially neutral, later affiliated itself with the ANC, which espoused a 'non-racial', supra-ethnic policy. The worker poets, in redeploying a traditional Zulu genre associated with royalty and chiefs, were thus risking accusations of Inkatha-style ethnic nationalism; and while 'being Zulu' had long meant different things to people differently positioned in the political spectrum (Marks 1986; La Hausse de la Louviere 2000), every cultural affirmation was potentially explosive. Some worker poets developed a style more reminiscent of reggae than *izibongo*, and this was especially popular with younger audiences. Those who followed Qabula's lead had to adapt the familiar, shared features of the *izibongo* tradition – which were the reason for the new genre's positive reception in the first place – in order to neutralize its potentially reactionary overtones.

The process of adaptation went beyond the shift in subject matter. The deliberately obscure, allusive, riddle-like mode of traditional *izibongo* was replaced by an explicit, immediately comprehensible style in which only general and publicly-available knowledge was required in order to grasp the meaning. The specific performance conditions played a part in this transformation. The 1980s were the decade of mass rallies, and worker *izibongo* were often performed on stages before huge crowds – in some cases as many as 100,000 people – and beamed out to them through massive banks of amplifiers. These large venues brought together not only union members but also large numbers of ANC supporters of diverse ethnicities, communities, occupations, ages and religions. The performers had no choice but to concentrate on a galvanizing vocal and gestural delivery and a broad, easily grasped message, the performance of which was often preceded by chanting a series of slogans. The 'interpretive community' which Kromberg believes made the success of worker poetry possible was not a local, stable, residential community with an accumulated depth of shared knowledge based on daily interaction over many years. The 1980s Durban public for worker poetry was a fragile coalition drawn from widely dispersed constituencies with deep cultural and ideological fissures, which the rallies and meetings were precisely designed to bridge over. The shared cultural knowledge on which the worker poetry drew was genuine but very limited – not only because of the diverse backgrounds of the participants, but also because for almost all of the urban lower classes, the *izibongo* tradition was only known in scraps and flashes, and not as the central, vital presence it had once been to their rural kin.

As is demonstrated by these last two examples – new-style *nnwonkoro* and trades union *izibongo* – the expanded public convened by mediatized oral genres can be a national 'imagined community' or a particular strategic combination of interest groups. Though the idiom of the nation state is prominent in many broadcast genres, the exuberant proliferation of genres in African languages rules out any simple one-to-one correspondence between listening audience and a single, national, imagined community. Every African-language performance has the potential to foster local ethnic-nationalism or 'tribalism' as well as to present the local culture as one component of an orchestrated national 'unity in diversity'.

MEDIA AND POPULAR CULTURE NOW

In the 1990s, very widely across Africa, the state-controlled media were at least partially privatized and pluralized. The deliberate attempt to consolidate a national public through the media fell by the wayside and the media became a marketplace, a free-for-all where interest groups of all sizes and persuasions could take to the airwaves (Fardon and Furniss 2000). The relaxation of official control also meant the diminution of programming oriented towards development goals. Orderly but extremely dull programmes designed to inform and educate (Bourgault 1995) were replaced with chaotic but lively and entertaining talk shows and a huge increase in popular music channels featuring local rap and other youth genres. The first commercial community radio station in Kenya, Kameme FM, launched in March 2000, was so successful that the government was pushed into setting up its own version of it (Ngumo 2004). A Kikuyu-language station with an interactive approach, Kameme stimulated Kikuyu listeners to consolidate their linguistic and cultural repertoire; but at the same time the high proportion of popular music in its programming meant that large numbers of non-Kikuyu listeners also tuned in. However, Ngumo observes that political 'liberalization' has not led to more open discussion of political issues in Kameme FM broadcasts; censorship is now practised by advertisers rather than government, and if advertisers pull out, the radio station may be forced to sack employees and even close down. In Ghana, privatization of radio stations has fomented disorderly but highly interactive talk shows in which managerial control and traditional norms of respect have been hilariously brushed aside (Sika Ahadzie, personal communication). Local interest groups are buying up airtime and even opening their own broadcasting stations in order to push their messages, often evangelical and fundamentalist in nature.

How the media function, how they convene audiences and how people's relations to older oral traditions of knowledge are transformed are vitally relevant to Africa's present and immediate future. Sociality in many parts of Africa is in unprecedented crisis, with the HIV plague eroding community and family; with religious organizations setting up what amount to parallel states within the state (and establishing their zones of influence precisely through astute use of the media); with the proliferation of local political autonomy movements, border wars and inter-state looting. The privatization and fragmentation of media echo the privatization and fragmentation of the state. Authoritarian governments which formerly attempted to control the media through monopoly and censorship are now less able to do so. But the threats to freedom of expression and the impediments to a genuinely popular media, operating in the interests of the people, remain.

Nonetheless, wherever there is a chance, acerbic criticism, hilarious mockery and mesmerizing tales of wrongdoing in high places break out in popular media and quickly spread from one medium and genre to another, creating a politically charged super-medium continually refreshed by gossip. Sometimes lampoons of the mighty have to be hidden in sleazy performance venues or disguised as fiction, like Wahome Mutahi's bar-room satires and comic newspaper columns (Mwaura, this volume; Ogola 2004). In the more liberal context of Ghana, scandalous allegations were recently broadcast live while 'the nation stood still' in shock and amazement (Sika Ahadzie, personal communication). Sometimes the mediatized zone of popular culture in Africa seems like a site where political and social forces can be cloudily discerned in the very process of taking shape.

REFERENCES

Abu-Lughod, Lila (1990), 'Shifting Politics in Bedouin Love Poetry'. In Catherine A. Lutz and Lila Abu-Lughod (eds), *Language and the Politics of Emotion*. Cambridge: Cambridge University Press, pp. 24–45.

Anyidoho, Love Akosua (1993), *Gender and Language Use: The Case of Two Akan Verbal Art Forms*. PhD thesis, University of Texas at Austin.

Appadurai, Arjun (1996), *Modernity at Large: Cultural Dimensions of Globalization*. Minneapolis: University of Minnesota Press.

Arhin, Kwame (1986), 'The Asante Praise Poems: The Ideology of Patrimonialism'. *Paideuma* 32 (163–97).

Barber, Karin (1987), 'Popular Arts in Africa'. Special issue of *African Studies Review* 30, 3 (1–78, 105–32).

— (1991), *I Could Speak until Tomorrow: Oriki, Women and the Past in a Yorùbá Town.* Edinburgh: Edinburgh University Press for the IAI.

— (1997), 'Introduction'. In Karin Barber (ed.), *Readings in African Popular Fiction.* Oxford: James Currey, pp. 1–12.

— (2000), *The Generation of Plays: Yoruba Popular Life in Theatre.* Bloomington, IN: Indiana University Press.

— (2007), *The Anthropology of Texts, Persons and Publics: Oral and Written Culture in Africa and Beyond.* Cambridge: Cambridge University Press.

Bourgault, Louise M. (1995), *Mass Media in Sub-Saharan Africa.* Bloomington, IN: Indiana University Press.

Chadwick, H. Munro (1926), *The Heroic Age.* Cambridge: Cambridge University Press.

Diawara, Mamadou (1997), 'Mande Oral Popular Culture Revisited by the Electronic Media'. In Karin Barber (ed.), *Readings in African Popular Culture.* Oxford: James Currey, pp. 40–53.

Durán, Lucy (1995), 'Jelimusow: The Superwomen of Malian Music'. In Liz Gunner and Graham Furniss (eds), *Power, Marginality and African Oral Literature.* Cambridge: Cambridge University Press.

Fardon, Richard and Graham Furniss (eds) (2000), *African Broadcast Cultures: Radio in Transition.* Oxford: James Currey.

Galand-Pernet, Paulette (1998), *Littératures berbères: des voix, des lettres.* Paris: Presses Universitaires de France.

Gunner, Liz (1989), 'Orality and Literacy: Dialogue and Silence'. In Karin Barber and P. F. de Moraes Farias (eds), *Discourse and its Disguises: The Interpretation of African Oral Texts.* University of Birmingham, pp. 49–56.

Ignatowski, Clare A. (2006), *Journey of Song: public life and morality in Cameroon.* Bloomington, IN: Indiana University Press.

Jeyifo, Biodun (1984), *The Yoruba Popular Travelling Theatre of Nigeria.* Lagos: Nigeria Magazine Publications.

Kiguli, Susan (2004), *Oral Poetry and Popular Song.* PhD dissertation, University of Leeds.

Kromberg, Steve (1993), *The Problem of Audience: A Study of Durban Worker Poetry.* MA thesis, University of the Witwatersrand, Johannesburg.

La Hausse de Lalouviere, Paul (2000), *Restless Identities.* Pietermaritzburg: University of Natal Press.

Lawuyi, O. B. (1997), 'The Political Economy of Video Marketing in Ogbomoso, Nigeria'. *Africa* 67, 3 (476–90).

Manuel, Peter L. (1993), *Cassette Culture: Popular Music and Technology in North India.* Chicago: University of Chicago Press.

Marks, Shula (1986), *The Ambiguities of Dependence in South Africa: Class, Nationalism and the State in Twentieth-century Natal.* Johannesburg: Ravan Press.

Ngumo, Danson (2004), 'The Place of FM Stations'. Paper presented at conference on *Media and the Construction of African Identities*, IAI and Twaweza Communications, Nairobi.

Njogu, Kimani (1997), 'On the Polyphonic Nature of the *gĩcaandĩ* Genre'. *African Languages and Cultures*, 10, 1 (47–62).

— (2004), *Reading Poetry as Dialogue.* Nairobi: Jomo Kenyatta Foundation.

Ogola, George (2004), 'The Idiom of Age in a Popular Kenyan Newspaper Serial'. Paper presented at 'Idiom of Age' workshop, University of Birmingham.

Rennie, J. K. (1984), 'Cattle, Conflict and Court Cases: The Praise Poetry of Ila Leadership'. *Research in African Literatures* 15, 4 (530–67).

Rouget, Gilbert (1971), 'Court Songs and Traditional History in the Ancient Kingdoms of Porto-Novo and Abomey'. In Klaus P. Wachsmann (ed.), *Essays on Music and History in Africa*. Evanston, IL: Northwestern University Press, pp. 27–64.

Spitulnik, Debra (1994), *Radio Culture in Zambia: Audiences, Public Words and the Nation State*. PhD dissertation, University of Chicago.

For a richly suggestive discussion on the consumption of videos in southwestern Nigeria, see Lawuyi 1997.

THE MEDIA IN SOCIAL DEVELOPMENT IN CONTEMPORARY AFRICA

If communication is the lifeblood of human interaction, the media constitute the veins through which it flows. The media have a multiplicity of forms, functions, and impacts. They exist in oral, literary and visual forms; they are transmitted through print, audiovisual, and digital technologies; and they play communicative, creative, and representational roles. As a whole, or in specific artifacts and genres, the media have varied social, economic and political effects that can promote democracy, development, nation building and inclusion as much as they can sustain authoritarianism, exploitation, conflict and exclusion. Media infrastructures, practices and policies are embedded in the prevailing material conditions of production, the ideologies of current political economies and the discourse networks of particular periods. In short, the media, ancient and ubiquitous in all human societies, develop in complex and contradictory ways. They are a reality and social practice whose construction, dissemination, consumption vary and change in time and space, subject to the shifting materials and imperatives of production, communication, transport, and power configured around the historical markers of nation, class, gender, race, religion and other social inscriptions.

Communicative spaces in Africa have expanded remarkably in recent years, owing to wider transformations in the continent's political and cultural economies. They remain unstable, unequal, and uneven in their development within and among countries, however. Media, moreover, are and have been integral to Africa's social development. They have been crucial to the development of African socialities, and in the construction and articulation of collective identities at various social and spatial scales from gender to generation, and from the local to the global.

CONCEPTIONS OF MEDIA AND SOCIAL DEVELOPMENT

In examining the intersections between the media and development, it is important to analyze the role of the media, and to distinguish their various forms, as well as to identify and unpack the paradigms of development. Of the media's many roles, four can be singled out for emphasis. To begin with, media serve as a vehicle for the transmission of ideas, images, and information. Moreover, they are a communicative space for public discourse and of the discursive public. The media are also an arena of sign-communication and sign-communities. Finally, the media constitute a process for performing social identities and identifying social performances.

As for the media forms, we can fruitfully differentiate between three: mass communication media, interpersonal media, and what Debra Spitulnik (2002) calls 'small' media. This tripartite typology seems to have more explanatory power than the binary distinction between 'formal' and 'informal' media made by Hydén and Leslie (2002). Mass communication media refer to media produced and distributed for, and consumed by, mass publics. Interpersonal media apply to communication that is produced for more limited consumption and is distributed along interpersonal channels. 'Small' media, which are also sometimes referred to as 'personal', 'popular', or 'community' media, are a hybrid of the two modes – mass and interpersonal media – and occupy an intermediary position between them. The scale of production, distribution and consumption is smaller than that of the mass media, but larger than that of interpersonal media. Also, small media blend old and new technologies, which gives them an innovative and transitory edge, a textual and iconographic intertextuality of different communication media, thereby making them a dynamic, fluid, multi-sited and multi-media phenomenon and process. Types of 'small' media include posters, flyers, graffiti, cartoons, underground cassettes, independent videos, internet listservs, web pages, jokes, parodic or cynical genres (for example, poaching and reworking slogans of state or corporate power), rumours, and radio trottoir ('pavement radio'). This paper largely deals with the developmental implications of contemporary mass communication media in Africa.

Development as a process of sustainable socioeconomic change, of material societal transformation, has long been a preoccupation of African states, leaders and social movements. The development project has been articulated through four paradigms – modernization, dependency, Marxist, and free-market fundamentalist theories – each of which has been dominant in different periods for different states.

During the twilight years of decolonization and the early post-independence period, the precepts and prescriptions of modernization theory held sway. In this paradigm, development was seen largely in terms of importing Western models, capital, technology and market institutions and ideologies. However, dissatisfaction with the tepid performances and promises of modernization, or growth without development, led many African states to join the broader Third World plea for a new international economic order. This call was rooted in the insights and implorations of dependency theory that ascribed underdevelopment in the global South to the enduring inequities of the international division of labour. The more radical among them, especially those which achieved independence through protracted, armed liberation struggles, embraced the socialist path to development. This paradigm derived its ideological imprimature from Marxist theory, which valorized class struggle and collective ownership of the means of production, and from the models of Soviet industrialization and Chinese peasantization. In the 1980s, a neoliberal paradigm of development arose. This constituted a fierce regime of free market fundamentalism, and gained ascendancy on the backs of a new wave of capitalist globalization as Keynesian welfare capitalism in the global North was abandoned, Soviet communism began to disintegrate, and the nationalist project in the global South collapsed under the weight of proxy wars and rising indebtedness.

The interactions between media and social development are mutually reinforcing. The media facilitate development as much as the state of development sets the contexts for the operation of the media. Society and the media are connected and interrelate in various ways. There is a technological dimension to the interaction – exchanges of technologies and techniques between the media and various sectors of society. In addition, there is a cultural dimension, in so far as media contents are cultural products. Moreover, a sociopolitical dimension exists in the fact that the media have an impact on society as much as society impacts on the media. Finally, there is an economic dimension in the form of media markets and investments. To put it differently, in many countries the media constitute an important industry, one of the most vital service sectors.

Thus, the media have several roles to play in social development in contemporary Africa. Politically, there is the question of the impact of the media on the democratization of society, as well as the impact of democratization on the media itself. Economically, at issue is the development of the media as a service industry. This would include growth and ownership patterns, as well as levels of profitability and competitiveness. Culturally, the media can contribute to the development of social capital – that is, relational networks involving social interaction, civic trust and normative behaviour that can benefit or harm society – as well as to the articulation and performance of cultural identities. Technologically, the media have played a crucial role in the ways in which they introduce and incorporate technological innovation.

THE CONTEXTS OF MEDIA DEVELOPMENT IN CONTEMPORARY AFRICA

The African media in 2004 were more vibrant, diverse, competitive, larger, and freer than they were in 1994, let alone in 1984. The transformations in the media landscape can be attributed to changes associated with democratization, globalization, the information technology revolution and the emergence of knowledge society and knowledge economies as material and discursive processes and regimes. Much has been written about each of these factors, how they have altered, separately and collectively, Africa's political and cultural economies and its media systems and practices (Ogundimu 2002; Girard and O'Siochru 2003).

Democratization in contemporary Africa can be analyzed from various angles, in terms of processes, paradigms and prescriptions. As processes, focus is often on the manifestations of democratic transformation, the modalities of transition to democracy, and the visions of democracy in the social imagination. There can be little doubt there have been changes in the organization of state power and civil society in much of Africa, despite retreats, reversals and resistance by some of the continent's wily and obdurate dictators. From the 1990s, state power became increasingly subject to the strictures of electoral politics and multipartism, all of which represented the emergence of at least minimalist democracies with regard to the rules and patterns of regime change and legitimation. The expansion of political space and the pluralization of associational life reflected, in part, the growth of civil society and its compulsions and capacities to play a more dynamic role in the public arena. Across Africa, the transition to democracy took different paths.

Also varied were visions of democracy. There was, first, what I call the nativist model. This invokes the ethos of traditional or communal democracy. Second, there is the liberal model, which is confined to multipartism, periodic electoral contests and good governance. Third is the popular democratic model, seeking the construction of distributionist democratic developmental states. Fourth is the theocratic model, which envisions the creation of a new social and political order sanctioned by religion. Fifth is the transnational model, which aspires to the construction of democratic regional federations and a Pan-African dispensation (Zeleza 2003a).

Analyses of Africa's democratization – the 'second independence' as it was once called in popular circles when the continent began to reel from the winds of democratic change in the early 1990s – have centred on four key debates concerning the relative roles of internal and external factors behind the democratic wave, historical and contemporary dynamics, structural and contingent factors, and economic and political forces. The dualities embedded in these analytical paradigms, in which scholars stress either side of the explanatory coin, yield insights as much as they obscure the complex and often contradictory pressures, possibilities and perils of democratic renewal and consolidation in contemporary Africa. In my view, the struggles for democracy from the 1990s represented the latest moment of accelerated change in the continent's long history of struggles for freedom (Zeleza 2004).

Central to the analytical and popular conceptions of democratization is the instrumental value placed on democracy, in which two sets of emphases can be identified. First there is the trope of good governance, centred on the propensity of democracy to facilitate, indeed deliver, administrative efficiency, transparency, accountability and popular participation. The second expectation is that democracy promotes human rights. In so far as the current wave of democratization in Africa is occurring in the context of prolonged historical movements for decolonization and development and against postcolonial authoritarianisms, there is an overriding hope that democratization will entail the respect for and implementation of the so-called three generations of rights: political and civil rights, social and economic rights, and development and solidarity rights.

Democratization has been critical to the growth of the media, and the media have been critical to the growth of democracy in contemporary Africa (Hydén and Okigbo 2002). The struggles for democracy opened up space for, and were facilitated by, the explosion of the press, followed later by the broadcast media. The emergence of new democratic and human rights regimes affected the media in several specific ways. National constitutional reforms involving the separation of powers, strengthening the power of the judiciary, and the legalization of multiparty politics created a more auspicious environment for the media. In addition, many African states incorporated in their national legal systems the relevant international instruments that protected and promoted media freedoms. The body of human rights particularly pertinent to the media includes the right to communicate (freedom of expression and access to information) and the right to culture (participation, protection and language) (Hamelink 2003). But it is one thing to reform constitutions and pass progressive media laws, and another to enforce them. The problems of enforcement often reflect the weaknesses of formal enforcement mechanisms as well as various economic and political pressures, ranging from the commodification and commercialization of communication to the subversion of human rights under the guise of protecting national security, especially since the onset of the current American-led 'war on terror' (Zeleza 2005a).

Besides democratization, globalization constitutes another important context for the development of the media in contemporary Africa. Whether understood as a historical process or an ideological project, globalization bears serious implications for the media (Zeleza 2003b). As a process, globalization refers to greater interconnectedness among communities, countries and continents in the spheres of economy, culture, politics and technology. It is marked by increased flows of capital and commodities, ideas and images, values and viruses, and people and problems, as well as the growth of global reflexivity and transnational constructions of identities and collaborations in knowledge production. As a project, globalization is synonymous with global capitalism – the drive to institute a global regime of neoliberal restructuring. The implications of globalization as both process and project are quite grave for the African media and for African social development. The developmental perils of structural adjustment pro-grammes, the primary face of globalization for Africa in the 1980s and 1990s, are well known, but no less important are the possibilities of political and economic liberalization and new information technologies in breaking the oppressive monopolies of the postcolonial state.

The impact of the revolution in information and communication tech-nologies (ICT) in the growth and transformation of the media cannot be overemphasized. The new information technologies have had a profound impact on the production, dissemination and consumption of information, which has affected all forms of media communication. Specifically, the ICT revolution has eroded the capacity of governments to control information, facilitated the faster transmission of information, and encouraged the emer-gence of new communication spaces and sign-communities such as online media and transnational and diaspora networking. Slowly at first, but growing more aggressively, Africa has been trying to catch up with the ICT revolution.

The emergence of these technologies has facilitated the rise of what are variously described as information or knowledge societies and economies. Academic definitions of knowledge societies are often framed in epistemo-logical, sociological and economic terms (Zeleza 2003c). Knowledge soci-eties and economies are characterized, variously, by the emergence of new digital and electronic spaces and increased flows of computer-mediated information, images and ideas, the growth of information and knowledge as a critical factor of production, the increasing importance of trade in knowl-edge and information products and services, and the rising application of proprietary and profit norms to knowledge and information through various intellectual property regimes including the World Intellectual Property Organization (WIPO), and the General Agreement of Trade in Services (GATS) under the auspices of the World Trade Organization (WTO). In the 1970s, the debate about the new world information society was driven by states, whereas the current debate about the information society is driven by corporate interests (Raboy 2003). The new information and communication technologies and networks are, simultaneously, constitutive of new social dynamics and derivative of, embedded in, and contributary to the repro-duction of older societal structures and power dynamics inscribed by the enduring hierarchies and divisions of gender, class, nationality and location (Plou 2003).

Table 2.1 Number and Circulation of Daily Newspapers, 1980–2000

38 countries	Number of daily papers				Total average circulation (000s)			
	1980	1990	1997	2000	1980	1990	1997	2000
Totals	148	192	212	276	6,734	8,870	9,165	9,418

Source: United Nations Statistics Division, Common Data Base

CHANGES IN AFRICA'S MEDIA LANDSCAPE

The changes in the scale, size and structure of the African media are exceedingly complex and contradictory. In general, four major trends can be observed, although of course they manifest themselves quite differently and in varied combinations within and among different countries. First, there is greater liberalization and commercialization of the media. Second, the pluralization and concentration of the media have yielded increases of media practitioners and entrepreneurs which are counterbalanced by the rise of larger media concerns. Third, simultaneous media localization and transnationalization, whereby local media outlets (such as ethnic media) coexist with elements of the global media establishment (such as CNN). Fourth, the tabloidization and fragmentation of the media is increasing (in print media especially) as they become less text heavy, more visual and graphics rich, more sensational and parochial. As might be expected, specific trends characterize each of the major forms of mass media: print, radio, television and the internet.

For the print media, one of the obvious changes can be seen in the expansion in the number and circulation of newspapers. As shown in Table 2.1, the number of daily newspapers for the thirty-eight countries for which data was available increased from 148 in 1980 to 276 in 2000, a growth rate of 84.5 per cent, or 4.3 per cent per annum, while the total average circulation grew from 6.7 million in 1980 to 9.4 million in 2000, an increase of 2.7 million, or nearly 40 per cent. The expansion in the number of newspapers occurred fastest between 1990 and 2000 (by 84, compared to 44 for the previous decade), while average circulation did so between 1980 and 1990 (by 2.1 million, as compared to 548,000 for the following decade). Circulation peaked in 1990, when struggles for democracy were at their height. This suggests the pivotal role the press played in these struggles. In addition to the proliferation of newspapers, the African print media were increasingly marked by a growing focus on lifestyle agendas and business at the expense of developmental journalism that was dominant in the 1960s and 1970s. There was also a growing propensity for sensationalism, and the emergence of parochialism in the

Table 2.2 Radio Broadcast Stations and Ownership, 2001–2+

46 countries	Radio stations AM FM SW			Radio sets (000s)	Radios per capita per 1,000
Total	414	925	141	172,269	208.78

Source: http://www.nationmaster.com

form of ethnic and religious journalism, as has been reported from Nigeria.

Radio has always had a much greater impact as a medium of mass communication than newspapers. The role of clandestine radio in galvanizing nationalist movements fighting against colonial rule is well known (Van der Veur 2002). Precisely because of radio's popular appeal, most postcolonial governments imposed stringent controls over radio broadcasting, which remained a state monopoly until the democratic wave of the 1980s and 1990s. Democratization led to, and was increasingly measured by, the liberalization of public broadcasting. That liberalization also fostered the freeing up of political space and public discourse.

By the turn of the twenty-first century, patterns of radio broadcasting, ownership and programming had changed profoundly from what the situation had been in the first three decades after independence. The sheer scale of radio penetration can be seen in Table 2.2, which shows that more than a fifth of all Africans had access to radio, a figure unmatched by any other mass media, or by any services sector or industry for that matter.

Besides the exponential growth of radio broadcasting, ownership and access, several other trends can be identified. First, there was the expansion of commercial radio that offered a lot of music and little news. For news, many commercial radio stations often rely on rebroadcasting from the BBC, Voice of America, or Radio France International. Second, there has been the remarkable development of non-profit community radio. By 2003 there were an estimated 450 community radio broadcasting stations in West Africa alone, and 100 in South Africa. Third, there has been the rise of talk radio, which some have called the rebirth of oral tradition. Fourth, religious broadcasting has increased as religious organizations, including Islamic and Christian fundamentalists, have taken to the airwaves to defend their faiths and win new converts in the face of the religious revivalisms and rivalries sweeping the continent. Fifth, more foreign broadcasters have entered the scene, thanks to the relative decline of short wave radio and the growth of FM stations. The tendency of commercial radio to rely on news from international feeds has facilitated the trend. The impact of all this has been a crisis of public broadcasting, which has seen both its subsidies from the state and appeal to previously captive audiences dwindle (Deane et al. 2003).

Table 2.3 Growth of Television, 1980–2002

45 countries	Television stations, 2000–2	Receivers (000s)			Receivers per 1,000		
		1980	1990	2000	1980	1990	1996–2002
Total	901 (+652 repeater stations)	8,083	25,204	45,804	18	42	60

Source: World Bank 2004: 249, United Nations Statistics Division – Common Data Base

Like radio, television has also become increasingly commercialized, although, given the higher investment required in television broadcasting, the number of television stations lags behind that of radio stations. Also, the relatively high cost of television sets means that far fewer people have access to television than to radio. In 1996–2002, for Africa as a whole, radio was available to 213 people out of every 1,000, while the per capita rate for television sets was eighty-nine out of 1,000 (World Bank 2004: 249). Nevertheless, television has also grown rapidly during the past two decades. This can be seen in Table 2.3, which shows that the number of receivers for the forty-five countries surveyed grew by more than 5.5 times between 1980 and 2000, and that the receivers per capita more than trebled. Altogether, these countries boasted 901 television stations.

Another notable feature in the television industry has been the growth of satellite television, which has accelerated the transnationalization of television broadcasts. In many urban markets, viewers now have access to international and regional television stations, most prominently CNN from the United States and the BBC from the United Kingdom, as well as Al-Jazeera from Qatar and M-Net from South Africa. The first three provide round-the-clock news, whereas M-Net represents the growing number of stations that mostly provide entertainment. Although entertainment programming continues to be dominated by American movies, soaps and comedies, especially in English-speaking countries, local and regional content has also expanded. Particularly impressive has been the growth of the video film industry in Nigeria and Ghana, whose products are shown on televisions in many countries across the continent (Dogbe 2003). Thus, the television scene in contemporary Africa is more diverse and complex than ever, characterized by products and viewing habits that promote, simultaneously, transnationalization, regionalization, nationalization and localization. The proliferation of television outlets is fragmenting audiences and reconstituting them in new ways, providing a mosaic of mirrors of social identities and aesthetic pleasures.

Table 2.4 Telephone, Computers and Internet Availability (1998–2002)

Country					Computers (per 1,000 people)		Internet users (000s)	
	Telephones (000s)							
	Mainlines		Mobile					
	1998	2003	1998	2003	2001	2002	2001	2002
Africa	16,442.3	24,624.6	4,156.9	51,024.5	10.9	12.9	6,162	9,954
World	838,848.8	1,143,084.1	317,674.8	1,404,844.4				

Source: World Bank (2004: 249–50); ITU (2005)

Print, radio and television are relatively old technologies, even if they are being reconfigured technically and socially. Critical to the notion that the world is undergoing a revolution in information and communication technologies is the spread of computers, the internet, and cellular telephony, and the complex convergences of all these technologies, thereby blurring the old distinctions between telecommunications, computing and broadcasting. This has created a nomenclature problem, as former definitions of services and markets within the information and communications industry erode. It is also causing regulatory hurdles (Osiro 2003; McIver 2003). The growth in cellular telephones has been so spectacular that by 1996–2002, twice as many people already used mobile phones as landlines (see Table 2.4). In fact, mobile phones grew faster in Africa than anywhere else in the world, by more than 1,000 per cent between 1998 and 2003. By the beginning of 2005 there were more than 82 million mobile phone users on the continent, which was revolutionizing not only interpersonal communication and business, but also the media (BBC 2005).[1]

Compared to mobile phones, computer and internet use have experienced slower but steady growth since the mid-1990s, although Africa still lags behind the rest of the world and there are huge disparities among and within countries structured along the enduring social and spatial hierarchies of location (urban-rural), class, gender, and age.[2] As Table 2.4 shows, computer use for Africa as a whole rose from 10.9 per 1,000 people in 2001 to 12.9 in 2002, and internet hosts per 10,000 people rose from 1.99 to 2.71 as the number of internet users rose from 6.2 million to nearly 10 million during the same period. By the beginning of 2005, as depicted in Table 2.5, the number of internet users across the continent had reached 12.9 million. There are wide national variations in internet usage among African countries. South Africa has the largest number of users, at 27.2 per cent, followed by Egypt with 20.9 per cent, which gives these two countries almost half of the continent's total number of internet users.

Africa's internet usage grew faster than the world average between 2000 and 2005 – at 186.6 per cent compared to 125.7 per cent for the rest of the world (see Table 2.5). For some countries the rates of growth achieved several hundred, even exceeding 1,000 percentage points, although beginning at very low levels. Indeed, at the start of 2005, Africa only comprised 1.69 per cent of internet users worldwide, and had a low penetration rate of 1.4 per cent, as compared to the world average of 14.6 per cent. Only the island nations of Seychelles and Reunion approximated or surpassed the average world penetration rate. The rates of penetration were below half a percentage point for twenty-one out of Africa's fifty-four countries. Thus, Africa has enormous ground to cover in joining the internet revolution by increasing both internet usage and African content on the internet. Additionally, Africa has to raise its capacity for producing electronic software and hardware – in short, to become a major producer, not simply a consumer of electronic products and services.

Despite the challenges of access, connectivity and content, the internet has clearly been beneficial to the African media. Hundreds of African newspapers are now available online and individuals and institutions on the continent are setting up new websites, weblogs and discussion groups all the time. Also remarkable has been the explosion of the diaspora presence on the internet. Diaspora groups have established numerous ethnic, national, regional and continental websites and electronic networks linking their compatriots at home and abroad. The internet has expanded the communicative horizons of citizens and empowered journalists to overcome government censorship and reach beyond their domestic audiences. In the case of Zimbabwe, the closure of several opposition newspapers as the country descended deeper into tyranny before and after the 2000 parliamentary elections only served to turn the opposition press increasingly to the internet (Ebeling 2003). Some studies suggest that the internet may be forcing greater transparency among leaders in the public, private and civic sectors (Leslie 2002). Thus, the internet and online activism have been an integral part of the liberalization and democratization of the media and communication in Africa, notwithstanding all the well known infrastructural problems and social inequalities reflected in, and reproduced by, the new information technologies.

THE CHALLENGES FACING THE MEDIA

The African media have made many strides in the last two decades, and are better poised than they have ever been to contribute to Africa's social and political development. It cannot be overemphasized, however, that the mass media face formidable challenges. First, there are the infrastructural constraints – the investments and costs associated with the construction of

Table 2.5 Internet Usage in Africa, 2000–5

Region	Population (2005 est.)	Pop as % in world	Internet users (3 February 2005)	Usage growth (2000–5)	Penetration (as % of population)	% Users in world
Africa	900,465,411	14.0%	12,937,100	186.6%	1.4%	1.6%
Rest of the World	5,511,601,774	86.0%	804,510,047	125.7%	14.6%	98.4%
World Total	6,412,067,185	100.0%	817,447,147	126.4%	12.7%	100.0%

Source: http://www.internetworldstats.com/stats1.htm

extensive and efficient information and communications systems, from energy to education. This also includes the question of literacy and the use of African languages in expanding communicative spaces to make them more relevant for more people. Second, there are regulatory issues. Inadequacies in the legal systems of many countries, especially in the form of clawback clauses that operate as derogable measures, make press freedom conditional. Additionally, the extra-legal sanctions of arbitrary political action, including the confiscation of media properties and harassment of journalists, continue to exact a toll on the media (Ogbondah 2002). Further, institutional mechanisms essential for balancing the private and public interests, which often take the form of self-regulating media councils or independent media commissions, remain relatively weak or are inadequately developed in most countries. A third set of challenges centres on access issues, the media's access to official information, and the access for different groups to information and the media (referred to as universal access)[3] – particularly for those inscribed by the marginalities of social difference: women, the rural areas, the working poor and peasants, and the young and elderly.

Corporate pressures pose their own difficulties for the mass media through the negative effects of corporate ownership, the tyranny of advertisers, and the emerging global regime of trade in services. In much of the global North, the media has become more concentrated as it has become more corporatized, a threat that is growing in Africa as the mass media is liberalized and becomes a more lucrative business. It is certainly an issue in post-apartheid South Africa, where the interpenetration of black and white capital has led to, according to Keyan Tomaselli (2002), the deradicalization of the black press. Of more immediate concern is the commercialization of the mass media, as the public media face reductions or withdrawals of subsidies and the expanding private media face more competition, thereby forcing all media outlets to scramble for advertisements, sponsorship and donations. In this environment, audiences and the public interest matter far less than the private interests of those who pull the purse strings. Media products are also increasingly subject to commoditization as trade in services has grown – faster, in fact, than trade in goods – and has become subject to international trade and intellectual property rules of the WTO and WIPO. Even scholarly publications on the internet have not escaped the drive to redefine what Jean-Claude Guédon calls 'the boundaries between infrastructural commons and the proprietary commons' (Guédon 2003: 187). The potential impact of GATS on the African media, as well as on other social and services sectors, such as education, deserves closer scrutiny (Zeleza 2005b).

These developments are connected to two other sets of challenges. One concerns the international dimensions of Africa's media, both the presence of the international media in Africa and of Africa in the international media. In addition to the Western news agencies and wire services, upon which many African newspapers have traditionally depended for foreign news stories and the importation of television programmes, European and United States media powerhouses like CNN and BBC now directly broadcast to Africa, or they are carried by private radio and television stations anxious to fill empty time slots and bask in borrowed credibility.

As already noted, the internet has opened new avenues for Africa to broadcast itself at home and abroad, and thus to increase its global presence. Numerous African newspapers and radio stations can now be readily accessed on the internet, not to mention exclusively online sites created by people and organizations on the continent and in the diaspora. Nevertheless, the flow of news is still predominantly from the global North to Africa rather than the other way round, and Africa lacks a BBC, a CNN, or even an Al-Jazeera that can project its presence to the rest of the global village. This is a challenge African media entrepreneurs must address, if Africa is to acquire the global capacity to define itself rather than always to be defined by others, especially those invested in perpetuating negative images of Africa. For example, the mainstream American media reserves a special derogatory vocabulary for describing African events, in which 'tribalism' is applied to every conflict, whereas class, ideology, religion, resources or the grind of competitive politics are the 'normal' sources of conflict occurring elsewhere (Hawk 2002). This discourse of derision is rooted in the country's historic contempt for African Americans, and tells us far more about US race relations than about Africa as such.

Finally, there is the question of media hierarchies, the relationships among the three media systems noted earlier – mass communication media, interpersonal media and 'small' media. We need to know more about how they interact and are valorized. This is a call for more research into all forms of media, their complex and contradictory connections, and the role they play in constructing African identities and promoting or undermining social development. Who can forget the horrific role played by the mass media, especially radio, in inciting the Rwandan genocide of 1994? The media, in short, have the capacity for perpetrating both good and evil, ignorance and awareness, bigotry and fairness, development and destruction. It is a power too awesome to ignore.

NOTES

1. Despite this rapid growth, sub-Saharan Africa's teledensity (main telephone lines and mobile users per 1,000 inhabitants) remained among the lowest in the world. In 2002 it stood at 5.3 (up from 1.0 in 1992), which was higher only in

comparison with the Pacific with 4.7 (up from 2.3) and South Asia with 4.5 (up from 0.7). But it was much lower compared to the rates for the Caribbean with 52.6 (up from 9.8), developing Europe and Central Asia with 44.1 (up from 14.1), Latin America with 35.4 (up from 7.1), East Asia with 27.4 (up from 1.2), and the Middle East and North Africa with 18.0 (up from 4.5) (ITU 2004: 74).

2. One of the ways in which many African countries have been trying to deal with some of these disparities is to encourage the development of community tele-centres in the rural areas and in poor urban neighbourhoods. Typically, telecen-tres contain older technologies (telephone, television, videos, photocopying and facsimile) along with the newer ones (computers with internet connectivity). The telecentre movement is still in its infancy, so it has yet to be subjected to detailed research. For an informative recent study on the challenges facing telecentres, see Etta and Parvyn-Wamahiu (2003).

3. Universal access is defined or often described in terms of geographical avail-ability of ICTs within a country, their accessibility to all those who need them, their affordability, use of common technology standards, and participation.

REFERENCES

BBC News (2005), 'Mobile Growth "Fastest in Africa". <http://news.bbc.co.uk/1/hi/business/ 4331863.stm> March 3, 2005.

Deane, James, et al. (2003), 'The Other Information Revolution: Media and Empowerment in Developing Countries'. In Bruce Girard and Sean O'Siochru (eds), *Communicating in the Information Society*. Geneva: UNRISD, pp. 65–100.

Dogbe, Esi (2003), 'Elusive Modernity: Portraits of the City in Modern Ghanaian Video'. In Paul Tiyambe Zeleza and Cassandra Rachel Veney (eds), *Leisure in Urban Africa*. Trenton, NJ: Africa World Press, pp. 227–47.

Ebeling, Mary F. E. (2003), 'Going Global: The Internet Age and Freedom of the Press in Africa'. In Paul Tiyambe Zeleza and Ibulaimu Kakoma (eds), *Science and Technology in Africa*. Trenton, NJ: Africa World Press, pp. 291–307.

Etta, Florence Ebam, and Sheila Parvyn-Wamahiu (2003), *Information and Communication Technologies for Development in Africa*, Volume 2: *The Experience with Community Telecenters*. Dakar and Ottawa: CODESRIA and IDRC.

Guédon, Jean-Claude (2003), 'Locating the Information Society within Civil Society: The Case of Scientific and Scholarly Publications'. In Bruce Girard and Sean O'Siochru (eds), *Communicating in the Information Society*. Geneva: UNRISD, pp. 165–94.

Hafkin, Nancy (2003), 'The African Information Society Initiative'. In Paul Tiyambe Zeleza and Ibulaimu Kakoma (eds), *Science and Technology in Africa*. Trenton, NJ: Africa World Press, pp. 95–126.

Hamelink, Cees J. (2003), 'Human Rights for the Information Society'. In Bruce Girard and Sean O'Siochru (eds), *Communicating in the Information Society*. Geneva: UNRISD, pp. 121–63.

Hawk, Beverly G. (2002), 'African Politics and American Reporting'. In Goran Hydén, Michael Leslie, and Folu F. Obundiumu (eds), *Media and Democracy in Africa*. Uppsala: Nordiska Afrikainstutet, pp. 157–76.

Hydén, Goran, and Michael Leslie (2002), 'Communications and Democratization in Africa'. In Goran Hydén, Michael Leslie, and Folu F. Obundiumu (eds), *Media and Democracy in Africa*. Uppsala: Nordiska Afrikainstutet, pp. 1–27.

Hydén, Goran, and Charles Okigbo (2002), 'The Media and the Two Waves of Democracy'. In Goran Hydén, Michael Leslie, and Folu F. Obundiumu (eds), *Media and Democracy in Africa*. Uppsala: Nordiska Afrikainstutet, pp. 29–53.

International Telecommunications Union (ITU) (2004), *World Telecommunications Development Report 2003: Access for the Information Society*. Geneva: ITU.

— (2005), World Telecommunications Indicators Database. Geneva: ITU. http://www.itu.int/ITU-D/ict/publications/world/world.html.

James, Tina (ed.) (2004), *Information and Communication Technologies for Development in Africa*, Volume 3: *Networking Institutions of Learning – SchoolNet*. Dakar and Ottawa: CODESRIA and IDRC.

Leslie, Michael (2002), 'The Internet and Democratization'. In Goran Hyden, Michael Leslie, and Folu F. Obundiumu (eds), *Media and Democracy in Africa*. Uppsala: Nordiska Afrikainstutet, pp. 107–28.

McIver, William (2003), 'A Community Informatics for the Information Society'. In Bruce Girard and Sean O'Siochru (eds), *Communicating in the Information Society*. Geneva: UNRISD, pp. 33–64.

Ogbondah, Chris W. (2002), 'Media Laws in Political Transition'. In Goran Hyden, Michael Leslie, and Folu F. Obundiumu (eds), *Media and Democracy in Africa*. Uppsala: Nordiska Afrikainstutet, pp. 55–80.

Ogundimu, Folu Folarin (2002), 'Media and Democracy in Twenty-First century Africa'. In Goran Hydén, Michael Leslie, and Folu F. Obundiumu (eds), *Media and Democracy in Africa*. Uppsala: Nordiska Afrikainstutet, pp. 207–38.

Osiro, Deborah Akoth (2003), 'IT and telecommunications: Legal implications'. In Paul Tiyambe Zeleza and Ibulaimu Kakoma (eds), *Science and Technology in Africa*. Trenton, NJ: Africa World Press, pp. 201–22.

Plou, Dafne Sabanes (2003), 'What about Gender Issues in the Information Society?'. In Bruce Girard and Sean O'Siochru (eds), *Communicating in the Information Society*. Geneva: UNRISD, pp. 11–32.

Raboy, Marc (2003), 'Media and Democratization in the Information Society'. In Bruce Girard and Sean O'Siochru (eds), *Communicating in the Information Society*. Geneva: UNRISD, pp. 101–19.

Spitulnik, Debra (2002), 'Alternative Small Media and Communicative Spaces'. In Goran Hydén, Michael Leslie, and Folu F. Obundiumu (eds), *Media and Democracy in Africa*. Uppsala: Nordiska Afrikainstutet, pp. 177–205.

Tomaselli, Keyan (2002), 'Media Ownership and Democratization'. In Goran Hyden, Michael Leslie, and Folu F. Obundiumu (eds), *Media and Democracy in Africa*. Uppsala: Nordiska Afrikainstutet, pp. 129–55.

Van der Veur, Paul R. (2002), 'Broadcasting and Political Reform'. In Goran Hydén, Michael Leslie, and Folu F. Obundiumu (eds), *Media and Democracy in Africa*. Uppsala: Nordiska Afrikainstutet, pp. 81–105.

World Bank (2004), *African Development Indicators 2004*. Washington, DC: World Bank.

Zeleza, Paul Tiyambe (2003a), 'Imagining and Inventing the Postcolonial State in Africa', *Contours: A Journal of the African Diaspora* 1(1): 101–23.

— (2003b), *Rethinking Africa's Globalization,* Volume 1: *The Intellectual Challenges.* Trenton, NJ: Africa World Press.

— (2003c), 'Knowledge, Globalization, and Hegemony: Production of Knowledge in the Twenty-First Century', keynote address presented at the First Global Research Seminar on Knowledge Society versus Knowledge Economy: Knowledge, Power, and Politics. Organized by UNESCO's Forum on Higher Education, Research, and Knowledge. Paris, December 8–9.

— (2004), 'The Struggle for Human Rights in Africa'. In Paul Tiyambe Zeleza and Phil McConnaughay (eds), *Human Rights and the Rule of Law in Africa.* Philadelphia: University of Pennsylvania Press, pp. 1–18.

— (2005a), 'Human Rights and Development in Africa: Current Contexts, Challenges, and Opportunities'. In Lennart Wohlgemuth (ed.), *African Commission on Human and People's Rights and the Current Challenges of Promoting and Protecting Human Rights.* Uppsala: Nordic Africa Institute.

— (2005b), 'Transnational Education and African Universities'. *Journal of Higher Education in Africa.*

Zeleza, Paul Tiyambe, and Ibulaimu Kakoma (eds) (2003), *Science and Technology in Africa.* Trenton, NJ: Africa World Press.

LANGUAGE AND THE MEDIA IN AFRICA: BETWEEN THE OLD EMPIRE AND THE NEW

Peter Mwaura, former director of the School of Journalism of the University of Nairobi, has argued that 'if the communication media [in Africa] are to be part of our culture as indeed all effective and meaningful communication should be – then they must use the local language[s] of our culture' (1980: 27). Mwaura's reasoning derives from the idea that:

> Language influences the way in which we perceive reality, evaluate it and conduct ourselves with respect to it. Speakers of different languages and cultures see the universe differently, evaluate it differently, and behave towards its reality differently. Language controls thought and action and speakers of different languages do not have the same world view or perceive the same reality unless they have a similar culture or background. (1980: 27)

Mwaura then concludes that there is a real sense in which 'the medium of communication is also the message' (1980: 27).

This position, of course, is one that is widely held in African intellectual circles, and has sometimes led to the conclusion that the 'domination of a people's language by languages of the colonizing nations was critical to the domination of the mental universe of the colonized' (Ngugi 1986: 16). The postcolonial hold that European languages inherited from the colonial legacy continue to have on African nations is often seen as a continuation of the cultural and intellectual domination by the West. Against this backdrop, after noting that 'Colonialism created some of the most serious obstacles against African languages . . . [which] still haunt independent Africa and continue to block the mind of the continent', the 2000 Asmara Declaration on African languages concluded that 'African languages are essential for the decolonization of African minds and for the African Renaissance'.

A central objective of this essay is to interrogate the terms of this debate as it relates to the media in Africa specifically, drawing examples from both the old empire of European colonial rule and the new empire of a globalizing world under the hegemony of the United States. I use the term 'new empire' to designate the so-called 'new world order', whose logic is framed

> not by an explicit contrast between the colonizers and the colonized, superior and inferior races, but rather in the language of laws, the injunction to be moral, the apparent concern for lives (there must be no American casualties, in any case), and the ethic of caring. The imperative to punish and kill is now derived by designating entire states as rogue or outlaw formations, who invite retribution by having stepped outside the pale of law of what American politicians call international community. (Lal 2002: 10)

And, like the old empire, the new American empire has its own political, economic and cultural articulations rooted in the encounter with the imperial 'center'.

This African debate is, of course, part of a wider contest of ideas that has taken place within linguistics between advocates of relativism and those of universalism. The terms of this debate, their implications and the limitations of both positions are explored in greater detail elsewhere (Alidou and Mazrui 1999).

LANGUAGE AND THE MEDIA IN THE OLD' EMPIRE

The African colonial experience, especially as it relates to the mass media, provides numerous examples that contradict a monolithic reading of European colonial language policy. While newspapers like *Muigwithania* (1925) in Kenya and *Sauti ya Tanu* in Tanganyika (1957) demonstrate how nationalists made use of African language media to protest against colonialism, there are numerous examples of the so-called vernacular papers that were launched with the specific objective of furthering the ends of colonialism. A good early example of the colonial use of African language media is drawn from what was then Tanganyika under German colonial rule. Under the influence of Carl Meinhof, attempts were made to 'dis-Islamize' Kiswahili, transforming it into a medium of Christian-oriented journalistic ventures like *Msimulizi, Habari zo Mwezi, Pwani na Bara* and *Rafiki*, all with the objective of consolidating German rule (Mazrui and Mazrui 1999: 58).

Another example is from southern Africa where, in 1931, the Bantu Press was formed with the explicit intention of diverting Africans away from political engagement to other pursuits at a time when socialistic ideas were gaining currency in the region. In 1944, when it expanded its operation to what was then Southern Rhodesia, it began to produce Ndebele and Lozi versions of the *Bantu Mirror* and Shona and Chinyanja editions of its *African Weekly*. The Bantu Press was itself a project of the South African Argus Group. This was largely controlled by Cecil Rhodes, who insisted on a conservative, pro-colonial approach to political reporting (Bourgault 1995: 160). Similar colonial ventures in print media can be found elsewhere in Africa.

It is in the electronic media, and especially the radio, that we find more compelling examples of the use of African languages for colonial ends. Radio has been one of the most powerful instruments of electronic communication, due to its relative affordability, its accessibility to both literate and non-literate audiences, and the scope of its demographic reach. The use of local languages in radio transmission was widespread in British colonies. France, on the other hand, had a policy of (linguistic and cultural) assimilation, and therefore tied radio services in its African colonies directly to France. In fact, the French regarded radio broadcasting in the French language as an inexpensive means of counteracting 'the discussions of educated Africans turning rapidly to subversive and anti-governmental ideas' (Tudesq 1983: 15).

The average citizens of French colonies, however, soon learnt to turn to the radio broadcasts in local languages coming from neighbouring countries under British rule. People in the West African French colony of Niger, for example, would listen to radio broadcasts in Hausa from neighbouring (British-controlled) Nigeria. In an attempt to counteract the influence of these radio services, the French began providing indigenous language broadcasts to Africans in their own colonies (Bourgault 1995: 71). Even staunchly assimilationist France, with its deliberate policy banning the use of African languages in formal domains, was ultimately compelled to resort to African languages when political circumstances made it expedient to do so.

A similar change of colonial language policy took place in African colonies held by the Portuguese. The Portuguese also pursued an assimilationist policy whose objective, according to a document from the colonial Service for Psycho-Social Action, was to teach the Portuguese language so as to 'instill [in the native] the desire to learn Portuguese so they will speak of it as "our language"' (quoted in Ferreira 1974: 159). Before the beginning of the armed struggle for independence, broadcasts in Portuguese colonies were exclusively in the Portuguese language. However, once the war for liberation broke out, the Portuguese colonial administration found it necessary to broadcast programmes in African languages in order to communicate their propaganda in words that the colonized majority could understand.

Though itself not a colonizing power in Africa, the United States began to take an interest in African languages in the concluding years of Africa's colonization. Area studies, into whose ambit comes the study of African languages, developed in the United States partly in response to the Cold War, when the US government decided to lay claim to certain regions of the world and 'protect' them from the 'communist' threat, or to penetrate regions that had already come under Soviet influence. Expectedly, the end of the Cold War turned area studies (and African languages) into an engagement of relatively low priority in the US government's agenda on foreign nations, as seen in the decreasing funding for international education and cultural exchanges. However, in light of new technological advances, the needs of capital, combined in the aftermath of the Cold War with the unfolding of new political conditions, gradually stimulated a new kind of interest – part economic and part political – in the languages of the 'other'.

LANGUAGE, GLOBALIZATION AND THE MEDIA IN THE NEW EMPIRE

Political and economic developments in the world are postured towards a hegemonic world culture. Being the only super-power in the post-Cold War period, the United States has naturally become central in this globalization process. The globalization of empire that the British attempted in the formal sense has been carried further by America in a different sense to the point where 'Americanization in its current form is a synonym of globalization, a synonym that recognizes that globalization is not a neutral process in which Washington and Dakar participate equally' (Readings 1996: 2).

But the centripetal dimension of globalization with an American face has often had its centrifugal counterpart. In many instances the momentum for democratic change in parts of Africa was spurred and supported by the United States and its NATO allies. Throughout the Cold War period, the United States was known to support all sorts of tyrannical regimes in the Third World if, by so doing, it would prevent the Soviet Union from establishing a foothold in the respective countries. The end of the Cold War, however, saw a US government eager to encourage political liberalization, partly because of its greater conformity with the globalization agenda of its market ideology. The expression of democratic pluralism that resulted from this process often assumed an ethno-nationalist articulation.

These expressions of democracy in Africa, with their ethnic and nationalist aspects, have had a direct impact on the media, leading to a flowering of the press, both in European and African languages. There are many variations in this development from region to region, and from one form of media to another. 'Francophone' African countries, for example, seem to be far behind their 'Anglophone' counterparts in newspaper production in African languages. 'Lusophone' African nations seem to have the least amount of print media in African languages. Television in Africa is far less multilingual than radio: one can listen to radio news in Lutooro, for example, but not watch it on television. In spite of these variations, however, it is still true that media in African languages received a boost from the democratization momentum.

At the same time, post-Cold War globalization has compromised the sovereignty of nation states in Africa (Readings 1996: 47). One of the results of this decline in state-nationalist ideologies has been the momentum for privatization, often imposed by the World Bank and the International

Monetary Fund, in a way that no longer questions the domination of African electronic and cyber spaces by foreign services. In the process, the new imperial centre has increasingly come to have unfettered access to the African public. Here, too, the issue of language has come into play.

The philosophy of universalism (in linguistics) has contributed significantly to computer-language research, thereby helping to perfect a technology that has rationalized the world market in favour of the North and to the detriment of the South (Mazrui 1992: 71). The computer and the internet increasingly dominate the global network of communication, serving as a relatively new engine of empire building and the creation of a homogenized, transnational, consumerist capitalism.

For a long time, computer-based communication was regarded as the domain of the English language – it began, in fact, with American English and the Roman script (Jordan 2001). More recently, however, this linguistic pattern seems to be shifting, as American businesses realize that 'Web users are three times more likely to make purchases at sites that are presented in their native language' (Biggs 1999: 52). A whole new industry – the so-called localization industry – has emerged, seeking to adapt products and services to the languages and cultures of target audiences in distant lands.

When it comes to computer-based communication, it is becoming increasingly clear that the forces of economic globalization have developed a great interest in penetrating local markets through local languages, and that they are working hard to transform these languages into commodified instruments of economic and cultural domination. In spite of the fact that economic globalization has spurred the spread of English globally – which the greater fluidity of internet communication makes it easier to domesticate – there is the centrifugal effect which creates new avenues for the advancement of certain African languages in the service of that same economic globalization.

In the colonial period, some African languages were selected for standardization and codification to serve imperial ends, whereas others were not so privileged. As Johannes Fabian (1986) and others have demonstrated, African languages became an important part of the colonial project of command and control. In this era of the new empire, we are again witnessing a selective process, controlled from the centre of global economic power, by which some languages will get 'scientificated' and 'technologized' and, thus, pushed to new positions in the global constellation of languages, to give fresh momentum to new engines of the new empire. This linguistic dynamic in computer communication also prevails, although to a lesser extent, in other domains of the electronic media.

The US invasion of Iraq provides a good example of a new understanding of the role of language on US television. At this time, the term 'embedded journalism' was coined to refer to the arrangement whereby US journalists wishing to cover the war could do so only under the cover of the US military, having access only to events, sites, and people that the military made available to them. But the term 'embedded' can also be understood metaphorically, to describe the extent to which the US media at home sees itself as an extension of the US government. It is not at all unusual, for example, to hear US journalists making use of an inclusive 'we' when referring to US government actions in Iraq.

The US media is constantly feeding its 'captive' public – to use Ginsberg's term (1986) – with inscriptions of new meanings of English words, suggesting, for instance, that 'occupation' (the loss of sovereignty) actually means 'liberation', and that the strugglers who resist occupation are exclusively terrorist insurgents who hate the idea of 'freedom'. The construction of the new empire is, thus, not simply a matter of political and economic domination. It is also a matter of informational and epistemological control, with the media sharing platforms with education to constantly (re)shape the lenses, the categories and terms of reference, through which we perceive and understand the world.

While such disinformation in the English language is primarily intended for the American audience, its demographic reach is quite global. It may be true that, in print media, US newspapers like the *New York Times* and *Washington Post* have less influence in Africa than the British *Financial Times* and the *Guardian*; but US magazines like *Time* and *Newsweek* are not only widely read but widely imitated by other publications. Similarly, British English is probably heard more widely than American English on the radio, in Africa and in the rest of the world – not just from the BBC but from almost all European broadcasting channels using English. But on television it is American English that predominates. Worldwide, US television occupies a disproportionate share of the electronic space.

In spite of the global tentacles of US television, the reality of the resistance in Iraq forced the US government to reconsider its exclusive reliance on the English language. US attempts to change the image of the US empire in Arabic-speaking populations, in particular, have led to the launching, on 14 February 2004, of Al-Hurra ('The Free'). With a first year budget of some US$62 million, Al-Hurra is operated by the Middle East Television Network, a corporation funded by the US Congress through the Broadcasting Board of Governors that oversees all government-sponsored international broadcasting. Targeted at about twenty-two Arab-speaking countries in North Africa and the Middle East, the new television project has recruited some of the best Arab journalists to Washington DC to launch an ambitious media campaign to 'win the minds' of the Arabic-speaking world. Al-Hurra has been projected as an antidote to Al-Jazeera, an Arabic-language station that the founders of Al-Hurra consider to be unduly anti-American. In this self-contrast with Al-Jazeera, Al-Hurra claims full custody of 'truth' – not to *a* truth but, like the Bible and the Qur'an, to *the* truth – implying, of course, that Al-Jazeera operates in the realm of falsehood.

The new realization that the Pax Americana needs the language of the 'Other' to prevent it from plunging into a crisis of legitimacy has led to a totally new emphasis in area studies and foreign (including African) language study in the American academy. This change of academic course is well captured in the International Studies in Higher Education Bill (HR 3077), passed by the US Congress on 21 October 2003 (though later revised). According to the summary of the bill,

> America's international interests and national security concerns have taken on new importance in the post-9/11 era. Whether in business and industry, education, politics, trade and commerce, or national and international security, America's interests are tied to . . . a group of programs at colleges and universities which work to advance knowledge of world regions, encourage the study of foreign languages, and train Americans to have the international expertise and understanding to fulfil pressing national security needs.

As we now well know, the fulfilment of these 'pressing national security needs' has included gunboat democracy, with the self-censoring US mass media playing an important role in the ideological arsenal. Academic emphasis has shifted from the study of languages once connected with Cold War politics to, especially, Arabic as the language of Islam. There is even evidence that the United States has cut its media services to Eastern Europe – the former communist bloc – because broadcasting funding has shifted to the Arab world. After all, as John Woods, the esteemed professor of Middle Eastern history at Chicago University, once remarked, 'Almost immediately after the collapse of Communism, Islam emerged as the new evil force in the Western imagination' (*New York Times*, 28 August 1995).

In addition to the space for covert action opened up by this policy towards the study of foreign languages, however, there is the attendant concern that the languages of the Other will be invested with the discursive terms of reference of the new empire, especially through the power of the media. Will the Kiswahili of East African media be reconfigured in the image of the English of American hegemony? It is unsurprising that the words of George W. Bush, spoken in English in the immediate aftermath of September 11, migrated rapidly to Daniel Arap Moi's Kiswahili within the East African context, with all the attendant violation of rights, freedoms and justice that they implied.

It is evident that there is no deterministic correlation between European languages and imperial domination, on the one hand, and African languages and cultural liberation, on the other. It is true that in both the old and the new empires, European languages have served the ends of imperialism, but they have not necessarily done so as a consequence of imperial imposition. In both German East Africa and apartheid South Africa, the languages of the dominating class were deemed to serve the interests of domination best by being made inaccessible to the African. Furthermore, while African languages have indeed been mobilized in the struggle against imperial domination, there are many instances, then and now, where they have been transmuted into instruments of domination. This complex linguistic equation cannot be explained by either a universalist or relativist reading of language, precisely because both of them espouse an ahistoricity that predicates social progress on a pre-existing order of things rather than on the politico-economic dialectics of a dynamic and constantly evolving society.

AFRICAN LANGUAGES AND REGIONAL INTEGRATION

If lessons of history have led to this conclusion, however, they do not imply that African languages have no special role to play in the media that cannot be performed by European languages inherited from the colonial tradition. There are indeed several areas of development that require the primacy of African languages. For instance, African languages are crucial to fostering cultural convergence on the regional level.

Experience from the European Union (EU) suggests that efforts towards economic and political integration are likely to be more successful if some degree of cultural convergence has already taken place. It was out of this cultural convergence that Europeans began to regard themselves as European and sought to give expression to their collective identity in a new, modern economic community. In time, the EU has come to insist on a shared liberal political culture before a European country could apply for membership. Similarly, governments in Africa that seek regional integration may have to give the issue of cultural integration more serious thought than they have done in the past.

Language is no doubt an indispensable instrument in cultural integration. In East Africa, for example, English has played an important role in the process, but mainly at the upper (elite) level of society. At the level of non-elites, Kiswahili continues to serve as a facilitator of regional cultural convergence. While there are fewer speakers of English than there are of Kiswahili in Kenya, Tanzania and Uganda, the number of speakers of both languages seems to be rising all the time. This linguistic trend is likely to help the consolidation of the East African community.

Cultural convergence is also aided by the media. Whenever Kenyan newspapers are permitted to enter Uganda, they are met with great demand. Today, virtually all Kenyan newspapers, in both English and Kiswahili, find their way to Uganda on a regular basis. Likewise, Uganda's *New Vision* has become a common item in some stalls in Kenya. The same kind of exchange is taking place between Kenya and Tanzania, on the one hand, and Tanzania and Uganda, on the other. The launching of the English-language *East-African* newspaper, with its focus on regional coverage, is a particularly important development in fostering East African cultural integration. What now remains is to design a sister paper, with a similar regional focus, in Kiswahili.

At one time, one of the reasons for the popularity of East African newspapers across their own borders concerned the limits of censorship within each partner state. There were occasions when the most candid news about Kenya could only be read in a Tanzanian newspaper. In a sense, then, there was a kind of decentralized press freedom in Africa during the heyday of tyranny, provided that newspapers of partner states were given general free circulation. Today, of course, the demand for newspapers and magazines from across the border has a lot to do with the general increase in human traffic, trade and commerce. All this international activity promotes an interest in what newspapers from the various nations have to say about events in their own countries as well as in the region as a whole. Trade and journalism, therefore, have combined in East Africa to foster cultural convergence, with both Kiswahili and English as primary linguistic facilitators of the process.

DEMOCRATIZATION OF INFORMATION

The construction and durability of a genuinely democratic order depends, to a very significant extent, on the democratization of information, to the extent that as large a proportion of the citizenry as possible has access to information about the important events happening in their country. Such information cannot be the exclusive preserve of the few that are proficient in the languages of the former European colonizers. It is only by providing access to information in the languages that the people understand that will allow them to participate in political reconstruction towards a healthier future. As Ngugi wa Thiong'o points out, 'as long as the ideas are available in African languages [to those who have no competence in the Euro-languages], even anti-African ideas, the people will start developing them in ways that may not always be in accordance with the needs of the national middle classes and their international allies' (Ngugi 1998: 97–8). Ngugi here is raising the question of class struggle over meanings assigned to ideas and concepts in African languages, and the possibility of their semantic transformation in the struggle for a new order.

Bourgault has made the observation that a healthy trend in recent years has been 'the growth of groups founded in the Southern Hemisphere, assemblages of persons promoting communitarian politics, grassroots awareness, feminist consciousness of peace and equality, and environmental stewardship, all within an ethical or religious framework. African groups have also participated in this process, many in connection with the flowering of democracy movements' (Bourgault 1995: 247). With these grassroots initiatives there has also emerged a communitarian model of the media, especially in electronic media. This development not only favours the use of African languages, but provides excellent opportunities for the inscription of alternative and independent ideas and discourses outside the confines of the epistemological empire imposed by the West.

The existence of counter-hegemonic ideas and concepts in a language is, of course, important. Conveying those ideas to the public is equally so. The mere existence of ideas does not imply, in every case, their conveyability. The first depends on a language's own capacity for expansion; the second on the social rules on how language is to be used. That is why some women writers regard European languages in Africa as both a blessing and a curse – as potential instruments of liberation and, simultaneously, as malleable vehicles of domination. For Assia Djebar, for example, the French language provided her with the space for 'self-unveiling' – to do with the language what the patriarchal society of Algeria considered taboo for women to do in the Arabic language. But she understood, at the same time, what she and the rest of her society stood to lose by a total 'capitulation' to a Western tongue (Lionnet 1996: 331–3).

The point raised by Assia Djebar's experience, though based on Arabic, can easily be extended to other African languages. The bottom line is that the act of creating a counter-discourse cannot be restricted to the generation of alternative meanings. Often it has to involve a certain degree of linguistic transgression, challenging the social rules and cultural politics that govern language use, that determines who says what to whom, how, when and where.

AFRICAN LINGUISTIC ENRICHMENT THROUGH TRANSLATION

The exclusive reliance on imperial languages in Africa has fostered a certain degree of media (and intellectual) dependency on the West. As a result, even much of the international news that is transmitted in African languages by the African media is based on translations of texts in European languages, especially English, released by media syndicates. Can Africa capitalize on this to its own benefit? Yes, if there is sufficient appreciation that the value of translation transcends the imperative of communication. Translation can be an instrument of enrichment for target languages and cultures. Referring to the impact of biblical translations in Europe, for example, Lowry Nelson has argued that:

> at every turn translators of the Bible had to make difficult choices reflecting accuracy, intelligibility and idiomatic grace. Those choices . . . helped to fashion not

only medieval Latin as a living language, but also a wide array of vernaculars in
Slavic, Germanic, Romance, and other language groups. (Nelson 1989: 19)

Indeed, there is an entire heritage of idioms – such as having 'one's cross to
bear', 'washing one's hands' of responsibility, and 'crossing one's fingers' –
which have emerged as a direct result of the availability of the Bible in the
English language.

The translation exercise in the African media needs to respond to a whole
range of vocabulary regarding world politics, for example, including such
terms as the Cold War, the Iron Curtain and North-South relations. There
is also the challenge of translating euphemisms: How can one discuss 'homosexuality' without being morally judgmental? Kiswahili words like *ukhanithi*,
ushoga or even the quasi-religious *uliwati* are not as morally neutral as
'homosexuality' or the euphemistic term 'gay'. In any case, the challenge of
translating news of the world is bound to enrich African languages, rendering them even more potent media tools in the process.

At the same time, the media in Africa needs to adopt a more interventionist
mode of translation. News in English from US-based syndicates, for example,
repeatedly reproduces the discourse of domination. At the same time that it
conquers new regions, new people and new cultures, the American English-
language media carries with it a neoliberal ideology that seeks to legitimize
the market philosophy of 'profit over people', the unequal power relations
between North and South, and the ongoing construction of global apartheid
(Chomsky 1999). The effect is to preclude any imaginable possibility of an
alternative system or credible path of revolutionary action. As a transmission
belt of neoliberalism, in other words, the English-language media from the
West have the capacity to numb our consciousness and reduce the democratic
struggle to party politics and the periodic exercise of voting. If African trans-
lators are to avoid reinforcing the globalization of this neoliberal ideology,
then they must be boldly creative in inscribing new categories of meaning in
the contested space of political semantics. In this way, translation can play a
counter-discursive role against the logic of the new imperialism.

STABILIZING AFRICAN LANGUAGES

The electronic media (especially radio and television) can constitute a major
force behind the standardization of pronunciation. BBC radio and television, for example, have popularized a particular upper-class, British accent
in Britain and abroad. The print media, on the other hand, constitutes a
major force behind the standardization of spelling. Both forms of media
encourage and reinforce the standardization of usage. The development
and stabilization of standard varieties of African languages can benefit
immensely from their more extensive use in the media.

In the final analysis, then, while this paper has concentrated disproportionately on the place of African languages in the media, the media has its own impact on African languages. Like the relationship between the global and the local, the story of the interplay between language and the media in Africa must be seen as one of reciprocal effect. Language makes it possible for the media to have a global reach and impact. In turn, the media can empower languages in a way that extends their capacity for local cultural resistance against the global hegemony of the imperial center.

REFERENCES

Alidou, Ousseina and Alamin Mazrui (1999), 'The Language of Africa-Centered Knowledge in South Africa: Universalism, Relativism, and Dependency'. In Mai Palmberg (ed.), *National Identity and Democracy in South Africa*, Cape Town: Human Science Research Council; Uppsala: Nordic Africa Instituet and Cape Town, Mayibuye Center, pp. 101–18.

Biggs, Maggie (1999), 'Globalization Issues Force to the Front Lines by Changing Online Demographics'. *InfoWorld*, 21(36): 52.

Bourgault, Louise M. (1995), *Mass Media in Sub-Saharan Africa*. Bloomington: Indiana University Press.

Chomsky, Noam (1999), *Profit over People: Neoliberalism and Global Order*. New York: Seven Seas Press.

Chomsky, Noam (2001), *9–11*. New York: Seven Seas Press.

Fabian, Johannes (1986), *Language and Colonial Power: The Appropriation of Swahili in the Former Belgian Congo, 1880–1938*. Cambridge: Cambridge University Press.

Ferreira, Eduardo de Sousa (1974), *Portuguese Colonialism in Africa: The End of an Era*. Paris: UNESCO.

Fukuyama, Francis (1992), *The End of History and the Last Man*. New York and Toronto: Free Press and Maxwell MacMillan Canada.

Ginsberg, Benjamin (1986), *The Captive Public: How Mass Opinion Promotes State Power*. New York: Basic Books.

Jordan, Tim (2001), 'Measuring the Internet: Home Counts versus Business Plans'. *Information, Communication, and Society*, 4(1): 34–53.

Lal, Vinay (2002), *Empire of Knowledge: Culture and Plurality in the Global Economy*. London: Pluto Press.

Lionnet, Françoise (1996), 'Logiques Metisses: Cultural Appropriation and Postcolonial Representations'. In Mary Jean Green et al. (eds), *Postcolonial Subjects: Francophone Women Writers*. Minneapolis: University of Minnesota Press, pp. 321–44.

Mazrui, Alamin (1992), 'Relativism, Universalism and the Language of African Literatures'. *Research in African Literatures*, vol. 23, no. 1, Spring 1992: 65–75.

Mazrui, Ali A., and Alamin M. Mazrui (1999), *Political Culture of Language: Swahili, Society, and the State*. Binghamton, NY: IGCS, Binghamton University.

Mchombo, Sam (1998), 'National Identity, Democracy, and the Politics of Language in Malawi and Tanzania'. *Journal of African Policy Studies*, 4(1): 33–46.

Mwaura, Peter (1980), *Communication Policies in Kenya*. Paris: UNESCO.

Nelson, Lowry (1989), 'Literary Translation'. *Translation Review*, 28: 17–30.

Ngugi wa Thiong'o (1986), *Decolonizing the Mind: The Politics of Language in African Literature*. London: Heinemann.

Ngugi wa Thiong'o (1998), *Penpoints, Gunpoints and Dreams: Towards a Critical Theory of the Arts and the State in Africa*. Oxford: Clarendon Press.

Readings, Bill (1996), *The University in Ruins*. Cambridge, MA: Harvard University Press.

Searle, Chris (1983), 'A Common Language'. *Race and Class*, 25(2): 65–74.

Shakespeare, William (1963), *Julius Caesar*, trans. Julius Nyerere. Nairobi: Oxford University Press.

Tudesq, André-Jean (1983), *La radio en Afrique noire*. Paris: Editions A. Pedone.

REFLECTIONS ON THE MEDIA
IN AFRICA: STRANGERS IN A MIRROR?

INTRODUCTION

As a result of advances in information and communication technology (ICT), the world has shrunk to a global village, where we can learn about events happening anywhere in the world as they take place, or soon after, largely courtesy of the mass media. However, although we have all become citizens of the global village, we are not equal partners. There are disparities in access to information and communication channels, as well as disparities in the levels at which individuals may participate in, and benefit from, the production of information.

In a typical African village, people were expected to know one another and they received information from all corners of the village, such that each member of the community felt part of the communication process and could identify with what was being communicated. Ideally, media should act as a mirror to reflect in structure and content the various social, economic and cultural realities in which the societies and communities operate (McQuail 2000: 171). However, the problems of imbalances in communication that the MacBride Commission (MacBride 1980) tried to address in the 1970s are still evident to date. Looking at the media in Africa, can the majority of Africans easily identify with most media content, or do they simply see forms of strangers reflected in the mirror?

The discussion in the paper is premised on theory of political economy and how this has influenced African media. Different perspectives related to globalization and information dualism, which contribute to the distorted images that give the reflection of strangers in a mirror, are explored.

TRADITIONAL COMMUNICATION PATTERNS

In most parts of Africa, the major traditional sources of information were the family and the local members of the community. People largely depended on interpersonal communication, which was predominantly verbal. Written culture and formal education were introduced to the African continent by Christian missionaries. This was later reinforced during the colonial period.

Ugboajah (1985) coined the term 'oromedia' to designate indigenous, speech-based African channels of communication. He describes them as highly distinctive and credible, unlike the electronic media, which can be elitist, vicarious and urban. He points out that the distinctive feature of oromedia is their capacity to communicate with the common person in their own language and idioms, as well as dealing with problems that are directly relevant to his situation. Nyamnjoh (1996) argues that, even now, ideas, information and knowledge can be effectively transmitted using such indigenous forms of communication, which are characterized by simplicity of technology and directness of information. Accordingly, such communication takes place in a non-artificial milieu, involving the use of gestures, body language, facial expression, symbols and folklore. In Africa, the ability to speak well with oratorial power constitutes a highly valued attribute in many oral cultures (Peek 1981).

Another characteristic element of traditional African oral communication was its emphasis on community participation. Even if only one person actually spoke, others were an important part of the communication process, directly or indirectly. Traditional communication was participatory, unlike communication through the mass media, which is mainly a one-way flow of information, with minimum participation by the receivers.

However, in the largely patrilineal African societies, differentiation in gender roles was clearly exposed in the dynamics of the traditional communication process, reflecting the subordinate status of women. Because men were not restricted to the domestic domain, as girls and women were, they had an exposure to influences beyond their immediate environment, giving them greater access to new ideas and information. For example, the men of East Africa who migrated to townships usually learnt Swahili and English, along with other local languages. This meant that they could interact or communicate with other people who came from far beyond their home communities. Few women had access to such experiences. This imbalance is reflected in today's media. Women are given much less coverage than men; the little coverage provided tends still to portray women in traditional gender roles.

Traditionally, if people wanted to communicate over long distances, they adopted various systems. One of these, particularly used by chiefs and kings, was the use of messengers to relay information to the people. These messengers can be compared to the journalists whose major function is to keep society informed. Like today's journalists, messengers enjoyed the privilege of working close to the centre of power (government), where major political and economic decisions are made. Messengers occupied a special position within society, serving as the link between the people and the centre of power (kings and chiefs). Other channels of long distance communication were the use of drums and musical instruments like the flute.

Drama has been, and continues to be, an important means of communicating messages in African societies. Drama possesses a strong power of sensitization and education, which attracts people's attention due to its conformity with the social, educational and interactive nature of communication (Ahade 1999). In certain places, particularly among the royalty, there were people who were designated as keepers of tradition. These individuals served both as entertainers and as 'points of reference' with regard to historical events.

Despite the apparent advantages of non-oral (especially visual) media over traditional oral forms, the latter remain important. For example in Uganda, the Population and Housing Census (2005) found that 49.2 per cent of respondents depended on 'word of mouth' as their main source of information.

The transformation from traditional communication styles to mass communication in most parts of Africa was largely precipitated by the coming of the missionaries and colonial rule. Both these forces brought with them a change in the people's allegiance and general way of life, necessitating new forms of communication structures. The missionaries set out from Europe with a mission of spreading Christianity in Africa. This could not be done by oral means alone. The people needed to be taught to read the Bible. This in turn necessitated the introduction of formal education in missionary schools and the development of print media. As schools spread, the culture of writing and reading also grew, leading to a reduction in reliance on traditional oral communication.

In addition, changes have taken place in family structures and patterns of living. These have led to the near-extinction of traditional oral culture in some parts of African society, such as the urban areas. The pressures of modern life leave no time for parents or other relatives to engage the children in 'informal learning' – through the use of stories, songs, poems, idioms, proverbs, and the like. Moreover, with the change from extended family structures to nuclear family units, elders who used to co-reside with the younger generations of their families and performed important educational tasks, now stay with the children only during brief visits.

Once people became literate, they recognized that knowledge is more efficiently stored and passed on through documentation than was possible using oral traditional. In addition, written materials could reach far more people. This inspired the creation of newsletters, which later grew into modern newspapers. By the 1960s, radio had been introduced into most African countries; by the 1970s, most countries had access to television. By 2000, internet services could be accessed in most countries.

AFRICAN MEDIA IN THE AGE OF GLOBALIZATION

Media theory based on the principles of political economy clearly explains what is taking place in the media industry at the global level and locally in African countries. This is reflected in the domination of the media by the minority wealthy class, while excluding the masses. Globally, Western media conglomerates and their multinational counterparts enjoy a monopoly in international communication, while at the national level, the media serve the interests of the minority urban elite. The importance of advertising revenue means that media content is tailored to meet the interests of advertisers, instead of addressing the public interest. Information has become commoditized, or priced for purchase, rather than serving as a social good, to which all people should have access. Market forces exclude the economically disadvantaged from media participation, while favouring the economically endowed.

Ramonent (cited in Moumina 2007: 4) explains this change from an economic perspective, stating that information initially was a rare good, which made it expensive, unlike today when it is superabundant and tends to be 'relatively free'. He says that while, initially, its value was based on the criterion of truth, today, the criterion is the number of likely interested buyers, thus subjecting media to the laws of supply and demand. He points out that since there are insufficient consumers of information who can pay the prices in Africa, most of the information targets the West. Hamelink (1996) criticizes the media-centred globalization processes, noting that these are largely driven by the economic interest of opening up new markets worldwide.

Analysing the impact the 'digital divide' will have on Africa, De Beer (2007: 206) predicts that the prosperity of Africa will depend on its ability to navigate the knowledge space, based on its capacity to engage in networks of knowledge production, transaction and exchange. He attributes the downfall of the communist governments to their incapacity to pursue collective intelligence, because of the crisis of social and cultural integration. This integration, he says, is a non-negotiable condition in the globalizing world for survival and prosperity. In order to participate in the knowledge space, one needs to have access to electronic communication, which unfortunately is still very low for most African countries. Looking at internet use, by June 2008, World Internet Usage Statistics (ww.internetworldstats.com) showed that Africa had 3.5 per cent of users, compared to Asia with 39.5 per cent, Europe with 26.3 per cent and North America with 18 per cent. Of those in Africa, 50 (91 per cent) of the countries had below 5 per cent users, with only five (9 per cent) of the countries (Nigeria, Egypt, Morocco, Algeria and South Africa), having 6 to 20 per cent.

A few people in the urban areas have gained access to the information superhighway and can access information readily. But as Nyamnjoh (1996) has ably described, the majority is silent, still searching for a footpath. In Uganda, for example, the urban population is only 12 per cent, much lower than the 34 per cent for Africa, and the 90 per cent for the United Kingdom (World Population Data Sheet 2007).

The debate on the causal dynamics of globalization has brought about three schools of thought: the globalists, the traditionalists and the transformationalists. The globalists believe that globalization cannot be resisted or influenced by interventions from traditional institutions like nation states. The traditionalists consider globalization as a myth that has been exaggerated, since they see nothing very new: the North-South gaps still remain. The traditionalists see a big role for nation states as they argue that most economic and social activities are regional, rather than global. The transformationalists take a middle road and see globalization as representing a significant shift, but they question the inevitability of its impact (Servaes and Lie 2003). What is happening in Africa would fit more with the globalists' view, as we are moving towards homogenous global (Western) culture. For instance, while initially the 'pure' or ideal community media were started in the 1990s, these could not withstand the global influence of media commercialization. What we have now is a hybrid of commercialized community media.

One of the major changes resulting from globalization, which Servaes and Lie (2003) identify, is the link between the global and the local, or what has been termed 'glocal'. In other words, how globalization has affected the local communities. Locality can be defined as a combination of ideology, culture, language and ethnicity, often seen in terms of a nation. The locality can be viewed from two perspectives: the globally oriented space and a geographically oriented place. It is noted that as oral communication has given way to mass communication, the mode of expressing locality and the focus of spatiality have changed. This is explained by the mass communication culture in transition societies, whereby in its search for a new locality, its focus tends to exaggerate the significance of the nation level and the urban components, while ignoring the rural and local elements in conventional mass communication (Kivikuru 1999: 78).

Hall (cited in Servaes and Lie 2003) acknowledges that it is human nature to want 'a place' to which a person feels he or she belongs, but it is also human nature to want to reach out to the strange, unknown world outside of this 'place'. Enhanced by globalization forces, we now have a melting pot where cultures have merged. Looking at the social impact of globalization, Appadurai (cited in Jacobson and Lang 2003) points to the key role played by modern communications, transportation and migration patterns in creating large populations around the world whose identities are attached in part to adopted lands, in part to original home lands, and in part to newly emerging global cosmopolitan identities. Due to conflicts, wars, civil strife, political differences or economic reasons (in search of greener pastures), one finds many Africans who have migrated to Western countries.

Relating globalization to the media situation in Africa, in his discussion of Africanity and modernity, Nyamnjoh (2005: 4) observes that the basic assumptions underpinning African journalism ignore the fact that ordinary Africans are busy 'Africanizing their modernity and modernizing their Africanity', in ways that are too complex to be captured by simplistic dichotomies. He opines that the precepts of journalism that apply currently in Africa are largely at variance with dominant ideas of personhood, society, culture and democracy on the continent. He attributes this practice to the assumption that there is a 'one-best-way of being and doing', to which Africans must aspire in the name of modernity and civilization. He observes that this leads to the journalism of bandwagonism, where mimicry is the order of the day.

Nyamnjoh (2005: 4) submits that African journalism needs to recognize and provide for the fact that the home village in Africa has retained its appeal both for those who have been disappointed by the town, and for those who have found success in the towns. He explains that even the most achieving and successful cosmopolitan individuals hesitate to sever their rural connections entirely, but take the 'world out there' as a hunting ground, and return to the home village at the end of it all. This attachment can be evidenced in the valued norm up to today of burying the dead at their ancestral home. Nyamnjoh regrets that the prescriptive journalism practised in Africa denounces this reality, and he calls for recognition of the importance of cultural identities.

MEDIA AND INFORMATION DUALISM IN AFRICA

For a long time, there were high expectations for the media's contribution to development through their ability to facilitate mobility. Greater mobility leads to the broadening of horizons, which increases a person's capacity for change, encouraging an orientation toward the future, and belief in one's efficacy. Lerner (cited in Hedebro 1986) noted that whereas mobility can be direct or physical, it could also be indirect, achieved through the media. He further argued that an expanding mass media system promoted the spread of modern attitudes, favourable to social change and development. He suggested that increased literacy led to increased media exposure, which in turn stimulates economic and political participation; and that increased urbanization tends to raise literacy levels. Media expansion and the processes of urbanization and modernization were thus seen as automatically leading to development. Other researchers add that the media play an important role in teaching knowledge and skills more rapidly and inexpensively. In this view, the media can compensate for the lack of teachers, schools and educational materials (Hornick 1988).

The development strategies of the 1960s shared a belief in the media's power to transform society, and therefore emphasized media expansion in the Third World. However, even after considerable expansion over the decades that followed and liberalization in many countries, the media industry has not contributed markedly to the progress of development in Africa. What happened along the way? Where did things go wrong?

After the 1960s, when most African countries gained independence, governments maintained control over the media. In most countries, government had a monopoly in the broadcast media. Although there were no legal provisions or other regulations preventing private newspapers, few could compete against the government-owned outlets, so the government presence was heavily felt in the media industry. By 2000, however, most governments had adopted a liberalization policy, and the media sector was opened up to private enterprises. In almost all African countries, media structures are similar. They are predominantly centralized and are concentrated in urban areas offering programming largely of interest to the urban elite. Karikari (1999) sums up the media systems in Africa pointing out that although each community has its own message and voice, existing media are not disposed to accommodate these different voices.

In his study *Mass Communication in Africa*, Mytton (1983) noted that because media are vital to the exercise of political power, they tend to come under political control, whether direct or indirect. He contends that the media may actually increase the widening gap between rural and urban life and culture. He observes that although the media are supposed to be a reflection of the whole of society, the attention given to urban affairs, urban problems and urban culture is nevertheless greatly disproportionate. Citing Tanzania and Zambia as case studies, he says that the media have failed to perform their primary function of informing society. Rather, they tend to cater more for urban demands, neglecting rural life.

In another study of the press in Nigeria, it was found that about 80 per cent of Nigerians were excluded from participation in mass media, largely because they were not part of the urban elite. Another media study in Francophone West Africa (Benin, Burkina Faso, Côte d'Ivoire, Guinea-Conakry, Mali, Niger, Senegal and Togo) revealed the same findings: that out of the estimated 80 million people in the region, 64 million individuals had no access to information, education or entertainment through the media (M'Bayo 1995).

Mytton (1983) noted that access to communication facilities and technology are closely associated with access to economic resources. He observes that indices of economic development and the development level of communications facilities are also closely related. In Uganda, for example, in a survey done to assess access to information delivery systems and media habits, of the 5.1 per cent who had access to the internet, 4.4 per cent were in Kampala and other towns (Nassanga 2002: 74). This confirms Mytton's (1993) conclusions about the communications gap that exists between towns and rural areas. He asserts that there are two types of communication networks operating almost autonomously: the urban communication network, which is not responsive to what takes place in the villages, and village level communication, for which information from the urban areas seems to contain little of local relevance.

An analysis of media content shows that most of it is by and about urban people. Media owners have argued that, like any other business, they must rely on market surveys to find out what consumers want. If consumers are mostly in the towns, the media must put out the kind of programming that the urban people are willing to buy. The few stories originating from or dealing with the rural areas are only those made relevant to an urban audience because they refer to a minister, government official or other celebrity visiting the areas. Chambers (1983) has termed this 'urban tourism', by which reporters concern themselves with rural areas only for short 'visits', before dashing back to the comfort of the towns. The short time spent in the rural areas does not allow journalists to truly understand the information needs and interests of rural people.

Of particular concern to the situation of information dualism are the big differences in living conditions among urbanites, as compared to rural people. Although the term 'poverty' is relative, it can be safely said that poverty is more prevalent in rural areas than in urban ones. One of the indices used to measure human poverty relates to knowledge levels, and the degree to which individuals are excluded from the world of reading and communication. This situation is pertinent to Uganda, where it may be noted that the rural poor suffer from social, economic and political marginalization, with lack of access to basic services, marketing information and opportunities for political participation to influence decision-making at local and national levels (UNDP 1998). In many rural areas, people live a hand-to-mouth existence, with little time to worry about other things apart from where to get the next meal.

Communication research has shown that information exchanges are related to power relations in society. Those with higher social-economic status and education tend to have more central positions within information exchanges (Hamelink 1988). As information facilitates change, those with better access to information are more likely to benefit from development. Advances in information and communication technologies have led to an information explosion, even spreading to the African countries. Although much information is now readily available, accessing that information is not free. Access to information and the media is largely dependent on socio-economic and educational levels.

MEDIA AND GENDER

Apart from the information dualism observable between the urban and rural societies, it is also visible in disparities of access and coverage accorded to men as compared to women. The majority of women are 'media disadvantaged' not just locally, but nationally and internationally, as well as being generally accorded a lower status than men. In Uganda, a baseline survey done by the Uganda Media Women's Association (UMWA) on the coverage and portrayal of women in the Ugandan media found that women received only 16 per cent of coverage (Nassanga 1994). Since information is a key factor in facilitating change and development, the fact that women have less access to the media means that they do not benefit as much as the men from development programmes.

The *Uganda Human Development Report* (1998) confirms the gender imbalances existing in Uganda. The report notes that women constitute a disadvantaged social group, with poverty being on the rise among rural women. The report further states that this situation has led to poverty being 'feminized', such that people talk of the 'feminine face of poverty'. Women generally have less income at their disposal, rendering them unable to afford the necessary instruments to access information: radio, printed matter, television, computers, internet and so on. Given that women make up more than half the population, their lack of access to information has a considerable negative impact on development.

MEDIA AND SOCIAL CONTEXTS

It is important to note that it is not only information *per se* that causes development. Social, cultural, economic, political and other aspects that influence people's way of life need also to be addressed. Gumucio and Tufte (2006: 157) observe that history has shown that development is accelerated not so much by the acquisition of information, but rather is dependent upon structural issues such as land ownership and human rights. They explain that even when armed with useful information, poor peasants usually do not break the vicious cycle of social injustice and exploitation. It is thus important not only to consider the availability of information but also the context within which the information is communicated, including the level of participation. As Hall (2000) submits, before a message or information can have an effect or be put to use, it must be appropriated as a meaningful discourse, and meaningfully decoded, explaining that it is the decoded meanings which have an effect on the receiver.

Another crucial aspect relates to the relevance of media content in Africa. Examining programming in most countries, one finds that a large proportion of time and space is given over to entertainment programming, rather than informational and educational or developmental programmes. For instance, in a national survey on the performance of the electronic media in Uganda (Chibita 2004: 37), when respondents were asked to rate the balance in the programming, less than half (45 per cent) were satisfied with the balance. This imbalance was explained by the predominantly private media, whose priority is to minimize costs, so as to maximize profits. So there is a tendency to look to entertainment programmes like music and sport, as investing in news collection and investigative stories is costly. Moreover, most of these entertainment programmes are sourced from the Western countries. For instance, Western music, soaps and sports account for a big part of local media programming.

The effect of such media content is that when the majority of Africans who live in rural areas turn to the media, most of the programme content is of little relevance to them. This is evidenced in Uganda, where one of the barriers to sustainable development identified by Uganda Sustainability Watch Report (2005: 18) was the lack of 'active local participation in national affairs'. It was found that the population was generally not well informed about government programmes, laws and policies, which created an information gap and resulted in the grassroots being detached from them.

Although the media are supposed to be a reflection of what is taking place in society, to the rural majority all that can be seen are strange reflections in the mirror. Hamelink (1995) terms this 'disempowerment', which he says refers to the process by which people lose the capacity to control decisions affecting their lives as well as the ability to define themselves and to construct their own identities. Hamelink notes that the strategy of disempowerment is based on deceit, by making people believe that existing conditions are desirable and that they have been accepted out of free will. When pan-Africanists express concern over the Western bias in media content, the ready reply from the media is that 'this is what the people want'. Hamelink's concept of disempowerment brings that reply into question. Are we really sure that this is what the people freely prefer, or have they been conditioned to accept this content?

It should be recognized that Africa has gained a lot from the West, but it has also to be noted that the West has much to learn from Africa's experiences. As Gumucio and Tufte (2006: 157) contend, cultural interaction is healthy when it happens within a framework of equity, respect, dialogue, debate and solidarity. Advocates for new development communication approaches have emphasized the need for a relationship based on an egalitarian principle. Gumucio (2001: 153) cautions that while globalization has been accepted as a phenomenon, it requires correction, short of which will lead to greater disempowerment of those outside of the economic network. Thus, this calls for a review of media systems at global, national and local levels, with a view to put strategies in place to counteract the existing imbalances.

PROSPECTS FOR THE FUTURE

Some regional media institutions in Africa have attempted to counteract the negative effects of globalization. These include the Media Institute of southern Africa (MISA), which brings together media institutions in southern and Central Africa; East Africa Media Institute (EAMI), bringing together thirteen countries in the eastern Africa region; West Africa Journalists Association (WAJA), Media Foundation for West Africa (MFWA), and the Middle East News Agency (MENA), which covers some countries of North Africa. The Africa Council on Communication Education (ACCE), the African Women Development and Communication Network (FEMNET), and the Union of National Radio and Television Organizations of Africa (URTNA) all need to be rejuvenated.

The media have undoubtedly contributed greatly to alienating Africans from their cultural norms, values and customs. Western languages like English, French, Spanish and German have facilitated global communication, but at the cost of marginalizing local languages. While embracing Western media products, Africans need to pick the good aspects from the West while maintaining the good that can be found in their traditional systems. Initiatives to make their own entertainment programmes like Nigerian movies or 'KinaUganda' movies should be supported by governments, for example by offering such companies favourable tax conditions.

It may be argued that multilingual media are not viable as the media cannot accommodate all that many languages and dialects in each country. However, using the existing regional media organizations, public media could be strengthened, allowing them to cater for the rural population as well as the urban elites. The development of community media should be encouraged. Community media, which are largely owned and managed locally, are by definition concerned with local issues. Through them, community members are better able to participate meaningfully and to influence programming so that it is relevant to their needs.

Through the community media and by strengthening the public media, the rural majority no longer need to see reflections of strangers. They may thus be de-alienated from their culture and local environment. Because the media, as a major source of information, play such a big role in the development process in Africa, it is imperative to review their focus so as to work towards reflecting the realities of Africa's constituent societies. Through this process, many Africans will no longer see strangers reflected but should be able to find media content relevant to their local environment.

REFERENCES

Ahade,Y. (1999), 'The Development of Community Media in French Speaking West Africa'. Paper presented at the Regional Seminar on Promoting Community Media in Africa, Kampala: 7–9 June.

Bennett, T. (1998), 'Media, Reality and Signification'. In M. Gurevitch, T. Bennett, J. Curran and J. Woollacot (eds), *Culture, Society and the Media*. Routledge: London, pp. 287–309.

Chambers, R. (1983), *Rural Development. Putting the Last First*. London: Longman.

Chibita, M. B. (2004), *The National Electronic Media Performance Study*. Kampala: Broadcasting Council.

De Beer, C. S. (2007), 'Africa in the Globalising World: Digital Divide or Human Divide?', *Communicatio. South African Journal for Communication Theory and Research* 33(2), pp. 196–207.

Gumucio, D. A. (2001), *Making Waves: Stories of Participatory Communication for Social Change*. New York: Rockefeller Foundation.

Gumucio, D. A. and T. Tufte (eds) (2006), *Communication for Social Change Anthology*. New York: Communication for Social Change Consortium.

Hall S., 'Encoding/Decoding'. In P. Marris and S. Thornham (eds) (2000), *Media Studies*. New York University Press: New York, pp. 51–61.

Hamelink, C. (1988), *Cultural Autonomy in Global Communication*. London: Centre for the Study of Communication and Culture.

— (1995), *World Communication: Disempowerment and Self-Empowerment*. London: Zed Books.

— (1996), 'Globalisation and Human Dignity: The Case of the Information Superhighway'. In *Media Development*. London: *Journal of the World Association for Christian Communication* (1).

Hedebro, G. (1986), *Communication and Social Change in Developing Nations*. Des Moines: Iowa State University Press.

Hornick, R. C. (1988), *Development Communication: Information, Agriculture and Nutrition in the Third World*. Longman: New York.

Jacobson T. L. and W. Y. Jang (2003), 'Mediated War, Peace and Global Civil Society'. In B. Mody (ed.), *International and Development Communication: A 21st Century Perspective*. Sage: New York.

Karikari, K. (1999), 'The Development of Community Media in English-Speaking West Africa'. Paper presented at the Regional Seminar on Promoting Community Media in Africa, Kampala, 7–9 June.

Kivukuru, U. (1999), 'Locality in Mass Communication: An Irreplaceable Quality or a Relic from the Past?'. In T. L. Jacobson and J. Serveas (eds), *Theoretical Approaches to Participatory Communication*. New Jersey: Hampton Press, pp. 77–104.

MacBride, S. (1980), *Many Voices, One World*. London: Kogan Page.

M'Bayo, R. (1995), 'Press Freedom and the Imperatives of Democracy: Towards Sustainable Development'. *Africa Media Review, Nairobi: ACCE* (9).

McQuail, D. (2000), *McQuail's Mass Communication Theory*. Sage: London.

Moumina, S. C. (2007), 'Information in Search of a Market'. *Rhodes Journalism Review* (27). Rhodes University: Rhodes.

Mytton, G. (1983), *Mass Communication in Africa*. London: Edward Arnold.

Nair, S. K. and S. A. White (eds) (1993), *Perspectives on Development Communication*. Thousand Oaks, CA: Sage.

Nassanga, G. L. (1994), *The Role of the Media in Creating Images of Women: A Survey of Women's Portrayal in the Uganda Mass Media*. Kampala: UMWA.

— (2002), *Improving Information Delivery Systems: Targeting Women Through Development Communication*. Unpublished PhD dissertation, Kampala: Makerere University.

Nyamnjoh, F. B. (1996), 'Africa and the Information Superhighway: Silent Majorities in Search of a Footpath'. *Africa Media Review*. Nairobi: ACCE, 10(2).

— (2005), 'Africanity, Modernity'. *Rhodes Journalism Review* (25). Rhodes: Rhodes University.

Peek, P. N. (1981), 'The Power of Words in African Verbal Arts'. *Journal of American Folklore* 94(371).

Population and Housing Census (2005), Kampala: Uganda Bureau of Statistics.

Servaes, J. and R. Lie (2003), 'Media Globalisation Through Localisation'. In J. Servaes (ed.), *Approaches to Development Communication*. Paris: UNESCO.

Uganda Sustainability Watch Report (2005). Kampala: Uganda Coalition for Sustainable Development.

Ugboajah, F. (ed.) (1985), *Mass Communication, Culture, and Society in West Africa*. Zurich: Hans Zell.

UNDP (1998), *Uganda Human Development Report*. Kampala.

Walgrave, S. and V. P. Aelst (2006), 'The Contingency of the Mass Media's Political Agenda Setting Power'. *Journal of Communication*. Blackwell: Washington, 56(1).

World Internet Usage Statistics (2008). *Internet Usage and Population Statistics*, www.internetworldstats.com. Accessed 15 September 2008.

World Population Data Sheet (2007). Washington: Population Reference Bureau.

5 Francis B. Nyamnjoh

AFRICA'S MEDIA: DEMOCRACY AND BELONGING

In popular as well as academic circles, there are varying degrees of certainty about the extent to which media influence Africans. Contrary to the popular understanding of the media as magic multipliers capable of stimulating or dulling the senses of those who receive them, media effects are neither direct, simple nor immediate. The audience, by extension, is neither altogether passive nor helpless, since members of the same demographic often get different messages from the same source. In other words, what people make of particular media contents depends, inter alia, on where their vested interests lie, interests which are not fixed. Media effects are usually gradual and cumulative, and dependent on other accompanying factors.

The media – conventional and alternative, old and new, traditional or modern, interpersonal or mass – can, in principle, facilitate popular empowerment as a societal project. If civil society is crucial for democracy, communication is even more so. For, as Philip Lee puts it, people can only participate and make their wishes known if public communication is made an integral part of political democracy. Effective democracy, he maintains, 'demands a system of constant interaction with all the people, accessibility at all levels, a public ethos which allows conflicting ideas to contend, and which provides for full participation in reaching consensus on socio-cultural, economic and political goals' (Lee 1995: 2). In order to participate meaningfully in discussions of public issues, people need both knowledge and education on how to use the information at their disposal. The media have an enormous potential to provide such knowledge and education, but the media can also be a vehicle for uncritical assumptions, beliefs, stereotypes, ideologies and orthodoxies that blunt critical awareness and make participatory democratization difficult. Thus, only when they empower individuals and communities to publicly scrutinize and contest decisions made in their name by the most powerful members and institutions of society can the media promote democratization.

However, the media do not have the same potential in every society, nor are they accessible to everyone in the same way or to the same extent. Because of unequal access to wealth and power, certain communities and individuals are less privileged than others. This can make a world of difference in terms of media access, content and practice. In a context where availability is not synonymous with affordability, media plurality is often miles away from media diversity. This makes of democracy and participation more of an illusion than a fact of life. This is the case even in the most privileged countries of the West, where quite often, 'political rhetoric about democracy denies the possibility of inequity, inaccessibility and marginalisation' (Lee 1995: 10).

Culturally, the media are subject to an imposed hierarchy of national and world cultures, and also of the cultural industries that have opted for routinization, standardization and homogenization of content. This has occasioned the exclusion or marginalization of entire world views and cultures that do not guarantee profitability. African world views and cultural values are doubly excluded: first by the ideology of hierarchies of cultures, and second by cultural industries more interested in profits than the promotion of creative diversity and cultural plurality. The consequence is an idea of democracy hardly informed by popular articulations of pluralism and social action in Africa, and media whose professional values are not in tune with the expectations of those they purport to serve. The predicament of media practitioners in such a situation is obvious: to be of real service to democracy in its contrived liberal form, they must ignore alternative ideas of pluralism and social action in the cultural communities of which they are a part. Similarly, attending to the interests of particular cultural groups risks contradicting the principles of liberal democracy and its emphasis on the autonomous individual.

Torn between such competing and conflicting understandings of democracy, the media find it increasingly difficult to marry rhetoric with practice, and for strategic and instrumentalist reasons may opt for a Jekyll-and-Hyde personality. This has meant propagating liberal democratic rhetoric in principle while at the same time promoting the struggles for recognition and representation of the various cultural, ethnic or sectarian groups with which they identify. The politics of belonging is thus central to understanding democracy in Africa and the role of the media in promoting democratic pluralism. The predicament faced by the media in this regard emphasizes the need for more domesticated understandings of democracy as mediated by the quest for conviviality between individual and community interests.

INFORMATION TECHNOLOGIES AND DEMOCRACY

There is an increasing tendency to claim that interactive information and communication technologies (ICTs) offer more control over the media by consumers, allowing them to choose and consume what, when and how they want. Power is said to lie not with governments or multinationals, but with individuals as autonomous citizens and consumers. But others deny this claim, arguing that the new technologies are conceived, designed, built and installed with the primary objective of maintaining economic, political and cultural privileges and advantage. This argument has only grown stronger with the reactionary 'global intelligence' measures adopted by the United States, the United Kingdom and other states following 11 September 2001 (Todd and Bloch 2003). Whatever one's political or ideological position, there is clearly a need to treat the notion of 'information society' as problematic, by investigating 'alternative options in the adoption of new technologies' and discussing various strategies for the 'social shaping' of these technologies (Lyon 1986: 585–6). Far from being 'a monolithic or placeless "cyberspace"', for example, the internet 'is numerous new technologies, used by diverse people, in diverse real-world locations', and therefore cannot be fully understood outside of how it is being harnessed and assimilated under differential political, economic, cultural and social circumstances of individuals and communities (Miller and Slater 2000: 1–25). It is regrettable that scholarly focus has been rather on what ICTs do *to* Africans, instead of what Africans do *with* ICTs. Underway are processes of 'enculturation' (van Binsbergen 2004) that are yet to be fully studied.

With the exception of South Africa, Africa still resides in a world of shadows as concerns the ICTs. So far, responses by African governments leave much to be desired. Despite the adoption in 1989 of a common African information and communication strategy, little has been done at the level of individual countries to start implementation. Indeed, Africa's response to ICTs has thus far proved to be simplistic and overly optimistic in its assumptions, objectives and timetable, in view of its lack of the basic capacity to adopt and adapt ICTs to local environments.

In May 1996, the UN Economic Commission for Africa (ECA) adopted its Africa's Information Society Initiative (AISI), 'a broad, long-term and ambitious programme, directed at the utilization of information and communication technologies to stimulate overall economic and social growth in Africa' (van Audenhove 1998: 76). But not only are these guidelines dependent on the goodwill of individual states for implementation, the leeway given to private initiative leads one to question whether such 'liberalisation would indeed foster the enabling environment in which services will or can be broadly generalised' (van Audenhove 1998: 79). Countries are joining the privatization bandwagon almost without exception, quite oblivious to or regardless of the fact that private ownership does not necessarily entail better or even cheaper services, especially in a global economy where states and labour are virtually at the mercy of multinationals and their thirst for profit. African subscribers to the new privately operated cellphone networks know this only too well, and have started speaking out against poor services and exorbitant charges.

Some scholars have criticized certain questionable assumptions in the ECA document, such as that information and technology are neutral, that technology is easily transferable, that access to information technology by Africa and Africans is necessary and sufficient to accelerate development, and that information will be free or almost free in the information society. They argue that the ECA's action framework fails to take into account the formidable economic, infrastructural, political and social constraints to the effective development and implementation of ICT services in Africa (van Audenhove 1998: 77–9). What is urgently needed in most countries is not so much privatization as the constitution of an independent national regulatory authority 'to regulate the market and to introduce fair competition in certain sectors' (van Audenhove 1998: 80–1).

A sustained interest in the information superhighway by Africa must entail the domestication and standardization of the information and telecommunication technologies, 'so that its countries become capable of easily reaching each other and exchanging experiences and training facilities' (Organization of African Unity 1995: 4). This calls for a concerted and organized approach by African countries and for appropriate policies on ownership and control, which is by no means easy, especially if Africans are determined to show that assumptions about internet configurations in North America or Europe need not necessarily be reflected in internet developments in Africa.

Estimates indicated in 2000 that Africa, with a population of 780 million, had around 500,000 internet subscribers and about 1.5 million users, with approximately 1 million of these users based in South Africa alone and mostly white (Jensen 2000: 217). Despite these modest statistics of connectivity, ordinary Africans are determined to be part of the global technological revolution, even if this means accessing the information superhighway on foot, horseback, bicycles, bush taxis, and second-hand cars, or relying on lifts and the generosity of the super-endowed driving the latest sports cars.

This makes the African mediascape a rich and fascinating blend of traditions, influences and technologies. Coexisting in conviviality and interdependence are the most modern forms of communications technologies and indigenous media. One finds on the continent pockets of people in tune with an internet facilitated by multi-media connectivity – perfect examples of first-class passengers on the information superhighway staking a claim to the global village. One finds also those whose hybrid realities dictate the need to straddle the worlds of indigenous and modern media, creatively drawing on both to negotiate the communicative hurdles and hierarchies of the continent. Africa's creativity simply cannot allow for simple dichotomies or distinctions between old and new technologies, since its peoples are daily

modernizing the indigenous and indigenizing the modern with novel out-
comes. No technology seems too used to be used, just as nothing is too
new to be blended with the old for even newer results. Such creativity is
not only informed by cultures amenable to conviviality, interdependence
and negotiation, but also by histories of deprivation, debasement and
cosmopolitanism.

The political advantages of a fully harnessed internet are obvious. It could
for example, offer Africans many avenues to address current predicaments
and promote good governance, thereby serving as 'the hope of many NGOs
world-wide, of scientists and community initiatives, of trade unions and critical journalists, of alternative movements and counter-movements, who
wish to avail themselves of an independent, inexpensive, non-state-
controlled, open communication network' (Becker 1996: 10). In the
Cameroonian city of Bamenda, for example, residential telephone lines are
grossly inadequate and often defective; and internet connections are difficult
and expensive. But the literate and illiterate alike, eager to stay in touch with
relations, friends and opportunities within Cameroon and in the diaspora,
daily flood the few internet points with messages to be typed and emailed
for them. Replies to their emails are printed out, addressed and pigeonholed
for them by operators who can only afford to check for emails twice a day.
What is noteworthy, however, is that the high connection charges do not
seem to discourage those determined to stay in touch with the outside world.
Through such connections, people are able to exchange news on family,
projects, events and developments of both a personal and general nature.
They are also able to learn about different cultural products and make
arrangements to acquire them. It is mainly through this means that
Cameroonians abroad do not lose out on local musical releases, publications, satirical humour, artifacts and fashion. Each visitor to the home village
is armed with a long list of cultural products to take back. Many bachelors
and spinsters in the diaspora would otherwise have given up on marrying
from their home village or country, and doing so in accordance with local
customs and traditions, were email not available to facilitate contacts and
negotiations with parents and potential families-in-law.

Among Anglophone Cameroonians, where feelings of marginalization by
the state and exclusion from the mainstream media are high, many people,
especially youths, are increasingly turning to the internet. They use it as a
vehicle to air their views on various aspects of their predicament, centring
mostly on their perceptions that their territory and communities are victims
of gross mismanagement by a corrupt and inefficient Francophone-
dominated state (cf. Konings and Nyamnjoh 2003). Their main outlets on
the internet include web pages and discussion and mailing groups. These are
created and managed by Anglophone youths, usually grassfielders of the
North-West Province, and mostly are based in the American diaspora.

Because of their influential nature, these mailing and discussion groups have even attracted the attention of the state. Previously indifferent to this traffic, government departments and members of the ruling party now monitor its content on a daily basis. Given the flexible nature of the internet, real identities of users can be hidden under ambiguous usernames, making provocative and fearless exchanges more possible. Those who participate in the discussions are Anglophones both in Cameroon and the diaspora, and their opinions run the gamut, from pro-government to pro-opposition to pro-southern Cameroons independence. Among their number can be found the most radical and most conciliatory alike. This clearly highlights the importance of the internet in providing the space for Anglophone issues in a state that has stifled such debate and monopolized the conventional media. Critics of the government no longer need to be physically located in Cameroon to be relevant to the ongoing struggles for democracy. Quite strikingly, discussions even at this level tend to reflect the same tensions and multiple divisions that the politics of belonging and autochthony have brought to the fore. The internet discussions not only shape what is discussed in society, they also reflect the inherent divisions that autochthony brings about.

Throughout Africa, young people are amongst the greatest internet enthusiasts. These youths are not only keen to stay in touch with family and friends, but also to enhance their knowledge of international affairs and to take advantage of new opportunities by becoming involved with people of other countries with different realities. Prominent among the enthusiasts 'are journalists and aspiring journalists who use the internet to research and send stories, either as employees of an African news service or as freelancers' (cf. Franda 2002: 18–19).

Again, African creativity and conviviality are already helping to combat the technological difficulties. Africans have been innovative in their responses to neoliberalism and the globalization of poverty, despite their perceived passivism and victimhood. Like other anti-neoliberal forces in the world, African activists have taken advantage of the new ICTs to mobilize and strategize against the multinational corporations and their unyielding access to the resources and protection of African governments. Prominent African activists are leading members of the anti-globalization coalition that has given the World Trade Organization a tough time in recent meetings. Formal and informal networks of various kinds are taking advantage of the internet to push ahead their own agendas in situations where the conventional media continue to blunt aspirations for creative diversity. True, the internet is not free from the logic of domination and appropriation typical of neoliberalism, but it clearly offers marginalized voices an opportunity for real alternatives.

The same is true of other technologies, such as the cellphone. Political dissidents or subversives are able to bypass conventional channels of control, and by using cellphones they can easily be tipped off of possible danger from collaborators in the centre of state power. Dissident action can be coordinated right up to the minute of execution by collaborators who do not have to be physically located in their national territories. At the social level, diasporic Africans or migrants collectively supply a free phone to someone in a village whom they can call. In South African townships and informal settlements, for example, the cellphone has been used creatively by poor urban dwellers to stay in touch with rural relatives and through them maintain healthy communication with ancestors (Thoka 2001). In the Bamenda grassfields of Cameroon, as well, marriages, feasts, funerals, death celebrations and village development initiatives can no longer pass by any grassfielder simply because they are in the diaspora. The cellphone has become like the long arm of the village leadership, capable of reaching even the most distant 'sons and daughters of the soil' trapped in urban spaces (Geschiere and Nyamnjoh 1998). The dramatic increase in the sale and theft of cellphones is an indication that this technology has been eagerly grasped by Cameroonians exploring ways of denying exclusion its smile of triumph.

Most cellphone owners in West Africa and central Africa serve as connectivity points for their community, with others paying or simply passing through them to make calls to relatives, friends and contacts within or outside the country. Thus, for example, Nigerians actually own fewer phones than most countries in the West, but the country generates higher average cellphone revenues per month. This can be explained by the fact that Nigerians receive more calls than they make, and also by the reality of single-owner, multi-user communities. It suggests that the economic and social value of a cellphone in countries like Nigeria, with its higher volume of single-owner, multi-user communities, is much higher than for the countries with single-owner, single-user communities. Contrary to popular opinion, sociality, interdependence and conviviality are not always a liability to profitability.

Any analysis of the media's role in promoting democracy in Africa should be made against this background of a global scene marked by rapid advances in ICTs on the one hand, and the inequalities they occasion or reinforce at international, regional and national levels on the other. Such analysis should engage critically with conventional ideas of liberal democracy which focus on individuals as 'citizens', in relation to a continent where individuals and communities, for various political, economic and cultural reasons, may be forced (or willingly offer) to be 'subjects' or to straddle the worlds of liberties and subjections.

PRESS FREEDOM AND DEMOCRATIZATION IN AFRICA

The current democratic process in Africa has brought with it not only multipartyism, but also a sort of media pluralism. In almost every country, the number of private newspapers increased dramatically with the clamour for more representative forms of democracy in the early 1990s. In 2004, four-teen years into the second wave of liberation struggles, most countries liberalized the airwaves as well. More and more countries are opening up to satellite television, with little indication of any large-scale efforts by govern-ments to regulate its reception, even though satellite television is known to threaten public broadcasting by pulling away audiences and available adver-tizing funds. Digital, flexible, global and quality broadcasting is now a reality.

West Africa has experienced a boom in private, local and commercial radio stations. In Burkina Faso and Mali, where there has been a real explo-sion, the majority of these stations are rural. Most are non-profit, public service organizations, and most prefer to stick to music, sports and other 'innocent' content in order to avoid interference and possible closure by nervous governments. In Cameroon, such closures are the order of the day. South Africa, Uganda, Rwanda, Burundi, Zambia, Namibia, Senegal and Botswana are other leading examples of private involvement in broadcast-ing. Malawi launched its first national television station in January 1999, and Botswana did the same in July 2000. Lesotho and Swaziland have recently mobilized a South African commercial broadcaster, M-net, to provide a pseudo-national television system, and have also allowed the establishment of private radio stations. Zimbabwe is the exception in the region. Its gov-ernment has yet to liberalize broadcasting or to tolerate a critical private press.

South Africa, with democratic intentions and equity in mind, has not only reformed the South African Broadcasting Corporation (SABC) that served as the mouthpiece of apartheid into the early 1990s, but has also opened up to satellite television greatly. The subscription satellite television service M-net has been operational since 1986 and is owned by a consortium of South African newspaper publishers. It has rapidly spread its tentacles throughout the continent and, together with Multi-Choice and Canal Horizon of France, it virtually dominates the scene of satellite entertainment television. These providers specialize in routinized, standardized or 'McDonaldized' international sport and entertainment, which they serve to every subscriber on the continent, regardless of region, nationality or cultural preferences. This approach has occasioned renewed criticisms of Western cultural impe-rialism through South African and French media. It is hoped that increased local production and programme exchange through such organizations as the Union of National Radio and Television Organizations of Africa (URTNA), will correct the dependence on cheap, imported programmes and sports of little direct relevance to Africa.

Southern Africa has also witnessed an explosion in community radio sta-tions. In South Africa alone, more than 100 licences have been granted. It is estimated that there will be more than 200 community radio stations in the near future. According to veteran community broadcaster Zane Ibrahim of Bush Radio Cape Town, a proliferation of stations is not necessarily a good thing, because those likely to benefit most 'are the 'consultants' and the many new broadcast equipment supply companies who are more likely to be 'laughing all the way to the bank' than serving any community interest. Ibrahim is equally critical of government involvement with community radio, as such involvement can only be detrimental to 'communities not overly friendly with the ruling party of the day' (Ibrahim 1999: 15).

Although the media have seen themselves, and have been seen, as key players in the democratic process, they do not seem to be doing enough to promote democracy. There is little evidence that the media have undertaken systematic voter education during campaigns, for example, nor have they explained the electoral process to the voters. These shortcomings may be due to bias, but also to lack of professionalism and other factors. But placed in perspective, such shortcomings are hardly surprising, given that the task for the media has been rendered difficult, if not impossible, by the failure almost everywhere to give democracy an 'identity' relevant to the experiences and marginalized value systems of ordinary folks.

If the private press and private radio stations of Africa are often independent and critical of government, they have not always succeeded in displaying a similar attitude vis-à-vis opposition or other pressure groups and lobbies (ethnic, religious and regional). Instead of seeking to curb intolerance, fanaticism or extremism of all kinds, some of the media have actually fuelled them. Examples abound of newspapers in Senegal, Mali, Niger, Côte d'Ivoire, Kenya, Madagascar, Cameroon and elsewhere that have served as mouthpieces for divisive forces, often reproducing calls to murder, destruction and hatred, and generally keeping everyone fearful of a Rwanda-type situation wherein Radio Mille Collines proved what the media can do to spur ethnic cleansing. In the early 1990s in Mali, for example, elements of the press exacerbated ethnic tensions and conflicts in the north, encouraged striking students to paralyse the educational system for three years, and allowed themselves to be manipulated by 'certain leaders of the opposition, in order to attempt to make the country ungovernable' (Sangho 1996: 70–1).

In Kenya, the ethnic violence that occurred in Laikipia and Njoro in January and February 1998 exposed the press as being keener to promote 'hate journalism' through exaggeration and politicization of ethnic tensions than to provide accurate and responsible reporting. Those elements of the private press that were critical of the government tended to portray the Kalenjin (former President Moi's ethnic group) 'as the villains in the clashes' and the other ethnic groups, the Kikuyu especially, as innocent victims. Conversely, the state-owned Kenya Broadcasting Corporation and pro-government print media focused on the Kalenjin as victims. As a whole, the press 'settled on politics as the cause' and whipped up ethnic or political emotions, often without bothering 'to venture into the battlefront' (Charo and Makali 1998: 1–2).

In most countries, journalists are perceived as mouthpieces for competing political pressure groups. The pressures on them to please those for whom they work or with whom they are allied are such that they cannot report fairly on all sides of an issue, suppressing personal prejudices and sticking to the facts. The private press indulges in half-truths or blatant lies, yet claims infallibility. Although hostile to criticism of their *manière de faire*, journalists often do not hesitate to judge, instruct, moralize about or condemn others. For instance, on the front page of the Cameroonian newspaper *The Messenger*, the editor-in-chief himself ran the headline 'Kill this Man', referring to the governor of the South West Province. Such excesses are common, and refresh memories of the atrocities in Rwanda. In the name of freedom and the right to inform, the media at times have abused certain human rights.

In South Africa, newsrooms tend to reproduce 'prior metanarratives of social schisms, even when those narratives may be radically inappropriate and counter to available evidence' (Fordred 1999: iv, 215–20). It is often a case of much reporting without listening and of an exaggerated sense of self-righteousness on the part of journalists, who often do not hesitate to sacrifice truth for 'a good story'. This tendency of 'twisting or falsifying the supposed news to fit a journalist's opinion about where the truth really lies' is not exclusive to Africa. It is also 'typical of much of modern British journalism', as demonstrated by Lord Hutton's recent inquiry into a report by BBC correspondent Andrew Gilligan which accused the government of having deliberately 'sexed up' an intelligence-based dossier on Iraq's weapons of mass destruction, in order to justify going to war. However, the tendency among African journalists and media to serve ethnic, religious and regional interests is also indicative of their predicament as professionals and institutions that are expected to fulfil liberal democratic functions in a context where people are clamouring, as well, for recognition and representation as cultural, religious, and regional communities. Such competing claims for attention help explain the media's apparent contradictions, hypocrisy and double standards.

POLITICS OF BELONGING

Ethnicity and an obsession with belonging remain active forces on the African political scene. Rights articulated in abstraction do not amount to much. For one thing, political, cultural, historical and, above all, economic realities, determine what form and meaning the discussion and articulation of citizenship and rights assume in any given context. Having rights is something individuals and groups may be entitled to in principle, but who actually enjoys rights does not merely depend on what individuals and groups wish, or are entitled to under the law, by birth, or in the Universal Declaration of Human Rights.

Along with this growing obsession with belonging arise new questions concerning conventional assumptions about nationality and citizenship (Englund and Nyamnjoh 2004). The questions concern not only how nationals and citizens perceive and behave towards one another, but also how they behave towards immigrants, migrants or foreigners. Even in countries where ethnic citizenship and belonging had almost disappeared in favour of a single political and legal citizenship, there has, in recent years, been a resurgence of identity politics and overt tensions over belonging, as various groups seek equity, better representation and more access to national resources and opportunities. In such situations, while every national can claim to be a legal citizen, some see themselves or are seen by others to be less authentically so. The growing importance of identity politics and other exclusionary ideas of citizenship are paralleled by increased awareness of and distinction between 'locals', 'nationals', 'citizens' or 'autochthons' on the one hand, and 'foreigners', 'immigrants', 'outsiders' or 'strangers' on the other, with an emphasis on the opportunities, economic entitlements, cultural recognition and political representation due to each category. Customary African values and policies of inclusion, and a mainstream philosophy of life, agency and responsibility that privilege wealth-in-people over wealth-in-things, are under pressure within the struggles and politics of entitlements in an era of sharp downturns and accelerated flows of opportunity-seeking capital and migrants. The situation is complex and the choices often unclear for the various actors involved, the media included.

The media reflect as well as shape African societies, which are themselves marked by continuities, interconnections, convivialities and creative marriages of differences. Competing for the attention of the media are the notion of liberal democracy on one hand, and popular ideas of democracy informed by African notions of pluralism and social action on the other. If the media are sensitive to these apparent contradictions, as they are expected to be, their content should reflect ongoing efforts to negotiate conviviality between competing traditions, influences and expectations. Their success as mediators will depend on the indicators of democracy used, and also on how sensitive to the predicaments of ordinary Africans those indicators are. However, liberal democratic rhetoric has dominated the struggle for democracy in Africa. If the political and legal cultures of the larger society are not democratic, therefore, it is highly unlikely that the media will be any different or that they will have the political and legal freedom to endorse or pursue any democratic agenda. The media can only play an effective role, in this regard, if the law and its application are democratic.

Conducive political and legal environments, important as they may be for press freedom, are hardly enough to guarantee liberal democracy if the media operate without regard to the need to be ethical and professional in their approach to journalism. For the conventional mass media to be meaningful in the process of empowerment of civil society in Africa within the current liberal democratic framework, they, as institutions, must embody the virtue of tolerance.

On its own, liberal democracy is much too parochial for Africa's sociality, negotiability, conviviality and dynamic sense of community. Since liberal democracy appears uncomfortable with salient relationships, community and creative diversity, African leaders, journalists or media practitioners who subscribe to its rhetoric find themselves reduced to a Jekyll-and-Hyde democracy: tolerant in principle but stifling in practice. Such African leaders and media practitioners, whether in government, the opposition or civil society, are forced to keep up appearances with liberal democracy in a context where people are clamouring for recognition and representation as cultural, religious and regional communities. The competing claims for their attention by internal interest groups and external forces explain the apparent contradictions, hypocrisy and double standards when their actions are appreciated exclusively from the standpoint of liberal democracy.

The greatest shortcoming of liberal democracy is its exaggerated focus on the autonomous individual, as if there is anywhere in the world where individuals are capable of living their lives outside of communities or in the total absence of relationships with others. Losing the weight of community, solidarity and culture is not easy, even for the most dedicated of disciples of neoliberal tradition. By investing so much rhetoric in the rights of the independent person, liberal democracy is left without a convincing answer pertaining to the rights of dependent persons and communities. Although, in principle, liberal democracy promises rights to all and sundry as individuals, not everyone who claims political rights is likely to have them, even when these are clearly articulated in constitutions and guaranteed legally. The American system, which champions liberal democracy, offers some interesting examples of how Americans, assumed to be autonomous individuals by law, find themselves bargaining away their political, cultural and economic freedoms in all sorts of ways under pressure from the consumer capitalist emphasis on profit over people.

If there is an illusion of democracy and participation in communication in the West, the situation is even more critical in Africa where, in most cases, the media are the privilege of a relative few. In some countries the electronic media, both satellite and terrestrial, mean very little in language and content to the bulk of the population that is rural and has a limited understanding of the Western languages of local broadcasts. The term 'mass media' thus is often a misnomer in Africa, given that literacy in French,

English, Portuguese or Spanish is a prerequisite for access to and participation in the media, a privilege too remote for both rural and urban illiterates.

The future of democracy in Africa – or anywhere else for that matter – lies in recognizing and providing for the fact that societies are and have always been cosmopolitan and multicultural. Although we live in an age of growing uncertainties and anxieties, we cannot hope to succeed through narrow and abstract definitions of rights and citizenship, nor by preoccupying ourselves with the politics of exclusion and difference within and between groups, local or foreign. On the contrary, the answer to the impermanence of present-day achievements is to be found in a cosmopolitanism informed by allegiances to cultural meanings drawn from different sources in the rich repertoire of multiple encounters by individuals and groups in all societies. Governments, the media and other social institutions must therefore allow individuals and communities the creative interdependence to explore various possibilities for maximizing their rights and responsibilities within the confines of the economic, cultural and political opportunities at their disposal. Inclusion, not exclusion, is the best insurance policy in the face of the uncertainties to which individuals and collectivities are subjected under global consumer capitalism.

The media can find in this philosophy the inspiration needed for a vision and coverage in tune with the predicaments of their audiences, be these individuals or groups, minority or majority ethnic communities, citizens/ nationals or immigrants. The challenge for the media is to capture the spirit of tolerance, negotiation and conviviality beneath every display of difference and marginalization, encouraging acceptance as the way forward for an increasingly interconnected world of individuals and groups who long for recognition and representation.

REFERENCES

Becker, J. (1996), 'The Internet, Structural Violence, and Non-Communication'. *Media Development* XLIII(4): 10–12.

Charo, T. and D. Makali (1998), 'New Media and the Hate Campaign: Ethnic Conflict Brings Out the Best of Hate Journalism'. *Expression Today* 4: March.

Englund, H. and F. B. Nyamnjoh (eds) (2004), *Rights and the Politics of Recognition in Africa*. London: Zed Books.

Fordred, L. J. (1999), *Narrative, Conflict, and Change: Journalism in the New South Africa*. PhD dissertation, Department of Social Anthropology, University of Cape Town, South Africa.

Franda, M. (2002), *Launching into Cyberspace: Internet Development and Politics in Five World Regions*. Boulder, CO: Lynne Rienner Publishers.

Geschiere, P. and F. B. Nyamnjoh (1998), 'Witchcraft as an Issue in the "Politics of Belonging": Democratization and Urban Migrants' Involvement with the Home Village'. *African Studies Review* 41(3): 69–92.

Ibrahim, Z. (1999), 'What Does "Community" Mean for Community Radio?: Reality Check'. *Rhodes Journalism Review*, p. 15, December.

Jensen, M. (2000), 'Making the Connection: Africa and the Internet'. *Current History* 99(637): 215–20.

Konings, P. and F. B. Nyamnjoh (2003), *Negotiating an Anglophone Identity: A Study of the Politics of Recognition and Representation in Cameroon.* Leiden: Brill.

Lee, P. (1995), 'Introduction: The Illusion of Democracy'. In P. Lee (ed.), *The Democratization of Communication.* Cardiff: University of Wales Press, pp. 1–14.

Miller, D. and D. Slater (2000), *The Internet: An Ethnographic Approach.* Oxford: Berg.

Organization of African Unity (1995), 'OAU'. Paper presented at ICC workshop on New Information Technology and Standardization of Communication Equipment in Africa, Yaoundé, 29–31 May.

Sangho, O. S. (1996), 'Problems of Ethics in the Media of Mali'. In K. Karikari (ed.), *Ethics in Journalism: Case Studies of Practice in West Africa.* Paris and Accra: Institut Panos, pp. 69–90.

Thoka, M. D. (2001), 'Cellphones, Ancestors and Rural/Urban Connections. Report of Research Conducted in Monwabisi Park in November 2000'. Paper presented at Joint Conference of AASA and SASCA, UNISA, South Africa.

Todd, P. and J. Bloch (2003), *Global Intelligence: The World's Secret Services Today'.* London: Zed Books.

Van Audenhove, L. (1998), 'The African Information Society: Rhetoric and Practice'. *Communication* 24(1): 76–84.

Van Binsbergen, W. (2004), 'Can ICT Belong in Africa, or Is ICT Owned by the North Atlantic Region?'. In W. van Binsbergen and R. van Dijk (eds), *Situating Globality: African Agency in the Appropriation of Global Culture.* Leiden: Brill, pp. 107–46.

REPRESENTATION OF AFRICA IN THE WESTERN MEDIA: CHALLENGES AND OPPORTUNITIES

Most Westerners have never visited and may never visit Africa, yet they hold an image of Africa in their minds (Hawk 1992). Their knowledge of Africa is formed from sources like school textbooks, the news media, church mission reports and the entertainment industry, all produced by fellow Westerners. These images provide the context for Westerners' interpretation of media coverage of Africa.

A common theme running through the Western understanding of Africa is the metaphor of the 'dark continent', an illusion not only to the skin colour of its inhabitants, but also to their perceived ignorance (Hawk 1992). Another is that Africa is the setting for wild adventure stories. These are essentially negative portrayals of Africa, and they date back to the formative sources of Western culture. In the fifth century BC, the Greek Historian Herodotus wrote *The Histories*, portraying Africa as inhabited by savage and even non-human creatures and, by comparison, presenting the Greeks and Caucasians as the epitome of creation.

This stereotype was carried down through the years, and in the mid-1800s Charles Darwin reaffirmed them in the application of his theory of evolution. The original title of his most famous book was *The Origin of the Species by Means of Natural Selection, or the Preservation of Favoured Races in the Struggle for Life*. Later editions dropped the second part of the title, probably in reaction to its racist undertones, but it remains clear that, according to Darwin, Africans were still evolving and therefore did not fall within the 'favoured races' category with the same status enjoyed by Europeans.

In the eighteenth and nineteenth centuries, European explorers became the main source of media images of Africa. Their books denigrated Africans in their accounts and, according to Allimadi (2003), the more they exaggerated their tales of African savagery, the more books they would sell. By the early twentieth century, these negative characterizations permeated the Western view of Africa. Just as the explorers drew their preconceptions of

Africa from Herodotus and Darwin, twentieth-century Western journalists drew their stereotypes from the books written by the explorers. These stereotypes still inform Western understandings of Africa by providing the context for media coverage, both explicitly and implicitly.

THE ESSENTIAL AFRICAN STEREOTYPE AS PORTRAYED IN WESTERN MEDIA

Africa in the Western media is constructed through metaphor. The metaphors selected for the communication of Africa's stories, however, do not come from Africa, but from the stereotypes of Africa that have permeated Western culture. These metaphors are largely negative, and rest on the opposition of 'primitive' (Africa) versus 'modern' (the West). Implicit in this opposition is the idea that Africans do not behave rationally. This is evident even in the language used. For example, communities in Africa are generally referred to by the term 'tribe'. Yet this term is not used in comparable situations if they take place in Europe, where the term 'ethnic group' is preferred. The use of terms like 'tribes' and 'tribalism' serves the purpose of dehumanizing the people being described and reducing events to peculiarly racial terms.

Throughout their various histories, Africans have distinguished themselves from one another, recognizing differences in linguistic and cultural variations. They are no more culturally monolithic than the peoples of the West, and it therefore should not be surprising when there is political conflict among them. Yet reports on Africa present the continent as essentially homogeneous and disorderly. The essential characteristics of the received stereotype are the following:

1. The inhabitants of the African continent are all black.
2. Black people are morally, physically and intellectually inferior to white people.
3. The black race has made no contributions to world history, nor has it contributed any cultural, social, artistic or scientific developments.
4. Africa is uncivilized and barbaric.
5. The African continent itself is inhospitable.

The negative representations, echoing back to Herodotus, remain pervasive and effective. Worse still, many black Africans have internalized them, becoming convinced that indeed they are the most inferior human race (Allimadi 2002). Together they provide the context for modern media stories about Africa, which has powerful negative implications for Africa's place in Western foreign policy decisions, and negatively impacts the judgment of news agencies regarding the relevancy of African events to Western media consumers.

According to Ungar and Gergen (1991), part of the explanation for the paucity of news about Africa and the predominantly negative focus of such coverage as exists lies not with the media, but with the institutions they represent. In their view, the press is a follower, not a leader – it usually takes its cues from the government and industry. If these institutions do not pay attention to Africa, neither will the media. In the case of the United States, for example, both the White House and Congress place Africa low on their list of foreign policy priorities. Since the end of the Cold War, Africa has been seen as geopolitically unimportant.

CRITERIA FOR COVERAGE: WHY AFRICA IS NEGLECTED

According to Ebo (1992), the neglect and/or negative portrayal of Africa by Western media is both deliberate and systematic. The selection process employed by Western media when choosing what stories to cover can be understood by examining three types of criteria: the commercial, the political, and the sociocultural. Regarding the commercial criterion employed in determining if a story is newsworthy, Phil Harris notes: 'The production and distribution of news stories in the present international arena is in fact the production and distribution of commodity information – within an international system whose base lies in a free trade concept of a market society economy' (cited in Ebo 1992: 16). News, like any other commodity, is subject to commercial imperatives. Simply put, the need for profit maximization influences the determination that events are newsworthy. The implication, then, is that Western correspondents in Africa look for news stories that are easy and convenient to gather, and that will be attractive to viewers. As a result, they choose exceptional and aberrational news stories. Western media are not interested in meaningful development stories about Africa because such stories are, by media standards, mundane and unattractive.

Further complicating the economic aspect of Western journalism about Africa is the cost of resources and manpower. Maintaining a news bureau on the continent can cost as much as US$200,000 – about the same as a bureau in Tokyo, currently the most expensive city on the planet. The political significance of a country or a geographical region also raises the newsworthiness of a story and provides an incentive to allocate resources and attention. However, the Western media judge that significance only in terms of Western interests. Because Africa is not considered an important player in global politics, particularly since the collapse of the Soviet Union, the continent is equally unimportant to the media. As Mary Ann Fitzgerald has noted, 'Africa is no longer politically fashionable, instead the content presents a repetitive litany of coups, corruption, and famine' (cited in Ebo 1992: 17). The only time Africa gets attention from Western media outlets is when major political events take place that threaten Western political interests. This interest, however, is short-lived. As soon as the temporary political significance of the crisis dies down, the media lose interest.

Finally, most journalists from the West are not sensitive to cultural nuances in covering stories set in African countries because they do not have the necessary training or background to explain the historical and cultural significance of African social events to Western news consumers. The result, at best, is that Western correspondents deculturalize news from Africa by stripping it of its social relevance and value. At worst, the context provided is drawn from the negative stereotypes that have long influenced the Western image of Africa and its peoples. Further, African stories are disadvantaged because of the strongly held Western belief in a particular hierarchy of international social relationships that places the cultures of industrialized nations at the top, and the cultures of developing nations at the bottom. The further apart two nations stand in this hierarchy, the greater the imbalance in the flow of news between the two nations, to the disadvantage of the nation in the lower level of the hierarchy.

A SELF-PERPETUATING NEGATIVITY

The lack of broad-based Western public interest in the African continent helps to perpetuate the negative images that prevail in the press. According to Ungar and Gergen (1991), Americans seem only rarely curious about Africa, especially about its customs, political institutions and economic development. The fact that most Westerners, and particularly most Americans, know so little about Africa contributes to the reluctance of many editors to run stories on Africa. Western news consumers have become weary of Africa's problems and generally perceive those problems to have no direct impact upon their own lives. They are more likely to display an interest in the continent's wildlife than its poverty, and this is reflected in the stories the Western press chooses to cover.

Racism may also play a role in the way that Western (especially the American) press covers Africa. There are very few blacks in the newsrooms or in decision-making positions within the media. According to Roger Wilkins (cited in Ungar and Gergen 1991), what is news and what is newsworthy is basically decided by middle-class, middle-aged white males who have a very limited slice of human experience and who overvalue the ability of their limited experience to give them a broad world view. The fact that media decision makers are predominantly white may explain why, although more black people died in Natal under apartheid than in the violence of Lebanon and Northern Ireland combined, the deaths in Africa received far less coverage.

The situation is further exacerbated by the fact that Western correspondents rarely take the trouble to learn the local language (or languages) of the countries in which they are stationed. While it is true that more than half the nations of Africa have designated English as the official (or one of the official) languages, the farther away one gets from the cities, the more likely

it is that people do not speak the language. By refusing to learn local, indigenous languages, Western journalists have to rely on interpreters, which limits
their ability to explore the nuances of local culture. Forced to rely on local,
unreliable sources for details of the story they have been sent to cover, and
lacking an adequate grasp of Africa's issues, Western journalists are generally unable to probe African officials and judge their statements critically
(Ungar and Gergen 1991).

AFRICA'S CONTRIBUTION TO ITS NEGATIVE COVERAGE

The lack of press freedom in Africa is one of the most important obstacles
for foreign journalists trying to gain access to news and information there.
Many African governments distrust the press, and obtaining interviews with
their leaders is almost impossible. The lack of an open and thoroughgoing
domestic press corps, and the reluctance of many African journalists to write
critically about their own or their neighbour countries makes it hard for
foreign journalists to do a good job. Only recently have the African media in
general become liberalized – in the past, most press outlets were owned by
governments.

Africa's relative lack of infrastructure also contributes to the problem.
Logistical barriers to effective news coverage are at least as high as those
found anywhere in the world. Simply getting to the site of a story can be a
problem, since local airlines can be undependable and their schedules a
matter of conjecture, and visas are often difficult to obtain. Moreover, once
they arrive on the scene, it is often a struggle for Western journalists to get
the story out of Africa. There is no established system to provide local television networks with adequate pictures of the news. Satellite dishes, telephones and electrical equipment are in scant supply. This is a particular
problem for television, which is so strongly visual. For television news
producers, if there is no footage, there is no story.

IMPLICATIONS FOR AFRICA

According to the *Tyndall Report*, only 5.6 per cent of the total time devoted
to international news on the three major US television networks from 1988
to 1990 was concerned with Africa. This is unsurprising since, as Ungar and
Gergen note, Americans are at best indifferent and at worst hostile towards
outside cultures, especially those in the Southern hemisphere. Historically,
the United States has been an insular, ethnocentric nation, looking upon
other peoples with suspicion.

In attempting to cover Africa, American reporters face numerous obstacles at home and abroad. These problems are compounded by deficiencies
in the ways that Africa's representatives are themselves prepared for their

task. In Washington, for example, the spokespersons for African embassies are often uninitiated in the ways of the Western press. When approached by journalists to comment on breaking news stories that involve their countries, representatives often react quizzically, if not rudely, or simply fail to respond to telephone messages. Many of these spokespersons often have mandates from their governments *not* to provide information, and those who have been forthcoming have sometimes got into trouble at home. Regarding African spokespersons abroad, Ungar and Gergen note that the unreliability of certain African embassies in providing information to the press has led reporters to ignore them entirely, relying on US State Department officials for information instead.

As a whole, Africa has not always been so ignored by Western media. During the Cold War, for example, certain African nations were of interest as the site of competition between the interests of the US and the USSR. Nelson Mandela's visit to the United States in 1990 marked a high point in media interest in Africa: coverage of his visit attracted a broad audience, although it was racially skewed. Fifty-eight per cent of the black audience tuned in, whereas only 20 per cent of white viewers did so. The white audience was by far more interested in other, contemporaneous stories, such as those concerning the Supreme Court's flag-burning decision, the president's call for higher taxes, brush fires in southern California, and a new machine to help terminally-ill people commit suicide.

Compounding the problem is a general decline in interest in the news, particularly in the United States. Between 1970 and 1980, the American adult population increased by 36 per cent, but the circulation of newspapers increased by less than 1 per cent. The number of people claiming to read at least one daily newspaper fell 10 per cent in the decade leading up to 1989. A similar demographic trend can be observed in the viewing habits of the television audience. The baby-boom generation does not appear to be as concerned about the news as their parents' generation. A Gallup survey in 1965 found that 87 per cent of Americans had read a newspaper the day before, but by 1990, only 30 per cent made the same claim. Why are young people paying little attention? Part of the reason may be that they are reflecting the American cynicism toward public affairs. Many people appear to feel that Washington, let alone distant nations, has little relevance to their daily lives, unless there is a threat of war.

With audience interest falling and costs rising, many news executives feel caught in a bind. To keep their audience, many news organizations are scrambling 'down market', offering up more fluff, more glitz and more consumer information, taking up air time that might otherwise be devoted to the coverage of world affairs. Many news organizations have opted to devote their resources on these 'viewer friendly' stories rather than invest in maintaining correspondents in Africa.

POSSIBLE CORRECTIVE MEASURES

Among Africans, there is a tendency to hold the Western press solely responsible for the poor public perceptions of Africa that prevail in Europe and the
United States. In this view, the press must be seen as the primary vehicle for
improving public understanding, but a vehicle that is failing to do its job. It
is inappropriate, not to say impossible, for African interest groups to attempt
to reach in from outside and 'reform' the Western media's coverage of the
continent's nations and issues. Nonetheless, there are some areas in which
there may be room for Africans to take the initiative.

The most obvious first step would be to increase the exchange of information between African and Western journalists, particularly by bringing
journalists from every part of Africa to the West for extended working visits.
Both sides in such an exchange will benefit. From the African point of view,
such exchanges would help Africans deal with the philosophical attitudes,
the practical needs and the folkways of the Western media. At the same time,
the most meaningful way to help the Western public develop a deeper understanding of African issues is to send more Western journalists (especially
editors and senior representatives of the press) on extended working visits
to Africa. Existing exchange programmes are too heavily dependent on
funding from Western governments to be effective and credible. A system of
carefully planned two-way exchanges, underwritten by private-sector or
non-profit funds, could provide instant credibility to expanded exchange
programmes. A similar effect of increasing Western sensitivity to African
news items possibly could be achieved if there were an increase in the
hiring of Africans in Western newsrooms. Even though there is no guarantee that recruitment and training of Africans would necessarily produce
more voluminous and sympathetic coverage of Africa, it might have a subtle,
gradual effect, particularly if and when these people move into management
positions.

The news organizations in African countries can help to improve the
current state of affairs by strengthening their own journalist traditions. If
Africans covered their own countries with greater freedom and depth, this
would improve and also awaken the outside world to the richness and vitality
of African life. It would also encourage Western journalists to build a broader
variety of contacts within the African press, who would then help to shape coverage in the West. Moreover, Western news organizations that are unable to
afford full-time representation in Africa could develop a reliable corps of
African stringers. One way to encourage this would be the establishment of
annual prizes for excellence in reporting from Africa.

It would also help if governments would ease journalistic access to Africa.
With an investment of funds in infrastructure, particularly in travel and in
communications technology, some of the current difficulties can be quickly

overcome. More difficult would be to achieve the loosening of restrictions of press freedoms. Authoritarian regimes have a vested interest in controlling the news flow from Africa, particularly if they are engaging in behaviour not condoned by the world community. By restricting the news flow, they can avoid international scrutiny of their behaviour. Similarly, something could be done to reverse the current inability or unwillingness of many African representatives abroad to provide reliable information about their countries or their continent. Serious consideration should be given to setting up an African society along with an African house to act as an information clearing house, provide regular public dialogues, draw speakers, and show films (among other things) so that Africa is more in the mainstream of Western attention and not relegated to the fringes.

The immensity of Africa's problems and its potential to affect the Western world politically and economically can no longer be minimized. There are ways of ensuring that this complex continent does not remain relegated to the backwater of the news, brought to light only during clashes, coups and natural catastrophes like floods and drought. To cover Africa with the thoroughness and competency it deserves requires imagination, effort and financial resources. To fail to do so is to deny its present and future importance on the world stage.

REFERENCES

Allimadi, M. (2002), *The Hearts of Darkness: How White Writers Created the Racist Image of Africa*. New York: Black-Star Books.

Ebo, B. (1992), 'American Media and African Culture'. In B. C. Hawk (ed.), *Africa's Media Image*. New York: Praeger Publishers, pp. 15–25.

Hawk, B. G. (1992), *Africa's Media Image*. New York: Praeger Publishers.

Kasoma, Francis P. (1999), *The Neo-multiparty Theory of the Press: Donor Aid and Other Influences on the Media in Africa*. Zambia: The University of Zambia.

Mills, M. N. (1998), *Africa, U.S. Foreign Policy, and the American Media: Somalia, South Africa, and Rwanda in the Headlines*. Cambridge, MA: Harvard University Press.

Ungar, S. J., and D. Gergen (1991), *Africa and the American Media*. New York: Columbia University Press.

MEDIA CONSUMERISM AND CULTURAL TRANSFORMATION

The so-called information and knowledge age has been characterized by the dominance of two related movements, which serve the age-old human pre-occupation with capitalist accumulation. These movements are economic globalization and the revolution in information and communications tech-nologies (ICT). These are movements that may be seen as the engines of the contemporary global economy. They drive the new information world order, in which most of the continent of Africa is not faring too well. The expan-sion of globalization and ICT is itself largely driven by the logic of the market (Etta and Parvyn-Wamahiu 2003).

This has given rise to a new age that commoditizes knowledge, ensuring that the information- and knowledge-rich countries are also rich by other, more conventional measures. It is a new world order in which there are sig-nificant changes in the nature of human interactions and relations between peoples and nations (Etta and Parvyn-Wamahiu 2003). Globalization has resulted in greater integration in the world market than has ever been seen before. Many scholars underscore the cultural dimensions of globalization and argue that the process of marketing has gained a new impetus through the role of the media. Many of them are not interested in the effects that the social and cultural repertoires of a given economy help to define consumer behaviour, yet these operational dynamics make the economy a problematic social process. The effect of media advertizing on consumer behaviour cannot be explained outside an exhaustive analysis of such social variables as access to capital (particularly financial capital), poverty, health, literacy and the accessibility of marketing centres. The whats, whys, whens, wheres and hows of buying are part of the consumer problematic that needs to be investigated, interpreted and discussed.

GLOBALIZATION, MODERNITY AND MARKETING

Media-based marketing strategies are carried out in the name of providing customer value, but they must be interpreted in terms of the complexities of the social process that characterizes the market economy and its own distinctive allocation of values. Societal responses to the prospects and dangers of globalization are increasingly coming under study, in an attempt to explain the character of social transitions in the present era. Some scholars have argued that modernity is inherently globalizing, that globalization is the intensification of worldwide social relations which link distant localities, and that, therefore, the trajectory of social development is away from the institutions of modernity towards what Antony Giddens identifies as a new and distinct type of social order (Giddens 1990). This new social order, in Giddens' view, is dominated by sophisticated marketers, syndicates and profiteers – many of whom care little about the public interest.

Despite the existence of such actors, the media play an influential role in the transformation of communities with regard to such areas as identity, technology, economics, globalization and surveillance. The importance of the media in some of these realms is located in the forms they take as fundamental mediating agencies. Nonetheless, the prevalence of marketers, profiteers, and syndicates within the media ensures that they are driven by the profit-seeking motives that underpin international capitalism.

Through the media, the globalization process generates transformational dynamics that have a negative impact on a whole range of pre-modern cultures of the pastoralist or agrarian types throughout Africa. It creates complex interfaces of behaviour and social action that, in turn, generate new rhythms of interactivity and, at times, illegality. The whole gamut of pre-modern social orders on the continent is rapidly being brought into the ambit of Western-driven globalization. The thrust of this trend is toward a hegemonic, imperial and incorporative dynamic that encourages, even demands, local community identities to absorb and internalize the inherent values of contemporary globalization (Slater 1995).

Local transformation processes can thus be seen as part of the trend toward globalization, and media projects can be understood in postmodernist terms. Originating in theoretical trends that evolved out of French anthropology, postmodernity theorizes the powerlessness of individuals in the face of diverse globalizing encounters. There is, however, an alternative theoretical approach. Some scholars argue from the standpoint of localization theory, arriving at a theoretical hybrid that may be termed 'glocalization'. The counter-penetrative power of a glocalist approach runs counter to the postmodernist assumption of individual (and local) powerlessness in the face of Western-originated trends of globalization.

Antony Giddens proposes such a dialectic of powerlessness and empowerment that encompasses both experience and action (Giddens 1990). The extent to which the media is embedded in a nationalist discourse directed at the intensification, clarification and crystallization of identity needs to be critically highlighted in view of glocalist realities such as the legitimation of forms and structures of political authority that are critical in the social transformation of societies. During the first wave of independence movements in Africa, idioms of identity were encoded in nationalist constructs that were held to be integrally linked to notions of self-determination. Yet these notions lacked any expression of ontological transcendence that could lead to the growth of supra-ethnic African identities. Expressed through the various nationalist media, idioms of identity became the basis for organizing and challenging the participatory experiences of those who contested the colonial order. As such, idioms of identity became the basis of the invention of the imagined political communities.

IDENTITY CREATION AND TRANSFORMATION

The dynamics of identity transformation cannot be understood without inquiring into the process of cultural contestations and negotiations by which norms may be transformed. This process takes place in the context of social encounters as a means of resolving any resultant fractures and tensions. These fractures are situated in the complex registers of the theoretical, cultural and representational politics of identity.

Obviously, cultural productions, including language and technology, are central to identity politics. There is, therefore, a need to examine the ambiguities and conflictual principles that emanate from such shifts in the representational sensibilities of societies, particularly when considering the case of Africa. As A. O. Mojola has noted, Africa and most of the so-called Third World were never part of the modernity project, even though they were caught up in it, mostly as victims rather than beneficiaries through the slave trade, colonization, neo-colonial imperialism, the Cold War and global transnational capitalism (Mojola 2002).

GLOBALIZATION AND THE RISE OF CONSUMERISM

In the process of globalization, as in much else, the media create the agenda. Noam Chomsky states that the media drive this agenda by creating panics and crises to further their own agenda and those of their political masters (Chomsky 1997). Consumerism, which is the predictable result of capitalist ethos and norms, characterizes the postmodern condition. It is fostered and fed through the plethora of signs that crowd today's media, but which have, on the whole. no basis in reality – they are, in other words, simply illusions.

The illusory nature of signs is a central fact of marketing and particularly that of advertisement in this postmodern age. In cyberspace and virtual worlds, such signs are parasitic on an already experienced reality – that is to say, on memory. To a certain extent, media images are a pack of lies, concealing or misrepresenting the truth, because, at base, the media are concerned with the sanitization of information, presenting it in accordance with the profit interests of their proprietors.

In this context, consumerism must then be recognized as a media-driven pattern of behaviour predicated on access to money and a drive to purchase and use particular goods. Hidden in the false images presented via the media is the fact that this behaviour often contributes to the destruction of the human social and physical environment, undermines personal financial and physical health, and operates contrary to the common good of individuals and human institutions. Throughout its history, the culture of consumerism has taken variegated forms to suit the range of geographical and historical settings in which it has arisen.

Consumerism, along with secularization, materialism, market totalitarianism and syncretism, is a product of the project of modernity that is enhanced by the so-called information society. Media consumerism is a particular sub-category of the larger concept, and involves establishing a means of information flow and its control. Such means must be grounded and supported by powerful infrastructural, economic and technological forces that are largely monopolized by the West. Nonetheless, this cannot accurately be seen as a one-way relationship. Ever-changing geographies of aesthetic self-expression and other social forces are also implicated in media consumerism. Understanding these forces is critical to media producers who seek to nuance their studio narratives in the name of information production and dissemination.

The assembly and consequent dissemination of media-generated information – in radio or television news bulletins or in print – has yet to be adequately addressed by scholars in cultural studies or other disciplines. Yet it would be useful to ascertain whether current production trends in Africa's electronic media industries are merely exercises in mimicry of the West or represent an authentic African creativity. This needs to be ascertained in a serious social science inquiry. Entertainment and advertising, along with educational and public informational programming, play a critical role in changing or generating individual and collective perceptions and behaviour. The media are therefore critical to the creation of the global village, especially in this new world of crass, materialistic consumerism. The emerging perceptions of agency fostered by the media houses and applied to their policies regarding entertainment, advertising, news gathering and news reporting is bound to lead to the definition of new forms of etiquette and social dispositions.

CONCEPTUALIZATIONS OF IDENTITY

It is worth noting that politics, sport and economics are key elements of the content provided by the media. A proper understanding of the media must be within the basic institutional structures and relationships within which they operate. The provision of these three content elements enables media providers to set the terms of the domestication of popular knowledge and to inscribe it in a rational field that informs cultural identity and its dynamics, manifesting them as project and invention. Already, a number of scholars are at pains to explain and employ ideas of modernity and postmodernism in an effort to decipher how these imported content elements participate in the conceptualization of a new African gnosis (Mudimbe 1994).

While a number of African scholars have embraced postmodernism, there seems to be lacking a serious exploration of other possible theoretical approaches. For instance, none appear to have explored the possibility of re-working Saussurean semiotics in their exploration of these issues. Nor do scholars appear willing to attempt a fundamental re-thinking of recent anthropological studies dealing with postmodernist trajectories of thought by subtly re-introducing and reinforcing Durkheimian and Lévi-Straussean discourses on myth and ritual (Comaroff and Comaroff 1997). Finally, there is the absence of any ongoing re-interrogation of Marxist theory. Yet the assumptions of these theoretical approaches ought to be explored. Their analyses of social questions offer real, often controversial, insights into the issues and politics of difference in terms of genre, gender, race, culture and/or ethnicity.

How do African intellectuals who employ aspects of postmodern theory and criticism to a contemporary media work integrate these views into the African project of social transformation? Postmodernism articulates agendas of de-centring of culture, and its discourses legitimize unmediated consumerism. Both of these trends, while celebrating technology and the representations it perpetuates, are likely to have a negative impact on African societies, particularly on their children and youth. The postmodern project is positioned to enhance a form of digitized techno-industrialism amidst contradictions of race and ethnic politics whose social permutations generate news, yet their influence is hardly accounted for.

The lack of any adequate textual analysis of news coverage raises fundamental questions about the semiotics of reporting. It also leaves unexplored the changing character of media identities and advertizing as they respond to imperialist assignments. Literary criticism has shown a preoccupation with analyzing media productions that are critical of so-called progress, such as the satirical commentaries of the Late Wahome Mutahi and his regular newspaper column, 'Whispers'. However, most of this criticism ignores the language and rhetoric of media advertizing and fails to take into account the naiveté with which people take in information.

Regardless of the positions adopted by literary critics such as Egara Kabaji and Barrack Muluka, or their predecessors Chris Wanjala and William Ochieng, culture remains best understood as a fundamental social process that provides a matrix within which different forms of behaviour are displayed. Some behaviour is accorded public approbation, while some meets with public disapprobation. Identity is culturally constructed, and this is as true of individual identity as it is of political identity (Mamdani 2001). Contemporary, Western-driven consumerism appears to be self-perpetuating, especially given the West's pursuit of domination of information flow. However, this consumerism offers only short-term gratification for those who can afford the luxuries it represents, whereas it engenders frustration for those who cannot.

This is the paradox of modernity and postmodernity – they are social orders that give excessive freedom to social identities to self-destruct in their pursuit of happiness, through the very operation of their efforts to dominate, control, exploit, manipulate and even misuse resources. In light of this, the belief in the right of every individual to self-fulfilment and self-gratification, and the belief in the logic and goodness of the free market – both of which are fundamental to the concept of consumerism – are critical assumptions that need to be revisited. When reassessed in this way, consumerism as constituted under contemporary capitalism is exposed to be an incomplete and inadequately engineered system of values substituted for a waning cultural heritage that nevertheless seeks to assert dominance. Even in the United States, society is awakening from its fascination with television, video, and internet-based entertainment to find itself stripped of its tradition, controlled by an oppressive power structure, and bound to the credit obligations of a defunct American dream.

For the public at large, the integrating and transformational experiences of culture have been replaced by the collective viewing experience and by participation in consumer trends defined in the West. Further exacerbating this trend is the accelerated pace of corporate mergers and acquisitions affecting the media industry. The market has become ever more rapacious in expanding the territory served by modern materialism, and consumerism has ever been at its service.

THE CHOICES AHEAD

Culture, religion and ideology are the spheres in which values, standards and norms are defined within society. It is to them, unmediated by the demands of consumerism and postmodernism, that we must turn if we wish to regain the hope of recovering our individual and collective selfhood. The media, therefore, must begin to interrogate the modern capitalist order within which they thrive. They must begin to explain the implications of certain trends of consumer behaviour. They must begin to question the blind consumerism inherent in contemporary broadcasting.

Contemporary consumerism is more than simply a means by which corporate entities ensure a profit. It is also the means by which the new capitalism maintains control of its public. In corporate (monopolistic) capitalism, the consumer is a target whose interests and actions are to be controlled. Operating without reference to the public interest, capitalism and consumerism merely commoditize culture in order to sell it to a gullible public. However, many consumers are beginning to realize the political power they wield – for instance as a collective buying force. Through the use of union pickets and boycotts, a number of communities have tested this power at the grassroots level. In the process, it is true that selection is reduced, but the sacrifice is made not in response to what would yield the greatest profit for the capitalist stockholder. Rather, it is made in the name of what the moral public wants, what it will accept as congenial to its own interests. Our choices and freedoms should not be limited by corporate policy despite the growing façade of corporate social responsibility that is spreading like wildfire. It has become clear that in the so-called project of postmodernity, what constitutes human authenticity remains a big problem.

Postmodernism is rooted in the perversion of the essence of being and the perception of authenticity, and can only be countered by taking an active stance in opposition to the representations it thrusts upon us. The African media, however, have failed to aggressively market an African identity and authenticity to challenge the one imposed by the West. This has led to an evasion of responsibility and the obfuscation that is characteristic of inauthentic existence.

In this postmodern age, as we sit around the television sets, as we watch movies or soap operas and collectively strive to acquire the media-produced images of 'the good life', let us remember that our choices are made for us if we relinquish our mediatory positions and initiatives. When choices are made for us, those choices are reduced to the equivalent of a brand name. We sacrifice our self-knowledge, our values and our purpose, and attempt to fill the resulting gap with sheer consumerism. But consumerism offers only the illusion of choice. Beneath its pretensions of a utopia achieved lies real suffering, stress and anxiety that, because of its failure to address basic social issues around the world, has led to the emergence of dangerous fundamentalisms. In capitalism's seduction of the television audience, especially among the Third World's youth, who want to imitate everything American and have a hope to immigrate to America, the individuating personality identifies with advertising fantasies and consumer ideals. Is it any wonder, then, that more than 60 per cent of African students who go to the United States to study do not come back to Africa, even though the bulk of Africans who remain in American end up underemployed?

In recent years, the leading engines of globalization have championed what have come to be called structural adjustment programmes, to be embarked upon within the Third World (Aseka 1999). These programmes are an affront to community values, and their immediately observable effect has been an erosion of social infrastructure in Africa. This affront has been accentuated by the disrespect of human values by mass media advertizing which has left a well actualized consumer but a poorly individuated personality. The effectiveness of the socio-cultural symbol has diminished in the wake of a new market fundamentalism. This capitalist exploitation of the media is carried out in various mechanisms, ranging from the broadcast of biased news analysis to invasive and intrusive advertisements. Thus have the media become a power agent, tasked with the responsibility of spreading Western-defined consumerism. As the power of culture is depleted by the parasitic deconstruction of the commercial production, the spine of social cohesion and moral rectitude is being broken in the process.

The process of globalization has exacerbated the commercial exploitation of culture. As advertising duplicity invades the realm of ideals where traditional guidance and counselling takes place, it appropriates subjective values and forces them into the service of capitalist consumer product enhancement. The substantiating experiences of culture seem to recede into the shadow, as society in Africa disintegrates into market materialism and changing consumer behaviour. With the push for liberalization and privatization that is inherent in the concept of structural adjustment, this process has been further enabled. For instance, markets have come to be seen as maximizing individual choice, and the process of product marketing has become a major ideological apparatus by which societies are brought in line with the interests of capital. The shaping of attitudes toward certain products, the identification (creation) of new needs based on products available in the market, and the instigation of financial expenditure are all strategic goals of professional marketers.

CONCLUSION

Our society is today marked by a growing addiction to over-consumption of products and services ranging from car alarms to TV news programmes. Addictive consumerism, and an adherence to narrow beliefs about products, is bringing to birth a new social reality. A vibrant and functional democracy depends on the honest dissemination of information. The corporate media, in their rightward drift and easy compliance with political power, are failing the general populace because of their patron-client links. But citizens can hold the corporate media responsible for perpetrating violence and consumerism under the guise of news and entertainment. We can start by being conscious of just what they are serving up as our media diet. The egocentricity of

Western society has made the African community an easy target for the transition to a consumer society. Its deceptive advertising and academic nihilism guts our cultures and erodes our values, rendering us easily swayed on to the path of consumerism. The reduction of cultural values to economic worth has produced a situation in which product availability, as opposed to survival needs, becomes the ethical justification for political oppression.

At present, African cultural values are losing out to consumerist values. Economic worth has displaced self-worth as the measure by which we value one another. You can see it in the haughty and demanding attitude of the consumer as he stands before the cashier. As America settles into its nightly routine of television viewing, Africa follows suit in sheer mimicry, and corporate profiteers are quick to substitute the lure of material luxury and consumer gratification for the fading community spirit that is cultural. As the media continue to advertize products in the market in the name of selling an image of the postmodern personality, which is an empty shell because it has lost its moral essence, Africa will continue to be hollow and vulnerable to imperial manipulation.

In the economic and political orthodoxy fostered by the values of corporate America and exported to Africa, this imperialism will continue to throttle the public with images manufactured in the West and relayed through its dominant media houses and their surrogate African outlets. This outcome falls short of the public morality we desire to see created in African communities. We can challenge this situation by recognizing that corporate priorities are not intrinsically humanitarian or ecologically sensitive, and that they are, in the end, oriented solely towards the profit motive.

REFERENCES

Ake, C. (1981), *A Political Economy of Africa*. London: Longman.
Aseka, E. M. (1995), 'Postmodernism and History: The Fallacies of a Theory without Theoretical Rigour'. Staff seminar paper, History Department, Kenyatta University.
— (1999), 'The Political Economy of Panopticism: Interrogating the Neo-Liberal Discourses in the Globalization Process'. *Chemchemi* 1(1).
Atieno-Odhiambo, E. S. (1999–2000), 'From African Historiographies to African Philosophy of History'. *Afrika Zamani* 7–8: 41–89.
Carman, T. (2000), 'Must We Be Inauthentic?'. In M. Wrathall and J. Malpas (eds), *Heidegger, Authenticity, and Modernity: Essays in Honour of Hubert L. Dreyfus*, vol. 1. Cambridge, MA: MIT Press.
Chomsky, Noam (1997), *Media Control: The Spectacular Achievements of Propaganda*. New York: Seven Stories Press.
Comaroff, Jean and John Comaroff (1997), 'Postcolonial Politics and Discourses of Democracy in Southern Africa: An Anthropological Reflection of African Political Modernities'. *Journal of Anthropological Research* 53(2): 123–46.

Etta, F. E. and Parvyn-Wamahiu (eds) (2003), *Information and Communication Technologies for Development in Africa*. Vol. 2: *The Experience with Community: Telecentres*. Nairobi: IDRC.

Friedman, J. (1994), *Cultural Identity and Global Process*. London: Sage Publications.

— (1999), *The Rational Choice Controversy: The Economic Model of Politics Reconsidered*. New Haven: Yale University Press.

Giddens, A. (1990), *The Consequences of Modernity*. Stanford: Stanford University Press.

Havas, R. (2000), 'The Significance of Authenticity'. In M. Wrathall and J. Malpas (eds), *Heidegger, Authenticity, and Modernity: Essays in Honour of Hubert L. Dreyfus*, vol. 1. Cambridge, MA: MIT Press.

Khamisi, L. (1981), *Imperialism Today*. Dar-es-Salaam: Tanzania Publishing House.

Mamdani, M. (2001), *When Victims Become Killers: Colonialism, Nativism, and the Genocide in Rwanda*. Princeton, NJ: Princeton University Press.

Meyer, B. (1998), 'Communities and the Power of Prayer: Pentecostalist Attitudes towards Consumption in Contemporary Ghana'. *Africa Zamani* 6.

Mojola, A. O. (2002), 'Modernity, Post-Modernity and the Information Age: Prospects and Challenges for African Theological Education in the Twenty-First Century'. *Chemchemi* 2(1).

Mudimbe, V. Y. (1994), *The Idea of Africa*. London: James Currey.

Mueller, D. (1996), *Constitutional Democracy*. New York: Oxford University Press.

Slater, D. (1995), 'Challenges of Western Visions of the Global: The Geopolitics of Theory and North-South Relations'. *European Journal of Development Research* 2(7).

Zafirovski, M. (2000), 'Extending the Rational Choice Model from Economy to Society'. *Economy and Society* 29(2).

AFRICAN INTELLECTUALS IN A HOSTILE MEDIA ENVIRONMENT

The African intellectual faces a hostile media environment because the media are largely foreign owned or dependent on foreign sources and programming. The symbiotic relationship between foreign-based media ownership and local media providers is one in which the local elites are the agents of the foreign elites. The foreign elites decide what everyone else is to think and, using their local agents, force it on the Africans. Olatunde A. Oladimeji of Nigeria has argued that Africa has been the target of a new kind of 'war without missiles', in which the African elites are the 'victims of the war on our minds' in many guises (1987).

The media are also involved in a new form of indirect rule, postmodern colonialism, in which the local media try to give the impression of being independent, while all the time getting guidance from Paris, London, Brussels, or New York and Washington. Should a local editor exercise independence on matters of interest to the foreign controllers, that local editor quickly loses his or her job. This happened in Kenya when George Githii, editor in chief at the *Nation,* failed to understand instructions from the Aga Khan in Paris. And, according to Mitch Odero, the local representative of the Lonrho Group, Mark Too, 'kept a close eye on the editorial performance of the [*East African*] *Standard* and literally killed its passion for investigative journalism'. The parameters of discussions are predetermined in such a way that the interests of the foreign elites are not questioned. Yet it is only in the questioning of those parameters that the African can try to fight back against the intellectual warfare that relegates him to the bottom of the international order.

STRATEGIES OF COLONIAL RULE

Arguments about who should interpret Africa can be traced to the onset of classical colonialism following the meeting of European powers at Berlin in 1884–5. At that time they established the rules they would follow in grabbing up African territories. Having agreed that the brutal rule of Africans was good for Africans and for humanity, these powers then proceeded to impose their rule through the creation of material and mental poverty amongst the Africans.

First was the deliberate effort to make the African materially poor. In imposing colonialism in Africa, writes Alex de Waal (1997), 'conquerors often created famine' as a controlling mechanism by which to entrench European interests. Entrenching European interests meant destroying African industries, turning the people into peasants and cheap labourers, and forcing them to live from hand to mouth by blocking avenues of independent economic activities. It also often meant enforcing the compliance of otherwise recalcitrant Africans by burning villages and confiscating livestock, and by punishments ranging from public whipping, to cutting off their hands and limbs.

Effective physical and material control also called for the mental impoverishment of the Africans. This required both cultural and intellectual justification. Colonial officials were assisted in this enterprise by missionaries who were deployed to Africa to deprive its peoples of their heritage under the pretext of spreading Christianity. Among the earliest missionaries was Mary Kingsley, a believer in the mental inferiority of Africans, who called for finding the best way to govern them.

THE AFRICAN RESPONSE

An alternative to Kingsley came from W. E. B. DuBois, a black American, who questioned the prevailing views about Africa and black people. He founded and edited *Crisis*, an organ of the National Association for the Advancement of Colored People (NAACP). DuBois's *Crisis* and Marcus Garvey's *Negro World* were banned in the colonies but were influential for many Africans, including Jomo Kenyatta of Kenya, who edited the journal *Muiguithania*. Kenyatta exposed the lie behind colonial 'benevolence' in his book *Facing Mount Kenya*, in the acknowledgements to which he sardonically thanked 'those professional friends of Africa' who struggled hard to ensure that Africans remained ignorant. Those professional friends, he wrote, were 'prepared to maintain their friendship for eternity as a sacred duty, provided that the African will continue to play the part of an ignorant savage so that they can monopolize the office of interpreting his mind and speaking for him'.

Another challenge to colonial benevolence was the Mau Mau war that forced Great Britain and the United States to rethink their positions in Africa and led to a behind-the-scenes rivalry between London and Washington. Although most media went out of their way to ridicule African aspirations, the war forced Britain to create 'new' African leaders, the most important of whom was Tom Mboya. The British built up Tom Mboya in order 'to create a new and, hopefully, more pliant leader'. The United States stole Mboya from the British, however, and showered him with praise. In the 16 May 1956 edition of the *New York Times*, it was asserted that Mboya 'had become the chief spokesman of Kenyan Africans' and a messenger 'for African freedom and democracy'. The project to make Mboya Africa's spokesman, however, was contradicted by Jaramogi Oginga Odinga's claim that all the real African leaders were in jail.

Daniel Arap Moi became president in 1978, after Kenyatta's death. Determined to entrench himself, he proclaimed a slogan of *'Nyayo'*, meaning that he would follow in Kenyatta's footsteps. At the same time, however, he adopted the symbol of a well polished *fimbo* (stick), in contrast to Kenyatta's political trademark, the flywhisk. Out of Moi's trademark would emerge an ideology of the *fimbo*, and the media were key to its evolution. Previously 'independent' media intellectuals became apologists for Nyayoism. State pressure was successfully put on the *East African Standard* to appoint former *Nation* editor (and Moi loyalist) Githii as its chairman and, later, editor in chief. Githii turned the *East African Standard* into a promoter of the idea that some people were better Nyayo followers than others, and that Nyayoism could be measured with some exactitude.

Ng'weno, publisher of the *Weekly Review* and the *Nairobi Times*, also succumbed to government pressure. *The Times* was officially transformed into a press organ for the Kenya African National Union (KANU) in April 1983 and renamed the *Kenya Times*. The new publication's mission, asserted in its first editorial, was to project KANU 'policies in an unequivocal manner . . . [and that its] editorial policy will be the furtherance of the aims and objectives of the ruling party'. The paper, Moi argued, was a response to popular demand, then pleaded: 'It needs your support. Long Live Kanu, Nyayo.' With support from government and advertisement revenues from parastatal corporations, the *Kenya Times* initially attracted journalistic notables to its masthead, including those that the government had previously detained. They became instruments of Moi's news judgment, which required every Kenyan to sing the praises of the president.

With such effective control, the mainstream domestic media became agents of the *fimbo* ideology, justifying it through a process of 're-education'. To deal with dissent, mainly concentrated within the universities, Moi accused professors of being intellectual terrorists who indoctrinated students, and ordered them to be sent to re-education centres. 'I see no systematic alternative to the intellectual re-education of staff for the purpose of reforming the learning atmosphere in order to achieve a balance and articulate preparation of the students for the realities of life', Moi wrote in his book *Kenya African Nationalism: Nyayo Philosophy and Principles*. Students who are thus prepared, he went on, would 'evolve into intellectual home guards against intellectual terrorism, political agitation and subversion in the universities'.

NEW INTELLECTUAL CLIMATE

Moi's effort to re-educate lecturers, however, collided with a new Western re-assessment of its relations with Third World countries. The United States led the way by rejecting the essence of its previous, Cold War foreign policy, and, looking for a way to restore to itself a sense of self-worth and purpose, concluded that it needed to distance itself from perceived autocrats. Among the strategies employed in this effort was one to emphasize multilateralism in place of its previous reliance on bilateral relationships. The strategy crystallized in the early 1980s and coincided with the rise of 'conservative' leaders in the West who controlled such multilateral institutions as the International Monetary Fund and the World Bank. These leaders appeared to glorify inequality as a social good, rejecting 'special consideration' for poor countries and insisting that poor countries compete with the 'developed' ones in a neoliberal economic framework. As a result, according to the noted academic Paul Tiyambe Zeleza, African states were pressed to liberalize their economies internally while accepting global 'uniformity', and to believe that 'the god of capitalism . . . has won [and that] history is over'.

Another strategy in this re-assessment was the adoption of a new rhetoric in international discourse that targeted particularly Third World countries. The rhetoric was meant to make the United States appear to identify with the aspirations of ordinary people instead of catering for the wishes of the ruling elites. To further this end, the National Endowment for Democracy was created in 1982, and was tasked with the mission of promoting such 'American' values as freedom of the press, trade unionism and political activism. It entailed support for non-governmental organizations and, most important, the promotion of 'civil society'.

In Kenya, the changing international climate coincided with the interests of local intellectuals who had been agitating for political change. With some external support, the elites founded an alternative press to counter docile local mainstream media. Leading the alternative press was the *Nairobi Law Monthly*, founded in September 1987 by Gitobu Imanyara to cater for Kenya's small legal fraternity. It captured public attention by questioning court decisions and by publicizing human rights abuses and the harassment of judicial officers. Njehu Gatabaki's *Finance* also attracted attention. In 1983 the magazine had pandered to industrial and financial tycoons who advertized in its pages. Gatabaki ultimately changed his editorial policy and assumed a stance of crusading zeal against the Moi regime. In 1989, Pius Nyamora, a former *Nation* and *Kenya Times* employee, founded *Society* magazine, which specialized in providing relatively light content. After he joined the multi-party crusade in 1990, however, his attitude and editorial policy changed. In October 1991 Nyamora complained of newspaper and magazine vendors being harassed by security men and urged these men to 'put the interest of the country before the selfish interests of those local godfathers'. These three magazines, *Finance*, *Nairobi Law Monthly* and *Society*, were largely responsible for bringing multi-party politics to Kenya and giving a voice to dissenting intellectuals.

RECENT TRENDS

The growing activism of the alternative press in Kenya that has given the opportunity to intellectuals to speak their minds has attracted two types of reactions in Tanzania. On the one hand, there are those who admire the trend, perhaps best exemplified by Mwesiga Baregu. Baregu, a political scientist, has lamented that Tanzanian intellectuals, unlike their Kenyan counterparts, were too docile and were not participating in the liberation of their country from state oppression. On the other hand, Issa Shivji, a law professor, represents a more disapproving perspective. He takes issue with African intellectuals and media who accept the 'neo-liberal images and ideologies of democracy, constitutionalism, pluralism, and the "free market"'. The danger, he has argued, is that, instead of critically assessing the implication of globalization, 'our political leaders, publicists, and intellectuals are mesmerized' and thus fail to see that this 'glib talk of democracy, human rights, and "free" markets' was just the old imperialism presented in a new and more pleasant looking guise. To Shivji, neoliberalism and globalization threaten Africa, being mere euphemisms for mechanisms by which the West can continue controlling African states. By promoting the neoliberal discourse, therefore, the media and African intellectuals fall into the trap of being 'missionaries' of corporate capitalism.

But missionizing for corporate capitalism is not restricted to the print and electronic media; it is also to be found in academia and the book industry where decisions are made as to what will be taught and read at the universities. Since the selection of knowledge is part of power politics that can be used to keep some down while upholding the favoured, it becomes a way of depriving certain people of their human rights. Africans are among those whose knowledge has long been denied, supplanted by the knowledge that is promulgated by the master states. Further, access to knowledge of any kind is hindered; when multilateral funding institutions show an interest in education, their focus is on the primary level, and they enforce cuts in higher education.

In certain quarters during the 1980s and 1990s, there was an intellectual preoccupation with proving that Africans are incapable of being democratic. An example of this can be found in Jean François Bayart's *The State in Africa:*

The Politics of the Belly (1993), which argues that the only thing that matters in Africa is the 'politics of the belly'. Patrick Chabal and Jean-Pascal Daloz contributed to this trend with their 1999 *Africa Works: Disorder as Political Instrumental*, in which they argue that African leaders actually thrive in chaos and disorder. They claim that the seeming disorder in Africa is actually logical, because it is designed to ensure the continuity of the ruling clique which has found ways of brushing aside pressure from the international community, or bending that pressure to serve their personal desires.

One conclusion that can be drawn from these trends is that there is a war going on – one that is waged against Africans on a primarily intellectual level. It has been going on for a long time, and many instruments of control have been used – from religious missionaries to corporate missionaries to the media. The media have been very noisy about 'freedom of the press' which has often meant 'freedom for those who own the press' to do whatever they want. Since the mainstream media in Africa tend to be externally controlled, however, this has meant the freedom of outside interests to determine what knowledge is to be made available to Africans.

It is ironic that, while this war is going on, emphasis is placed on importing knowledge from the enemy. When African intellectuals try to respond, they land in trouble because the enemy constitutes a kind of monopolistic intellectual tribunal that decides what is to be published and publicized. The media in Africa, mainly controlled externally, have become part of the instruments by which the natives can be controlled. The media shape the political and economic agenda and they define the perceptions of African intellectuals, as a community. Instead of fostering free thought, the media become part of a political machine that controls thought, thus frustrating any challenges not only to local political potentates, but also to their external manipulators. The African intellectual, therefore, operates and barely survives in a hostile media environment.

REFERENCES

Apple, Michael W. (1996), *Cultural Politics and Education*. Buckingham: Open University Press.

Ayittey, George B. N. (1993), *Africa Betrayed*. New York: St Martin's Press.

— (1998), *Africa in Chaos*. New York: St Martin's Press.

Bayart, Jean Francois (1993), *The State in Africa: The Politics of the Belly*. London and New York: Longman.

Bennett, George (1963), *Kenya, A Political History: The Colonial Period*. London: Oxford University Press.

Carter, Gwendolen M. (ed.) (1962), *African One-Party States*. Ithaca, NY: Cornell University Press.

Chabal, Patrick and Jean-Pascal Daloz (1999), *Africa Works: Disorder as Political Instrument*. Oxford and Indiana: James Currey Publishers.

Diouf, Mamadou and Mahmood Mamdani (eds) (1994), *Academic Freedom in Africa*. Dakar: CODESRIA.

Domatob, Jerry, Abubakar Jika, and Ikechukwu Nwosu (eds) (1987), *Mass Media and the African Society*. Nairobi: ACCE.

Gilder, George (1981), *Wealth and Poverty*. New York: Basic Books.

Gudkind, Peter and Peter Waterman (eds) (1977), *African Social Studies: A Radical Reader*. New York: Monthly Review Press.

Hancock, Graham (1989), *Lords of Poverty*. London: Macmillan.

Harrison, Pau (1993), *Inside the Third World: The Anatomy of Poverty*. New York: Penguin Books.

Hawk, Beverley G. (ed.) (1992), *Africa's Media Image*. London: Praeger.

Herman, Edward S. and Robert W. McChesney (2001), *The Global Media: The New Missionaries of Corporate Capitalism*. London: Continuum Paperbacks.

Hochschild, Adam (1999), *King Leopold's Ghost: A Story of Greed, Terror, and Heroism in Colonial Africa*. London: Macmillan.

Kenyatta, Jomo (1978), *Facing Mount Kenya: The Traditional Life of the Gikuyu*. Nairobi: Kenway Editions.

Kissinger, Henry (2001), *Does America Need a Foreign Policy? Toward a Diplomacy for the Twenty-First Century*. New York: Simon & Schuster.

Moi, Daniel arap (1986), *Kenya African Nationalism: Nyayo Philosophy and Principles*. Nairobi: Macmillan.

Mudimbe, V. Y. (1988), *The Invention of Africa: Gnosis, Philosophy, and the Order of Knowledge*. Bloomington: Indiana University Press.

Ochieng, Philip (1992), *I Accuse the Press: An Insider's View of the Media and Politics in Africa*. Nairobi: ACTS Press.

Odero, Mitch (ed.) (2000), *Media Culture and Performance in Kenya*. Nairobi: Friedrich-Ebert-Stiftung.

Oladimeji, Olatunde A. (1987), 'War Without Missiles: Need for Effective Propaganda Machinery in Africa'. In Jerry Domatot, Abubakar Jika and Ikechukwu Nwosu (eds), *Mass Media and the African Society*. Nairobi: ACCE, pp. 254–9.

Palmer, Robin and Neil Parsons (eds) (1977), *The Roots of Rural Poverty in Central and Southern Africa*. Berkeley: University of California Press.

Parenti, Michael (1986), *Inventing Reality: The Politics of the Mass Media*. New York: St Martin's Press.

Risse, Thomas, Stephen C. Ropp and Kathryn Sikkink (eds) (1999), *The Power of Human Rights: International Norms and Domestic Change*. Cambridge: Cambridge University Press.

Shivji, Issa G. (1988), *The Concept of Human Rights in Africa*. Dakar: CODESRIA Series.

Timberlake, Lloyd (1995), *Africa in Crisis: The Causes, the Cures of Environmental Bankruptcy*. Nairobi: East African Educational Publishers.

Waal, Alex de (1997), *Famine Crimes: Politics and the Disaster Relief Industry in Africa*. Oxford: James Currey.

Zartman, William (ed.) (1993), *Europe and Africa: The New Phase*. London: Lynne Rienner.

Zeleza, Paul Tiyambe (1997), *Manufacturing African Studies and Crises*. Dakar, Senegal: CODESRIA.

PART II

THE MEDIA AND IDENTITY: THE GLOBAL MEDIA

9   Cecilia Kimani

PUBLISHING IN AFRICA

Many people believe that the surest path to success in the largely capitalistic world economy is through information. Information is the most valuable resource – it is the common denominator for managing other resources. The notion that material poverty is directly related to lack of access to information is gaining credibility, especially in the so-called Third World countries. Africa, perceived as the epitome of human desperation according to some retrogressive minds in the West, is generally depicted as riddled with poverty, illiteracy, poor governance, disease and superstitions. Information about the continent is routinely misrepresented, often deliberately doctored by agents of hate to ensure that nothing good comes from the continent.

HISTORICAL UNDERPINNINGS

Much has been written on the history of publishing in Africa (see, for example, Chakava 1996). The earliest printed books on the continent came from North Africa, and were spread along with the expansion of Islam. However, soon after most countries had attained their independence, multinational publishing houses trooped to the continent, ostensibly to provide educational materials for the new nations. In Ghana, for instance, Christian missionaries established schools and brought in supplies of books. During the colonial era, the print media was introduced in the continent, albeit not for the mutual interests of the parties involved. It seems to have been a well orchestrated approach to facilitating the adoption of a foreign culture by the indigenous people and to make it easy to colonize the continent. All governments have invested heavily in educational initiatives in the quest to attain self-sufficiency in skilled manpower.

In South Africa, even after its many years of isolation due to its apartheid policies, the publishing industry has remained strong. In fact, its isolation probably helped, because it allowed the local media companies to grow without foreign competition, and there was a great demand for information in the racially volatile country. Media houses thrived on spreading political propaganda. It is obvious that the political transformation of the 1990s has not relieved the historical racial and cultural disharmony of the country. The consequent effects of history and the transformation from apartheid have affected the development of the publishing industry both positively and negatively. As a result, despite the perceived high level of development in the country, South Africa suffered an educational book crisis in the mid-1990s. This served as a wake-up call to the country to redefine the future of its publishing industry.

Nigeria has the largest independent publishing industry on the continent, centred in the Igbo city of Onitsha, where novels, self-help and religious books are the speciality. Sharing the aspirations of many newly independent African countries, Nigeria started with the objective of achieving self-sufficiency in the production and distribution of educational materials. However, economic and political instability occasioned by the numerous coups d'état in the 1980s had adverse effects on the development of the publishing industry. Efforts have been made through the various task forces established by the government and civil society to reverse the downward trend in the book industry, and some gains have been realized. As in many African countries, 90 per cent of the books published in Nigeria are educational.

The current state of publishing industry in Africa can be analysed according to several broad spheres of engagement. The roles of the government, donors and multinationals on the continent are three important areas of concern. Also important are the legal aspects of publishing, issues of language diversity and illiteracy rates, as well as the level of publishing expertise available within a given country. In addition, the state of technology and the printing sub-sector, the state of African economies, and the general conditions of infrastructural development all contribute to the challenges facing the publishing industry in the continent.

ROLE OF GOVERNMENT AND DONOR ASSISTANCE

The development and publication of educational materials has been largely a government affair in most African countries. Initially, this was a noble mission, but, ultimately almost all government institutions failed to deliver on their promises due to rampant inefficiency and corruption. By monopolizing publishing activities, the governments robbed (and, in places, still rob) the private sector of any real opportunity to participate. For example, the publishing industry in Ghana is mainly state-controlled through the curriculum Research and Development Division of the Ministry of Education. Private publishers can access only a small share of the market and this, compounded by the lack of a requisite capital base, has locked out most of the would-be publishers. Most of the few private publishers, such as Sedco, have had to enter into trade agreements with multinational publishers. The same is found in Kenya and Zimbabwe.

State-run publishing firms share a number of negative characteristics. The civil servant mentality of its management, for instance, leads to reactive responses to the market, a lack of skilled input in decision making, and a failure of accountability regarding results. In addition, states fail to provide adequate financial resources to their publishing enterprises and tend to rely on coercive or corrupt practices. Finally, states tend to focus on textbook publishing at the expense of other types and genres of books.

Not all state involvement has been negative, however. In Ghana, for instance, the Public Library Act of 1950 helped to equip and maintain public libraries in the country. The same is true of the Kenya National Library Act. This has helped to foster the growth of publishing activities, although most of the books used in the national libraries are still imported or are donations from foreign publishers. Nonetheless, the common assumption that state firms perform poorly compared to the private sector deserves re-evaluation. There are as yet no studies to show whether public firms could be as efficient as private firms in competitive environments. The Kenyan book industry is a good example of a case where, due to stiff competition from the liberalized market, the state publishers, notably Kenya Literature Bureau and the Jomo Kenyatta Foundation, have made tremendous improvements in their operations.

It is worth noting that Africa's national governments are gradually liberalizing their book industries. Already, in some countries, the private sector plays a significant role in publishing. However, publishers need to operate in a generally favourable economic climate and with appropriate government policies in order to be successful. In most countries, governments work in partnership with donors in all sectors of their economies. This presupposes the involvement of government in the formulation and implementation of policies to govern the industry activities. Many countries still lack a coherent book policy, and this has led to the lack of proper coordination of publishing activities in the country. In Nigeria, for instance, there is no National Book Development agency, and the belatedly launched National Book Council (2000) has had no significant impact. There is, however, the Nigerian Book Foundation, a non-profit organization that helps to coordinate efforts by the various stakeholders in the industry. Carefully crafted book policies would recognize the strategic importance of the publishing industry and provide a comprehensive framework to govern and regulate all activities in the book sector and to guide actions of all players involved. Unfortunately, most countries still lack both national information policies and book policies. This has led to significant problems and abuses within the industry.

In Nigeria, for example, the book industry is largely unregulated. This has occasioned the mushrooming of many publishing houses, most of which operate in total disregard of conventional publishing ethics and copyright provisions. It is worth noting that, despite the gloomy picture, some government initiatives, in partnership with the private sector players, have helped to revamp the industry. There was a time when the government had the prerogative to decide who won tenders to publish and print books for use in public schools and colleges. This approach failed, however, due to rampant inefficiency and corruption.

Finally, it is disheartening that, after many decades of self-rule, many of Africa's national governments still rely on the developed nations for economic and infrastructural redemption. A quick check of the publishing activities in most African countries reveals a sad picture of the industry's dependence on donor aid. All the major publishing projects allocate to donors the control of about 80 per cent of their activities. Donors set the conditions of the projects, provide funding, and ensure their interests are satisfied first. And yet, international donor support for book projects remains uncertain. While it can be said that this international support has helped many book industries in Africa to grow, donor support has also always been accompanied by a dereliction of duty in serving the literary interests of the citizens.

PRIVATE FIRMS AGAINST MULTINATIONALS

The winds of change are blowing towards private-sector development initiatives in many African nations. This fact has been noted in the various conferences focusing on the industry. Most industry observers recognize that the production and marketing of books is best left to private sector firms that are professionally equipped to do the job.

This idea is gaining currency. Even in countries with strong state-run publishing interests, there are initiatives to involve and consult with the private sector in the development of reading materials in many countries. In Ghana, for example, there is a new development and distribution policy that has been established for basic-education textbooks. In Kenya, the industry was liberalized in 1993 when the Kenya Institute of Education stopped publishing school textbooks and allowed private publishers to compete freely.

But even as private publishers are finding more freedom to operate, they face a further challenge from the multinational publishing houses. In Africa, multinationals are seen as powerful, uninvited guests, who regard the countries of the continent either as mere export markets or as a source of profit for their shareholders back at home. Their policy of repatriation of profits leads to capital flight, damaging the already fragile economies of their African host companies. The multinationals were the first companies to run publishing activities on the continent.

Today, most publishing activities in many countries are controlled by multinationals. As evidenced in various countries, multinationals inevitably kill indigenous firms due to their superior financial base, access to manpower and technologies. Although it has been argued that competition promotes quality, this David versus Goliath scenario is unhealthy. Foreign control – economic and, sometimes, political – has sometimes occurred. For instance, in Kenya, there is a free primary education project. This is a donor initiative that has been perceived by many in the book industry as a way to funnel profits directly to the multinational publishing firms in the country. The donor agencies dictated the bid evaluation criteria, which effectively locked out most local publishers. In a few countries, the situation is different. For example, in South Africa, previously independent publishing houses and booksellers have been acquired through mergers by large media conglomerates that are looking for synergy between traditional publishing and other forms of media.

At the end of the day, local publishing firms need protection from foreign competition. A strategy is needed to monitor and appraise the maturity level of the local firms, so that they can be allowed to compete on equal terms with the multinational firms. In most countries however, this may be difficult to achieve. Local firms benefit from being considered 'immature' because they receive legal protections, and no company will want to come from behind that protective wall to compete head-on with the multinationals.

In 1978, the Nigerian Enterprises Promotion Decree required that at least 60 per cent of the publishing industry be owned by local investors. Many foreign publishers were forced to either reduce their equity participation or leave the scene altogether. Some of these foreign publishers simply changed their names: Oxford University Press became University Press, for instance. A similar situation (but triggered by different legislation) occurred in Kenya, where Longman sold most of its equity shares to Longhorn. Unfortunately, the same foreign publishers have come back, and they dominate the publishing sector in Africa.

THE IMPACT OF STRUCTURAL ADJUSTMENT PROGRAMMES

Colonization of the African continent by the West in the nineteenth century, followed much later by the economic crises of the 1980s, has affected every aspect of African society. In the publishing industry, which depends heavily on imports, the effect has been profound.

The introduction of structural adjustment programmes (SAPs) in the early 1990s stimulated donor activities on the continent. Book policies were developed to cater for the donor-aided projects, particularly those that focused on the procurement of textbooks. Whether they went into it blindly or as a result of pressure from the donor agencies, most governments have embraced such programmes. Yet, in the one area where donor assistance was needed – to relieve the chronic shortage of books – no long-term solutions have been achieved. Perhaps the main problem with donor-based projects is that politics play too significant a role. The governments receiving donor aid must dance to the tune of the donating nations for the aid to continue flowing. This is a major impediment to the growth of a strategic industry such as book publishing.

PRINTING SERVICE PROVIDERS

Printing is an old tradition, dating back to the arrival of the missionaries, and new technologies have vastly improved the process. However, book-printing practices in most parts of the continent do not harness the new technological advances. Africa is technologically poor, and most of the technologies are imported from the developed world, making them too costly for most African countries. Because the publishing industry is currently in a slump, few investors are willing to venture into the printing business, as many consider it a high-risk endeavour. It requires a heavy initial capital outlay, but does not guarantee immediate returns. In addition, the seasonal nature of publishing activities in most countries in Africa makes the business less than reliable as a source of profit. The new 'print-on-demand' technology would be invaluable for small print runs, where books are required in small quantities, but virtually no publisher in Africa uses this technology.

It is, therefore, not surprising to find most printers specializing in the production of advertising materials, packaging materials and other small-time printing services such as printing cards, magazines and brochures. The overheads on printing facilities are very expensive in most African countries. In countries where donor-funded educational initiatives are vibrant, local publishers are often unable to afford local printing services, or cannot get their projects scheduled. Thus they are forced to seek printing services outside the continent. The most popular offshore printers are in Malaysia, Dubai and India. It is actually cheaper to print books in these countries than to print them locally.

This trend, however, is changing, and in some countries such as Kenya, Nigeria, and Egypt, liberalization of the publishing industry has made it possible to import printing technologies in anticipation of increased demand for printing services. Still, the number of printers offering high-tech options remains very low, and will remain so for at least the near future.

COPYRIGHT LAWS IN AFRICA

All countries in Africa are signatories to the international copyright convention. Copyright is rooted in certain fundamental ideas about creativity and possession. It springs from the idea that anything we create is an extension of 'self' and should be protected from general use by anyone else. Coupled with this is the idea that the person creating something has exclusive rights over the thing on the grounds of social justice, economic grounds and moral grounds.

Nigeria has a relatively comprehensive copyright law, administered by the Nigerian Copyright Commission. However, inconsistent implementation of the law is still a major problem and malpractices in the industry such as book piracy are evident. In his article 'Copyright and development', P. G. Altbach (1995) is sceptical about the role of copyright especially in Africa. He argues, 'the International Copyright Convention was created by the "haves" to protect their interests. It generally works against the interests of developing countries'. This raises the question of whether copyright is a means of protecting trade advantages or a system of knowledge distribution.

However, international copyright laws are necessary to govern knowledge-sharing across countries and continents. There is a need to develop an integrated copyright law for the African continent, if only to promote the exchange and sharing of intellectual works. In some countries, such as Kenya and Nigeria, copyright laws exist only on paper; there is little implementation of the copyright provisions. National copyright laws in Africa suffer from a variety of shortcomings. For instance, there is the lack of a functional implementing office, delays in the handling of court cases, and an unwillingness to take cases to court at all. In addition, there is a chronically selective application of the copyright laws, an absence of any truly deterrent punishment for those who infringe the laws, a lack of legal awareness within the industry (innocent infringement), and inadequate protection of works published in electronic formats. Therefore, although some success has been achieved in the enactment of copyright laws in most African countries, their implementation and safeguarding is still a major handicap.

THE OBSTACLE OF ILLITERACY

A vibrant publishing industry can only exist in the presence of a reliable readership base. Books are published so that they can be read: to transfer knowledge using the printed word. High levels of illiteracy in Africa, however, have presented a major obstacle to the growth of publishing. More than half of populations in African countries comprise people who can neither read nor write. This problem is aggravated by the fact that the majority of reading materials are published in foreign languages that can be read or understood by less than 30 per cent of the people, including those who may be literate in one or more indigenous languages. In Ghana, for instance, the literacy level is only about 40 per cent. This provides a small market for books.

A related problem is the highly fragmented nature of the local market. To appeal to as broad a public as possible, most published materials must contain content that transcends local or ethnic borders. Thus, published works tend to focus on subjects of interest to the whole nation, or to concentrate on academic subjects. Initiatives to eradicate illiteracy in Africa have faced problems ranging from cultural resistance to a shortage of money and manpower to implement literacy programmes. Research indicates that there are over 1,000 languages in Africa. It would be useful to publish materials in some of these local languages in order to attain wide readership.

PUBLISHING, MARKETING AND DISTRIBUTION

For a long time, publishing was not recognized as a strategic domain of knowledge, especially at the higher levels of the education sector. People had to go abroad to be trained in book publishing and printing. The situation is slowly but steadily improving, with the establishment of training institutions in the continent. Currently, there are only two institutions of higher learning in Africa that offer a substantive degree course in publishing. These are the Faculty of Information Sciences at Moi University in Kenya, and the University of Botswana. There is, therefore, a need to develop training facilities in publishing and to encourage people to take publishing as a career. Until publishing is recognized as a profession, few will be willing to pursue careers in the industry.

In any industry, the effective distribution of goods and services from the points of manufacture to the points of sale or consumption is of paramount importance. The book business is only viable if the books are produced at the right period and distributed to the right people and places at the right time. Distribution has faced major problems throughout the continent, however. There is a general dearth of transport and communication facilities. Most roads are poorly developed and limited to urban areas. Publishers therefore incur huge transport costs, because they must rely on hired transport for long distances. In Nigeria, for example, many publishers do not have the capacity to market and distribute their books in the country. Efforts are being made to develop a national book distribution network however.

TECHNOLOGY AND PROFESSIONALISM

There is an emerging paradigm shift – from the conventional publishing approach to the one-stop publishing approach. The rise of these 'briefcase publishers' has been facilitated by the rapid growth in publishing technology and the need to cater for smaller-scale publishing initiatives. Desktop publishing is mainly confined to those projects which require minimal capital investment and a less complex mix of publishing skills. In South

Africa, the publishing industry is relatively more developed and has embraced many aspects of modern day publishing, including desktop publishing (DTP) and computer-to-plate (CtP). Overall, however, it is in the area of vanity publishing and self-publishing that the new technologies find the greatest use.

To promote professionalism, the publishing industry in Africa has many related associations, which integrate their efforts to ensure that there is efficient production and adequate supply of reading materials. The most common associations target the publishers, the printers and the booksellers. African publishers also belong to international associations and agencies such as the African Book Collective (ABC). The ABC has also facilitated the translation of some books, mainly novels and children's books, into foreign languages such as French.

Publishing associations are relatively active in many countries, and where there is positive and adequate government and civil society support, the associations are doing a good job. Printing associations are not as active as the publishing associations, however. This is mainly due to the lack of recognition that printing is a structured profession requiring guiding rules and professional principles, and the dominance of the sub-sector by Indian companies which view competition as unhealthy.

CHALLENGES AHEAD

It is well accepted today that textbooks constitute the bread and butter of book publishing in the developing world. In most countries, there are no properly constituted, governmentally established guidelines to regulate the activities of the publishing industry. In such uncertainty, it is unlikely that publishers can indulge themselves in underwriting expensive, long-term projects. They prefer to operate in the safe textbook market, where immediate returns are assured. In addition, textbook publishing benefits from donor and government funding. For example in Kenya, the donors have funded a new curriculum in partnership with the government to the tune of Kshs 6 billion.

Unless publishers make sacrifices and agree to stretch their investment over longer periods, key publishing areas are likely to remain neglected for a long time. However, in some countries such as Nigeria, Cameroon, and Ghana, some publishers have successfully ventured into other areas of publishing. Generally, there is insufficient supply of locally developed reading materials for children, pulp fiction and other forms of creative writing. This is in sharp contrast to the anticipated response to demand from the emerging African readership for relevant homegrown reading materials.

Despite the many challenges facing the publishing industry on the continent, great strides have been made within the industry since its early

beginnings. Individuals and organizations have initiated activities and projects. Although many of the publishing associations in most of the countries
of Africa have long lain dormant, efforts made by some of them have been
commendable. For instance, the Douala Writers Club and Cameroon
Publisher Association in Cameroon, the Nigerian Publishers Association,
the Kenya Publishers Association, and the South African Publishing Association have all been active in advancing the professionalism of the industry.

INCENTIVES TO EXCELLENCE

Some national book associations have been at the forefront in recognizing
works by local authors and publishers through awards. In Ghana, for
example, the Ghana National Development Council sponsors an annual
award ceremony where authors are feted for their works. The Noma Award
for Publishing in Africa provides another incentive for the industry. This is
was the first major continent-wide award for the publishing industry in
Africa, and was established in 1979 by Shoichi Noma, the former president
of the Japanese publishing house Kodansha. The Noma award is given to the
winner of a competition among African publishers to develop world-class
reading materials that are relevant to the needs of the continent. The award
is offered every year to writers and publishers working in three categories:
academic and scholarly books, children's books, and literature and creative
writing. Among previous years' winners are Kimani Njogu and Rocha
Chimerah, who won in 2000 for the book *Ufundishaji wa Fasihi: Nadharia na
Mbinu* ('The Teaching of Literature: Theory and Method'), which was published in Kiswahili by the Jomo Kenyatta Foundation. In 1981, the prize
went to Kenya's longest-serving author and publisher, Gakaara wa Wanjau,
for the publication of his prison diary, which had been written in his native
language, Gikuyu. This book, titled *Mwandiki Wa Mau Mau Ithamirio-ini*
('Mau Mau Author in Detention'), was published by East Africa Educational
Publishers.

Other competitive awards include the Caine Prize for African Writing, the
Grand Prix du Roman de l'Académie Française, the Booker Prize, and the
Commonwealth Writers' Prize. Awards like these have contributed a great
deal to book writing and publishing in Africa. The 2005 Caine prize winner
was a Zimbabwean, Brian Chikwava, with the title, *Seventh Street Academy*,
and the winner of the twenty-fifth Noma award was a Cameroonian woman,
Werewere-Liking, who wrote *La Mémoire amputée*.

More Africa-based awards could go a long way in extending and enhancing the growth and vitality of the book industry. Already in some countries,
national award schemes have been established to reward publishers and
writers in various categories of book writing. For example, in Kenya, the
Jomo Kenyatta Prize for Literature was established in 1972 by the Kenya

Publishers Association. The scheme plays a significant role in the growth and development of literary works and talents in the country.

CONCLUSION

In the mid 1990s, the wind for political party pluralism blew across the African continent. Most incumbent presidents were adamantly against allowing the registration of multiple political parties and were averse to the freedom of press. As the revolution became unstoppable, however, most countries adopted a politically pluralistic approach, and many newspapers and magazines were introduced to steer national political agendas. In Malawi, Kenya, Uganda, Zambia, and many other African countries, there were just two or three newspapers and magazines before the 1990s. Since then, the situation has changed drastically. There are many newspapers and magazines on the streets, and even the alternative press has not been silenced.

In sum, the major problems facing the print media in most countries in Africa are the lack of media laws and regulation policies, the dwindling purchasing powers of people on the continent, and an over-reliance on the Western media for international news. The only sustainable approach to the growth of the book industry in Africa is the development of local publishing firms to ensure that they compete favourably with multinational publishers, the establishment of appropriate and proactive policy measures to regulate the industry, the development of institutions to provide training in publishing, and the embrace of modern technologies in publishing.

REFERENCES

Albach, P. G. et al. (ed.) (1985), *Publishing and Development in the Third World: Knowledge and Development*. Portsmouth, NH: Heinemann.

Altbach, P. G. (ed.) (1993), *Publishing in Africa and the Third World*. Chestnut Hill, MA and Oxford: Bellagio.

Brickhill, P. (1996), 'The Transition from State to Commercial Publishing System in African Countries'. In Phillip G. Altbach (ed.), *The Challenges of the Market*. Chestnut Hill, MA and Oxford: Bellagio.

Chakava, H. (1996), *Publishing in Africa: One Man's Perspective*. Oxford and Nairobi: Bellagio Publishing Network and East African Educational Publishers.

Chege, J. W. (1978), *Copyright Law and Publishing in Kenya*. Nairobi: East African Literature Bureau.

Makotsi, R. and L. Nyariki (1997), *Publishing in Kenya*. Nairobi: East African Educational Publishers.

Tanzania Ministry of Education and Culture (1998), 'New Approval System for Educational Books'. United Republic of Tanzania, Ministry of Education and Culture, circular no. 7.

UNESCO (1993), *Formulating the National Book Policy: Need and Guidelines*. New York: UNESCO.

PENTECOSTALISM AND MODERN AUDIOVISUAL MEDIA

In recent years, Pentecostal charismatic churches (PCCs) have gained increasing popularity throughout Africa (Corten and Marshall-Fratani 2001; Gifford 1998; Meyer 2004a). Situated in a genealogy of Christianity in Africa, these churches espouse significant continuities with mission churches, African Independent Churches and even the African religious traditions which they despise as being the realm of the 'powers of darkness'.[1]

Nonetheless, a contrast exists between the familiar image of the African Zionist, Nazarite, or Aladura prophet dressed in a white gown, carrying a cross, and praying for the afflicted in the bush, on the one hand, and, on the other, the exuberant appearance of the immaculately dressed born-again Pentecostal pastor, driving no less than a Mercedes Benz, addressing mass audiences in mega churches, performing miracles in front of the eye of the camera, using high-tech media to spread the message, and celebrating his prosperity as a blessing of the Lord. Preachers such as Benson Idahosa, Mathew Ashimolowo, Nevers Mumba and Mensa Otabil are new icons of success. They serve as role models, speaking to millions of young people in Africa who set their hopes – against all odds – on the Pentecostal theology of prosperity that understands wealth as a divine blessing and empowers born-again believers to get in touch with God through the intermediation of the Holy Spirit.

PCC EXPANSION IN AFRICA

Significantly, PCCs proliferate at a time marked by policies instigated by the International Monetary Fund (IMF) to encourage the democratization, liberalization and commercialization of the media. These policies entail the reconfiguration of postcolonial states and the emergence of new public spheres which give much room to religion. Contrary to expectations generated within theories of modernization and development, which expect a decline of the public role of religion, the phenomenal spread of these churches occurs together with the turn to democratization, a deliberate embrace of global capital in the aftermath of structural adjustment programmes, and the increasing privatization of the state (Hibou 1999).

One of the most salient characteristics of this new type of churches is their skilful use of audiovisual mass media, such as television, video and DVD (Hackett 1998). The most successful of these churches run well equipped media studios which allow them to design and spread their own audiovisual religious products and control their public image. They also accommodate their services and other events to the requirements and opportunities of the new media. Spreading out into the public sphere and reconfiguring modes of worship within the church, PCCs contribute to the rise of a new Christian mass culture. Independent cultural entrepreneurs in the spheres of theatre, popular painting, music and videos tend to surf along with the popularity of Pentecostal Christianity, thereby blurring boundaries between religion and entertainment.

These processes raise intriguing questions. How does the adoption of new mass media relate to, and possibly transform, religious practices and ideas? And how do Pentecostals experience and manage the apparent tension between the emphasis placed on the deep and sincere faith in God that goes together with being 'born again', on the one hand, and the spreading out into the world via media that have a close affinity with mass entertainment, on the other? These questions will be addressed by focusing on southern Ghana, which offers one of the best researched instances of the rise of Pentecostalism, its public presence, and its symbiosis with mass entertainment (Asamoah-Gyadu and Kwabena 2004, 2005a, 2005b; Gifford 2004; De Witte 2003, 2005; Meyer 2004b). Before doing so, however, it is necessary to explicate the understanding of the relation between religion and media that informs this reflection.

RELIGION AND MEDIA

Concomitant with the appearance of mass-mediated religion across the globe, the relation between religion and media has become subject to research and debate in the fields of anthropology, religious studies, media studies and philosophy (De Vries and Weber 2001; Horsfield, Hess and Medrano 2004; Meyer and Moors 2006; Stolow 2005). It has been argued that religion and media are entangled in complicated ways that subvert facile oppositions such as spirituality and technology or faith and reason (De Vries 2001; Plate 2003). Far from describing a recent development, this entanglement expresses a characteristic feature of religion: the positing of a distance between human beings in the world and the divine realm. This distance can only be overcome through mediation. Once religion is understood as a practice of mediation, media – such as images, written texts, film and television – appear neither as alien to religion nor as alienating forces, distracting from the true religious essence. Rather, the media appear as an inalienable condition on which any attempt to access and render present the divine and to communicate among religious practitioners ultimately depends. Therefore religion needs to be analyzed in the context of the forms and practices of mediation that define it.

Insisting that media are intrinsic to religious mediation, however, does not imply that the adoption of new media would necessarily be smooth. On the contrary, as media play a key role in authorizing and authenticating religious experience, the possibility of adopting new media may be experienced as difficult and unsettling, and as possibly challenging established power structures. Media are defined by their particular technology, but they are also socially and culturally embedded, thus producing a variety of different genres, cultural forms and styles that address audiences in particular ways. In studying how new media are adopted into existing religious traditions, the central question concerns not only the impact of new media as technologies, but also the ways in which the forms and styles that proliferate through particular media are matched – or clash – with already existing religious modes of approaching the divine and communicating among religious practitioners.

PENTECOSTAL MEDIATIONS

In 1992, a new democratic constitution was adopted in Ghana which entailed the liberalization and commercialization of hitherto state-owned media. In the wake of this development, a new type of media personality appeared on radio and television: the exuberant Pentecostal-Charismatic pastor. In contrast to the mainstream Protestant, Anglican and Catholic Churches, PCCs immediately took advantage of the liberalized media policies which reduced the possibility of the state to control what was being broadcast to the nation. They eagerly and skilfully made use of such new and comparatively cheap media technologies as video in order to spread the Gospel. Patterned upon American televangelism, a host of new Ghanaian-made Pentecostal programmes emerged, usually recorded and produced by church-owned media studios staffed with the latest equipment.[2]

The example of post-Reformation iconoclasm reminds us that the incorporation of new mass media into practices of religious mediation may be subject to considerable conflicts and debates, but the PCCs' adoption of and adaptation to new mass media occurred rather smoothly. This suggests that existing Pentecostal mediation practices had an almost natural affinity with newly accessible mass media such as television and radio.

HAVING VISION — MAKING IMAGES

Pentecostal understandings of vision and new audiovisual media intersect in interesting ways. The link between Protestantism and vision has been well established ever since nineteenth-century Western missionaries propagated Christianity as throwing light into the darkness of heathendom. Missionary Protestantism operated not only as a harbinger of a more enlightened, modern attitude towards life. Certainly for converts at the grassroots, the enlightenment espoused by the new religion was also expected to yield particular visionary capacities allowing for a deep insight into the invisible realm, so as to grasp how it impinges on the visible world. This attitude towards vision as a spiritual way of looking into what remains invisible to the naked eye, of course, is reminiscent of traditional vision practices, such as interrogating spirits, divination or interpreting dreams (Meyer 2005).

Mainstream churches did not find it easy to accommodate divine revelations (for instance through dreams), and preferred to stress the necessity of reading the Bible and prayer. In the African Independent Churches that seceded from the mission churches, however, vision and prophecy played a far more important role. Here the Bible was not so much a text demanding interpretation but a resource called upon to verify the authenticity of messages received from God.

Contemporary Pentecostals, too, attribute much importance to having visions and looking into the spiritual realm. The so-called Spirit of Discernment empowers them to look behind the surface of mere appearance and, thus, to lay bare the operations of the 'powers of darkness'. When explaining how such vision works, people frequently refer to modern mass-media devices, drawing analogies between spiritual vision and X-ray machines, or to the screening devices at the airport, which make it possible to look right into the interior of bags and see what is concealed to the naked eye. They also mention that God's omniscient eye was just like film technology: God carefully registers every person's life, including his or her secret encounters with occult forces and amoral behaviour, and stores it as on film. The Spirit of Discernment is, in principle, available to all born-again believers, and in the PCCs, many testimonies circulate in which people claim to have seen, via a dream, a certain danger threatening them and their beloved ones, or to have received the revelation of a person's true demonic identity or evil plans. Above all, the capacity to see is mobilized as a key power resource by Pentecostal pastors, who at least partly owe their charisma to being recognized as seers. They seek to enhance their stature by using audiovisual technologies to spread their fame as a new kind of religious superstar (Gifford 2004). As ultimate embodiments of Pentecostal-Charismatic theology, with its emphasis on prosperity and success, pastors not only see, but are also made to be seen. Their carefully crafted images are icons created to testify to Pentecostalism's success all across public space (Asamoah-Gyadu 2005b; De Witte 2005).

MASS MEDIA — MASS AUDIENCE

Many PCCs advertise themselves as masters of new media technologies, thereby stressing their modern identity, international orientation and global connections. Not only do they videotape church services and use big screens so as to project what happens on stage, where the pastors and his entourage are seated, to all visitors within the church hall, they also produce and sell videos of their sermons and other carefully edited church events to a mass public outside the church. In addition, they produce regular television and radio programmes (De Witte 2003, 2005; see also Gordon and Hancock 2005).[3] Pentecostal mega-churches, seating up to 5,000 people, celebrate Christianity en masse. A huge following is taken as the ultimate sign of success.

Marleen de Witte has studied *Living Word*, the televised programme produced by the International Central Gospel Church (ICGC), a mega-church founded and run by Mensa Otabil (see also Gifford 2004; Hackett 1998). She has shown that editing is a crucial tool in the creation of the pastor's image as an icon of piety and spiritual power who embodies the ideal born-again believer (De Witte 2003). In televised broadcasts, the pastor (Otabil uses the term 'general overseer') is brought intimately close to his viewers by zooming in on his face; thereby transcending the distance between Otabil and his followers in everyday life. Inappropriate behaviour on the part of church members – dozing off, chewing gum, being distracted – is cut out; in their place, viewers see close-ups of persons praying with sincerity, listening attentively, or even taking notes during Otabil's sermon, each seeking their personal contact with God. The mass of believers is shown to consist of serious Christians, who are thus implicitly opposed to the so-called 'nominal' Christians that, according to Pentecostals, make up the majority of mainstream churches. In this way, broadcast services present role models to be simulated and internalized.

Addressing and representing the congregation as a mass audience, and speaking to the fragmented mass audience who view the proceedings on television screens, conveys an impression of ultimate organization and unbounded spread. This way of involving members and addressing viewers is remarkably different from the congregational model which characterizes mainstream churches. The latter are often still organized on the basis of ethnic identity. Yet, the mass approach imposes a great difficulty on the PCC leaders, who must find ways to effectively involve members, let alone television and radio audiences, in a moral-religious regime. The sheer size of PCCs makes it virtually impossible for church leaders to know and control the whereabouts of their audiences, both within and outside the church. Opting for a mass organization and expanding into the public sphere, therefore, may easily come at the cost of 'watering down' the message. The mainstream churches make this criticism regarding Pentecostal charismatic mega-churches, but it is also an often heard lament in Pentecostal circles.

MIRACLES

Teaching Christian understandings has became a trademark of the ICGC, which has cast Otabil as the 'teacher of the nation'. Other PCCs, however, place more emphasis on performing miracles – in churches and prayer camps as well as on-screen. The 'miracle ministry' of the German Pentecostal pastor Reinhard Bonnke (Gifford 1987), who organizes mass crusades throughout Africa, offers a role model for displaying the pastors' power to heal – in the name of the Holy Spirit – people who have been given up by medical doctors. Many PCCs organize what they call, in a self-assured manner, 'breakthrough events', promising that 'Your miracle is on the way!'

Many such events are broadcast on television, featuring sweating, yet ultimately victorious, pastors engaged in the performance of miracles. Such programmes – with names such as *Your Miracle Encounter* (by the Ghanaian Bishop Charles Agyen Asare, World Miracle Church International) or *God's Winning Ways* (by the Nigerian, London-based pastor Matthew Asimolowo) – are not broadcast live, but instead are subject to careful editing. The mode of address is such that spectators are made into eyewitnesses of the operation of divine power that is embodied by the pastor. At a certain moment, the pastor looks directly into the camera to address the viewers. He may ask them to join him in prayer, or even to touch the screen in order to be touched by divine power and receive healing. Many people claim that they have felt personally moved by a TV pastor, thereby suggesting that the medium of television is able to bridge the spatial and temporal distance between the pretaped, televised appearance of pastor and his viewers at home. In this way, television is authorized as suitable to convey immediate religious experience.

While faith in God is understood to yield spiritual vision, visibility is also mobilized as evidence in order to persuade followers and potential believers of the truthfulness of the miracle performed. In 2003, for instance, there was much talk about a particular videotape, circulated by a Nigerian Pentecostal church, in which a pastor had been able to raise a dead person, who had been brought to church in a coffin. This was taken as a proof of the superiority of Pentecostalism over other varieties of Christianity and, above all, over science and positive knowledge. The message was that faith can achieve the impossible, if only one believes in the power of God. Interestingly, in April 2004, the Nigerian Broadcasting Corporation banned the broadcasting of this kind of miracle on TV and radio because, as it was put, the pastors could not verify them. Those defending the miracle broadcasts argued that faith exceeds reason, and claimed that the ban violated the constitutional right to freedom of religious expression.

CHRISTIAN ENTERTAINMENT

The performance of miracles and the celebration of vision – consonant with the adage that seeing is believing – draws contemporary Pentecostalism close to the realm of entertainment. This is also apparent in the use of audio-visual media such as video, television and radio, all of which have become widely accessible with the liberalization and commercialization of hitherto state-controlled media.

Locally made Ghanaian and Nigerian movie videos offer a very interesting example of Pentecostalism's closeness to the realm of mass-mediated entertainment. Taking up the popularity of this brand of Christianity (a popularity also reflected in the rise of prayer groups in the mainstream churches), such movies present stories that display a remarkable similarity with the confessions and testimonies elicited in PCCs. Based on a dualistic structure that casts the world as the site of the spiritual (end time) war between God and Satan, one of the attractions of these movies is that they offer insight into its spiritual, normally invisible dimension (Meyer 2005; Oha 2000). Pentecostal modes of looking are thus transposed on to film, substituting the omniscient eye of God with the camera, and the 'film' He is held to record people's secret lives with the revelation visualized on screen. In offering such revelations, this kind of video offers highly stereotypical representations of traditional religion. These images echo the diabolization of traditional religion that stands central in Pentecostalism, and that can be traced back to nineteenth-century missionary representations of 'heathens' as devil worshipers (Meyer 1999).

In recent years, Nigerian movies have been far more successful in appealing to popular taste than Ghanaian ones. One important reason for this is the far more extensive treatment of occult forces (*juju*), horror, and violence in the former (which may be explained, at least in part, by the fact that Ghanaian films are more heavily censored). Special effects play a key role in simulating how the powers of darkness operate, and how divine miracles come about. Re-mediating Pentecostal concerns and modes of looking, movie videos give credibility to Pentecostal views, but also draw them into the logic of dramatization and spectacularization on which popular films thrive. In this way, these movies contribute to the spread of a Christian mass culture. Even a brief visit to southern Ghana reveals the presence of popular Pentecostalism in all spheres of life, and most certainly in the public realm. This imagery, with its representation of traditional religion as occult, dangerous and cruel, stands in remarkable opposition to the attempts of intellectuals and state-run cultural offices to upgrade local religious and cultural traditions (Coe 2005). In the period before 1992, the state still governed the representation of 'the national heritage' and sought to produce more positive images. Currently the popular Christian mass culture, with its stress on demons and the devil, its heavily melodramatic orientation, and spectacular special effects, has become the order of the day.

CONCLUSION AND OUTLOOK

Clearly, the adoption of audiovisual media into PCCs is quite unproblematic, in that these media are understood as almost natural extensions of already existing religious mediation practices in which having visions plays a central role. Not only is vision understood in analogy to modern audiovisual devices, the technological possibility to produce images is also seized upon. The proliferation of images of successful Pentecostal pastors throughout public space – from billboards to television screens – is part and parcel of the PCCs' assertion of their presence and power. This entails a deliberate act of imaging the Pentecostal imaginary, thereby turning it into a tangible, material reality that cannot be overlooked. Paradoxically, this imagery features images of wealth and success, making invisible the pain, poverty and overall suffering that attracts people to these churches (Asamoah-Gyadu and Kwabena 2004). The Pentecostal icons of good living represent the desires of PCCs' mass audiences, rather than mirror their predicament. It remains to be seen how far this more or less deliberate concealment and exclusion will cause cracks in the excessive presence of Pentecostal images of beauty and bounty that have, to a large extent, colonized the public sphere in southern Ghana.

Although they produce their own television programmes, PCCs are not entirely free to choose their own mode of representation. Taking up the televangelist format, especially regarding the miracle shows in which wonders are made to materialize (by any means possible), implies the adoption of the spectacle as a key mode of providing evidence for the power of God. While this resonates well with Pentecostal ideas about the amazing capacity of the Holy Spirit to surpass normal understanding and scientific knowledge, the emphasis on miracles draws Pentecostalism close to the realm of mass entertainment. How to convincingly authorize Pentecostal mass-mediated imagery as authentic and credible is a matter of ongoing concern for the media ministries of PCCs. Here, too, it remains to be seen how PCCs will manage to maintain the difference between God-sent miracles and technologically produced special effects, particularly as the televisual, televangelist format requires its miracles to occur in compliance with production values. Calling upon audiovisual mass media to provide evidence for the efficacy of divine power blurs the distinction between religion and technology. The credibility currently afforded to audiovisually simulated miracles may easily turn into a view that they are 'make believe' and faked.

In sum, adopting modern audiovisual mass media allows PCCs to expand into the world via a proliferation of imagery. However, though consonant with religious ideas about the need to preach the Gospel to the world and evangelize, this expansion has a compromising potential. Spreading images of success, speaking to mass audiences, embracing the representational modes of spectacularization and dramatization – all these assert Pentecostalism's presence in the world, yet make it increasingly difficult to maintain and safeguard the sincerity that characterizes a born-again believer as being in the world, but not of it.

NOTES

1. This essay has been written against the background of my engagement with questions concerning religion and media in the context of my PIONIER research programme, Modern Mass Media, Religion, and the Imagination of Communities, which has been generously sponsored by the Netherlands Foundation for Scientific Research (NWO).

2. In Ghana PCCs are seen by the public as a profitable industry. Not only do members vow to pay their monthly tithes, there also exists a culture of exuberant public gift giving through which the big men (and to some extent women) establish themselves as persons commanding respect. I heard pastors talk openly about the fact that the suits or lavish African clothes they wear, or the Mercedes Benz cars they drive, have been donated by rich business people who were thanking them for spiritual support. Successful PCCs have a substantial amount of funds for building huge churches and engaging in media enterprises. Their high-tech media studios, which often far exceed those of their state-owned counterparts, are also used by independent media professionals.

3. There is also an extensive Pentecostal literature. Sold in Christian bookshops, and at street corners, are a host of tracts and books written by Ghanaian, Nigerian and American Pentecostal pastors.

REFERENCES

Asamoah-Gyadu and J. Kwabena (2004), 'Pentecostal Media Images and Religious Globalization in Sub-Saharan Africa'. In P. Horsfield, M. E. Hess, and A. M. Medrano (eds), *Belief in Media: Cultural Perspectives on Media and Christianity*. Aldershot: Ashgate, pp. 65–80.

— (2005a), *African Charismatics: Current Developments within Independent Indigenous Pentecostalism in Ghana*. Leiden: E. J. Brill.

— (2005b), 'Of Faith and Visual Alertness: The Message of "Mediatized" Religion in an African Pentecostal Context'. *Material Religion* 1(3).

Coe, Cati (2005), *Dilemmas of Culture in African Schools: Nationalism, Youth, and the Transformation of Knowledge*. Chicago: The University of Chicago Press.

Corten, André and Ruth Marshall-Fratani (2001), *Between Babel and Pentecost: Transnational Pentecostalism in Africa and Latin America*. London: Hurst.

De Vries, Hent (2001), 'In Media Res: Global Religion, Public Spheres, and the Task of Contemporary Religious Studies'. In Hent de Vries and Samuel Weber (eds), *Religion and Media*. Stanford, CA: Stanford University Press, pp. 4–42.

De Vries, Hent and Samuel Weber (eds) (2001), *Religion and Media*. Stanford, CA: Stanford University Press.

De Witte, Marleen (2003), 'Altar Media's Living Word. Televised Christianity in Ghana'. *Journal of Religion in Africa* 33(2): 172–202.

— (2005), 'The Spectacular and the Spirits: Charismatics and Neo-Traditionalists on Ghanaian Television', *Material Religion* 1(3): 314–35.

Gifford, Paul (1987), 'Africa Shall Be Saved: An Appraisal of Reinhardt Bonnke's Pan-African Crusade'. *Journal of Religion in Africa* XVII(1): 63–92.

— (1998), *African Christianity: Its Public Role*. Bloomington and Indianapolis: Indiana University Press.

— (2004), *Ghana's New Christianity: Pentecostalism in a Globalising African Economy*. London: Hurst.

Gordon, Tamar and Mary Hancock (2005), 'The Crusade is the Vision: Branding Charisma in a Global Pentecostal Ministry'. *Material Religion* 1(3): 386–403.

Hackett, Rosalind I. J. (1998), 'Charismatic/Pentecostal Appropriation of Media Technologies in Nigeria and Ghana'. *Journal of Religion in Africa* XXVIII(3): 1–19.

Hibou, Beatrice (ed.) (1999), *Privatizing the State*. London: Hurst.

Horsfield, P., M. E. Hess and A. M. Medrano (eds) (2004), *Belief in Media: Cultural Perspectives on Media and Christianity*. Aldershot: Ashgate.

Meyer, Birgit (1999), *Translating the Devil: Religion and Modernity among the Ewe in Ghana*. Edinburgh: Edinburgh University Press.

— (2004a), 'Christianity in Africa: From African Independent to Pentecostal-Charismatic Churches'. *Annual Review of Anthropology* 33: 447–74.

— (2004b), 'Praise the Lord: Popular Cinema and Pentecostalite Style in Ghana's New Public Sphere'. *American Ethnologist* 31(1): 92–110.

— (2005), 'Mediating Tradition: Pentecostal Pastors, African Priests, and Chiefs in Ghanaian Popular Films'. In Toyin Falola (ed.), *Christianity and Social Change in Africa: Essays in Honor of J. D. Y. Peel*. Durham, NC: Carolina Academic Press, pp. 275–306.

Meyer, Birgit and Annelies Moors (eds) (2006), *Religion, Media and the Public Sphere*. Bloomington: Indiana University Press.

Oha, Obododimma (2000), 'The Rhetoric of Nigerian Christian Videos: The War Paradigm of the Great Mistake'. In Jonathan Haynes (ed.), *Nigerian Video Films*. Athens: Ohio University Press, pp. 192–9.

Plate, S. Brent (2003), 'Introduction: Filmmaking, Mythmaking, Culture Making'. In S. Brent Plate (ed.), *Representing Religion in World Cinema: Filmmaking, Mythmaking, Culture Making*. New York: Palgrave, pp. 1–15.

Stolow, Jeremy (2005), 'Religion and/as Media'. *Theory, Culture, and Society* 22(2): 137–63.

REKINDLING EFFICACY: STORYTELLING FOR HEALTH

Orality has been an important method for self-understanding, creating relationships, and establishing an equilibrium between body, soul and the environment. Through oral narratives, communities have been able to pass on values, attitudes, knowledge and modes of practice to generations. Because 'story telling occupies a natural role in many African cultures' (Pillay 2003: 109), it has the potential of functioning as a key strategy for the promotion of health and well-being. In many cases, therapeutic stories are transmitted through the mass media to be consumed by individuals in their homes or by groups in schools, orphanages, prisons, dispensaries, market places, and on public transport.

Because stories are non-threatening and emotionally engrossing in their presentation, they can allow for the release of intense feelings through the establishment of trust and identification. Stories can build confidence in one's ability to change existing circumstances. Equally, they are able to build a sense of community that could play a critical role in social change. Stories can serve as entry points into discussion, and as a soft and friendly exploration of the self. Used as a form of treatment, they establish a collaborative and non-hierarchical relationship with the counsellor, care-giver or discussion facilitator. Stories are at the centre of work with contemporary media in addressing issues of poverty, HIV and AIDS, unemployment and poor governance.

Below, I reflect on the issue of self and collective efficacy in media initiatives that seek to encourage behaviour modification and which view efficacy as a necessary condition for social change. Specifically, I discuss initiatives that relate to the health of individuals and communities. Pro-social interventions aim at change, although there are those which aim for information, discussion and choice around an issue, and those that seek quantifiable behaviour change, difficult though it is to measure. I am interested here in the health interventions. At the 1994 International Conference on Population and Development (ICPD) held in Cairo, it was recognized that empowering women and meeting the needs of citizens for education and health, including reproductive health, are absolutely necessary for development to occur. In paragraph 7.2 of the ICPD Program of Action, reproductive health is defined as 'a state of complete physical, mental, and social well-being, but not limited to the absence of disease or infirmity'. Thus, health is imagined broadly to include other spheres of life which bring equilibrium to the physical and mental state.

While recognizing that *majaaliwa* (fatalism) exists in many African societies, it would nonetheless seem that media efforts that anchor efficacy seek to challenge *majaaliwa* and, in the process, to activate individual and community action in social transformation. They attempt to engage audience members in a realignment of the understanding of the self, the environment and the community. According to Bandura (1986, 1997), self-efficacy is the belief in one's capabilities to organize and execute the sources of action required to manage prospective situations. It is the internal motivation that is vital in determining how people feel, think and behave. Self-efficacy may emanate from successful experience in overcoming problems: from the vicarious experiences provided by social models, from social persuasion in one's ability to perform, and from altering negative emotional proclivities and misinterpretations. According to Bandura:

> Personal efficacy is valued not because of reverence to individualism but because a strong sense of personal efficacy is vital for successful adaptation and change regardless of whether they are achieved individually or by group members putting their personal capabilities to the best collective use. (1997: 32)

Collective efficacy becomes possible through approaches that put people at the centre of social change interventions. It is more than critical consciousness because it is oriented towards action and the ability to take responsibility. But collective efficacy is also a consequence of community dialogue and interaction. It draws its impetus from inter-individual reflections made possible over time. Singhal and Rogers (2003) view health projects as effective when the cultural values, beliefs and practices of the targeted community are well understood. This can be achieved through a number of ways, including having an integral and ongoing audience research component in order to be in rhythm with the target community, and incorporating audience feedback. Effective communication strategies permit communities to engage in dialogue, becoming agents of change and agenda setters.

Within the context of HIV and AIDS, for example, effective communication influences the social and cultural environment for their prevention, treatment, care and support. Communication is key for grassroots advocacy, the mobilization of political action, and the harnessing of gender sensitive and culturally appropriate intervention strategies. The humanization and contextualization of messages call for greater sensitivity to existing social systems as well as acceptable modes of communication and delivery. In most of Africa, for example, oral communication channels and the use of proverbs, adages, riddles, folklore, story telling and subtlety in presentation are key tools for communicating life-changing messages.

A person who believes in being able to cause an event to happen and to determine its outcome can conduct a more active and self-determined life course. By proclaiming '*naweza!*' ('I can!') they are able to influence events around them and to have an impact on friends and neighbours. This self-confident and internally liberating 'can do' cognition suggests and mirrors a sense of authority and control over one's being and the environment. It reflects the belief in being able to intervene and to have power over challenging situations by means of taking adaptive action with far-reaching consequences. This articulation, the outer expression of self-efficacy, is also a humanizing experience.

Self-efficacy makes a difference in how people feel, think and act. A low sense of self-efficacy is associated with increased helplessness and pessimism, whereas a high sense of self-efficacy ignites hope and optimism at the possibility of success. Moreover, a strong sense of competence facilitates cognitive processes and performance in a variety of settings, including quality of argument, decision-making and achievement. When it comes to preparing for action, self-related cognitions are a major ingredient of the motivation process. Self-efficacy levels can enhance or impede motivation towards action. People with high self-efficacy are daring, internally driven and inspired, and are likely to choose to perform more challenging tasks (Bandura 1995). They are also likely to motivate others to act. Such individuals set themselves higher goals and stick to them, and have a better sense of their potential and abilities. Equally, such people may be important players in community organizing for change.

MEDIA INTERVENTIONS

How then can we invoke efficacy for health promotion? How can the people of Africa benefit from a heightened sense of faith in their own abilities? A strong sense of personal efficacy is related to better health (Bandura 1997) and could be encouraged in communities in the pursuit of healthy living. Media strategies have gained presence in many African countries, ranging from advertisements, folk media (storytelling, proverbs, riddling, song and dance), photography, street theatre and soap operas. These cultural productions contribute to increasing levels of knowledge around given subjects, and to the determination of an individual's view of the self and the environment. That reflection within and between individuals may lead to a process of dialogization which, in turn, may contribute to action with concomitant consequences for the individual and society.

It is recognized among media practitioners that the communication system operates though two inter-related routes. First, communication media may promote changes among individuals and communities by informing, motivating, facilitating, and guiding. This is achieved through an explication of the stages and processes to be undertaken for the successful completion of a task. Second, media strategies linked to social systems have a direct effect on communities and their settings. They can contribute to behaviour modification at the individual and collective levels. In a study on the mass media and reproductive health in Nigeria, Bankole et al. (1996) show that contraceptive use and intention are positively associated with exposure to mass media messages, and that women who are exposed to media messages are more likely to desire fewer children than those not exposed to media messages. By extension, the exposure of men to media messages may influence their behaviour towards reproductive health as well. Significantly, then, the reshaping of behaviour related to health can be facilitated through well designed media programming that is consistent in message content and well targeted.

According to Singhal (2003), the effects of behaviour modification are dependent upon infrastructural situations such as the extent of 'air cover' (for instance, on radio or television), the intensity of the messaging, and 'ground cover' (health centres and other infrastructure existing 'on the ground'). When media messages are supported by positive infrastructural events on the ground, they tend to be more effective. If learning occurs through direct experience and social modelling, then health programmes will surely benefit from an activation of models in society whose behaviour can be emulated. The media can identify and make visible these models. Media interventions that deliberately anchor modelling in order to reach communities in dispersed locales and new ideas, values and styles of social

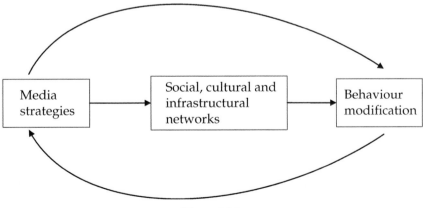

Figure 11.1

interactions are shared in a manner that can influence the consciousness of many simultaneously. Thus influenced, audience members may translate the consciousness into action which may lead to a shift in identity and practice. The mobilization of media outlets and the creation of a friendly and enabling environment to undertake health initiatives can positively transform African societies.

BEHAVIOUR-SHAPING PROJECTS

Most behaviour-modification interventions on the African continent use the radio to reach people. According to a BBC study, 'The Pulse of Africa' (August 2004), the main media used across Africa is radio at 95 per cent, followed by television at 65 per cent and newspapers at 49 per cent. The survey was conducted in urban areas, however, where TV is likely to be available. In rural Africa, the radio and word of mouth are key to the transfer of knowledge, mobilization and behaviour modification.

The radio drama *Our Neighbours, Ourselves*, implemented by Studio Ijambo in Burundi, features a Hutu and Tutsi family who live next door to each other. It relies heavily on humour to comment on the daily lives of rural Burundi, exploring such issues as police misuse of power, gender violence, family responsibilities, sexuality, HIV and AIDS, alcohol abuse and the reintegration of refugees. Studio Ijambo is Burundi's first independent radio studio and was set up by the US non-government organization Search for Common Ground in 1995. This use of the radio to create ethnic dialogue and harmony is critical, especially when one recalls the role played by radio in accentuating violence and genocide in Rwanda.

A radio soap opera called *Tembea na Majira* ('Move with the Times') deals with social, health and governance issues, and is broadcast in Kiswahili through the Kenya Broadcasting Station. The fifteen-minute programme, conceptualized by David Campbell of Mediae, was initially broadcast in Kimeru between 1993 and 1998. The Kiswahili version started broadcasting in 1996. Originally, the context was purely agricultural and may have been inspired by *The Archers* and another Kenyan soap, *Ushikwapo Shikamana* ('If Assisted, Assist Yourself'), both of which preceded it. It has covered issues such as milk production, marketing, domestic violence, child sex abuse, malaria, female genital cutting and pest control. The soap is supported by a magazine programme titled *Sikiza Uerevuke* ('Listen and Be Enlightened') which provides factual information on issues raised in the soap. The strategy of having another programme to provide concrete information to consolidate the soap opera's storyline ensures that correct information is shared. The creative, fictional genres are not designed to present dry facts. This function is better fulfilled by less emotional outlets, such as the magazine format, to answer key community questions.

In Tanzania, the radio serial drama *Twende na Wakati* (*TNW*) started in 1993 with financial support from UNFPA and Technical Assistance from Population Communications International, an NGO based in New York but with a regional office in Nairobi. This drama has since become a national institution. Through it, Tanzanians are able to engage in dialogue on health, gender relations, environmental conservation and the redefinition of masculinity. The character of Mkwaju embodies a re-examination of what it means to be a modern Tanzanian male. Exposure to *Twende na Wakati* produced a strong effect on HIV prevention behaviour. Seventy-two per cent of the listeners in 1994 said they had adopted an HIV prevention method because of listening to *TNW*, and this number increased to 82 per cent in a 1995 survey. The percentage of listeners who believed they could avoid HIV by using insect repellents (a commonly held belief, based on the idea that mosquitoes spread the virus) decreased from 24 per cent in 1993 to 14 per cent in 1995. *TNW* had debunked the belief in its storyline (Vaughan and Rogers 2000). In addition, 23 per cent of the listeners reported adoption of family planning methods because of exposure to *TNW* (Singhal and Rogers 1999: 134). The space created by *TNW* has ensured that hitherto taboo subjects are discussed openly, and intergenerational communication is improved. The drama, earlier broadcast on Radio Tanzania Dar-es-Salaam, has penetrated regional stations and hence reached wider audiences. It is supported by a discussion programme that irons out issues raised by characters in the drama.

Before the programme went on air, extensive formative research was undertaken in late 1992 by the Population Family Life Education Program (POFLEP), an organization based in Arusha. The formative research was used to develop a grid which covered health, economic, social and cultural values such as the favouring of male children over female children. The grid formed the basis for the storyline and characterization. Three character types guided the storyline to provide role models of alternative behaviours and their consequences, be they positive, transitional or negative. The shift in the behaviour of character is thought to inspire behaviour modification among the listening population.

Whereas the Tanzanian soap targets people in their reproductive age, the Nigerian soap *Ready or Not* targets the youth in urban areas, and it seems to affect the way in which sensitive issues are discussed. According to Margaret Adaba:

> In terms of real stories, there is no question that the lives of urban youth in Nigeria are touched by AIDS, ethnic violence, and poverty. Yet the picture of devastation, senseless sacrifice, and hopeless condemnation that the dominance of these images in world broadcasting implies is not the whole of their world. When youth were invited to speak for themselves, they described a richer, deeper, and much more complex picture. The authenticity of their hopes and their fears, of their

conflicts and their dreams of a better tomorrow is captured instead in the stories
created by an ensemble of characters like themselves in the infotainment drama
Ready or Not. (Kimani 2005: 114)

Ready or Not went on air in April 2000, and by September twenty stations
were airing the English series and eleven stations were airing a Hausa
version. Preliminary reactions from audience members were impressive,
with 88 per cent of the respondents saying that the stories were real and
true to life, and 92 per cent feeling that the messages were important to
youth.

Another intervention that is reshaping the way African families communicate is *Kati Yetu*, produced by Apex Productions for the Program for
Appropriate Technology in Health (PATH-Kenya). *Kati Yetu* has two segments: a radio soap opera (*Maisha ya Nuru*) and a radio magazine component that has interviews, discussions, quizzes, vox-pops, and health news.
The radio programme complements the work undertaken in the peer-
education intervention conducted by PATH. As the story unfolds, audience
members vicariously experience the challenges and dilemmas that face adolescent women, and explore the avenues that would allow them to lead a
quality life. Nuru's life is further developed in comic books and the Magnet
Theatre. It is enriched by feedback from listening groups located around
the country. By presenting a model character to youth, *Kati Yetu* is creating
an efficacious audience capable of confronting health challenges. In addition, in the Mathare slums of Nairobi, *Nairobits* is offering young people a
chance to share their dreams and hopes via the internet. Run by members
of the Mathare Youth Sports Association (MYSA), *Nairobits* has given
young people the opportunity to access information on healthy living, team
work and involvement in community improvement activities. The youth are
also addressing HIV and AIDS through sports. Before each game, players
listen to their peer educators and share their views on prevention of AIDS
in HIV-positive people. The anti-AIDS logo is printed on the Association's
sports equipment and the team bus. They have successfully integrated
sports and HIV and AIDS awareness:

> The senior soccer team – Mathare United – has not only performed . . . well . . .
> but has also represented the country in continental soccer tournaments. From
> this team, twenty-five young people were trained in 1994 as HIV/AIDS peer edu-
> cators . . . By taking AIDS seriously, these role models send an important message
> to their many fans. (Kiragu 2003: 136)

Role models are being created through sports in order to increase the feeling
of efficacy among fans.

Radio is the dominant medium in Africa, owing to its cost-effectiveness.
During the last four decades, the radio drama has established itself as an
important channel for entertainment and education. The radio is ideally

suited for re-energizing African oral forms to deal with local and global challenges. In West Africa, the griot tradition has found a space in radio productions and in Tanzania, *ngonjera*, the art of poetic duelling and dialogue, has been used to deal with issues of citizenship and health. The use of indigenous narrative structures – such as characterization and the melodramatic encapsulated in the trickster stories – has been utilized in radio dramas such as *Pwagu na Pwaguzi* ('The Thieves') and *Mahoka* ('Something Funny') in Tanzania and *Kapalepale* in Malawi.

Storytelling for health is a strong initiative for South Africa, including Soul City. Soul City is a South African multi-media project which combines education and entertainment to address critical social and health issues through radio, television and easy-to read-booklets. It also produces *Soul Buddyz*, a programme for children. Overall, Soul City reaches 79 per cent of the target population. Garth Japhet founded Soul City in order to use mass communications in the fight against HIV and AIDS and as a vehicle for promoting healthier lifestyles. In 1999 series, the media complex modelled a new style of collective behaviour in order to influence the way neighbours might intervene in a domestic violence situation (Singhal and Rogers 2003: 287–9).

Prior to the airing of that episode, the prevailing cultural norm was that neighbours would not interfere in a domestic abuse situation. It was treated as a private, not a public, matter. In the series, however, neighbours decided to break the cycle by gathering around the house of the abuser and collectively banging pots and pans, censuring the action of spousal abuse. Collective efficacy was modelled in that episode to give energy to neighbours to take action against violation of spouses. After this episode was aired by Soul City, pot-banging to spot and castigate partner abuse was reported in many communities in South Africa. This collective action, when multiplied, can drastically reduce spouse abuse. In an episode of *Soul Buddyz*, the prime-time TV series produced by Soul City to address issues of teenage sexuality and HIV/Aids, a grocery store owner fires a young employee when he finds that the employee is HIV-positive. Friends of the youth picket the store and urge the community to boycott it, forcing the employer to rehire the employee. Collective efficacy is here being used to combat stigma and discrimination, and to urge individuals and communities to show tolerance and compassion and to respect the rights of HIV-positive people.

There are also situations when cultural wisdom is re-activated in the mass media. The Story Workshop Educational Trust (SWET) in Malawi has been producing a radio soap opera called *Zimachitika* ('Such in Life'). *Zimachitika* began in 1997 as one-year programme promoting safe motherhood and family health, but has since broadened its thematic terrain to include women's political participation and food security. The theme of each show is captured in a proverb. The cultural heritage of Malawi is interwoven with new ideas in agriculture, environment, agro-forestry, family health, HIV and AIDS, gender equity and rural development. By drawing on ancient wisdom and retransmitting it through the electronic media, the Story Workshop seeks to empower individuals to take action in dealing with issues confronting them. The proverb serves to legitimize the action taken.

The Story Workshop seeks to encourage community dialogue on critical social and health issues. It was founded in 1996 by Pamela Brooke, an American educator and radio dramatist. *Zimachitika* is set in the fictional village of Mbonekera and portrays the misadventures of Nabanda, the beautiful but cruel gossip; Gogo, the grandmother with many tales of personal triumph and ancient wisdom; Gubudu, the traditional doctor; and Zakeya, the chief. The story revolves around the barriers to social change.

In Uganda, Africa Health and Development International (AHADI) is collaborating with the Central Broadcasting Corporation (CBS), and the Population Secretariat to develop a soap opera and magazine programme on adolescent sexuality – *Banadda Tweganda* ('Together We Will') in Luganda. The radio programmes are supplemented by a comic strip in the newspaper *Bukedde* as well as by stage performances, posters, T-shirts and caps. The UNFPA-supported intervention is opening ways for discussion on matters of sexuality in a culturally sensitive manner. Launched in June 2005, *Banadda Tweganda* shows the contradictions and challenges that face young Africans as they negotiate between the values taught them as they grow up and those brought about by modernization and globalization.

Many health soap operas follow a values grid that guides the writing team. The grid is extracted from the formative research conducted before the programme is put on air. Figure 11.2 is an example of such a grid, taken from the *Ushikwapo Shikamana* soap opera.

The grid captures the educational issue to be addressed in the drama, as well as the value(s) to be discouraged and the one targeted for erasure from the community. Characters are then crafted based on these values. The plot is also guided by the values grid so that as many issues as possible are discussed without the drama becoming didactic. Thematic trajectories are driven by story and by characters. The twice-weekly Kenyan serial drama *Ushikwapo Shikamana*, which was broadcast on the Kenya Broadcasting station between 1998 and 2004, sought to anchor self- and collective efficacy in characterization and plot. A young girl, Pendo, forcefully subjected to circumcision, rebels on learning that she is about to be married off to an old man, Mzee Konga. She runs away to Kanyageni. As the drama develops, women – such as Tatu, Chezi and Shikalao – assist many other girls, such as Zawadi from Langoni, to move away from their village in order to escape circumcision and forced marriage. The six-year radio serial argued for higher education and unconventional career opportunities for girls even as it tackled issues relating to HIV and AIDS. Through a multi-media strategy

Educational issues	Positive values (It is good that ...)	Negative values (It is bad that ...)
1. People do not understand that the major risk factors for HIV and other STIs are (1) promiscuity, (2) sex with commercial sex workers, (3) unsafe sexual practices, and (4) sharing of razors and needles.	... people understand the major risk factors for contracting HIV are having multiple partners, having sex with commercial sex workers, not using condoms, and sharing razors and needles.	... people do not understand the major risk factors for HIV, and wrongly believe that HIV is spread by (1) condoms, (2) hugging/kissing, (3) insects, (4) caring for an Aids patient.
2. People do not believe that there are means to protect themselves from getting HIV and other STIs.	... people understand that they can protect themselves from getting HIV and other STIs by (1) practising abstinence, (2) practising mutual monogamy, (3) using condoms, and (4) not sharing razors/needles.	... people wrongly believe that there are means to protect themselves from getting HIV and other STIs.

Figure 11.2

involving the radio serial, comic strips in the national Kiswahili daily news-paper *Taifa Leo*, comic books and listeners clubs, the initiative sought to model behaviour at the community level. By encouraging open dialogue on matters of sexuality within the family, the project urged for a re-envisioning of certain practices enshrined in culture that may be detrimental to health. Like *Twende na Wakati* and other socially committed soap operas, *Ushikwapo Shikamana* introduced characters into the lives of audience members, allow-ing that audience to share the characters' experiences vicariously. Both soaps put the education of girls at the centre of the campaign for better health.

It is now recognized that well designed models in the media can serve a range of functions, including giving instructions, information and guide-lines; as well as motivating individuals to act; prompting society to endorse a practice; and reconstructing social networks and processes. The media can be an indispensable engine for change in communities. When harnessed for social good, the media can help in the reformulation of identity. For example, well planned media strategies on health cannot ignore the status of women in society. Empowered women are likely to actively participate in decision-making and community initiatives. Although the soap opera can be essentialist and may tend to perpetuate stereotypes, it also has the potential to serve communities positively. For example, the serial drama has the capacity to be positively transformed into a kind of feminist discourse. It has the potential to act as a major communication channel that foregrounds female subjecthood. Although an essentialist femininity and masculinity does find expression in the genre, a gender-sensitive serial drama model has the potential of centralizing female subjectivity and positively influencing the educational and career ambitions of teenage women in Africa. It has the capacity to positively empower women psychologically, and their socio-economic development.

Through media interventions, girls' access to education could thus be improved. Health promotion efforts can, in fact, contribute to improving the access of girls to schooling. For example, when one or both parents get sick as a result of HIV and AIDS, it is the girls who carry the responsibility of taking care of their siblings and caring for the sick parents. The enrolment ratio for girls decreases with a rise in infection rates; and they are high in most of Africa.

The appeal of entertainment-education initiatives is a consequence of its narrative approach, essentially because human beings are storytellers who employ narrative logic in processing discourse. Entertainment-education soaps have complex plots and sub-plots, different levels of characterization, and conflicts and resolutions which are identifiable to audience members. These narrations designed with the use of formative research and a values framework are perceived by audience members as more involving, relevant, realistic, collaborative, coherent and believable than straightforward cognitive appeals associated with many educational programmes, which are often seen as 'preachy'. Entertainment-education programmes appeal to the emotional levels of audience members and, through parasocial interaction, the characters become personal friends and peers capable of influencing them. A balancing of the experiences of positive, negative and transitional characters creates conflicts and identification among audience members. The sense of suspense and solidarity with fictional characters becomes a learning experience for audience members.

Entertainment-education programmes that follow a clear social learning theory seek to engage communities in dialogue to pave the way for the reconfiguration of power dynamics and behaviour patterns within families and communities. They give voice to women and children and involve men in the deconstruction of masculinity. This is especially significant in situations where cultural practices hinder women's development and limit their life choices. In social change radio soap operas such as *Ushikwapo Shikamana* (Kenya), *Twende na Wakati* (Tanzania), *Mambo Bomba* (Tanzania), *Zimachitika* (Malawi), *Sarivolana* (Malagasy), *Tinka Tinka Sukh* (India), *Taru* (India) and *Apwe Plezi* (St Lucia), there are deliberate efforts to challenge existing gender relations and to reconstruct the way men and women relate to each other. Through social modelling, advocacy and collective organizing, harmful traditional attitudes and practices that put women and girls at risk of STDs, HIV and unwanted pregnancies are challenged.

In certain cases, cultural practices are reformulated simultaneously in the drama and in reality. One such situation involves the practice of female genital cutting. Over the years, female genital cutting (FGC) has been challenged by the media in Africa, and other ways have been proposed of defining what it means to be a woman in those communities that practise it. The practice of FGC is being replaced by alternative rites of passage, in which girls undergo life skills training during a period of seclusion and are declared as having undergone the rite of passage without the cut. The re-imagining, through the media, of a rite of passage in communities and the resultant practice of that rite may have far-reaching consequences for the community. In addition, by fostering and strengthening relationships, the media are also able to encourage African civil society, governments and citizens to increase women's participation in reproductive health and related development programmes; strengthen activities that link reproductive health with other critical sectors such as democracy and governance, economic growth and natural resource management; and promote the exchange of information between women's organizations, policy makers and researchers. In all cases, it is important to involve communities in the conceptualization of the alternative practice and to enter the culture with utmost respect. Indeed, the involvement of community members does not stop. They are involved before implementation of the intervention, during its implementation and afterwards.

The media can also play a major role in the development and eventual acceptance of the HIV and AIDS vaccine, which is key for the eradication of the scourge. As a mobilizing tool, the media can marshal support for organizations, such as the International Aids Vaccine Initiative (IAVI), which are committed to developing a vaccine. The IAVI is part of the global campaign to fight HIV and AIDS, a pandemic that has killed over 20 million men, women and children. Founded in 1996, the institution works in collaboration with local and international partners to speed the search for vaccines to prevent HIV and AIDS. The development of an AIDS vaccine in Kenya began in 1998, and testing began two years after in Nairobi.

The initiative works with individual healthy volunteers, regardless of sex, race or gender, across the world who seek to help find preventive methods for controlling HIV and AIDS. Prior to entering an agreement with the research body, a volunteer undergoes thorough counselling, where the merits and demerits of participating in the process are well elaborated. The information provided, including brochures, flyers and posters tailored to specific target audiences, also serve to educate the volunteer on the implications of the process.

In the fight against HIV and AIDS, preventive measures like safe condom use, abstinence, clean needle distribution, peer counselling and safe blood transfusion have considerable effect to control its spread. However, they have not stopped its spread. Development of a vaccine is the only sure way of erradicating HIV from the face of the earth. But this does not come without its challenges: lack of an animal model, lack of immune correlates,

lack of special strategies and HIV mutation are some of the scientific difficulties in vaccine development.

The clinical process also comes with its benefits and risks. The critical
benefit of the process is that a vaccine will be found and people's lives will
be saved. The risks include physical pain, social risks such as stigma and
discrimination, and misconceptions about the study. Coupled with other
socio-economic factors, these problems may make the volunteer opt out
of this research process, significantly reducing its effectiveness in the long
run.

CONCLUSION

Like sports, radio, television and film in Africa have tremendous potential.
Yet, owing to their origin in the colonial period and the presence of Western
values through programming and training, they are likely to contribute to
'cultural imperialism'. This imperialism may take different forms: media
systems consciously export media influence, media systems unconsciously
disseminate them, communities consciously adopt metropolitan values,
communities unconsciously integrate Western values. The questioning of the
values transmitted in communities could be facilitated in programming and
training, and it may be worth thinking about media forms that deny participation of communities, and media forms that integrate community voices
in the design; the set of industrial arrangements between media houses in
Africa and the metropole; the types of programming perpetuated by the
media houses.

The media dependence prevalent in Africa is, of course, accentuated by
poverty and the availability of a ready economic infrastructure in the metropole. Thus, African media houses end up using alien films and serials such
as *The Bold and Beautiful, Days of Our Lives,* and *The Young and the Restless.*
This cultural domination can be quite frustrating because of its ability to
interfere negatively in the public's tastes, modes of thought and decision-
making processes, and because of the way they can manipulate individuals
and communities to imagining that the West provides the ideal solution for
their predicament and that their identity should be pegged on that received
from the Western media. But it is important to recognize at this point that
media workers in Africa, despite the fact that their training is oriented to the
West, have not always been channels for the perpetuation of alien cultures.
There has always been a deliberate and systematic effort to inscribe an
African media culture. In the recent past, this has been manifest in the
development of health-related media interventions. E-media and the reha-
bilitation of such genres as the soap opera become key to the creation of
those moments of sharing, especially when people listen to or view it
together. Other opportunities include the sports field, the youth centre, the

performance stage, the churches and the dance floors. These are the spaces we want to start inhabiting more deliberately.

Health-related cultural productions from many African countries are multi-pronged and integrative in approach. The integrative capacity is at the centre of ancient creative traditions, such as the mode of storytelling. Audience members are also creators. Indeed, orature from Africa teaches us that intersubjectivity is a necessary condition to completion. Every proverb is a story, and every story can be compressed into a proverb; just as every riddle can be the subject matter of a longer narrative rendition. The artist is also an audience member, and each audience member an artist. This multi-voiced interrelation between apparently discrete phenomena, encapsulated in most African artistic productions, is finding expression in the contemporary entertainment-education work on important human experiences, and is reshaping identities in Africa. Identities are not fixed and muted; they are malleable and constantly shifting. Global diseases and technological opportunities are contributing to these shifts.

The site of storytelling is an important one for our reflection on identity formation. It is also an important space for intellectual work, especially because some of the creative cultural interventions being undertaken therein are spearheaded by people who may have certain theoretical assumptions about social transformation and who may have taken positions on matters of language and community, and the social function of art. They are bringing the theory of community and social change into popular productions. Although some stories may perpetuate *majaaliwa*, others have the capacity to question fatalism and inscribe the agency of the individual and the community. The stories are telling, not only because they are therapeutic and liberating to the individual, but equally because of their ability to engage communities for action.

REFERENCES

Bandura, Albert (1997), *Self Efficacy: The Exercise of Control*. New York: W. H. Freeman and Co.

Bankole, A., C. Rodriguez and C. F. Westoff (1996), 'Mass Media Messages and Reproductive Behaviour in Nigeria'. *Journal of Bioscience*, 28, 227–39.

Brooke, Pamela (1995), *Communication Through Story Characters*. Institute for International Research: University Press of America.

Kimani, Njogu (ed.) (2005), *Culture, Entertainment and Health Promotion in Africa*. Nairobi: Twaweza Communications.

Kiragu, Wambui (2003), 'For the Sake of the Children: Community Based Youth Projects in Kenya'. In Arvind Singhal and Stephen Howard (eds), *The Children of Africa Confront AIDS: From Vulnerability to Possibility*. Athens, OH: Ohio University Press.

Pillay, Yegan (2003), 'Storytelling as a Psychological Intervention for AIDS

Orphans in Africa'. In Arvind Singhal and Stephen Howard (eds), *The Children of Africa Confront AIDS: From Vulnerability to Possibility*. Athens, OH: Ohio University Press.

Singhal, Arvind and Stephen Howard (eds) (2003), *The Children of Africa Confront AIDS: From Vulnerability to Possibility.* Athens, OH: Ohio University Press.

Singhal, Arvind and Everett Rogers (eds) (2003), *Combating AIDS: Communication Strategies in Action*. New Delhi: Sage Publications.

Vaughan, P. W. and E. M. Rogers (2000), 'A Staged Model of Communication Effects: Evidence from an Entertainment-Education Radio Drama in Tanzania'. *Journal of Health Communication*, 5(3): 203–27.

THE MEDIA IN EDUCATION

The role of media in supporting and promoting education has been acknowledged globally and attracts a lot of documentation. The World Conference on Education for All (EFA), held in Jomtien, Thailand, in 1990 recognized this role and underscored the need for nations to involve the media in delivering and advocating for education. The World Forum on EFA held in Dakar, Senegal, in 2000 reaffirmed this position and reiterated the need for involving the media in education campaigns. These two world conferences, it is now acknowledged, gave birth to an expanded vision of education. No longer do we look at education as a regimented system of instruction moving from one point to another and conducted within a fixed environment, but rather as an all-encompassing system that involves formal, informal and non-formal modes of delivery (Aduda 2003).

As 2015 (the target date for achieving 'education for all') approaches, many of the countries of sub-Saharan Africa have yet to realize the set goals. There is evidence that laudable achievements have been made in various spheres: 20 million more children were enrolled in primary schools in sub-Saharan Africa between 1998 and 2002; primary school enrolment for girls, especially in poor countries of sub-Saharan Africa, has increased; and there was a doubling of aid for basic education between 1989 and 2003. Nonetheless, the majority of countries are failing to meet their targets, which include gender parity in primary and secondary education by 2005; achieving 50 per cent improvement in adult literacy by 2015; and the provision of quality education (UNESCO 2006). Tertiary education in Africa, which is expected to promote life-long learning and improve the quality of pre-university education, is itself in a serious crisis characterized by stringent economic conditions, rising graduate unemployment, premature departure of qualified and experienced faculty, declining quality of academic programmes, rising enrolment, and increasing demand at a time of decreasing funding.

How can these challenges be addressed? Aware that most sub-Saharan African countries have increased public expenditure on education to an average of about 20 per cent of their national budgets, it is impractical to mobilize more financial resources in direct proportion to the total demand for schooling. The media may be one of the main hopes of enhancing advocacy and increasing educational opportunities as well as its quality. This paper attempts to explain the role of the media both as a channel for the delivery of learning content to learners in Africa and as a venue for advocacy aimed at changing societal attitudes and setting educational agendas.

THE MEDIA AS A MEDIUM OF EDUCATIONAL DELIVERY

Pressure to expand and democratize educational opportunities has increased enormously, driven in part by population expansion and in part by the need to prepare people for jobs in ever more complex and interdependent societies. Planners have sought strategies that make education available to greater numbers of learners, while reducing the level of investment and administrative structure associated with the traditional system of education. Through the media, the benefits of education are being extended beyond the four walls of the school to embrace a wider spectrum of people, old and young, rural and urban.

What is needed to solve today's educational problems is nothing less than a revolutionary change in education. Developing countries must increasingly look to the application of mass media and modern technology – mass communication, mass transmission techniques, educational radio and television, and the like – with a view to reaching previously untouched millions in isolated regions and customarily neglected groups such as women. In addition, they must find ways to meet the growing shortage of teachers and to raise the content of what is taught to the highest standards (Bishop 1986: 184). There is compelling evidence that the use of technology, if properly designed, is a strategy that could be exploited to expand the provision of education. Opportunities inherent in the mass media to deliver education are enormous. The media cater for all types of learners regardless of age, social standing, commitment and geographic location.

INTERACTIVE RADIO LEARNING

Developments in technology have made both transmission and reception of radio over large areas considerably less costly. This, in turn, has made radio one of the most important instruments of the mass media in helping African countries surmount their massive problems in education. Educational radio programming addresses two needs. First, it supports classroom teachers with effective radio programmes for the learners. Many countries in Africa have used this device, including Tanzania, Kenya, Togo, Nigeria and Botswana. For instance, the Kenya Broadcasting Corporation, in partnership with the Kenya Institute of Education, aired school programmes to all parts of the country until 1992 and, while they lasted, the broadcasts provided invaluable inputs for learners in terms of richness of content, topicality and incisiveness. Further, they were used to share teaching expertise and provided a model of excellence for classroom teachers. All primary schools were sent (at no charge) accompanying materials that had been pre-tested for vocabulary and comprehension levels in a number of urban and rural schools. Interactive radio learning has been used with similar success in other countries and is believed to be particularly effective in schools characterized by a poor educational environment.

Radio programmes also enhance access to basic education in nomadic pastoralist communities where there are no conventional schools. For example, an interactive radio instructions (IRI) approach can provide primary school education. Children come together for an hour or two each day under the supervision of an adult from the community (whether qualified or unqualified as a teacher) in order to listen to and participate in the radio lessons.

Nigeria, one of the most populous countries in sub-Saharan Africa, has used this initiative to expand educational opportunities and improve the quality of education for its nomadic communities through the mobile school programme, in which IRI was one of the main mechanisms for disseminating education to children of pastoralists. When the programme was launched in 1990, total enrolment of nomadic children stood at 18,831. By 1998, enrolment had risen to 155,786. During the same period, the enrolment of girls rose from 5,068 to 65,855. The gap between male and female enrolment has been reduced by 85 per cent. Transition rates from primary to junior secondary school rose from 45 per cent in 1992 to 53 per cent in 1998, higher than the national average of 47 per cent. The number of students completing primary school rose from 2,077 in 1994 to 7,632 in 1998. In 1990, there were 329 schools and 886 teachers; by 1997 there were 1,098 schools and 3,355 teachers.

The mobile school programme for nomadic communities in Nigeria was developed jointly by national and external partners with various educational inputs that included curriculum and didactic materials based on the mainstream curriculum. However, these inputs were adapted to suit the needs and lifestyle of the nomads and teachers were retrained to handle the new curriculum and the new client. A programme to train twelve-to-eighteen-year-old nomads as teachers was also established. This was extremely important, because many teachers are unwilling to travel with the nomadic communities. Delivery systems with flexible schedules and shifts to allow room for children to work were also developed. Radio was used for the delivery of instructions through 198 nomadic radio listening groups. Collapsible classrooms made of aluminium were provided for the pastoralists, whereas canvas, motorized boat schools were developed for fishing communities. Standardized performance indicators and monitoring instruments were employed, resulting in a system for assessing the validity of this new type of school (ADEA 2001: 35). Encouraged by these results, the Kaduna State of Nigeria, in collaboration with Kaduna State Media Corporation, established an IRI in 2002. In 2003, Yobe Broadcasting Corporation established an IRI for Shuwa Arabs and Kanuri nomads in the Borno and Yobe states of Nigeria.

A significant target audience for interactive radio learning for other countries in Africa (including Uganda, Somalia, Djibouti, Sudan, Ethiopia, Mali, Senegal and Kenya) are nomadic pastoralists who live in sparsely populated and semi-arid areas of their respective countries. School enrolment among these pastoralists is quite poor, and where there are schools, multi-grade classrooms are common and the qualifications of most teachers are inadequate. Unless African countries that host nomadic pastoralists and other disadvantaged groups adopt the interactive radio learning approach as part of their strategy to promote equity in reaching disadvantaged groups, the quest for EFA will remain a pipe dream on the continent. The campaign for EFA in Africa should enlist the support of all the media – print, radio, television talk shows, and the like – to help in creating awareness about this strategy and how it has worked successfully elsewhere.

The advantages of using radio as a medium of instruction notwithstanding, it is not as effective a medium when used alone as it is when used in association with other media, particularly printed materials. There is no substitute for print as a tool for development. No other medium can store information so efficiently or convey such a quantity and technical detail as print. The *Accion Cultural* Popular Radio Project in Colombia, launched in 1947, has shown that a single medium, normally radio, is not in itself a sufficient teaching vehicle. Printed matter, in the form of text books, special readers and newspapers, are also needed to reinforce the radio messages (Bishop 1986: 190).

TELEVISION AS AN INSTRUMENT OF EDUCATION

Although radio combined with print can be used to increase educational opportunities and enhance its quality, televised education has an advantage over both radio and print. Several countries in Africa have had success in using television in education. For instance, when the Côte d'Ivoire attained its independence in the 1960s, enrolment was low due to inadequate access to schooling opportunities. Every sub-sector of the education system faced considerable difficulties. The physical infrastructure was inadequate; teachers were underpaid, undertrained, and demoralized; and management and planning were poor at all levels. Textbooks, teachers' guides and other essential instructional materials were in short supply, making both teaching and learning extremely difficult. These problems notwithstanding, education in the newly independent Côte d'Ivoire was expected to produce mature and dedicated Ivorians who loved their nation, took pride in their culture, possessed skills vital to the task of improving their living standard, and became active participants in the development of their country. The government initiated a televized education programme to develop the nation's education system.

Côte d'Ivoire was fortunate in having a television network that covered almost the whole country. In 1968 the government was given assistance by the United Nations Development Programme to set up a training school for primary teachers aimed at carrying out research towards a global solution to the problem of education for development. A teacher training school was set up in Bonake, along with a centre for the production of scripts for television, film, radio and other media. This was supported by a unit devoted to research in applied educational psychology. Substituting television for traditional teaching procedures not only meant a change in teaching methods, but also required that teachers be retrained in new subject matter as well as in the use of audiovisual techniques, communication psychology, group dynamics, new evaluation techniques and after-school activities. In September 1971 the first programmes, aimed at beginners in primary school, were broadcast. About 450 classes representing some 20,000 pupils took part in the televised lessons. Three years later, at the beginning of the 1974–5 school year, there were 3,800 primary school classes – about 170,000 pupils – participating in the programme, and when the schools opened in 1975, 260,000 pupils were distributed in over 5,000 classes. By 1980, plans were in place for the installation of 20,000 television receivers, providing schooling for 830,000 children, or 80 per cent of the six-to-eleven age group. Using traditional methods, it would have taken thirty years to achieve this result (Bishop 1986: 213).

In addition to using television to extend access to basic education, the medium has also been used to enhance the quality of classroom instruction. This is achieved by recruiting television teachers with a strong command of the subject matter, excellent language skills and superior teaching techniques. Classroom teachers use teachers' guides that are prepared and distributed in advance. These help teachers to prepare their learners for the day's television lesson with suggested activities and topics for discussion.

Universities in Africa are making efforts to improve their information and communication technologies (ICT) infrastructure so as to expand the provision of higher education and reduce the cost of teaching programmes while enhancing quality education. The African Virtual University (AVU) project and e-learning programmes are two strategies that exemplify the direction that African higher education institutions are taking.

THE AFRICAN VIRTUAL UNIVERSITY

In sub-Saharan Africa, the African Virtual University (AVU) project is the first of its kind. The AVU is a satellite-based, interactive, instructional telecommunications network. The initiative was launched in 1997, at a time when university programmes in sub-Saharan Africa were grappling with declining budgets, outdated equipment, inadequate staff, limited space, and an inability to mount effective engineering and technological disciplines. The goal of the AVU was to assist African universities in addressing these challenges. Using an exciting mix of videotaped courses and live interaction, AVU sessions allow students to interact with their professor, ask questions and solve problems. A local facilitator usually helps students with their questions.

The AVU programmes target post-secondary students and corporate employees throughout the region. The ultimate objective is to build capacity and support economic development by leveraging the power of modern telecommunications technology to provide world-class quality education and training. To realize its mission, the AVU harnesses the power of interactive satellite and computer-based technologies in order to share some of the highest quality academic faculty, library resources and laboratory experiences available worldwide. Using technologies that provide the flexibility and cost-effectiveness of a virtual academic infrastructure, the AVU is in a position to produce large numbers of scientifically and technologically literate professionals and to support them with lifelong learning opportunities. In so doing, the AVU seeks to bridge the digital divide by training world-class scientists, engineers, technicians, business managers and other professionals who will promote economic and social development and help Africa leapfrog into the knowledge age.

The AVU has sites in twenty-seven universities distributed throughout sixteen Anglophone and twelve Francophone countries, including Uganda, Zimbabwe, Kenya, Ethiopia, Mauritania, Rwanda, Niger, Burundi and Senegal. The AVU collaborates in teaching and research with universities and training institutions in the United States and Canada through a delivery model that combines a creative integration of satellite and internet technologies. These technologies allow the AVU to provide quality education from all over the world at an affordable cost. The other educational services that the AVU provides include a sophisticated internet-based digital library of journals, research reports and textbooks that allow both students and lecturers alike access to the world of database information. This web resource provides a one-stop-shop for research materials unavailable in local libraries.

The AVU also serves as a distributor of textbooks and other school supplies via its online bookstore. Partnerships with major online booksellers and publishers such as Amazon.com and McGraw Hill are currently being explored. Building upon the success of its pilot phases, the AVU has transitioned from a World Bank project to establish itself as an independent non-profit organization headquartered in Nairobi, Kenya. It plans to expand to more countries in Africa and reach undergraduate students, faculty and professionals through three main avenues: learning centres established in public and private universities, private franchises, and on-site professional learning centres housed in corporations and non-governmental organizations (NGOs). When fully operational, it is hoped that the AVU project will expand to all sub-Saharan African countries.

E-LEARNING PROGRAMMES

Learning has developed from the traditional model of classrooms to distance learning and, now, interactive virtual learning and e-learning. A key feature of this rapidly developing concept is the use of available technology to deliver the highest quality of learning content at minimal cost and to an unprecedented number of learners.

In Africa today, as elsewhere in the world, the demand for increased knowledge, skills development, capacity enhancement and a work-life balance have never been greater. To fill this need, individuals and industry are investing heavily in education and job training. The expectation is that the individual will be able to remain at the cutting edge of his or her industry or profession. This has ultimately stretched the traditional institutional providers of such education, leading many professionals to seek the same services abroad. E-learning has emerged as an opportunity for the African society to receive the benefit of world-renowned educational resources, delivered to the desktop computer at minimal cost, conveniently, and in a package flexible enough to suit the individual's specific needs, whether the individual is a senior executive or a newly recruited employee.

Proponents of this initiative argue that the cost to individuals, governments and institutions are dramatically reduced. If one were to go abroad for such a training programme, the costs would include visa fees, travel costs, accommodation, spending allowances and other hidden costs. E-learning eliminates these costs and thus makes the knowledge sought more affordable. With higher education having become an international business, thanks to globalization, foreign universities are aggressively advertizing their technology-driven programmes in Africa.

These aggressive attempts by foreign universities to gain an advantage in the marketplace over African universities has served as a wake-up call for African institutions of higher learning. As a result, African universities are also aggressively marketing themselves through the liberalization in higher education and by launching e-learning programmes. In Kenya, for example, Kenyatta University has embraced the e-learning initiative. The institution is in the process of converting its eight open learning centres, currently scattered across the country, into the interactive electronic learning mode. E-learning programmes use the blackboard learning management system, which is currently used by over 2,000 institutions in Europe, America and Australia and has over 20 million subscribers. Kenyatta University is one of the few higher learning institutions in Africa to adopt the infrastructure to accommodate this software (Kiprotich 2006: 6).

Universities in Africa are not taking up the e-learning programmes as fast as their counterparts in developed countries because of a variety of constraints. According to Frederick Muyia Nafukho, a reporter for the *Nairobi Standard*, in an article published in December 2005, the problems are manifold, but so are the possibilities of learning from others' experience. For instance, the cost of setting up e-learning programmes is astronomical, whereas the returns from this investment take a long time to realize. Columbia University, in the United States, spent US$25 million building a suite of online classes. When the time for implementation came, the university discovered that prospective students were not prepared to pay for the e-learning courses. New York University spent US$25 million to develop online courses, but only attracted 500 students. The University of California closed down its online division. The London School of Economics does not charge for its e-learning courses, but only uses them to promote conventional learning environments. This means that African universities must conduct needs assessment before designing and launching e-learning programmes.

Research has shown that, while online instruction has many advantages, e-learning courses may not work for everyone, especially undergraduate students. The arguments against e-learning often focus on the potentially negative impact of not having face-to-face contact, and on the anxiety caused by the nature and quantity of information transmitted through technology (Nafukho 2005: 13). Lack of a well-developed internet infrastructure and slow bandwidth is a further major challenge that universities in Africa must be prepared to address. For instance, according to a report prepared by the Bandwidth Consortium of the Partnership for Higher Education in Africa, consumers in Europe and North America typically pay US$100 per month for more bandwidth than African universities obtain for US$10,000 per month (Adam 2003; Nafukho 2005). This problem is aggravated by the fact that, in many African countries, less than 2 per cent of the population has online access. Other impediments against the fast adoption of e-learning programmes by African universities include limited technological and computer skills by students and their lecturers, and the tendency for learners to focus on the technology instead of the content being taught. Thus, the design and successful launch of e-learning programmes in Africa will require careful planning, adequate needs assessment, wide consultations with relevant stakeholder groups, and sharing experiences with institutions involved in the e-learning project both inside and outside Africa.

THE MEDIA AS A MEDIUM OF ADVOCACY

Throughout history, the media has played a critical role in information dissemination, awareness creation and influencing opinions. The media can inform the public about emerging educational challenges and empower it to make informed choices on education programmes and opportunities through its capacity to change societal attitudes and also through agenda setting and gatekeeping.

Research into causes of under-participation in education in several countries in Africa points to domestic poverty and low levels of parental education as causes of weak family commitment to the long-term education of children. Faced with the rising costs of schooling and limited socio-economic returns from investing in their children's formal education, many poverty-stricken and illiterate parents do not enrol their children at school, or withdraw them after one or two years of primary school. Rates of non-enrolment and early school attrition are higher among girls than boys. Although there are economic reasons for this, evidence indicates that in many situations, socio-cultural factors are at the heart of gender imbalances in education. For example, girls are widely valued for their reproductive capacities and domestic labour. Neither of these attributes requires lengthy attendance in schools. Likewise, because education is a form of social security investment for many families, the education of girls – most of whom are likely to be married before they reach the age of twenty – is often seen as potentially unrewarding, since the fruits of women's labour are usually reaped by husbands and in-laws, not by the woman's family of origin. Owing to these prejudices about female roles in African societies, deep-seated socio-cultural norms often impede the development in girls of behaviours that are necessary for scholastic achievement, such as out-of-class reading, doing regular homework in the evenings, and volunteering for in-class oral expression (Maclure 1997: 37).

How can the media alleviate such obstacles? The capacity of the mass media to reinforce existing cultural values, traditions, norms and mores of their societies has been widely acknowledged. Through the mass media, people learn the codes of conduct and behaviour of their society, which ensures conformity with basic values and cultural and behavioural patterns. The media must therefore de-emphasize those codes of behaviour that assign specific roles on the basis of gender. Such codes promote sexism and gender-related prejudices that deter the integration and assimilation of African girls and women into the educational, political, economic and social arena. Mass media have also demonstrated the capacity to change people's

perceptions of traditional social values and culture that are based on prejudices against a race, ethnic group, religion, and so on. In modern societies, the mass media are well established as effective agents of enforcing
norms and mores. (The laws against racial segregation introduced in the
United States of America in the 1960s and 1970s succeeded to a large extent
because of the media's capacity to influence the public to change its perception of the black race. According to Uka Uche (1997), the media's role
in the re-orientation of the American public to the reality of the anti-
segregation laws is one of the landmark achievements of the twentieth
century.)

This situation is relevant to the question of pastoralists and education in
Africa. Most pastoralists on the continent occupy the arid and semi-arid
lands (ASAL) within their countries. The aridity experienced in most of the
regions occupied by pastoralists, coupled with the vast expanse of the terrain
characteristic of the ASAL areas, engenders harsh climatic and ecological
conditions. The pastoralists try to adapt themselves to these harsh climatic
and ecological realities by migrating in search of water and pasture for their
animals. Under this system, pastoralists engage in labour-intensive forms of
animal herding and dairy production, and only occasionally sell off slaugh-
tered animals.

Nomads are often seen as conservative, inclined to avoid the sale of their
animals and accumulating huge herds, regardless of the cost (Ezeomah
1997: 4). Rigby (1969) explains that this causal link between pastoralism
and conservatism results from the problems of adaptation to a harsh environment, and the value system commonly referred to as the 'cattle complex'
(Schneider 1959). Together, these attitudes narrow the opportunities for the
youth to take on new ventures such as school education. The media,
however, can highlight the unique attributes of pastoralism that impact on
the education of their children. Education of nomadic children is constrained by unique sets of environmental and ecological barriers. Therefore,
education modelled on the pattern of the regular and conventional school is
inappropriate for children of pastoralists communities. The media must raise
awareness about the pastoral way of life, which relies heavily on the labour
of its youth, beginning at around the age of six years. This over-reliance on
youth for pastoral labour greatly jeopardizes their primary school enrolment.
To address this problem, there is a need for mobile schools responsive to the
lifestyle and needs of nomadic pastoralists. Through sustained social campaigns by the media, employing radio and television programmes and talk
shows, theatre plays and investigative journalism, societal attitudes towards
pastoralist communities and other normally disadvantaged groups can
begin to change.

AGENDA SETTING AND GATEKEEPING

One way in which the media influences the public is through agenda setting. This is the ability of the media to give prominent and persistent focus and emphasis to any issue considered important enough to warrant the attention of its audience. The media provide pictures of social interaction and social institutions that, by their sheer repetition on a daily basis, play an important role in shaping public opinion. Ideas and attitudes that are routinely included in media become part of the legitimate public debate on any particular issue. Conversely, ideas that are excluded from the media or appear only to be ridiculed have little legitimacy (Uche 1997: 5; Croteau and Hoyness 1997; Aduda 2003). Thus by emphasizing the education of girls and pastoralists as well as other minority groups in Africa, the media can set the agenda for this crucial development area.

The media also exert their influence through their tremendous power of gatekeeping. This is the practice of determining which news items get aired or published, and which do not. It also involves the amount of airtime or space allocated to a story, and the prominence given to news items through their positioning within the broadcast. Gatekeeping influences the orientation of audiences through the selective exposure of issues.

Two overwhelming challenges face stakeholder groups involved in campaigns for the attainment of quality education for all in Africa. First, they should mobilize the media to exercise their strength in agenda setting and gatekeeping to promote and support programmes of education that are designed to reach all learners in Africa – including girls and women as well as minority groups. This can be achieved by highlighting successful educational innovations for replication and emulation, and by reporting on emerging challenges and then encouraging governments and the public to address them. Second, they should campaign for the adoption of distance-teaching approaches, which are much less costly than traditional schooling. While the cost of conventional school systems will increase in the future, the cost of media-supported instructional technologies such as interactive radio learning will either remain at current levels or even decrease. It is probably not an exaggeration to say that the future of the African continent may depend on technology-based learning. Geographic distance, regional borders and language can no longer be regarded as obstacles to the movement of ideas and intellectual capital, as we have entered into the phase of knowledge-based economic development.

REFERENCES

Adam, Lishan (2003), 'Information and Communication Technologies in Higher Education: Initiatives and Challenges'. *Journal of Higher Education in Africa* 1(1): 199–221.

ADEA (2001), *What Works and What's New in Education: Africa Speaks*. Paris: International Institute for Educational Planning.

Aduda, David (2003), 'Using the Media to Promote Adult Literacy and Continuing Education'. Paper presented at the National Symposium on Adult Education at the Kenya School of Monetary Studies, Nairobi, Kenya.

Bishop, G. (1986), *Innovation in Education*. London: Macmillan.

Croteau, David and William Hoyness (1997), *Media and Society*. London: Pine Forge Press.

Ezeomah, C. (1997), *The Education of Nomadic Populations in Africa*. Dakar: UNESCO.

Kiprotich, Alex (2006), 'KU's e-Learning Project Running at Full Throttle in the *Standard* Newspaper'. *School and Career*, 19 January.

Maclure, Richard (1997), *Overlooked and Undervalued: A Synthesis of ERNWACA Reviews on the State of Educational Research in West and Central Africa*. Washington, DC: USAID.

Nafukho, Fredrick Muyia (2005), 'E-learning: African Universities Should Learn from Mistakes of the World's Best Institutions', *The Nairobi Standard*, 20 December.

Rigby, P. (1969), *Pastoralism and Prejudice: Ideology and Rural Development in East Africa*. Kampala: Makerere University, Institute of Social Research.

Schneider, H. (1959), 'Pokot Resistance to Change'. In W. Bascon and N. Herskovits (eds), *Continuity and Change in African Cultures*. Chicago: University of Chicago Press.

Uche, Uka (1997), 'Putting Girls' Education on the Media Agenda', *Fawe News* 5(1).

UNESCO (2006), *EFA News*. Nairobi: UNESCO.

13 Ann Biersteker

HORN OF AFRICA AND KENYA DIASPORA WEBSITES AS ALTERNATIVE MEDIA SOURCES

Internet websites of Horn of Africa and Kenyan diaspora groups (broadly defined to include exile, transnational, emigrant, expatriate and refugee communities) provide alternative media sources to Kenya and Horn of Africa based media as well as to the media of the United States and Europe. These alternatives affect the internet, print and broadcast media, news and opinion media, and arts and entertainment media. The alternatives presented by these websites address specific diasporic and exile communities, transnational diasporic communities, and African and global audiences. They include what is excluded by other media sources and demonstrate creative use of technology, they challenge the views presented in other sources, and they provide services for and work to organize and mobilize diaspora communities.

NEWS AND OPINION MEDIA

Numerous Horn of Africa and Kenya diaspora websites provide news and opinion media not available from media sources in Kenya or Horn of Africa or elsewhere. These websites provide news and opinion media about diaspora communities, about events in the Horn and East Africa, and about events elsewhere in the world. Two Eritrean diaspora websites, asmarino.com and awate.com, provide news, information and opinions about Eritrea that are not available from heavily government controlled Eritrean media sources, nor from US and European media sources that provide scant coverage of events in Eritrea. Both websites include their own news stories, as well as access to news coverage in Eritrean and international print and internet sources. Sources cited on a recent asmarino.com news page include awate.com, shaEbia.org, VOAnews.com, and an Amnesty International report. An audio source on the page provides the testimony of a refugee who escaped from an Eritrean prison and was subsequently deported from Malta. The site also provides its own editorial and opinion pieces, as well as access to other opinion sources. The website includes both text articles and radio broadcasts. The Eritrean website awate.com is more exclusively focused on news and opinion coverage, and provides original articles in Arabic as well as in Tigrinya and English. This website also cites a wide range of Eritrean and other sources and provides a discussion forum and a variety of means for reader participation. The Rahwa Media Association, www.democracy.nu, provides original video programming in both English and Tigrinya and states on its website that it 'strives for the empowerment of civil societies that will check and balance abuse by state powerholders' and 'will work for the revival of civil societies, both in Eritrea and among Eritreans in diaspora'.

There is also a wide range of Ethiopian diaspora websites that provide news and opinion media. CyberEthiopia, based in Switzerland, provides original articles and links to internet sources of news about Ethiopia. This website reports that it averages 2,500 unique visitors per day and 15,000 hits. Ethiomedia.com refers to itself as 'an alternative source of Ethiopian news and views'. This site provides original articles in its writer's forum and links to other articles. The site also links to twelve Ethiopian and eleven non-Ethiopian online journals and newspapers and news sources. The site also provides links to four human rights websites, four press freedom websites, six opposition party websites, two non-governmental organization (NGO) websites, and four internet radio broadcast sites. Tigrai_net states that it is 'an Ethiopian news and information site focusing on educational communications, [and] technology'. This site provides original articles and commentary and also links to eleven other news sites.

Ethiopianforum.com is a fourth source of news and opinion media. This site links to news sources and provides original commentary and editorials. Ethiopian News and Views is an online journal that is focused on freedom of the press. An issue begins with the following statement:

> This website was reactivated in February 2003 in response to the first draft of the press law, and the alarmingly ignorant comments of Information Minister Bereket Simon. This website will not respect the new press law *and will work openly to subvert it.* [emphasis in the original]

Based on consideration of Ethiopian diaspora chatroom discussions of the 2000 war between Ethiopia and Eritrea, John Sorenson and Atsuko Matsuoka argue that:

> Neither the experience of life abroad nor the supposedly boundary-transgressing qualities of cybercommunication created any alternatives to Abyssinian fundamentalism among Ethiopian exiles. Indeed, rather that posing any challenge or counter-narrative to Ethiopian nationalism and the regional cult of militarism, the Abyssinian cybernauts reinforced and intensified this discourse. (2001: 61)

These Ethiopian websites contradict the observations of Sorenson and Matsuoka and demonstrate the weakness of studying cybercommunication based only on consideration of a limited number of chatroom discussions. The diaspora websites do not merely challenge the media policies of African governments. For instance, mwambao.com, a Swahili website based in Toronto, published pictures of the flag-draped coffins of soldiers being transported home to the United States from Iraq – pictures that the US government tried to suppress – and provides links to anti-Iraq war websites.

Websites that challenge official government media sources are abundant in the case of Eritrea and Ethiopia, but even where media sources are much more open, diaspora websites provide access to opinions and perspectives not easily available in Africa-based media sources. For example, although media sources in Kenya frequently criticize the Kenyan government, they rarely do so from the perspectives available on the website of the Kenya Socialist Democratic Alliance. The KSDA website includes articles on a wide range of topics and also interviews with activists and workers.

Even sites such as mambogani.com offer a wide range of opinions in a wider range of Kenyan languages and dialects than do Kenya-based media sources. Websites such as Eristart.com, all-links-kenyan.com, Ethiopian News and Views, and jamhuriclub.com also provide convenient access through links to a wide range of news sources. Eristart provides links to twenty-seven news sources and thirteen radio and television broadcast services. Similarly, all-links-Kenyan.com links to fifteen news sources and four radio and television broadcasting services. Ethiopian News and Views links to three Ethiopian news search engines and more than fifty news and information sources, including Eritrean, Somali, Kenyan, Yemeni and Sudanese sources as well as the web sites of the Oromo Liberation Front and Ogaden Online. Jamhuriclub.com provides streaming TV news coverage from Kenyan television two hours after the programmes have been aired in Kenya.

The best available sources for news and opinions about Somalia and the Somali diaspora seem to be Somali diaspora websites. Somaliuk.com provides original news stories and opinion pieces and also provides links to other news media. Somalinet.com provides minute-by-minute access to international coverage of events in Somalia. Sources cited on the sample page include the *Independent Online* from South Africa, the Minneapolis *Star Tribune*, *Al-Jazeera*, the *New Zealand Herald*, AllAfrica.com, Reuters, the UN News Centre, and the *East African Standard*. The site says that it is 'one of the largest virtual communities on the net' because its SomaliNet Forum has 'over 20,000 registered members and more than 200,000 articles'. Somaliuk.com also includes original articles, as well as links to a wide range of other sources. Gedonet Online is edited by two graduates of the University of Wisconsin. Italosomali.org provides news about Somali in Italian as well as news about the Somali community in Italy. Somaliweyn.com provides an online radio service, as well as a wide range of text news and information resources. Its coverage of Somali diaspora community sporting events is a unique feature. This site also provides an extensive listing of Somali and Horn of Africa websites. There are at least two additional internet radio stations operated by Somali diaspora groups: www.radiogolis.com, based in Toronto, and Radio Dalmar (www.soneca.nl), based in The Hague. According to a BBC monitoring report, the primary audiences for these stations are diaspora Somalis.

Additional websites focus on specific regions and a greater number of stories in Somali. Ogaden Online provides original news stories and opinion pieces, and provides links to a wide range of radio services and Somali and Horn of Africa related webites. Allpuntland.com is a news and information source that focuses on the Puntland region. According to a BBC monitoring report, this site 'supports Colonel Abdullahi Yusuf Ahmad, the leader of Puntland'. The report also indicates that:

> The Ottawa-based Radio Somaliland site and the Vancouver-based Somaliland Net (http:/www.somalilandnet.com) support the government of Somaliland and appeal to an audience of emigrant Somalis who come from that region. An Arlaadinet site, based in Bankstown, Australia, supports the Rahanwein Resistance Army faction and appeals to Somalis originally from the southwest towns of Bay and Bakool.

The coverage of Somalilandnet.com emphasizes Somaliland but includes coverage of other regions and topics, and links are provided to a wide range of additional sources. This site also conducts opinion polls. Of course, African diaspora communities are not constituted exclusively on the basis of national or regional affiliation. Opposition and liberation groups have websites that provide news and opinion media as do groups affiliated on ethnolinguistic bases. The Oromo Liberation Front's (OLF) stated goal is:

> [T]o exercise the Oromo peoples' inalienable right to national self-determination to terminate a century of oppression and exploitation, and to form, where possible, a political union with other nations on the basis of equality, respect for mutual interests and the principle of voluntary associations.

The OLF's website is based in Washington, DC. The OLF provides radio broadcasts over the internet as well as clandestinely within Ethiopia. These broadcasts, as well as archives of broadcasts, are available on the internet at www.oromia.org/rsqbo/rsqbo.htm for Radiyoo Sagalee Qabsoo Bilisummaa Oromoo and at www.oromoliberationfront.org/sbo for Sagalee Bilisummaa Oromoo. The OLF website's front page focuses on news and commentary. Original articles are included, as are articles from a wide range of sources, including Eritrean newspapers, the Pan African News Agency, the BBC, Reuters, The *East African Standard*, Amnesty International, The Oromo

Community Forum in the UK, and the World Organization Against Torture. The site also provides a list of OLF press releases.

The newsletter Oromia Online is available at www.oromia.org. The site includes original articles and letters from expelled university students and from the Oromo Community of North America. The Oromia Support Group is based in the United Kingdom and issues a newsletter on human rights abuses, *Sagalese Haaraa* ('New Voice'). Human rights are also the primary emphasis of the site sidamaconcern.com. This site also provides information about the history and culture of the Sidama people of southern Ethiopia.

The website of the Ogaden National Liberation Front (ONLF) provides original articles and press releases and also links to ten online radio and television services. The site provides the ONLF's detailed political programme, interviews with ONLF spokesmen, and a list of military communiques. The website of the Ogaden Human Rights Committee lists addresses in Switzerland, the Netherlands, Canada and Minneapolis, Minnesota. The committee issues an annual report that is available and updated on its website, and also recommends actions that individuals, organizations and governments should take.

The website of the Kenya Somali Community of North America (KSCNA) states this organization was 'born out of the need to expose the long-term perpetration of injustices inflicted upon the Kenya Somalis living in the Northern Frontier Districts by the Kenyan Government'. This site brings together articles from a wide range of sources about injustices committed against Kenyan Somalis. Garissa.net states that it is the 'brainchild of youths from North Eastern Province of Kenya who are currently in studies or other intellectual fields of work across the globe in order to put back something to the community via the current Technology'. This site provides news articles, primarily from Kenyan sources, as well as a wide range of articles by diaspora and Kenyan writers from North Eastern Kenya.

ARTS AND ENTERTAINMENT MEDIA

What most clearly distinguishes these websites from alternative internet news sources focused on Africa, such as allafrica.com, swahilinews.com, or the Africa pages of Z-net, is the emphasis that these sites place on the arts, culture, entertainment and language. In addition to its news and opinion coverage, Asmarino.com provides unique arts and entertainment coverage. This coverage, like its news and editorials, challenges Eritrean government censorship. At the April 2004 meeting of the African Literature Association, Charles Cantalupo screened a film edited in Eritrea about the January 2000 Asmara conference on African languages and literatures, *Against All Odds*. The film provides excellent coverage of many of the main conference speeches and events, but those who attended the conference could not help but recognize that government censors had edited the film footage to eliminate Eritrean writers who, subsequent to the conference, criticized government policies. The late Reesom Haile is Eritrea's most renowned writer. His poetry readings at the conference were attended by hundreds, and he was a central figure in the conference's major events. He was edited completely out of the official conference film, presumably because of his criticism of the government. Nonetheless, his poetry is available in Tigrinya on Asmarino.com, and is also available to order in print or CD versions. In addition to providing the poetry of Reesom Haile, the Asmarino.com website includes examples of the works of other Eritrean poets, musicians and artists.

Additional diaspora websites also provide literary, artistic and cultural sources and links. Eristart.com links to four Eritrean poetry websites. Cyberethiopia provides links to five Ethiopian literature sites. Mwambao. com provides examples of Swahili poetry, taarab lyrics, stories, proverbs and riddles. The site also provides photographs. Similarly, Swahilionline provides proverbs and poetry. This site also provides audio music files and examples of arts and crafts. Both Swahili sites include information on Islam and links to other Islamic sites. Ogadenonline provides an article by Dinitia Smith from the *New York Times* about Nuruddin Farah. Eristart.com also provides links to the websites of art galleries. The website of the Horn of Africa Community Group describes that charitable organization's Somali women's drama group. Mwambao.com, Swahilionline and Rainbownation.com provide cuisine pages.

Numerous diaspora websites provide access to music. The websites www. all-links-kenyan.com, www.mashada.com, www.ukkenyans.co.uk, www. sikokas. com and www.mshenga.com provide a wide variety of Kenyan music for download and for purchase. All-links-kenyan also provides a guide to disk jockeys and sources of information about Kenyan music. In addition, it lists two dance groups. The Eritrean websites asmarino.com and eristart.com provide access to Eritrean music. Eristart.com provides links to twenty-five sources of Eritrean music, including video clips of the Lula band. Somaliuk and Somaliland.net provide links to Somali music sites. Access to Ethiopian music websites is available on the music page of Cyberethiopia.com.

LANGUAGE

The diaspora websites considered may most obviously be alternative media in their use of language. Nearly all of the websites considered provide news, opinion, and arts and entertainment coverage in African languages. Some sites articulate language policies that encourage use of African languages. For example, two of the stated objectives of CyberEthiopia are to:

foster dialogue, collaboration, and knowledge sharing among Ethiopians (both inside and outside the country), in particular by offering appropriate e-forums in local Ethiopian languages as it fits a democratic and free Ethiopia . . . [and to] initiate an Ethiopian 'cyber' culture by encouraging information exchange and content creation in local Ethiopian languages.

Some of these sites are entirely in African languages, for example, jaluo.com. Others, for example, AllPuntland.com and somaliweyn.com, are primarily in African languages. Most of these sites do not have explicit language policies and provide media in one or more African languages as well as in English. A number of the Eritrean and Ethiopian sites provide content using the Ge'ez script and provide downloadable fonts. Awate. com provides articles in English, Arabic and Tigrinya using both Ge'ez and Arabic scripts. Translations are generally not provided, although exceptions are found on the 'about us' page of Swahilionline.com and on the Oromia.org website, where a poem is provided in Oromia with an English translation.

Two of the websites focus on Swahili language and culture. Jamal Hadi (of Ottawa, Canada) initiated Swahilionline.com. Originally called Bwambadi, this website provides 'information on Swahili culture, "Kiswahili" language, and other related information'. Membership on the mailing list is restricted and 'requires approval from preceding members only' but the site states that this policy is subject to future change. In the meantime '[f]riends from all over the world have the opportunity to submit questions or comments regarding the content within these pages. Criticisms are equally welcome!' Mwambao provides similar content but also takes stances on political issues.

These websites present a wide range of content in African languages and also access to instructional materials and sources of information about specific languages. Somalinet.com provides an online magazine in Somali, as well as access to Somali/English and English/Somali dictionaries. Asmarino.com provides Tigrinya language lessons. Eristart.com provides links to websites that provide information on Bilin and Kunama, two minority languages that are spoken in Eritrea.

The types of language and code mixing, switching and linguistic play that occur on diaspora websites are well illustrated by the editor's note to the 2 April 2004 issue of the online journal *Seleda*. This sort of mixing takes place occasionally on other websites in articles, but most often takes place in forums and chat rooms.

SERVICES

The most obvious service that these websites provide is to foster communication among diaspora communities across the world. They also foster community by providing a wide range of additional services to diaspora communities. Ethiopiandiaspora.info, a website funded by the Italian government, provides information on investment, starting a business, finding a job and resettling in Ethiopia. The website of the Horn of Africa Community Group is that of a charitable organization based in the United Kingdom. Ethiopianamerican.org provides a listing of opportunities for volunteering, as well as other services. Eristart.com provides listings of Eritrean and Eritrean diaspora organizations and of Eritrean diaspora youth organizations.

Asmarino.com, Ogadenonline, somalilandnet, Ethiopian Students Association International, mashada.com, and ukkenyans.co.uk provide calendars of community events. The Ethiopian Students Association International also provides descriptions and videos of the meetings of local Ethiopian student groups. Listings or links to dating services are provided by Eristart.com, Somalinet, Misterseed.com and Mashada.com. Misterseed.com and Somaliland.net also provide wedding announcements and obituaries.

A number of sites promote and/or sponsor get-togethers, trips and events. For example, ERISTART.com promoted a July 2004 boat trip and musical event in San Francisco, California. Similarly, Mashada.com promoted a get-together and trip to Orlando, Florida. Other sites provide services relevant to particular communities. For example, somalilandnet provides a listing of missing persons and information on immigration. Rainbownation.com also provides information on immigration.

ORGANIZATION AND MOBILIZATION

The websites provide ways not only to become engaged in issues but also ways to take action. The Kenyan Community Abroad website provided a petition to the Attorney General of Kenya on child molestation. Users could sign the petition online. The Kenya Democratic Socialist Alliance (KDSA) also includes a letter on passports addressed to the Kenya Principal Immigration Officer that supporters may sign. Like many of the other sites, the KDSA site also encourages membership in the sponsoring organization.

The Ogaden Human Rights Committee provides 'recommendations and appeals' asking 'individuals, local human rights and humanitarian organizations' as well as 'governments, United Nations, international human rights and nongovernmental humanitarian organizations' to take action. Individuals are asked to write letters to their governments with copies to Ethiopian diplomats in their country of residence and to the United Nations High Commissioner for Human Rights. Somalilandnet conducts opinion polls on issues such as, 'What should Somaliland do about the border?' Ethiopiandiaspora.info conducted a poll asking, 'How would you like to participate in Ethiopia's development?' Ethiopianforum.com provides links to fundraising drives for schools and hospitals.

It is unclear whether the internet media efforts of the Oromo Liberation Front and the Ogaden National Liberation Front have been as successful as the internet media practices of the Zapatistas, the anarchist McSpotlight website, or the Indymedia network as described by Chris Atton (2003), yet it is clear that the internet is relevant to the objectives of these groups. Patience Akpan (2000) has argued that Africa 'must negotiate the terms of its engagement with the global network society in ways that benefit its populations. Sub-Saharan Africa cannot successfully go global until it has met its local obligations'. It seems evident that the producers of diaspora internet websites have begun to engage successfully in this process. These are not simply local ethnic media in the sense of the newspapers and websites described by Kathryn Mae Mogol, but are media that meet local needs as they engage with transnational global communities.

LIST OF WEBSITES SITED

www.africawired.com (Kenyan, based in San Francisco)
www.allafrica.com (continent-wide)
www.all-links-kenyan.com (Kenyan)
www.allpuntland.com (Somali)
www.asmarino.com (Eritrean, based in US, comprehensive)
www.awate.com (Eritrean, based in US, news and commentary)
www.cyberethiopia.com (Ethiopia, based in Switzerland)
www.democracy.nu (Rahwa Media Association, Eritrean)
www.ERISTART.com (Eritrean, based in US, extensive listings)
www.esai.org/services/forums/portal.php (Ethiopian Students Association
    International)
www.Ethiomedia.com (Ethiopian, media focus)
www.ethiopianamerican.org (Ethiopian, US based)
www.ethiopiandiaspora.info (Ethiopian)
www.Ethiopianforum.com (Ethiopian)
www.gedonet.com (Somali)
www.geocities.com/~dagmawi/Zebenya/Zebenya.html (Ethiopian News and
    Views)
www.italosomali.org (Somali)
www.jamhuriclub.com (Kenyan, provides streaming television news)
www.jaluo.com (Kijaluo online magazine)
www.kabugionline.com (Kenyan music site)
www.kenyaleo.com (magazine published in the United Kingdom)
www.kenyaniyetu.com (Kenyan chat site)
www.kenyasocialist.org (Kenya Socialist Democratic Alliance)
www.kenyansabroad.org (Kenya Community Abroad)

www.kenyasomalis.org (Kenya Somali Community of North America (KSCNA))
www.mambogani.com (Kenyan)
www.mashada.com (Kenyan)
www.misterseed.com (Kenyan, UK based)
www.mshenga.com (Kenyan)
www.mwambao.com (Swahili, based in Toronto, Canada)
www.ogaden.com (Ogaden Online)
www.ogadenrights.org
www.oromo.org (Website of the Oromia Support Group)
www.oromoliberationfront.org (Oromo Liberation Front)
www.onlf.org (Ogaden National Liberation Front)
www.oromia.org/rsqbo/rsqbo.htm (Radiyoo Sagalee Qabsoo Bilisummaa Oromoo)
www.radiogolis.com (Somali diaspora radio station based in Toronto, Canada)
www.rainbownation.com (South African)
www.refugeesonline.org.uk/hacg/ (Horn of Africa Community Group)
www.seleda.com (Ethiopian)
www.sikokas.com (Kenyan)
www.somalilandnet.com (Somali)
www.somalinet.com (Somali)
www.somaliuk.com (Somali, UK based)
www.somaliweyn.com (Sweden based, Somali site)
www.soneca.nl (Radio Dalmar: Somali diaspora radio station based in The Hague)
www.sudan.net (Sudan)
www.swahilinews.com
www.swahilionline.com (Swahili, Canada based)
www.Tigrai.org (Tigrai_net)
www.tisjd.net (Tigrean International Solidarity for Justice and Democracy)
www.ukkenyans.co.uk (Kenyan)
www.unity1960.com (Nigerian radio)
www.wakilisha.com (Kenyan music site)
www.zanzinet.org (Zanzibar)
www.zmag.org/racewatch/africawatch.cfm

REFERENCES

Akpan, Patience (2000), 'Africa in the Age of a Global Network Society: The Challenges Ahead'. *African Studies Quarterly* 4(2).
Atton, Chris (2003), 'Reshaping Social Movement Media for a New Millennium'. *Social Movement Studies*, 2(1): 3–15.

BBC (2003), *BBC Monitoring International Reports, Somalia: Survey of the Country's Media Environment*. London: BBC, 6 June.

Mogol, Kathryn Mae (nd), 'The Internet and the Ethnic Press of New York and New Jersey', <www.scils.rutgers.edu/jri/ ethnicmedia/ethnicpressresearchreport.pdf>

Sorenson, John and Atsuko Matsuoka (2001), 'Phantom Wars and Cyberwars: Abyssinian Fundamentalism and Catastrophe in Ethiopia'. *Dialectical Anthropology* 26: 37–63.

POPULAR DANCE MUSIC AND THE MEDIA

The record business in Ghana (and indeed West Africa) began in the mid-1920s, when the British Zonophone/HMV company first issued recordings of West African popular music and local 'spirituals'; and particularly after 1928, when the United Africa Company (UAC) became their distributor. In 1930 the Zonophone/HMV company sold 181,484 shellac 78-rpm records, and between 1930 and 1933 this company and the German Odeon company (working out of Lagos, Nigeria) sold 800,000 records in West Africa. This was possible because lucrative cash crops (like cocoa and oil palm) enabled many Ghanaian and Nigerians, even farmers, to buy wind-up gramophones and enjoy local as well as imported music records.

In Ghana, some of the early Zonophone recording stars were the Fanti guitarist and accordion player George William Aingo, who recorded in 1927, and guitarist Kwame Asare (Jacob Sam), whose Kumasi Trio recorded the earliest version of the archetypal Ghanaian highlife song 'Yaa Amponsah' in 1928 at Kingsway Hall in London. In the following year, Zonophone published a thirty-five page catalogue of recordings by 'native artists' in eighteen West African languages, primarily featuring popular songs and hymns. Besides the Ghanaian music of Aingo and Asare, this catalogue includes banjo songs, 'negro spirituals', music by a 'native jazz orchestra', and fox-trots and one-steps ('turkey trots') in the Akan and Ewe languages. In 1929 Zonophone also released music by the West African Instrumental Quintet that included 'Tin Ka Tin Ka', an instrumental version of the Trinidadian calypso 'Sly Mongoose' (recorded in 1923 by Phil Madison with Lionel Belasco) that later supplied the melody for the popular highlife song 'All for You'.

During the 1930s a host of guitar- and accordion-playing recording artists emerged in Ghana. They played the Fanti coastal style of Aingo and Asare as well as the slightly later and more rural early highlife style known as 'Akan blues', 'odonson', or 'palmwine music'. Among these performers were Kwesi Pepera, Appianing, Kwame, Mirelou, Osei Bonsu, Kwesi Menu and Kamkan. The internal African market was so lucrative that, up until the Second World War (which temporarily put an end to the record industry), other companies entered the Anglophone West African record market. Among these were Parlophone and the Basel Mission through its trading house, the United Trading Company (UTC).

IMPACT OF RECORDS AND SHEET MUSIC ON GHANAIAN DANCE ORCHESTRAS

An idea of the variety of imported dance music available in West Africa during the 1920s and 1930s on record (and sheet music) can be appreciated from the repertoires of some local dance orchestras that played everything from European ballroom waltzes and quicksteps to African American ragtime, jazz and foxtrots, Latin-American sambas and Caribbean congas and calypsos. The earliest of these symphonic-like dance orchestras in Ghana was the Accra Excelsior Orchestra, formed in 1914, followed by the Jazz Kings and Cape Coast Sugar Babies. Elsewhere in the region, Freetown had its Triumph Orchestra and Dapa Jazz Band, and Lagos had its Maifair Orchestra and Chocolate Dandies.

At sometime in the 1920s the name 'highlife' was coined by the poor, who gathered around the prestigious ballroom clubs of the Ghanaian elite when these 'high-class' dance orchestras began to play local street-songs. At the same classy shows where the top-hatted African elite would dance to ballroom music and an occasional refined 'highlife', they would also be entertained by a 'concert party'. This consisted of local 'blackface' minstrels and lady impersonators doing tap-dances, ragtime and vaudeville sketches, and by silent movies.

THE FIRST IMPORTED FILMS

Silent films got off to an early start in Anglophone West Africa. They began to be shown at Glover Hall in Lagos, Nigeria, from 1904; at Wilberforce Hall in Freetown, Sierra Leone, from 1925 (Leonard 1967; Nunley 1987); and at Azuma House in Jamestown, Accra in 1908. Then, during the 1920s, the Ada businessman Alfred Ocansey established a string of cinema houses in Ghana, including the Palladium cinema-cum-theatre built in 1925. The British merchant company, John Holt Bartholomew, used some of its premises in Accra for film screenings at this time. On occasion during the 1920s, films were taken out of the big towns by itinerant operators, such as Attah Joe, who supplied the provincial and rural cocoa-rich areas of southern Ghana with Charlie Chaplin comedies and westerns.

Charlie Chaplin films, singing cowboys and minstrel 'blackface' comedians like Al Jolson (who starred in the first 'talky') had a profound effect on

Ghanaian performing artists, such as the pioneering 'concert party' actor and singer Bob Johnson, who went on to do vernacular renditions of concert party music when he took the genre to Ghana's provincial towns and villages in the 1930s (Sutherland 1970).

From the late 1930s, it was swing-type jazz that became all the rage in Ghana through imported records and American 'jazz shorts' films. These featured such performers as Cab Calloway, Louis Armstrong, Lena Horne, Duke Ellington and Glenn Miller, and they influenced a whole generation of Ghanaian dance-band highlife musicians who came to the fore after the Second World War. Among these were Guy Warren (Ghanaba), Joe Kelly, E. T. Mensah and King Bruce.

WORLD WAR TWO AND GHANA'S MEDIA INFRASTRUCTURE

The need to disseminate wartime propaganda in Africa led to the expansion of the mass media there. A famous example is the powerful radio transmitter that the Americans built for General de Gaulle and the Free French in Congo-Brazzaville. In Ghana, the rediffusion 'Station ZOY' started operating in Accra in 1935. As a part of the war effort, in 1940, this became the country's first short-wave 'wireless', with a 1.3 kilowatt transmitter. It was also in 1940 that the British colonial administration in Ghana set up 'Aban' (or 'government') cinema to convey news and films such as the 'British Empire at War' series. These were not only shown at urban cinemas. Four mobile units took them, together with slapstick comedies, to the rural areas as well.

An economic boom followed the war, and the colonial powers thought their investments and regimes in Africa were safe. This helped spur a further growth in the mass media. In 1954 Radio ZOY became part of the Gold Coast Broadcasting System, and even earlier (in 1948) 'Aban' cinema became the colonial information service's Gold Coast Film Unit Service that produced many educational and propaganda films. Among these were the films *Towards New Farming* and *I Will Speak English*. These were shown in the rural areas using the wartime mobile units, as well as in the numerous urban cinema houses, there being eight in Accra by 1955.

In the immediate postwar period, the wartime limit on the production of records (plastic being needed for the war effort) was lifted and the West African record industry was re-started, mainly by the Western multinationals. These included the French Pathé-Marconi, the American Warner Brothers, the Dutch Phillips, and the British EMI and Decca. Some of these established recording studios, like the one Decca opened in Ghana in 1947 which pressed 47,000 records a year. Besides the activities of the big companies there was in the early 1950s also an efflorescence of small indigenous record labels in Ghana established by record store dealers. These labels included ECB (run by Mr Chebib, a resident Argentinian), TM (by

H. Teymani, a resident Lebanese), and the Kwahu Wago (by the Ghanaian Atakora brothers).

INDEPENDENCE AND THE AFRICANIZATION OF THE MEDIA

Ghana became independent in 1957, and its first leader, Kwame Nkrumah, facilitated the Africanization of film and broadcasting. The radio transmitting power of Accra Station was increased 100-fold from its wartime level, and a television service was begun in 1965. Both became part of the state monopoly called the Ghana Broadcasting Corporation (GBC). As the one-time director of state broadcasting, Fifi Hesse, put it in a personal communication in 1985, 'Kwame Nkrumah had strong ideas on Pan-Africanism and knew the important role the media could play in diffusing ideas and knowledge'. GBC not only transmitted patriotic and traditional Ghanaian ethnic music, but also popular songs, for Nkrumah recognized that the country's numerous highlife bands and concert parties had played an important role in the anti-colonial struggle. The GBC organized highlife competitions and from the early 1970s launched a number of long-running concert party serials on television, such as *Osofo Dadzie* and, in 1982, *Obra*, run by Grace Omaboe.

After independence, the Gold Coast Film Unit evolved into the government-run Ghana Film Industry Corporation (GFIC). Besides newsreels and government propaganda films, GFIC also produced films that involved popular music and drama. There was the 'Band Series' of artists such as the Tempos, Workers Brigade Band, Ramblers, and Joe Kelly's and the Black Beats highlife dance bands. Then, in 1970, came a full length GFIC feature film *I Told You So*, based on a concert party play and which included concert party actors and highlife singers.

In addition to state radio and film, the newly independent governments of Nkrumah and those that followed encouraged private music production ventures, and so by the end of the 1960s, Ghana had two record pressing plants. First was Ambassador Records, built in 1965 by a Kumasi businessman (Mr A. K. Badu) and capable of pressing 10,000 vinyl records (in 45-rpm and LP formats) a day. The other was the jointly-owned Ghanaian/Polygram Record Manufacturers of Ghana, established in 1969 by Dick Essilifie-Bondze (of the Essilfie-Bondzie record label) and pressing half a million singles and 100,000 albums a year.

THE INFLUX OF WESTERN AND AFRICAN AMERICAN POP MUSIC AND FILMS

From the beginning of independence the imported popular music styles were introduced through records and films that sometimes involved pop stars coming to tour in Ghana. An early example was the 1956 trip to Ghana by Louis Armstrong and his All Stars. They visited Ghana for three days as part of Armstrong's world tour, which was being made into a film entitled *Satchmo the Great* by the American Columbia Broadcasting System. He played in Accra to a crowd of 100,000, and his trumpet style influenced dance-band highlife musicians of the time, such as E. T. Mensah.

From the early 1960s a sequence of Western pop styles such as rock'n'roll, Chubby Checkers' 'twist', soul, and reggae came into Ghana through records. The rock'n'roll craze in Ghana was enhanced by films like *The Blackboard Jungle* and *Rock around the Clock*. As a result, numerous student and youth bands (the Avengers, Bachelors, Saints, and others) sprang up, emulating the songs of Elvis Presley, Cliff Richards, Sam Cooke and Fats Domino. Then came the soul and funk music of James Brown, who performed in Nigeria and Zambia in the late 1960s. He did not make it to Ghana, but soul artists Ike and Tina Turner, Wilson Pickett and Roberta Flack did, in 1971, when they were involved in the making of the American film of the 'Soul to Soul' concert in Accra.

The interactions going on between local and African-American music around 1970 are well captured in the feature film *Doing Their Thing*, produced by the Ghana Film Corporation (GFIC), which starred local Ghanaian soul artists Charlotte Dade and the El Pollos. This film, directed by Bernard Odjidja, is about two fans of soul music who are advised to tour the country in search of their musical roots, and find them in their own traditional music. Beginning in the early 1970s, imported soul records and films and their associated 'Afro' sentiments and fashions helped spark off the Afro-soul and Afro-beat music of Fela Anikikulpo Kuti and Segun Bucknor of Nigeria and the Big Beats, Sawaaba and Magic Aliens of Ghana.

DEMISE OF GHANA'S MUSIC INDUSTRY: LATE 1970S TO MID-1980S

By the early to mid-1970s Ghana had four recording studios, including one linked to the state-owned GFIC. Ghana also had two pressing plants making hundreds of thousands of records a year. These were Record Manufacturers of Ghana and Ambassador Records, which in 1975 published a thirty-page catalogue of 750 songs by sixty local bands that it had recorded and pressed. Everything seemed set for the Ghanaian music and entertainment business to progress. However, from the late 1980s, a number of socio-economic and political changes occurred that had a negative impact on the commercial entertainment industry.

In the latter part of the 1970s there was the decline of the whole Ghanaian economy due to the mismanagement and corruption of the Acheampong and Afuffo military regimes. Record production dropped to a quarter of its previous output, and many performing popular artists left the country in a musical 'brain drain' to settle in Great Britain, Germany and Nigeria (then at the peak of its oil boom). This was followed by two more military coups (in 1979 and 1981) and two and-a-half years of night curfews from 1982, which drastically curtailed the activities of commercial nightclubs and local 'pop', highlife, and concert party bands. Furthermore, the government then classed musical equipment as luxury items and imposed a 160 per cent import duty on band equipment. This prevented many of the local bands from operating again even after the curfew was lifted.

One immediate response to this vacuum of popular performing groups was that dozens of mobile disc jockeys, or 'spinners', who had previously operated in small, enclosed discotheques, invaded the open-air nightclubs and dancing spots, as their equipment was cheaper to buy and their operating overhead was lower than those of the larger highlife and concert bands.

Despite these problems affecting live performance groups, a number of films involving local music and musicians were still made until the mid-1980s. It was video that really destroyed the Ghanaian ciné film industry. One such musical film was *Roots to Fruits*, produced in 1982 by Essilfie Bondzie. His record company was unable to press records, so he involved many of the highlife artists on his record label in this musical odyssey. This was followed in 1984 and 1985 by two films from King Ampow's Afro Movies Company: the feature films *The Road to Kukurantumi* and *Juju*, whose soundtracks were supplied by Amartey Hedzolleh and Kris Bediako respectively. In 1986–7 came *Roots of Highlife*, a film produced by the Ghana Arts Council and by the record label manager Faisal Helwani.

A consequence of the demise of Ghana's record manufacturing industry was that, during the 1980s, commercial cassette production filled the vacuum, as it does not need the centralized and expensive matrix-cutting and steam-pressing plants that records require. Indeed, cassette production became so important that by the late 1980s there were an estimated 5,000 illegal, 'pirate' operators who transferred music from record to cassette in small kiosks. In 1987, 800 of these music pirates came together in an organization called the Ghana Tape Recordists Association which legalized their position with the Ghana Copyright Administration. In 1989, however, pressure from local and international phonogram associations re-criminalized the cassette manufacturers. Even today, the bulk of locally produced music in Ghana is in cassette form.

NEW FORMS OF TECHNO-POP

Disc jockeys with mobile sound systems, or 'spinners', gradually took over the live performance venues from the late 1970s, due to their low operating costs. This was followed by a number of 'techno-pop' music styles that utilized drum machines and, later, computers, and so were also able to do away with the large personnel required by the highlife and concert party bands of the pre-curfew era.

The first 'techno-pop' response was called 'burgher highlife', a cross between highlife and disco music whose drum machines and synthesizers replaced the numerous percussionists and horn players of earlier groups. This music was invented by an expatriate Ghanaian living in Hamburg, Germany, hence the name 'burgher'. It became popular in Ghana from the mid-1980s.

An even more drastic reduction of musical personnel emerged in the local rap groups of the early 1990s. In 1997 the name for this new type of group had been coined: 'hip-hop highlife' or simply 'hiplife'. In this genre, a single artist raps in a local language over pre-programmed imported beat-box rhythm generated by a studio engineer. This musical idiom is not performed live on stage by hiplife artists, but is rather mimed, or 'lip-synched'. The computerized and synthesized music, besides being cheaper to produce than the music of the old bands, has the advantage of providing the musically illiterate youth with a vernacular voice. This was a very important feature for the younger generation, because in 1988 the government discontinued music in the education system.

LOCAL VIDEO

A few films were still being made in the early to mid-1980s, but then came the video revolution of the late 1980s. This not only triggered the decline of expensive local cine films, but also drastically reduced the few touring concert parties that had managed to survive the 1980s by playing in the remoter towns and villages, as mobile videos began to follow the same route. On the positive side, however, local video productions employed quite a number of concert party actors and actresses. The themes of the local video productions continued to feature theatrical portrayals of dwarfs, demons and witches, for these fascinated the concert party audiences.

By 1988 there were 375 video centres in greater Accra alone, renting out imported and local films and, between 1987 and 1995, about 100 low-budget local video released in Ghana. This compares to the only twenty feature films in all that were made by GFIC from 1948 and other local films production companies from the 1970s. The final end of cine film production came in the late 1990s, when the state-owned GFIC was privatized and sold off to a Malaysian TV company (TV3).

The very first of the local videos was *Diablo* (1987, produced by William Nana Akuffo), about a man who makes money by turning himself into a magical snake. This was followed by *Zinabu*, about a women's battle with witchcraft, and *Ayalolo*, one of seven videos produced by musician Sidiku Buari at his Sid Studio in Accra. The music for these local videos was, and still is, usually supplied by a single synthesizer keyboard. Even the local African separatist churches got involved with video films, such as the Christo Asafo Mission's production, *No Easy Target*. However, the few hundred local Ghanaian video releases have been no match for the enormous output of Nigerian video (in 2000 about 500 per year) and so, in 2004, these imported 'Nollywood' films were monitored and partially restricted, causing some concern amongst Nigerian video producers, who claim to have lost 150 million naira.

MINIATURE AND DIGITAL RECORDING STUDIOS

In the late 1970s there were four recording studios in Ghana recording materials for vinyl records. When the record industry collapsed, these were whittled down to just one, the eight-track studio linked to the state-run GFIC. During the 1980s, Ghana switched from vinyl records to cassette production, and a number of analogue multi-track studios using new miniaturized components sprang into being, practically all of them set up by musicians. Bokoor Studio (owned by the author and established in 1982–3) was the first of these, and by the late 1980s there were seven more.

However, with the advent of digital studios in the 1990s, the industry had greatly expanded, and there are now well over 100 recording studios in Ghana, sixty in Accra alone, catering for the various techno-pop music styles (burgher and hiplife). In addition there are local gospel groups who utilize highlife and other popular dance-music styles and have so multiplied since the 1980s that they now generate around 70 per cent of the country's commercial releases of popular music.

THE OPENING UP OF THE AIRWAVES

The latest technology to positively affect the commercial music of Ghana has been made possible by the deregulation of the airwaves. Up until the mid-1990s there were just two government-controlled radio and TV stations in Ghana. However, when broadcasting equipment became digitalized and less expensive, the government began to allow the establishment of independent radio and television stations.

The first of the radio stations, established in 1994, was the 'pirate' station known as Radio Eye. As of 2006 there were about ten television channels and more than 100 commercial and community-based FM radio stations in the country. These put on specialized music programmes, live performances and music videos. Indeed, the video clip has became so important that a special category of award is given now each year to the top video production in contemporary highlife, hiplife and gospel music.

REFERENCES

Acquah, Ione (1958), *Accra Survey*. London: University of London Press.

Barber, Karin, E. John Collins and Alain Ricard (1997), *West African Popular Theatre*. Bloomington, IN: Indiana University Press.

Collins, E. John (1985), *Music Makers of West Africa*. Washington, DC: Three Continents Press.

— (1992), *West African Pop Roots*. Philadelphia, PA: Temple University Press.

— (2000), *The African Music Industry*. For Workshop of the World Bank and Policy Science Centre on Developing the Music Industry in Africa, available on <www.worldbank.org/research/trade/africa_music2.htm>

— (2004), 'Ghanaian Christianity and Popular Entertainment: Full Circle'. *History in Africa* (31) 389–91.

Leonard, Lynn (1967), *The Growth of Entertainment of Non African Origin in Lagos from 1866–1920*. PhD dissertation, University of Ibadan, Nigeria.

Mensah, A. A. (1971), 'Jazz: The Round Trip'. *Jazz Forschung/Research, Universal Edition Graz, Internationale Gesellschaft für Jazzforschung*, Nos 3/4.

Meyer, Birgit (1998), *Popular Ghanaian Cinema and the African Heritage*. The Hague, Netherlands: Netherlands Foundation for the Advancement of Tropical Research.

Nketia, J. H. K. (1956), *The Gramophone and Contemporary Africa Music in the Gold Coast*. Ibadan, Nigeria: Institute of Social and Economic Research.

Nunley, John W. (1987), *Moving with the Face of the Devil: Art and Politics in Urban West Africa*. Urbana and Chicago: University of Illinois Press.

Sutherland, Efua (1970), *The Original Bob: The Story of Bob Johnson, Ghana's Ace Comedian*. Accra: Anowuo Educational Publications.

Waterman, Christopher (1990), *Juju: A Social History and Ethnography of an African Popular Music*. Chicago: University of Chicago Press.

MEDIA PARENTING AND THE CONSTRUCTION OF MEDIA IDENTITIES IN NORTHERN NIGERIAN MUSLIM HAUSA VIDEO FILMS

In analyzing Muslim Hausa film viewing habits and the apparent preference for Hindi cinema, Brian Larkin (1997a) has coined the term 'parallel modernities' to refer to the coexistence in space and time of multiple economic, religious and cultural flows that are often subsumed within the term 'modernity'. He builds upon the concept of 'alternative modernities', introduced by Arjun Appadurai (1991). As he further argues:

> This formulation resonates with the term 'alternative modernities' . . . but with a key difference. Appadurai links the emergence of alternative modernities with the increased deterritorialisation of the globe and the movement of people, capital and political movements across cultural and national boundaries. While deterritorialisation is important, the experience of parallel modernities is not necessarily linked with the needs of relocated populations for contact with their homelands . . . My concern, by contrast, is with an Indian film-watching Hausa populace who are not involved in nostalgic imaginings of a partly invented native land but who participate in the imagined realities of other cultures as part of their daily lives. (1997a: 407)

Concurrent modernities may also contribute to explaining the behaviour of Muslim Hausa video film producers in their use of Hindi film motifs in their video films. Neither the parallel nor the alternative conceptions of modernities, as applied to the cinematic development of young urban Hausa film makers, takes into consideration the violent intrusion of small media technologies that help to create media identities, as opposed to social identities that are divorced from the religious, political and economic transnational flows alluded to by both Larkin and Appadurai.

In Larkin's theoretical framework of parallel modernities, the concept was used to argue for the emergence of 'imagined realities' of the Other as part of the Observer's daily lives. It may be argued, however, that these imagined realities of the Other help in constructing media identity, left in the realm of fantasy, and not 'downloaded' to the realm of daily life, at least in the social setting of Hausa Muslim societies of northern Nigeria. With extremely few exceptions, Hausa cinema is basically an adaptation of Hindi media reality. But whereas Hindi cinema reflects the cultural and moral spaces of the society depicted, the cloned media construct among the Hausa can be seen essentially as pure entertainment, and not a medium for supplanting an entrenched identity.

The rapidly changing pattern of transnational communication and the subsequent emergence of the new media and information revolution are often assumed to have a powerful impact on identities and cultures world-wide; but there is little agreement about how information flows actually interact with social processes, or even about methods for studying this interaction. Cultural and territorial boundaries have become much less coterminous, and new transnational identities are being created as a result of improved international travel and information technologies which no government can control. However, this does not mean the end for older identities which may also be strengthened by the opportunities provided by the communications revolution. It is within this context that the emergence of Muslim Hausa video films and their relation to Muslim Hausa cultural identity can profitably be analyzed.

MUSLIM HAUSA CULTURAL IDENTITY AND MEDIA DELUGE

Anthony H. M. Kirk-Greene (1973) has argued that the typical Muslim Hausa cultural mindset is characterized by about ten behavioural attributes. These include *amana* (strictly friendliness, but used to refer to trust), *karamci* (open-handed generosity), *hakuri* (patience), *hankali* (good sense), *mutunci* (self-esteem), *hikima* (wisdom), *adalci* (fairness), *gaskiya* (truthfulness), *kunya* (modesty, self-deprecation, humility, acknowledging others' opinion over one's own), and *ladabi* (respecting self and respecting others; also consideration for others, both older and younger).

In their 1982 study, Habib Alhassan, Usman Ibrahim Musa, and Rabi'u Muhammad Zarruk identified additional attributes, which included *zumunta* (community spirit), *rikon addini* (adhering to religious tenets and being guided by them with attributes such as truth), *dattako* (gentlemanliness), *kawaici* (tactfulness), *rashin tsegumi* (no idle talk), *kama sana'a* (engaging one in gainful employment), and *juriya da jarumta* (fortitude, courage and bravery). When Hausa drama evolved in the 1950s, these qualities became the main focus of the storylines, which also often reflected a bucolic or simplified urban lifestyle. These values became the standards which any new media attempting to re-mould Hausa society have to satisfy.

From 1937, when the first cinema was opened in Kano, to 1960, film distribution was exclusively controlled by a cabal of resident Lebanese merchants. These entrepreneurs sought to entertain the few British colonials and other, essentially Christian, workers in northern Nigeria by showing principally American and British films. There was no attempt either to develop any local film industry, or even to provide African-themed entertainment for the local people. After the 1960s there were a few attempts to show films from the Arab world and Pakistan. These were not popular with the audiences, despite their Islamic themes. However, the experimental Hindi films shown from November 1960 (after Nigeria became independent in October of that year) proved massively popular, and the Lebanese thus found a perfect formula for entertaining Hausa audiences. Throughout the urban clusters of northern Nigeria – Kano, Jos, Kaduna, Bauchi, Azare, Maiduguri and Sokoto – Lebanese film distribution of Hindi films in principally Lebanese-controlled theatres ensured the massive parenting of the Hindi film genre and storylines, and most especially the song and dance routines, on urban Hausa audiences.

From the 1960s to the 1990s, Hindi cinema enjoyed significant exposure and patronage among Muslim Hausa youth. Thus, films such as *Raaste Ka Patthar* (1972), *Waqt* (1965), *Rani Rupmati* (1957), *Dost* (1974), *Nagin* (1976), *Hercules* (1964), *Jaal* (1952), *Sangeeta* (1950), *Charas* (1976), *Kranti* (1979), *Dharmatama* (1975), *Loafer* (1974), *Amar Deep* (1958), *Dharam Karam* (1975) and countless others became the staple entertainment diet of Hausa urban youth, and were equally popular in the cinemas. However, the biggest boom for Indian films in northern Nigeria was in the 1970s, when state television houses were opened and became the outlet for readily available Hindi films on video tapes targeted at home viewers. For instance, the national television house in Kano presented 1,176 Hindi films on its television network from 2 October 1977, when the first Hindi film (*Aan Bann*) was shown, to 6 June 2003. At the time that Hindi films began to appear on Hausa television, children aged four to six and their youngish mothers (who were in their twenties) became avid watchers of these films. By 2000 the children had grown up. Many became film makers, and they used their Hindi cinema impressionistic conditioning as the defining template for artistic visual media.

Although the media outlets – both in the government-owned television stations and popular markets – had a large dose of traditional entertainment content, the barrage of Indian films on television, and the almost daily broadcast of Hindi film soundtracks on the radio, overshadowed the indigenous content. On television, for instance, indigenous theatre was restricted to thirty-minute dramatic sketches, while a full-blown Hindi, American or Chinese film lasted two or even three hours. Soundtrack music from the Hindi films was often played on the radio in rotation with indigenous music. This gave the impression of an absorbed, globalized Other by equating Hindi film music with Hausa music, because they shared the same cultural spaces. There was a comparative absence of indigenous traditional entertainment aimed at youth that could counter these foreign media influences, and little effort on the part of the government in northern Nigeria to promote traditional theatre and musical forms. Instead, indigenous genres were relegated to performances at quaint bucolic festivals or government functions.

After independence (in 1960), northern cities became open to an influx of other ethnic identities. As a result, the closeted Hausa society of the 1950s, which prided itself on its cultural homogeneity, was quickly opened up by the influx of other ethnic groups into predominantly Hausa and Fulani urban settlements. This created a category of settlers who did not share the same mindset as the Hausa, but who acquired the Hausa language and were ready to boldly experiment with new media technologies in Hausa entertainment. Unencumbered by the traditional mindset of the 'typical' Hausa, these incoming ethnic groups embraced the contemporary entertainment ethos, using 'modern' media instruments (guitars, drums, pianos and saxophones), and shunning traditional Hausa instruments such as the *kalangu*, *kukuma*, *goge*, *garaya* and *kuntigi*. Further, they used the vehicle of the Hausa language to spread their popular appeal.

These elements rapidly entered into the Hausa home video film industry, and in re-inventing entertainment, not necessarily targeted at Hausa groups only but at the Hausa-speaking audience, the Hindi film motif became the most digestible template for them. With religious and ethnic tensions leading to constant clashes in northern Nigeria, any video-film motif in a religiously mixed community had to balance between satisfying the religious conditions of Muslims, and at the same time remaining appealing to non-Muslims. Adopting a neutral song-and-dance, bubble-gum style, as performed by non-ethnic Hausa, would seem to provide an easy way out without ruffling any feathers.

Surprisingly, these linguistic minorities made no attempt to develop a new media-technology film culture in their native languages. When mainstream Hausa saw the success of the Hindi-style films, and the ease of their production (by simply appropriating a Hindi film rather than creating a fresh storyline), they also jumped on the bandwagon, and the line between non-ethnic and ethnic Hausa in terms of the quality of Hausa video film production disappeared. What caused the clash between these cosmopolitan acculturated Hausa and the mainstream Hausa culturalists was the assumptions of the latter that any Hausa-language medium entertainment targeted at a Hausa audience must essentially be Islamic and distinctly culturally Hausa. Neither the new entertainers (referred to as '*Yan Kwalisa*', or 'young dudes') nor the culturalists understood the reasons for this tension between the wider appeal of entertainment beyond mainstream societies and the more monocultural Hausa communities.

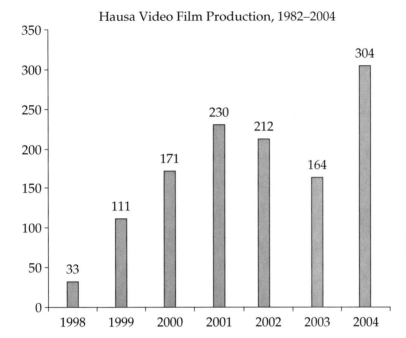

Figure 15.1   Official volume of Hausa home video output, 1998–2004.

National Film and Video Censors Board, *Directory of Video Films in Nigeria*. Abuja, 2002.
The 2003 figures were obtained from press releases from the Board; 1990–7 figures were
compiled in Kano, and not all were listed by the directory.

BOLLYWOODANCI' AND THE NEW WAVE OF HAUSA HOME VIDEO

The first commercial Hausa home video was *Turmin Danya*, released in
1990 by a drama group in Kano. From 1998 to 2004 the Nigerian Film and
Censorships Board recorded the volume of production of home videos in
Nigeria at about 1,180, as shown in Figure 15.1.

Three distinct characteristics have shaped the Hausa video film. The first
motif in Hausa home video is *auren dole*, or forced marriage. In this scenario,
which reflects outdated customs in a contemporary society, but nevertheless
provides a good storyline, a girl (or, more rarely, a boy) is forced to marry a
partner other than the one she (or he) would choose. Hausa film makers use
this theme to challenge traditional authority, and simultaneously provide
templates for youth rebellion against a system most youth see as unfair.

The second motif is the love triangle, with or without the additional
theme of forced marriage. It is inevitable that in a narrative conflict indicating rivalry between two suitors (whether two boys after the same girl, or two
girls after the same boy), antagonists will be given the opportunity to wax

lyrical about their undying love for each other. This is actually a reflection of
kishi – co-wife jealously in a polygamous Muslim Hausa household – which
the filmmakers use to attract housewives in particular to their films.
Although a unique characteristic of a typical Hausa Muslim household, the
love triangle is also a central feature of Hindi films, which makes it easier for
Hausa audiences to identify with them.

The third characteristic of the Hausa home video is the song-and-dance
routine, again echoing Hindi cinema style. These are used to embellish the
story and provide what the film makers insist is 'entertainment'. Indeed in
many of the videos, the songs themselves became sub-plots of the main
story.

The early producers of Hausa video films were young and sassy, called
'*Yan Kwalisa*', or 'young Turks'. They soon proved themselves to be the products of an acculturative media confluence, a mishmash of cultural influences
including American disco, rap and 'gangsta' culture that is applied to the
new-age, Bollywood ethos. The most successful of these producers were
acculturated, Hausanized Muslims and non-Muslim, non-ethnic Hausa. In
the main, they were originally Yoruba, Igbira, Beni, Nigeriène, Tuareg,
Yemeni, Kanuri and other 'minor' northern Nigerian groups whose parents
settled in the large, urban Hausa centres. They were born among the Hausa,
and most spoke the language fluently with only a trace of an accent. They
also attended school among the Hausa and perhaps, except for linguistic
difference and often mode of dress, would not be distinguishable from the
Hausa. According to Hausa industry insiders, these elements constituted as
much as 60 per cent of the Hausa home-video story content. In the April
2001 issue of *Mumtaz* magazine, published in Kano, it is revealed:

> whenever you mention Hausa home video it is assumed these are videos made by
> true ethnic Hausa. Surprisingly and annoyingly, in an investigation, we discovered
> this was not true; only few of those involved in production of Hausa home video
> are true ethnic Hausa. The ethnic tribes that overrun the Hausa home video
> industry include Kanuri, Igbos, and most significant of all, the Yoruba. In a table
> we drew, about 42% of the Hausa home video producers and artistes were of
> Yoruba extraction, 10% were Kanuri, 8% were Igbos. Thus only about 40% are
> true ethnic Hausa, and yet these videos are called Hausa videos . . . There is a
> dearth of true ethnic Hausa in Hausa home videos. (p. 12)

Many of the insiders (producers and directors) have argued that most of the
bold and experimental home videos, and especially the dance routines, had
to be performed by non-ethnic Hausa because they were not restricted by
the Hausa cultural and religious mindset that disapproves of such displays
of exuberance. These non-ethnic Hausa performers worked hard to hide
their actual ethnic identities, and invariably accepted roles of modernized
Hausa urban youth in the home videos, rather than appearing in traditional
Hausa or religious character portrayals. Even their dialogue was restricted

to urban Hausa lexicon, devoid of any references to the classical Hausa vocabulary typical of rural dwellers, for that might cause problems in pronunciation.

A second category of involvement of non-ethnic Hausa in Hausa video film production was exemplified by the participation of two of the larger ethnic groups in Nigeria, the Yoruba and Igbo, who had developed an extensive video film process far more advanced than the Hausa. Despite its ethnic and religious differences and flashpoints of conflict, northern Nigeria has been host to millions of people of southern Nigerian descent, many of whom were actually born in the north and had no other home but there. Although living in communities that are segregated from the predominant Muslim host community (often more by choice than by policy), they speak the Hausa language passably well and have excellent commercial links with the Hausa host communities. However, while some have a working knowledge of the Hausa language, many cannot speak the language and see the Hausa home video as merely another investment opportunity. Some of these businessmen have had prior experience of the Nigerian home video processes in Lagos and Onitsha.

When they realized that money could be made out of the Hausa home video industry, a few of these producers used their capital, expertise and superior technical skills and equipment to start producing Hausa-language home videos, using as many Hausa actors as they could. Interestingly, they seemed to prefer to feature the non-ethnic, Hausa-acculturated, Hausa artistes in their home videos. Examples of these videos include *Dan Adamu Butulu* (produced by Oscar Baker), *Halin Kishiya* (Tunji Agesin), *Zuwaira* (Matt Dadzie), *Almara* (I. Nwankwo) and *Matsatsi* (Taye Ukubardejo).

The production values of most of the new video moguls were not informed by the household dramas, rustic settings or moralizing sermons that appealed to the traditionalist establishment characterized by the old Hausa TV dramas such as *Hadarin Kasa, Hankaka, Dan Mogori, Zaman Duniya* and *Kuliya*. Rather, their main creative mechanism has been to 'rip-off' Hindi *masala* films and remake them into Hausa clones, complete with the original storylines, songs and choreography. About twenty of the 150-plus Hindi films so cloned into Hausa video films are shown in Table 15.1.

In this new age of Hausa home video, the genres of the industry's founding fathers disappeared, and a spicy *masala* mixture of videos appeared which combined several genres in one video and attempted to copy as many Hindi films as they could. This new genre can be called 'Bollywoodanci' ('Bollywood adaptation') to reflect the main mechanism used by this cluster of young and essentially urban film makers.

Table 15.1 Inspirations from the East – Hausa Hindi Video Films

S/N	Hausa video film	Hindi original	Element ripped off
1.	*Abin Sirri Ne*	*Judwa* (1997)	Storyline
2.	*Akasi*	*Sanam Bewafa* (1991)	Scenes
3.	*Al'ajabi*	*Ram Balram* (1980)	Song
4.	*Alaqa*	*Suhaag* (1940), *Mann* (1999)	Songs
5.	*Aljannar Mace*	*Gunda Raj* (1995)	Songs
6.	*Allura Da Zare*	*Sultanat* (1986)	Scenes
7.	*Almuru*	*Bhoot* (2003)	Storyline
8.	*Amira*	*Jodi No 1* (1999) *Khoobsurat* (1999)	Storyline
9.	*Aniya*	*Josh* (2000)	Song
10.	*Auwalu, Sani, Salisu*	*Oh, Jeh, Jagadish* (2002)	Storyline
11.	*Ayaah*	*Chandni* (1989)	Storyline
12.	*Badali*	*Hum Hai Rahi Pyar Ki* (1993)	Storyline
13.	*Bunkasa*	*Anmol* (1993)	Storyline
14.	*Burin Zuciya*	*Raazia Sultaan* (1961)	Storyline
15.	*Ciwon Ido*	*Devdas* (2002)	Storyline
16.	*Cuta*	*Qurbani* (1998)	Song
17.	*Da Wa Zan Kuka*	*Dil To Pagal Hai* (1997)	Song
18.	*Dafa'i*	*Ghayal* (1990)	Storyline
19.	*Danshi*	*Bazigar* (1993)	Storyline
20.	*Darasi*	*Hogi Pyar Ki Jeet* (1999), *Mann* (1999)	Song

RATIONALE OF MEDIA CHILDREN

The main reason advanced by Hausa home video makers – both those of the old school and those making up the new wave – for their strong focus on the love-triangle storylines and song-and-dance routines in their videos was that the 'Indian society' as shown in Hindi films is just like the Hausa society, at least in its approach to marriage, the main obsession of young Hausa home video producers. Hausa home video makers who seek their inspiration from Hindi commercial film sources focus on the visual similarities between Hausa culture and what they perceive as Hindi culture, rather than their divergences. As Brian Larkin has observed:

> Hausa fans of Indian movies argue that Indian culture is 'just like' Hausa culture. Instead of focusing on the differences between the two societies, when they watch Indian movies what they see are similarities . . . The wearing of turbans; the presence of animals in markets; porters carrying large bundles on their heads, chewing sugar cane; youths riding Bajaj motor scooters; wedding celebrations and so on: in these and a thousand other ways the visual subjects of Indian movies reflect back to Hausa viewers' aspects of everyday life. (1997: 12)

Ironically, the convergence of cultures, as perceived by Hausa video film makers, between Muslim Hausa society and 'Indian' society further accentuates the divergence of cultures between Muslim Hausa and other, Christian, Nigerians. Nigerian films were often used as templates by Hausa film makers – for example, *Dangerous Twins* (re-made in Hausa as *Auduga*), *Suicide Mission* (*Tsumagiya*), *Ungrateful* (*Akushi*) and *Break-Up* (*Kallabi*). However, the Christian-themed nature of Nigerian films are by and large avoided by Hausa film makers.

Public reaction to the Hindi film focus of Hausa video films has not always been favourable. A representative sample of this reaction can be seen in the comment made by Yusuf Muhammad Shitu, of the Kaduna Polytechnic in Zaria, quoted in the August 2001 issue of *Annur*:

> How can a person, claiming to be Hausa, producing a film for Hausa people, copy Indian and European cultural norms, and claim they are his culture? Film production (among Muslims) is good because it an easy medium for delivering social messages, but the way they are doing it now is mistake. (p. 24)

Hausa filmmakers whose techniques are entrenched in copying Hindi films insist that they will not stop copying Hindi films, even though it is against the Nigerian National Film and Censorship Board Enabling Law. They have good reason, because such conversions make money. In addition, they note that efforts to present Hausa culture in video films have met with little or no commercial success.

CONCURRENT MODERNITIES AND HAUSA HOME VIDEOS

There is no doubt that most Hausa youth cinema, especially from 2000 to 2003 – the 'golden age' of the industry – draws its creative inspiration and media identity from Hindi cinema. In drawing from such creative sources, young Hausa film makers rarely considered the disjointed interface between Hindu and Muslim Hausa cultures, especially as depicted in entertainment settings. As Brian Larkin points out:

> The iconography of Indian 'tradition', such as marriage celebrations, food, village life and so on, even when different from Hausa culture, provides a similar cultural background that is frequently in opposition to the spread of 'westemisation'. Indian films place family and kinship at the centre of narrative tension as a key stimulus for characters' motivations to a degree that rarely occurs in Western films. They are based on strict division between the sexes, and love songs and sexual relations, while sensuous, are kept within firm boundaries. Kissing is rare and nudity absent. These generic conventions provide a marked difference from Hollywood films, and many Hausa viewers argue that Indian films 'have culture' in a way that American films seem to lack. (1997a: 413)

Supplanting Hollywood for Bollywood, as done by young Hausa film makers – and certainly motivated by profit, rather than politics of nationalism or cultural imperialism – merely substitutes one imperial, and in this case religiously contrasting, mindset with another. As further pointed out by Larkin:

> the narrative structure of Indian films . . . is borrowed from the Indian religious epics the Mahabarata and Ramayana . . . The dependence upon the epics means that there is usually a fixed range of plots with clear moral contrasts that make the outlines of Indian films familiar to their viewers. The regularity of character types whose actions fall within a limited range of behaviour such as the hero, the mother, the comedic friend or the evil boss, with many of the lesser roles (such as boss or the mother) played by the same people in film after film, further aids the fixed parameters of plot structure within which the spectacle unfolds. (1997a: 412)

Thus, young Hausa film makers gloss over the religious disparities between Hindu and Muslim cultures and focus on the ceremonies embedded in the tradition of the two religions, extracting the basic entertainment elements they can adapt.

Yet Hausa Muslim communities have had a traditional structure infused with Islamic traditions since the twelfth century, hundreds of years before the advent of Hindi cinema in Hausaland in the late twentieth century. Consequently, the traditional Hausa lifestyle alone is thematically strong enough to inspire the exploration of *auren dole*, family values and love triangles, which obsess young Hausa filmmakers. Hausa traditional theatre and folktales were rarely considered for adaptation by Hausa home video producers; indeed only *Kogin Bagaja* and *Daskin Da Ridi* – both folktales (*tatsuniyoyi*) were made into home videos out of a repertoire of thousands of Hausa folktales. Even traditional Hausa songs, especially those of the *tashe* variety (games and street drama played from the tenth day of Ramadan fasting), were relegated to the background in favour of the urban glamour and glitz of Hindi-style entertainment.

The barrage of Hindi films shown in cinema houses and on government television stations ensured a high degree of acculturative bombardment of Hindi film messages, directed at the youth and at Hausa housewives. Further, it created the desire for Hausa-ized versions of these films, which the film makers were happy to provide, to the exclusion of any local entertainment traditions or creative inspirations. This entertainment strategy, informed by market-driven, supply and demand situations, rather than by the aesthetics of art and culture in dramatic representations, offers Brian Larkin an alternative interpretation of the role of media in mediating changes in social life. As he has stated:

> Just as I, growing up in London in a cinematic world dominated by American stars, incorporated American media as part of English popular culture, so it is for Hausa audiences. Indian films have been reworked and incorporated to form an integral part of contemporary Hausa social life. (1997a: 433)

This point is insufficiently defended by Larkin. The scale of similarities between American and British cultures – which makes it possible for a

British youth to be influenced by American popular culture – is not of the same magnitude as the scale of differences between Hindu culture as depicted in Hindi films and Muslim Hausa home videos. The flowing saris and long caftans of Hindi actresses and actors; the forced marriage scenarios; even the song-and-dance routines were integral icons of Hausa social life, with traditional equivalents, long before the widespread popularity of Hindi films in urban Hausa societies. Hausa home video producers – most of them acculturatively non-ethnic Hausa – merely 'modernize' these according to Hindi film templates.

Further, 'social life' has a wider scope of meaning than merely watching a clutch of Hindi films that have been translated into Hausa versions. The Hindinization of the Hausa home video cannot be equated with the Hindinization of Hausa culture. Such Hindinization of the home video, and creation of media identity, is essentially a stylistic entertainment strategy, and even at that, it is restricted to the urban clusters within the larger Hausa society. A total of about 1,180 home videos (from 1990 to 2004), no matter how much they copy Hindu motifs, cannot be a template for changing the 'social life' of more than 20 million people. It cannot be seen as a social pattern in which Hindi popular culture has become integral to Hausa social life. Hausa social life has remained Hausa. Indeed, the home video phenomena is essentially an urban process, unfelt and unaffecting in the rural communities of northern Nigeria, which are still wired to traditional festivals as a form of entertainment. Even in urban centres where Hausa home videos are watched, Hausa food, custom, mores and other indices of social life remain Hausa, perhaps borrowing, especially among the younger population, the fashion sense and musical tastes of the Western world. This borrowing is certainly not from India, no matter how many Hindi films the people watch.

In cases where there is a closer affinity between Hindi films and their audiences outside India, there is a relatively strong cultural link between the audience and the actors. This may be enough for the audience to feel a certain empathy for Hindu culture, and perhaps integrate it as part of their social life. For instance, in a fascinating application of Larkin's parallel modernities, we see correlations between the Hausa youth fascination for Hindi films and a similar addiction among Indonesian youth, who share the same media parents. This is because media parenting is a strong factor in Indonesian attachment to Hindi films. Cinemas in Indonesia have a long history of showing Hindi films, just as they do in northern Nigeria's major cities like Jos, Kaduna and Kano.

These developments in Indonesia have echoed the media parenting that northern Nigeria went through in order to entrench Hindi films in the entertainment mindsets of Muslim Hausa. But how is it that, in a mainly Islamic community, people are so enthusiastic about Hindi film? According to N. Samirah Khan (2003), writing on the subject online:

> Indonesia is called an Islamic country simply because the majority of population here is Muslim . . . However, Indonesians are much closer to Indians, not just geographically but also religiously and ethnically. For instance, most Indonesians . . . have a Hindu background. Their culture, dances, language (based on Sanskrit), philosophy, and their traditional ceremonies, all reflect this Hindu influence in their lives which has come to be a mix between Hinduism and Islam (Sufism).

Thus, if Indonesian youth seem affected by Hindu culture as depicted in Hindi films, one can say they share the same spiritual space. This is not the case with the Muslim Hausa youth of northern Nigeria, and therefore cannot be used to explain their fascination with the Hindi film. Instead, concurrent modernity may serve as a sociological model to describe the behaviour of Indonesian and Muslim Hausa youth in their imitation of Hindi cinema identity precisely, because of the convergence of cultural spaces (Hindu to Indonesian) or incidence of shared identity (Hindi to Hausa, via Islamic veneer in Hindi).

CONCLUSION

The 'Indianization', 'Indonesianization' and 'Hausanization' of media influences and the emergence of media identities are incidences of concurrent modernities, available via media technologies that have simply blurred the religious, cultural, economic and political divides and created a new techno-based entertainment culture. This is essentially because the flow is truly transnational, giving echoes and feedback in all directions. Larkin offers further insights into his parallel modernities theory as applicable to Hausa cinema viewing audiences, stating that: 'Indian films offer Hausa viewers a way of imaginatively engaging with forms of tradition different from their own at the same time as conceiving of a modernity that comes without the political and ideological significance of that of the West (1997a: 407)'. Yet much of the Hausa home video storylines, music, dance and style that was ripped off from Hindi films was itself stolen from Hollywood films. Thus *Fatal Attraction* was first copied by Hindi film makers as *Pyar Tune Kya Kiya*, which became the Hausa version in *Kudiri*. Also, *What Lies Beneath* became *Raaz*, before leap-frogging to Kano as *Salma Salma Duf*. Similarly, *Dead Poets Society* first became *Mohabbatein*, and then became *So* in Hausa, while *Sleeping with the Enemy* was remade into three Bollywood films (*Yaarana*, *Agni Sakshi* and *Darrar*) and subsequently into the Kano equivalents of *Hakuri*, *Izaya* and *Huznee*. The Hausa film makers who produced *So* have admitted that they were not even aware of Robin William's *Dead Poets Society*, and that their influence was *Mohabbatein*. In this case, where could the source of the media identity be housed for the Hausa audience – Hollywood or Mumbai? The Hausa Muslim conservative critical reaction to

Hausa home videos is certainly more to do with the singular obsession of the Hausa home video producers with love themes than a reaction against entertainment in a traditional Muslim culture, just as the same establishment reacted against Hausa novelists who focused virtually exclusively on *soyayya* (love) themes from 1980 to 2000.

Hausa television series drama such *Kuliya, Zaman Duniya, Mai Daki, Kwaryar Alawa, Taskira, Gajimarai, Hantsi, Sarauta Gado,* and others, were revered as a truer reflection of Hausa traditional theatre than the current crop of home videos produced by young Hausa and Hausanized film makers. As it is, the vast majority of contemporary Hausa home video can be called Hausa only because the dialogues are in Hausa language. In content, however, they do but increasingly reflect an urbanized Hausa worldview and mindset.

With the saturation of the Hausa home video market in 2003, when sales and production dropped drastically, many of the producers were squeezed out of the market. At that time, the Hausa home video genre started looking for an alternative to love stories for their thematic focus. Videos such as *Ruhi, Farar Aniya, Mahandama, Qarni, Kazar Sayen Baki, Kin Gaskiya, Ibtila'i* and *Judah* led the way towards the transformation of the genre into a more mature visual canvas. All that is required is the professionalization of the producers in order that they might take advantage of the rich Hausa literary heritage to create a truly Hausa cinema which reflects quintessential Hausa social and cultural identity.

REFERENCES

Adamu, Abdallah Uma (2003), 'Parallel Worlds: Reflective Womanism in Balaraba Ramat Yakubu's *Ina Son Sa Hak'*. *Jenda: A Journal of Culture and African Women's Studies* 4.

— (2005a), *Passage to India: Media Parenting and Changing Popular Culture in Northern Nigeria.* Kaduna: Informart Publishers.

— (2005b), ' "The Song Remains the Same": The Hindi Cinema Factor in Hausa Video Film Soundtracks'. In Mark Slobin (ed.), *Global Soundtracks: The Culture of World Film Music.* Middletown, CT: Wesleyan University Press.

— (2006), 'Loud Bubbles from a Silent Brook: Trends and Tendencies in Contemporary Hausa Prose Fiction'. In G. Furniss and K. Barber (eds), *Research in African Literatures.* Daytona, OH: Ohio University Press.

Alhassan, Habib, Usman Ibrahim Musa and Rabi'u Muhammad Zarruk (1982), *Hausawa.* Zaria: privately published.

Appadurai, Arjun, Frank J. Korom and Margaret A. Mills (eds) (1991), *Gender, Genre, and Power in South Asian Expressive Traditions.* Philadelphia, PA: University of Pennsylvania Press.

Bourgault, Louise M. (1995), *Mass Media in Sub-Saharan Africa.* Bloomington, IN: Indiana University Press.

— (1996), 'Television Drama in Hausaland: The Search for a New Aesthetic and a New Ethic'. *Critical Arts* 10(1).

Khan, N. Samirah (2003), 'Popularity of Hindi Movies in Indonesia'. Available online at <http://tamanbollywood.singcat.com/artikel/bollywood_in_indonesia.shtml>

Kirk-Greene, Anthony H. M. (1973), 'Mutumin Kirki: The Concept of the Good Man in Hausa'. Lecture delivered at the University of Indiana, 11 April.

Larkin, Brian (1997a), 'Indian Films and Nigerian Lovers: Media and the Creation of Parallel Modernities'. *Africa* 67(3): 406–39.

— (1997b), 'Bollywood Comes to Nigeria'. Available online at <http://wwwsamar-magazine.org/archive/article.jphp?id=21>

National Film and Video Censors Board (2002), *Directory of Video Films in Nigeria*. Abuja, Nigeria.

Nnoli, O. (ed.) (2003), *Communal Conflict and Population Displacement in Nigeria: A Research Report*. Enugu, Nigeria: Pan-African Center for Research on Peace and Conflict.

Owens-Ibie, N. (1998), 'How Video Films Developed in Nigeria'. *Media Development*, No. 1.

PART III

THE MEDIA AND IDENTITY: THE LOCAL MEDIA

'TO MAKE STRANGE THINGS POSSIBLE': THE PHOTOMONTAGES OF THE BAKOR PHOTO STUDIO IN LAMU, KENYA

The Bakor Studio in Lamu, situated on one of the main streets of the Old Town, was established in the 1960s. The founder, Mr Omar Said Bakor, born in 1932, was a self-made man and brilliant *bricoleur*, who never went to school. His family originated in Yemen. Before opening the studio, he worked for ten years as a street photographer. He experimented with various techniques of montage 'to make strange things possible and for fun', as one of his sons, Mr Najid Omar Said Bakor, explained to me in 1996. His father also recorded the history of Lamu in photographs and, like Dorris Haron Kasco in Abidjan, Côte d'Ivoire (1994), took pictures of insane people. In addition, he produced miniature portrait photographs suitable for mounting in people's watches. He died in 1993, and his sons continue to work in his studio.

Omar Said Bakor's photographic montages may serve as examplars in the discussion of the complicated processes of the localization and hybridization of a new global media: photography. Of interest in such a discussion are the points of contacts and 'third spaces' that come into being when images and visual media travel to and enter other cultures and representational regimes. Photography is connected to already existing local artistic traditions, and it is shaped and transformed by them. Through local interventions and the mediation of local social, religious and cultural values, photography is reworked to attract local customers. In the case of Bakor's photographic collages, these mediating forces specifically include the phenomenon of Islamic revival and the tensions between the new picture media and the Islamic prohibition of images.

A SHORT DIGRESSION ON THE HISTORY OF LAMU

To understand the special nature of Bakor's art, it is necessary to make a few remarks on the history of Lamu. In contrast to the more open and cosmopolitan character of Mombasa at the end of the last century, the old town elite of Lamu not only tried to keep strangers out of town, but also tried to keep up with traditions. In their view, as recorded by A. H. M. el-Zein, 'every innovation is an error, and every error leads to hell' (1974: 8). However, in the 1880s, when the old elite had already started to decline, a Jamalilil sharif named Habib Saleh reached Lamu. His family originated in the Hadramaut, on the Gulf of Aden. He succeeded in establishing an alliance with slaves and slowly gained power. He founded a new mosque and built up the famous Mosque College, which became a centre of Islamic scholarship. This mosque, and its yearly celebration of the *Maulidi* festival, attracted and still attracts thousands of participants from many countries. Thus, Lamu became, and remains, a very important centre of Islamic theology.

With the recent rise of Islamic fundamentalism in Lamu, the influence of Islamic laws on everyday life has increased and has triggered debates about modern media – film, video and photography – and the Islamic prohibition on the portrayal of human and animal images. Although the religious prohibition in the Qu'ran is debated, the ban on representing human beings and animals meets with wide agreement. Indeed, although many people did not renounce the pleasures of photography, their attitudes have modulated in recent years. Many households which, in the 1970s, ostentatiously displayed pictures of family members on the walls of the saloon had, by the 1990s, moved the display into the more private space of the bedroom or consigned the photographs to an album or a box hidden in a cupboard. Even some Islamic scholars who have accepted videos because the images are moving, fleeting and short-lived nonetheless resent photographic pictures of persons for fear that they will engender image-worship (especially when the picture is hung on a wall) and thus endanger Islamic monotheism.

THE PHOTOGRAPHIC COLLAGE

The collage as an art form was invented in the early twentieth century, making its appearance after the catastrophic experiences of the Great War. Various art historians, such as Werner Spiess (1988) and Rosalind Krauss (1985), saw it as the modernist art form *par excellance*, taking as its problem – and opportunity – the fragmentation and juxtaposition of cultural values (Clifford 1988). Collage, defined as a new combination of already existing visual material, places into doubt conventions regarding the proper arrangements of things and people, precisely because the juxtaposition of fragments makes obvious the degree to which the necessary relations implied by the original object are proven to be not necessarily so, after all.

Thus, collages are related to some sort of scepticism, to breaks and discontinuities, to semantic changes and the destruction of meaning. In addition, the process of producing a collage requires that the original images be cut into pieces – an aggressive, destructive act of protest against an apparently harmonious continuous world. The fragmentation of the modern world, which has been described by Walter Benjamin and others, and the dissociation of cultural knowledge into juxtaposed 'citations', are presupposed in collages. Furthermore, the collage attacks the aura of the traditional work of art in a double way: first, by using and recycling pre-existing images that have themselves been mass produced through reproduction technologies such as printing and photography; and second, by producing collages in series, as was done, for example, by Max Ernst.

ORNAMENTALIZATION OF PHOTOGRAPHS

Like the magic realists and surrealists in Europe, Bakor played with the relationship between humans and things, thus blurring boundaries and radically transforming photographic 'reality'. In relation to the code of mainstream photography, which puts its truth-value in the objectivity of its lens, Bakor's photographs are scandalous, as is all photography that resorts to construction, darkroom manipulations, and manipulation by scissors and paste (Krauss 1985). However, when seen in relation to already established art traditions on the East African coast, his photomontages do not appear strange or scandalous. On the contrary, they link up with diverse, long-established artistic traditions, such as the art of ornamental woodcarving, plasterwork in local architecture, embroidery, textiles and calligraphy. As can be seen in the portrait photographs included here (Figures 16.1, 16.2, and 16.3) Bakor's integration of photographic portraits in ornaments and arabesques yields photomontages which appear as a continuation of these art forms. Thus, as Oleg Grabar (1977) has noted, Bakor's photomontages give proof of the tendency inherent in Islamic art to ornamentalize whatever comes into its realm.

Bakor employs ornamentation for photomontages featuring non-human subjects as well (see Figures 16.4, and 16.5). On the East African coast, floral motifs like *waridi* (rose), *yungi-yungi* (water lily), *shoki-shoki* (a kind of lychee), *kilua* (a flower with a strong, sweet, aphrodisiac smell, also called *uvaria kirkii*), and leaves of various plants like *kulabu* form well-established, named patterns, some of which are widely used in textiles on *kanga*s, plasterworks, wood carvings and, of course, Bakor's photomontages.

Such ornamentalization must also be seen as an attempt to reduce the importance of the photographic portrait, in deference to the Islamic prohibition of images. Although the artist is not allowed to imitate Godly creation, he or she is accorded the freedom to experiment with the abstract depiction of various parts of God's world, and to recombine them within new ensembles.

Figure 16.1   Self-portrait of Omar Said Bakor against the background of Lamu.

Figure 16.2   Portrait.

As can be seen in the next three photographs (Figures 16.6 to 16.8), playing cards also seem to have inspired some of Omar Said Bakor's photomontages. Such cards were probably introduced by the Portuguese when they reached East Africa, toward the middle of the sixteenth century. The Swahili terms *kopa* (heart) and *shupaza* (inverted heart, or spade) were adopted from Portuguese words: *copa* (heart). and *espada* (sword). In Bakor's photocollages, these images are transformed into ornamental

Figure 16.3   Portrait.

elements that enrich and embellish the portrait while, at the same time, reducing the importance of the portrait, again deferring to the Islamic prohibition of images.

VISUALIZATIONS OF ABSTRACT THEMES, CONCEPTS AND TRADITIONS

On the East African coast there exists a highly complex culture of rhetoric, in which Swahili proverbs and sayings are printed on textiles (*kanga*), written on public taxis (*matatu*), and used in everyday speech to express knowledge, wisdom, moral instruction and the paradoxes of life. In some of his collages (see Figures 16.9 and 16.10), Bakor has taken recourse to this rhetoric, giving visual form to proverbs and sayings. Thus, he transposes a rhetorical tradition to the new visual media, and gives his pictures additional, conventionalized meanings.

Figure 16.4   *Waridi*, the rose.

In Bakor's collages, the proverbs are not only given visual form but also, in a certain sense, a voice. Their visuality is enriched with an auditory dimension, and thereby a dialogical quality of the photograph is enforced. Ghanaian photographer Philip Kwame Apagya has said that 'the picture is a silent talker', because, as it speaks, it requires an answer (cited in Pinther 1998: 37).

Just as Bakor has attempted to enrich the visuality of his photographs with the auditory, so also has he attempted to give them an olfactory dimension. This impulse is reflected in an anecdote collected and presented by Aziza Mohamed Aboubakar (1988). The tale takes place in the time before the Great War, when Bwana Tamu, an elder of Tundauwa, goes to an Indian photographer. He dresses himself carefully in his best clothes, takes a bottle of rose water he received from a pilgrim coming back from Mecca, and care-

Figure 16.5 *Shoki-shoki*, rambutan lychee, with Bakor's portrait (in the middle).

Figure 16.6 Inverted heart (spade) with arrow.

fully perfumes himself with the intention of impregnating his image with this precious scent. A few days later, when he enters the photographer's studio to collect his photographs, he is highly disappointed because his pictures do not have the smell of rose water. First he doubts that the photographs depict him; then, when he finally recognizes himself, he complains about the lack

Figure 16.7   Inverted hearts.

Figure 16.8   Inverted heart with flowerpot.

of scent and refuses to pay for the photographs. His children explain to him that photographs do not catch the smell of a person. He then puts the pictures into his *djellabia*, which he had perfumed strongly before going to the photographer. By this means the photographs are finally imbued with the rose water scent.

On the East African coast, perfumes, scents and incense are of great importance. They not only complete a person, but actually form a part of a social person. In the poem and song 'Full-Length Portrait of a Lady', for example, the lady's armpits are compared to sweet-smelling herbs with the scent of ambergris, and her navel has the pleasant perfume of jasmine or

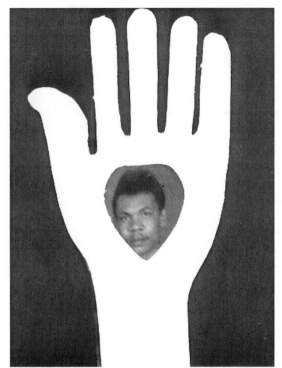

Figure 16.9   *Kua mkononi mwako*: to be in your hand.

roses. In addition, spirits, which are the doubles of human beings, are also associated with certain smells, and it is believed that they can be attracted by burning incense. In this context, the anecdote of Bwana Tamu clearly poses the problem of the absolute value of visuality in photography. The impoverishment of photography that arises from the separation of visuality from the auditory and the olfactory is nicely displayed in Bwana Tamu's disappointment and his futile attempts to regain the smell of rose water in his photographic portrait.

The roses Bakor uses in some of his photomontages must be considered in this context as well. The rose as a floral motif is extensively used in woodcarvings, plasterworks and textiles. This flower is not only an icon of love, pain and sexuality, but is also highly valued because of its sweet smell. This is clearly expressed in the proverb *'leso maua ni harafu si rangi'* ('the beauty of a flower is in its smell, not its colour'). In Figure 16.11 the heart and the rose's beauty and smell are nicely brought together in a strong, multisensory icon of love.

The long tradition of passionate, romantic love poetry is appropriated and given expression in many of Bakor's photographic collages. Many

Figure 16.10   *Umenikaa moyoni*: You live in my heart.

proverbs give warnings of the suffering, destructiveness, and asociality of
passionate love (Behrend 1998), for example *moyo huba ukingia ni heri
kuizuia* ('when love enters the heart, it is better to stop it'), and *mfuata moyo
mwiso huiyuta* ('the one who follows his heart will regret it in the end').
Nonetheless, it appears that the younger generation, in particular, make use
of photographs to give expression to their ideal of romantic love, which

Figure 16.11   Heart and rose as an icon of love.

sometimes strongly opposes the moralistic discourse of the older generation.
They use photographs, not only to represent and express their love, but also
to produce it. As M. Fuglesang (1994) argues, photos are not only
exchanged by lovers, but are also employed by women and men for love
magic. Furthermore, through his collages, Bakor has also fulfilled male
erotic fantasies by photographing young men with the poster image of the
famous Indian actress Sri Devi, providing the illusion that they are a loving
couple (see Figure 16.12).

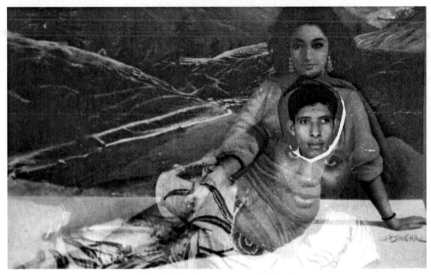

Figure 16.12   Actress Sri Devi.

In this photograph, the head of the young man has been montaged into the heart of the famous actress, but above his head, like a shadow, there is also a picture of a second woman. This second image appears to suggest the operation of some kind of love magic that brings the loved ones together through the mediation of an ideal woman (Sri Devi), thus representing a dream come doubly true. In addition, Fuglesang notes, these photographs show the increasing influence of Indian films in shaping gender relations and the ideal of romantic love.

ISSUES OF GENDER

In Figure 16.13 Sri Devi is depicted with a halo, like those appearing in images of Christian or Muslim saints. Bakor's use of the halo merges African and Indian aesthetic ideals with Christian and Muslim iconography. Thus, in the Bakor Studio, Sri Devi, the Bollywood superstar and unattainable icon of the seductive, ideal woman in movies, becomes not only *'l'être qui projette la plus grande ombre ou la plus grande lumière dans nos rêves'* as the surrealists wrote, she also became available, at one's disposal.

However, the photomontages in which Sri Devi appears must also be seen against the backdrop of Islamic prohibitions against images, and in the context of assumptions regarding the status of women. Among Islamic scholars, both male and female, there is a strong expectation that women, in particular, must lead a pious, pure life, according to the precepts of Islam. In the 1990s, the segregation of the sexes was far more strictly observed than

Figure 16.13   Actress Sri Devi.

it had been in the 1970s. Although, by this time, photography had intruded deeply into coastal life and was used extensively to celebrate and remember certain *rites de passage*, like weddings or birthdays, there remained (and remains) a strong urge to control the production and circulation of women's photographic images.

Because of the enforced separation of women and men, it is thought shameful for a male photographer to intrude upon the sphere of women in order to take their pictures. In response, a new professional opportunity for female photographers and video producers has opened up in recent years. Some of these women specialize in photographing and videotaping women at weddings and other celebrations. Their work is in great demand. Nonetheless, many Muslim women in Lamu take great care to prevent their image from being seen by strange men. Their photographic portraits, as well as their unveiled faces, are shown only to their husbands, close female relatives and girlfriends. They regard the idea of other men looking at them as shameful. This attitude, and the fact that Islamic women in Lamu are becoming increasingly hesitant about allowing themselves to be photographed with a man, has driven more men to take recourse to montages such as the one featuring Sri Devi.

Obviously, Bakor's collages play with themes of presence and absence, desire and imagination. They mix the fantasy space of Indian films with the indexicality of photography. And they intensify the play between transgression and conformity by using the technical media of photography to allow imaginative transgressions through disembodied representation. Under Islamic law, montages work because they keep the sexes apart physically, even while uniting them.

PHOTOGRAPHIC GENEALOGIES

Along the East African coast, as in many other areas of the world, genealogies play an important part in defining a social person. Bakor connects his collages to genealogical traditions, in order to give playful expression to genealogical relations. For instance, in Figure 16.14 he represents personhood in the form of patrilineal genealogy, amalgamating replications of himself and his sons.

In this photomontage, one of Bakor's sons holds in his hands the heads of both his father and his elder brother. The montage visualizes the notion of personhood as the aggregate of external relations, a familiar theme in African art. In addition, the ambivalence inherent in the relationship between father and sons is nicely displayed. Father and elder brother are upheld, elevated, maybe even glorified, by their son/younger brother, but at the same time they are represented as having been decapitated.

In depicting genealogical connections, cultures worldwide employ the metaphor of a plant which is growing out of an inverted, forked post, as is depicted in Figures 16.16. The leaves to the right and left sides of the plant carry identical photographic portraits of a young man who has not yet generated descendants. This correspondence between a tree or plant and genealogy derives from the analogy of plant propagation and human reproduction.

In Figure 16.17 Bakor transforms the genealogical tree into a plant growing out of a flowerpot. However, rather than depicting various people related to each other by descent, the montage presents the same person six times. Here, the multiplication of the portrait destroys the depicted person's singularity, while simultaneously displaying the capabilities inherent in reproduction. The resultant montage presents not the Western ideal of a unique, self-contained individual, but rather the 'dividuum', to use Marilyn Strathern's (1988) term. The divisible, multiple person is montaged in lots of images, sometimes as a series of portraits depicting the same person, as in Figure 16.18 or sometimes in a sequence in which the subject is presented in different guises, for example with and without spectacles, as in Figure 16.19.

As Alfred Gell (1998) and Strathern (1988) have observed, the notion of genealogy is the key trope for making plurality singular and singularity plural. Any individual is multiple in the sense of being part of a network of genealogical relations, an enchainment of people. Conversely, Gell goes on to note, an aggregate of persons forming a lineage or family can also be conceptualized as one person. In Bakor's photomontages, persons are seen to bud out of one another, in a paternal line, thus appropriating female reproduction.

Figure 16.14   Bakor and his sons.

Figure 16.15   Photographic genealogy.

Figure 16.16   Genealogical tree.

PEOPLE IN BOTTLES

In the 1970s, it became fashionable in Mombasa, Malindi and Lamu to montage people into bottles. Whisky bottles were the preferred container in which to portray a person. This echoes a tradition found in many parts of Africa, wherein containers are used to house spirits. According to Robert Faris Thompson (1983), in the Congo, at least as early as the 1700s, there was the tradition of trees garlanded with bottles, vessels and other objects, which were hung in order to protect the household through invocation of the dead (142). The practice was also found on the island of Dominica in the West Indies. Today, it flourishes in the Caribbean and in the United States – in South Carolina, Virginia, southern Arkansas, Mississippi and Alabama. In an article on Haitian studio photography, Marilyn Houlberg (1992) published a few images in which babies and children were montaged into milk bottles. She relates this practice to the voodoo religious tradition, in which different types of bottles and lidded jars are said to contain the spirits of

Figure 16.17   Flower-pot genealogy.

various *loa* or voodoo gods who can be invoked for protection, healing and harming. Houlberg also reported on women who give such photographs to their boyfriends as a sign that they have been 'captured' by them, as if in a bottle.

One of Bakor's photomontages depicts a woman contained in such a bottle. In his image, however, the bottle simultaneously resembles a fish and an airplane, thus modernizing the container. His variation on the 'children in a bottle' theme shows a man lifting up his children, who are captured in a sort of vase. The striped cloth that is shared by the two little girls and their father unites them, transforming them into a single social body.

MEN ON THE MOON

The moon, especially the *hilal*, the new or crescent moon, is a powerful emblem of Muslim identity. Since the nineteenth century, it has been officially adopted for use on flags, postage stamps and gravestones (for example, for Muslim veterans buried in national cemeteries in the United

Figure 16.18   Doubled portrait.

States). It has also been a popular motif in US photographic studios since the turn of the twentieth century.

At the end of the 1960s and in the 1970s, in many photographic studios in Kenya as well as in western Africa, it was highly fashionable to photograph people seated on the moon. Bakor also employed lunar imagery for his own purposes. As one of his sons explained, the image can be seen as an ironic commentary on man's first landing on the moon in 1969.

TRUE LIES

In his photo collages, Bakor playfully and often ironically explores a whole range of local artistic conventions, hybridizing them with photography. In his pictures, he not only transposes things and persons on to a different register,

Figure 16.19   Man with and without spectacles.

but he also attempts to transcend the pure, hegemonic visuality of photographic images. By giving visual form to proverbs and sayings, he gives a voice back to the silent photograph, and by montaging people into roses, he also alludes to the flower's scent. Corresponding to the multisensory concept of the person, his portraits attempt to complete their subjects by including allusions to other aspects of their identity, such as their voices and perfumes.

In addition, by integrating photographic portraits and ornaments, Bakor created a new technique of portraiture that can be seen as a 'technology of enchantment', in the words of Gell (1998: 74). The Islamic ban on the representation of living beings in Lamu seems to have inspired ever more effective attempts at captivation by visual artifice, mixing the non-mimetic appearance of animation (decorated surfaces are often referred to as 'animated') with mimetic photographic portraits. In the Bakor Studio, photography has been largely connected to and integrated in pre-existing art traditions and thereby has created new hybridizations, for example ornamental photographs and photographic genealogies.

Photography has also opened up a new field of production and consumption of self-images, even though this conflicts with Islamic prohibitions. Although there are attempts to control their circulation, especially the circulation of women's photographs, such photographs undermine the anti-imagistic strain of Islam and create a field of conflict that leads to debate and innovation. In his collages, Bakor did not so much attempt to fixate a reality, as attempt to outwit the fixed programme of the camera by shifting the creative process into the production of the collage. Yet, by using photographs as the material for his portraits (thereby producing a negative), his pictures also profited from the indexicality of photography. Although Bakor turned photography into a dream machine, his collages acquired an additional truth-value, for real people – actual women, men and children – were found in Bakor's collages of bottles, hearts or flowers, carried on hands, sitting on the moon, or budding out of a flowerpot.

REFERENCES

Aboubakar, Aziza Mohamed (1988), 'Quand Bwana Tamu alla se faire photographier'. In *Des Comores au Zaire Récits et poèmes Swahili*. Paris: Fleuve et Flamme.

Behrend, Heike (1998), 'Love à la Hollywood and Bombay: Kenyan postcolonial studio photography'. *Paideuma* 44: 139–53. Frankfurt: Kohlhammer.

— (2001), ' "Fragmented Visions": Photo Collages by Ronnie Okocha Kauma and Afanaduula Sadala in Kampala, Uganda'. *Visual Anthropology* 14 (33): 301–20. London: Routledge.

El-Zein, A. H. M. (1974), *The Sacred Meadows: A Structural Analysis of Religious Symbolism in an East African Town*. Evanston, IL: Northwestern University Press.

Flusser, Vilém (1997), *Für eine Philosophie der Fotografie*. Göttingen: European Photography.

Fuglesang, M. (1994), *Veils and Videos: Female Youth on the Kenyan Coast*. Stockholm: Stockholm Studies in Social Anthropology.

Gell, Alfred (1998), *Art and Agency. An Anthropological Theory*. Oxford: Clarendon Press.

Grabar, Oleg (1977), *Die Entstehung der Islamischen Kunst*. Cologne: Dumont Reiseveslag.

Houlberg, Marilyn (1992), 'Haitian studio photography: a hidden world of images'. *Aperture* 126: 59–65, Aperture Foundation.

Kasco, Dorris Haron (1994), *Les fous d'Abidjan*. Paris: Collection Soleil.

Knappert, Jan (1972), *A Choice of Flowers. Swahili Songs of Love and Passion*. London: Heinemann.

Krauss, Rosalind (1985), 'Corpus delicti'. In Rosalind Krauss and Jane Livingstone (eds), *L'Amour Fou: Photography and Surrealism*. Washington, New York: Abbeville Press.

Larkin, Brian (2003), 'Itineraries of Indian Cinema: African videos, Bollywood and global media'. In Ella Shohat and Robert Stam (eds), *Multiculturalism, Postcoloniality and Transnational Media*. New Brunswick: Rutgers University Press, pp. 170–92.

Lienhardt, Peter (1959), 'The Mosque College of Lamu and its social background'. *Tanganyika Notes and Records* 53: 228–42.

Pinther, Kerstin (1998), ' "Wenn die Ehe eine Erdnuß wäre . . ." Über Textilien und Fotografie in Afrika'. In Tobias Wendl and Heike Behrend (eds), *Snap me One! Studiofotografen in Afrika*. Munich: Prestel, pp. 36–41.

Schadeberg, Thilo (1991), 'Historical inferences from Swahili etymologies'. In S. Pilaszewicz and E. Rzewuski (eds), *Orientalia Varsoviensia: Unwritten Testimonies of the African Past*. Warsaw: Wydawnictwa Uniw. Warszakskiego.

Schuster, Carl, and Edmund Carpenter (1996), *Patterns that Connect: Social Symbolism in Ancient and Tribal Art*. New York: Harry Abrahams.

Spiess, Werner (1988), *Max Ernst*. Paris and Cologne: Dumont.

Strathern, Marilyn (1988), *The Gender of the Gift*. Berkeley: University of California Press.

Thompson, Robert Faris (1983), *Flash of the Spirit: African and Afro-American Art and Philosophy*. New York: Vintage Books.

Wendl, Tobias and Heike Behrend (eds) (1998), *Snap Me One! Studiofotografen in Afrika*. Munich: Prestel.

MUSICAL IMAGES AND IMAGINATIONS: TANZANIAN MUSIC VIDEOS

In Tanzania, multiple musical and cultural trajectories creatively coexist in music videos to form this decade-old popular art form. Music videos, also called 'music television', typically have been analyzed from the perspective of the visual, by people largely coming from cinema studies, with little attention to the music that gives rise to them, the cultures that inform them, or the histories that make them meaningful. Moreover, they equate music television with American and European rock music videos, because these are what the genre came to be defined by when it emerged in the West. The literature is thus badly in need of revision, given that an enormous variety of musical genres and cultures are finding representation in music videos in ever-increasing numbers. It is indeed time to decentre both the visual and Western rock biases of music video analysis.

The aural-visual forms represented in Tanzanian music videos must be understood as the combination of genres that they are – popular music, television, film – without privileging one over the other. Developments in mass media technologies, together with the advent of political and economic liberalization, facilitated the rise of music videos. Yet they continue to evolve in interesting ways that relate to broader social experiences and the shifting of social (and economic, political, cultural and geographic) boundaries. Tanzanian music videos thus should not be seen as amateurish mimicry of MTV, but rather as another creative outlet for the artistic skills and resources of Tanzanian musicians.

ON MUSIC VIDEOS

Music videos are a 1980s phenomenon, closely aligned with the 1981 debut of MTV, an American cable television network dedicated to the broadcast of pop and rock music videos. The small but growing literature on music videos has tended to focus on how they relate to the development of youth cultures and generational identities (Johansson 1992; Grossberg 1993;

Burns 1996; van der Rijt 2000; Juluri 2002), or their role as promotional advertising for artists, songs, albums, films or products (Berland 1986; Savan 1993; Straw 1993; Burns 1996). When discussed outside the context of the United States, they are identified as a key agent for Western cultural imperialism, alongside McDonalds, American situation comedies and CNN (Sturmer 1993; van der Rijt 2000; Juluri 2002). With very few exceptions, theorists share a presupposition that Western rock music constitutes music video content and postmodernism constitutes music video style. For many, music videos are the quintessential manifestation of postmodernism in their 'fragmentation, segmentation, superficiality, stylistic jumbling, the blurring of mediation and reality, the collapse of past and future into the moment of the present, the elevation of hedonism, the dominance of the visual over the verbal' (Tetzlaff 1986, quoted in Goodwin 1993: 45).

One artist whose music videos perfectly exemplify these traits, and who has received an inordinate amount of attention from music critics and cultural critics alike is Madonna (Allen 1993; Douglas 1994; Kaplan 1987; Lugo-Lugo 2001; McClary 1990; Savan 1993; Vernallis 1998). A key example of this attention would be the critical analysis of Madonna's 1993 video 'Fever'. This video presented her version of the 1956 song composed by John Davenport and Eddie Cooley that was first popularized by Little Willie John and subsequently covered by artists as wide-ranging as Peggy Lee, The McCoys, Rita Coolidge and Elvis Presley. The postmodern, hedonist style attributed to Western music video is clearly evident here in the lack of, indeed strict avoidance of, any sense of linear narrative beyond a vague evocation of erotic fantasy. This is underscored in the construction of the video by the deployment of a rapid succession of focal lengths, incomplete and jumbled cultural references, disconnected and unrelated visual tropes, and the frequent, sudden juxtapositions of a scantily-clad black male model and Madonna (in alternating pseudo-Thai and seductive siren outfits). This video perfectly exemplifies the breakdown of temporal, spatial, stylistic, moral and cultural coherence that is so frequently discussed in the literature.

Admirers celebrate music videos for rejecting assumed boundaries between high art and popular culture, abandoning grand narratives, and replacing them with unstable 'texts' that – in borrowing freely across genre, culture and time period – invite a reconsideration of assumed realities and can be considered a new form of political resistance (McClary 1990). Critics, on the other hand, argue that music television constitutes 'a "schizophrenic" abandonment of rational, liberal-humanist discourse which creates a nihilistic, amoral universe of representation' and contend that music television 'abandons the realm of political and social engagement' (Goodwin 1993: 46) leaving nothing but pessimism and emptiness in its wake.

Debates such as these dominated the early literature because music video first attracted the attention of cinema studies scholars who rarely, if ever, paid attention to the music. Whereas the *visual* component of Western music television often proves to be pastiche assemblages of disconnected fragments combining this and that, then and now, realism and imagination, the *music* is anything but unconventional. Western popular music is popular in large part because it follows an expected structure. Songs have lyrics that return in the form of a refrain that accompanies recurrent musical motifs. A regular, danceable rhythm grounds the song, and only rarely does the song deviate from that rhythm once it has been firmly established. Western popular music is thus 'organized around regimes of repetition and tonality that are highly ordered and predictable' (Goodwin 1993: 47). Western music videos, in turn, adhere to this musical form, which places limits on just how postmodern, fragmented and disconnected they can get. 'The relationship of song to visuals is . . . one between the basic demands of form (some elaboration of proposed themes, a movement towards closure) and the heterogeneity of codes and visual materials held in play by that form' (Straw 1993: 15). In other words, certain conventions in form and structure are nevertheless maintained and serve to identify the music video as a coherent genre. 'Across a series of music videos shown on music television or records occupying the pop charts, a consistency of rhythm and certain formal limits (verse-chorus structures and lengths) is likely to coexist with the invocation or reworking of a variety of historical styles and imageries' (Straw 1993: 14).

To be sure, these discussions take as their focus American music videos. An analysis of non-Western music videos raises questions regarding the assumptions forwarded about 'music video' as a genre, however, and constitutes an emerging field of research that includes Juluri's (2002) study of music television and youth culture in India, van der Rijt et al's (2000) exploration of the music video preferences of youth in the Netherlands, and the tantalizing references by Hamid Naficy and Louisa Schein to music video production in diasporic Iranian and Hmong communities in the United States. In all these cases, as in the case of Tanzanian music videos, one finds self-conscious efforts to localize music video and create forms that, in their content and editing choices, assert and affirm positive ethnicized values and nationalized identities, even as they celebrate global connections. This is not necessarily done in opposition to MTV, Western values and American identity, but certainly in relation to it.

SOME HISTORY

For the most part, broadcast television hit Africa in the 1950s and 1960s. The first television network in Africa, launched in 1956, was Radiodiffusion

Television Algerienne, followed by the Nigerian Broadcasting Corporation (1959), Egyptian Radio and TV (1960), Radiodiffusion Television Congolaise (1962), and the Voice of Kenya (1963). The United Republic of Tanzania, created by the 1964 merger of two formerly independent nations, Tanganyika and Zanzibar, evidenced its fractured national persona in this domain. Although Zanzibar inaugurated its television company, Television Zanzibar (TVZ), on 12 January 1974 as the first colour television broadcast on the entire continent, mainland Tanzania would wait a full two decades before initiating its own television broadcasts. Under the socialist austerity of Tanzania's first president, Julius Nyerere, it was argued that television was a luxury the nation could not yet afford. Moreover, Nyerere championed a philosophy and economic/political programme of 'African socialism', which was predicated upon a return to African communal roots. Consistent with this philosophy, Nyerere kept his country television-free for as long as possible, in an attempt to thwart Western cultural imperialism.

With the coming of liberalization, satellite dishes began appearing around the country, indicating that some elements of the population were hooked on television. In the face of these circumstances, the government revisited the question in 1989. By this time, televisions could be found in wealthier urban households that could somehow manage the 600 per cent import duty, and were used to view rental (mostly pirated) video cassettes. From 1989 through 1993, various government task forces and advisory committees explored the ways and means of introducing television to the mainland before issuing the first broadcast licence in February 1994 to the Coastal Television Network (CTN), a private station. CTN went on the air on 1 March 1994. Three months later, another private station, Independent Television (ITV), commenced broadcasting, and in December 1994, a third private station, Dar es Salaam Television (DTV), initiated its broadcast. It was not until 2002 that a mainland government station, Tanzania Television (TVT), finally emerged. Ironically, by the time the Tanzanian government accepted the inevitability of television and began issuing broadcast licences, its own economic reserves were too depleted to launch a government-controlled station to compete with the private stations that mushroomed in Dar es Salaam overnight. The result has been that Tanzania has more private television stations than any of its neighbours, and an overwhelming amount of foreign television content as a result of the need to fill all the available airtime.

TANZANIAN MUSIC VIDEOS

From 1992 to 1995, my work as an anthropologist and ethnomusicologist based in the northern Tanzanian city of Tanga and studying popular bands occasionally took me across the border to neighbouring Kenya, where the bands would often be invited to perform. On one occasion, in early 1993, I accompanied a band called Babloom Modern Taarab (*taarab* being a genre of sung Swahili poetry that was very popular along the coast, and which had Middle Eastern and Indian overtones) to its first television appearance, to be aired on the Kenya Broadcasting Corporation's (KBC) show, *Burudani* ('Entertainment'). Soon after the trip, my musician friends and I were sufficiently inspired by the experience to attempt our own music videos, using my fieldwork video camera – hardly a professional instrument, but more than adequate to our needs. In addition to the series of music videos made with Babloom Modern Taarab, we also made videos of a *dansi* (urban dance music) band, also from Tanga, called Watangatanga Band. After making enough of these to fill a video cassette, the bands sold and rented copies of their videos.

Given that we had no editing facilities, our videos had to be filmed in a single take. We were thus challenged to find means of varying the action, so as to maintain audience attention. No one in Tanga had seen a film crew before, motley and inexperienced though our crew was, so in the videos you can see passers-by walking and bicycling through the scene and casting curious glances at the musicians, who are lip-synching and playing air guitar to the pre-recorded audio track we fed into the camera. One of the best examples of our work is the Watangatanga video entitled '*Wanipenda Visa Wanitenda*' ('You Love Me Yet Treat Me Badly'). Because the song ends with a children's chant, '*Kinyuli nyulika*', we asked a group of children to play the hand game that goes with the chant in the opening and closing sequenc es. Without any rehearsal, the lead singers improvised a dramatic sequence to enact the song's lyrics, which speak of a love affair gone sour.

This song, in true Swahili fashion, blends elements drawn from a variety of local and distant cultures, including: (1) a coastal *ngoma* (traditional dance) rhythm called *chakacha*; (2) Congolese-style, hip-gyrations performed by the female lead; (3) a *taarab*-sounding melody; (4) *taarab*-like lyrical structure; (5) the formation of a circle (*duara*), a standard dance formation in Tanzania and other parts of East Africa; and (6) the local children's chant. No one at this time had heard of MTV, so the musicians were free, within technical constraints, to create their own genre of music video. Three points can be made when comparing this video to MTV-style music videos. First, drawing as this song does from a variety of local and global cultural resources, intertextuality is one of its main characteristics. Yet, whereas intertextuality is considered a primary feature of the visuals accompanying Western music videos, in this case it is the song, the audio component of the video, that quotes from multiple sites and genres. Second, the Tanzanian video embraces linear narrative. Third, in choosing to enact the lyrics, the musicians ensured that the visuals supported, rather than dominated, the music.

After a second trip to the KBC studios in early 1994 for the filming of additional videos with Babloom Modern Taarab, I met an executive, a fellow American, from the newly established ITV television network in Dar es Salaam. He was at that point in the midst of preparing for ITV's debut broadcast. I mentioned to him the popularity of the KBC show *Burudani* and suggested that ITV develop a similar show. Before I knew it, I was at work a few weeks later producing a series of music videos for ITV. The station manager provided me a with a crew that included a wonderful Moscow-trained director, Severine Kiwango; a camera man sporting a brand-new Betacam camcorder; and a bus to transport musicians to scenic venues (beaches, parks, hotels) to shoot our videos. We produced a total of ten music videos featuring three different bands and two genres: *taarab* and *dansi*. What became increasingly evident as we worked together was that our director's main reference point for filmed music was not MTV but rather Bollywood.

Bollywood is a favoured non-Western source of inspiration, with its extensive record in filming musical acts, and with its decided lack of the 'hedonism' sometimes associated with MTV. In this style, narrative spills into fantasy, as in a dream dance sequence that projects marriage and romantic bliss on a couple facing many obstacles that they have yet to overcome. Reality and fantasy blur together in much the same way that they do in the Madonna video and many other Western music videos (Kinder 1984), yet, once again, the visuals tend to support the aural track.

As we were embarking on music video production, other bands were starting to acquire access to consumer video cameras and experimenting with making their own music videos. A favoured editing style of Tanzanian music video in the 1990s was to tack back and forth between shots of a live performance and inserts of enacted scenes. Take, for example, music videos featuring the *taarab* orchestra of the *Jeshi la Kujenga Taifa* (JKT, the National Service Army), which displays a pronounced Bollywood influence by depicting a male-female couple strolling, then running, up a hillside. Upon reaching the top, the man mimes out his love for the lady, while the *taarab* performers sing about true love off screen. Reality (live performance) and mediation (enacted sequence) are blurred, creating an intertextual text on the visual level that nicely parallels the intertextuality of the audio level (namely, the combination of African, Egyptian and Indian musical elements).

Aside from Bollywood, the other primary source of video inspiration for Tanzanian music video hails from the Congo. Congolese popular music is, hands-down, the single most popular music throughout the continent. Spawning myriad dance forms, each named and affiliated with a particular band (for instance, *soukous, cavacha, dombolo, kwasa kwasa*), Congolese artists frequently make trips to Paris or Brussels to record their music and to make videos. The hip-gyrating dance move favoured by the female lead singer of the Watangatanga band is also featured prominently in videos by Zaiko Langa Langa (who perform in the *soukous* style), this time with men and women both performing it. Another trait shared with Watangatanga video is the formation of a circle. Yet, in content and style, the Zaiko Langa Langa video features many of the characteristics commonly identified with Western music videos: (1) lack of narrative; (2) cameras zooming in and out on body parts; (3) disjuncture between visual and musical levels; and (4) fast-paced montages. Editing follows the rhythm of the song, hence there is some correspondence, but, as with the Madonna video, attention is focused on singing and dancing. There are no instruments or shots of live perform-ance. Emphasis is thus placed on dance virtuosity, forcing both the lyrics and the music to take second place to the dance.

The most recent of the videos in my collection dates to April/May of 2004. Featuring the Zanzibari *taarab* band called the Island Super Stars Modern Taarab and their song '*Slogani ya Umbea*' ('Placard of Gossip'), this video exhibits greater editing capabilities and more skilled camera handling than that of the JKT video. Camera angles and perspectives, as well as the selection of scenes and costumes, alternate in tandem with the structural shifts of the poetry from verse to refrain to instrumental interlude. Musicians employ gesture and facial expressions to enact or emphasize the poetic lyrics. Yet, just as Madonna exoticized Thai culture and costume by appropriating it superficially and playing with it, so too do the musicians and videographer in '*Slogani ya Umbea*' play with and exoticize white tourists, who now con-stitute a significant sector in Zanzibar's postsocialist economy. Thus, fasci-nation with the foreign emerges as a shared theme. And even this video features the hip-rotating dance move that familiar from the Watangatanga and Zaiko Langa Langa videos. This time, however, the use of the dance is particularly notable. *Taarab* performers and aficionados continually aver that *taarab* is not dance music, but rather music one enjoys seated, listening carefully to the poetry.

Another variety of Tanzanian music videos is distinguished by the fact that shooting occurs entirely in a television studio. An example would be '*Chakubimbi*' ('Gossip Prostitute') by the All Stars Modern Taarab. This video was filmed in the ITV television studio in Dar es Salaam. A variety of camera angles and perspectives were achieved in a single take through the use of multiple cameras. This video features highly elaborate editing capa-bilities, what with the use of special effects, especially fancy fades, and added visual imagery. Because television studios upgrade their technological equipment somewhat regularly, music videos are increasingly being pro-duced within the confines of the studio. This is easily explained: it is easier and cheaper for studios to record on-site than to pay the cost of transport-ing musicians to different locations. Moreover, the studio has the theoretical capacity to record high-quality visual and audio tracks simultaneously (this is what distinguishes video from film), whereas, out on location, it is nearly impossible to capture high-quality audio, forcing performers to lip-synch.

From the musician's point of view, one problem with the emergence of Tanzanian music videos is that the bands typically are not paid for their television appearances. Studios argue that television appearances constitute free promotion of the artists' cassettes, CDs and concert performances. Musicians nevertheless dislike this arrangement, because the studio retains ownership rights to the videos. Thus, some musicians, wary of being taken advantage of, avoid the studio route and instead hire private videographers. The quality of the video may not be as high as that which television studios could achieve, but the artists retain ownership rights and can sell their videos in tandem with their audiocassettes and CDs. Additionally, if the quality of a privately-produced video passes studio inspection, musicians can deposit their videos for broadcast, thereby gaining the promotion without relinquishing their rights to the product. The studio accepts this arrangement because it gets product without having to finance or produce it.

CONCLUSION

Tanzanian music videos would be grossly misunderstood if represented as Tanzanian attempts to mimic the postmodern ways of Western, MTV-style music videos. This is not to say that there are no commonalities between the two styles of music videos, however. For example, both share understandings of music videos as sites of local/global engagements. However, in the Tanzanian case, the idea of 'global' is far from limited to Western cultural imperialism, as some critics would have us believe. India and the Congo carry far more influence than Euro-America. In addition, all music videos, regardless of their point of origin, share certain functions, such as the promotion of the artists, songs and performances featured in them. They also share some aesthetic qualities, such as tendencies to borrow across genre, culture, time and space. Yet, whereas the postmodern style arises more typically in the visual aspect of Western music videos, in the case of Tanzanian music videos, this inheres to the music itself. Sometimes it subsequently emerges in the visuals as well but, often-times, postmodern pastiche remains a musical feature, with Tanzanian musicians choosing to enact linear narratives as visual accompaniment.

In fact, it could be argued that Tanzanian popular music is more postmodern, in the sense of being experimental and open to the creative incorporation of diverse musical elements, than Western popular music, which is far more convention-bound in structure and style. Tanzanian popular music, especially in coastal and urban areas, manifests an aesthetic preference for

incessant innovation and the continual incorporation of new elements, both
local and foreign. This includes not only new musical elements, such as
melodies, instruments and rhythms, but also new dance styles, new costumes, new names and new locations for the production of music videos.
With this much investment in novelty, Tanzanian popular musicians can
afford to be less radically postmodern in their videos. Yet the flip side to this
argument also begs consideration. Could it be that Western music videos
prove particularly postmodern and intertextual as compensation for their
musical conservatism? Only with additional comparative research will we
be able to truly measure the relative merits and innovative/conservative
potential of music video around the world.

REFERENCES

Allan, Blaine (1990), 'Musical Cinema, Music Video, Music Television'. *Film
     Quarterly* 43, no. 3 (Spring 1990): 2–14.
Allen, Steve (1993), 'Madonna'. *Journal of Popular Culture* 27, no. 1 (1993): 1–12.
Askew, Kelly (2002), *Performing the Nation: Swahili Music and Cultural Politics in Tan-
     zania*. Chicago: University of Chicago Press.
— (2003), 'As Plato Duly Warned: Music, Politics, and Social Change in East Africa'.
     Anthropological Quarterly 76, no. 4 (Fall 2003): 609–37.
Aufderheide, Pat (1986), 'Music Videos: the Look of the Sound'. In Todd Gitlin,
     Watching Television. New York: Pantheon, pp. 111–35.
Berland, Jody (1986), 'Sound, Image, and Social Space: Rock Video and Media
     Reconstruction'. *Journal of Communication Inquiry* 10, no. 1: 34–47.
Björnberg, Alf (1994), 'Structural Relationships of Music and Images in Music
     Video'. *Popular Music* 13, no. 1: 51–74.
Burns, Gary (1996), 'Popular Music, Television, and Generational Identity'. *Journal
     of Popular Culture* 30, no. 3: 129–41.
Douglas, Susan J. (1994), *Where the Girls Are: Growing Up Female with the Mass
     Media*. New York: Times Books.
Dowmunt, Tony (ed.) (1993), *Channels of Resistance: Global Television and Local
     Empowerment*. London: British Film Institute.
Fiske, J. (1986), 'MTV: Post-structural Post-modern'. *Journal of Communication
     Inquiry* 10, no. 1: 74–9.
Frith, Simon, Andrew Goodwin and Lawrence Grossberg (eds) (1993), *Sound and
     Vision: The Music Video Reader*. New York: Routledge.
Goodwin, Andrew (1992), *Dancing in the Distraction Factory: Music Television and
     Popular Culture*. Minneapolis: University of Minnesota Press.
— (1993), 'Fatal Distractions: MTV Meets Postmodern Theory'. In Frith et al.
     (eds), *Sound and Vision: The Music Video Reader*. New York: Routledge, pp. 45–66.
Grossberg, Lawrence (1993), 'The Media Economy of Rock Culture: Cinema, Post-
     modernity and Authenticity'. In Frith et al. (eds), *Sound and Vision: The Music
     Video Reader*. New York: Routledge, pp. 185–209.
Johansson, Thomas (1992), 'Music video, youth culture, and postmodernism'.
     Popular Music and Society 16, no. 3.

Juluri, Vamsee (2002), 'Music Television and the Invention of Youth Culture in India'. *Television & New Media* 3, no. 4: 367–86.

Kaplan, E. Ann (1987), *Rocking Around the Clock: Music Television, Postmodernism, and Consumer Culture*. New York: Methuen.

Kinder, Marsha (1984), 'Music Video and the Spectator: Television, Ideology, and Dream'. *Film Quarterly* 38, no. 1 (Fall 1984): 2–15.

Lugo-Lugo, Carmen (2001), 'The Madonna Experience: a US Icon Awakens a Puerto Rican Adolescent's Feminist Consciousness'. *Frontiers* 22, no. 2: 118–30.

McClary, Susan (1990), *Feminine Endings: Music, Gender and Sexuality*. Minneapolis: University of Minnesota Press.

Savan, Leslie (1993), 'Commercials Go Rock'. In Frith et al. (eds), *Sound and Vision: The Music Video Reader*. New York: Routledge, pp. 85–90.

Schein, Louisa (2002), 'Mapping Hmong Media in Diasporic Space'. In Faye D. Ginsburg, Lila Abu-Lughod and Brian Larkin (eds), *Media Worlds: Anthropology on New Terrain*. Berkeley: University of California Press, pp. 229–44.

— (2004), 'Homeland Beauty: Transnational Longing and Hmong American Video'. *Journal of Asian Studies* 63, no. 2 (May): 433–63.

Straw, Will (1988), 'Music Video in its Contexts: Popular Music and Post-modernism in the 1980s'. *Popular Music* 7 (3): 247–66.

— (1993), 'Popular Music and Post-modernism in the 1980s'. In Frith et al. (eds), *Sound and Vision: The Music Video Reader*. New York: Routledge, pp. 3–21.

Sturmer, Corinna (1993), 'MTV's Europe: an Imaginary Continent?' In Tony Dowmunt (ed.), *Channels of Resistance: Global Television and Local Empowerment*. London: British Film Institute, pp. 50–66.

Sturmer, Martin (1998), *The Media History of Tanzania*. Salzburg: Afro-Asiatisches Institut.

Tetzlaff, D. J. (1986), 'MTV and the Politics of Postmodern Pop'. *Journal of Communication Inquiry* 10 (1): 80–91.

Van der Rijt, Gerrit A. J. et al. (2000), 'Young People and Music Television in the Netherlands'. *European Journal of Communication* 15 (1): 79–91.

Vernallis, Carol (1998), 'The Aesthetics of Music Video: An Analysis of Madonna's "Cherish"'. *Popular Music* 17, 2, 153–86.

POLITICAL RIDICULE: MEDIATIZED NOTIONS OF 'TRANSPARENT CONCEALMENT'[1]

In a website with the title 'art matters' (www.artmatters.info), Ogova Ondego publishes articles on arts and culture in Kenya. In one article, he reviews one of Wahome Mutahi's plays, summarizing Wahome's theatre as 'bar trivia and tribal drama'.

WAHOME MUTAHI AND WHISPERS

In the last couple of years before he passed on, Wahome Mutahi was acclaimed for his Gikuyu political plays, which he co-wrote, produced and performed widely across Kenya. However, Wahome was better recognized as a newspaper humour columnist. Indeed, Wahome Mutahi was synonymous with the ever-popular *Whispers* column that he penned every Sunday for more than two decades. The column was social commentary encapsulated within vignettes set in the household of the fictional protagonist, Whispers, a self-described 'son of the soil', along with his wife, Thatcher, and their two children, Whispers Jr and Investment (also known as Pajero). The fictional domestic setting was merely a façade for Wahome's lampooning of the ludicrousness and the intemperance of the national polity. Within the Whispers household, Wahome caricatured the fraudulent excesses of national politicians.

The *Whispers* column managed to escape the clampdown of the repressive regime of President Daniel Arap Moi in its worst period, the 1980s, although Wahome was imprisoned in the late 1980s on trumped-up charges of being a member of an outlawed political organization, Mwakenya.[2] Even after his stint in prison, Wahome continued to write and publish his *Whispers* column, without watering down his satire against political impudence.

Two reasons can be advanced to explain the continued publication of the *Whispers* column even after Wahome's imprisonment. One is technical: Wahome was not imprisoned for penning the column. More compelling, however, is the fact that the column was extremely popular, and so was a major contribution to a wider circulation of the newspaper publishing it. As long as it was not categorically banned, the newspaper was happy to continue carrying it. A third reason for the column's continued publication was the expectation that, by framing Wahome and imprisoning him for trumped-up charges, he would relent in his veiled criticisms and instead practise something much more effective: self-censorship. Finally, one could argue that, perhaps, the government simply (and foolishly) thought that banning a column so preposterous in its portrayal of its fictional characters would draw even closer attention to the characters' clear relationship to the outlandish actions of the government.

FROM NEWSPAPER TO PERFORMANCE

By the mid-1990s, Wahome's reputation as an unrelenting humorist who fearlessly pulled no punches in satirizing the politics of the day had ossified. It was also at about this time that Wahome, who was Ngugi wa Thiong'o's student at the University of Nairobi and also a student of the University's Free Travelling Theatre[3] under John Ruganda, ventured into co-writing plays in Gikuyu and 'taking them to the people'. In this endeavour, Wahome Mutahi decided to use the spaces that were readily available – as untheatrical as they may have been – in restaurants and pubs. This is a way of 'recuperating' non-theatrical spaces, such as the bar, in service of the theatre. The success of Wahome's Gikuyu plays cannot be extricated from the fact of their popular presentation in these non-theatrical spaces, in the pubs and restaurants. After all, Wahome's first play, *Mugaathe Mobogothi*, which was co-written with Wahome Karengo, had one of the longest runs in the history of Kenyan theatre.

But beside the notion of taking theatre to the people as he experienced it during the years of the Free Travelling Theatre at the University of Nairobi, there was another phenomenon that drove Wahome Mutahi's decision to take on the pub as a performance space for his Gikuyu productions. Long before he began exploring the pub as a performance space, the pub and restaurant scene had already been successfully tested as a venue for theatrical performance. To be sure, most of the performers prior to Wahome's companies put their primary focus on lewd, slapstick comedy, or offered adult-themed skits bordering on the vulgar. Wahome may have taken his cue from such a categorically different genre of performative entertainment – that is, the lewd comedy shows – but his theatre of political satire recuperated the pub as a discursive performatic space and sanitized it for family entertainment. One may argue that the pub or restaurant is not a entertainment venue for family audiences, given that the indulgence in alcohol is the primary attraction. However, a close look at the pub and restaurant industry in Kenya quickly discloses that the venue has become a popular place for family-style weekend entertainment, with many such enterprises offering a children's playground on their premises.

The state machinery did not categorically ban Wahome's plays, even though they were highly and directly political in their ridicule, possibly for the same reason that the Whispers column was not censored. As Mbugua wa Mungai (2003) has noted, 'By not interfering with Wahome's performances, the state seems to be operating on the assumption that since this drama is merely a part of general bar-room fun, drunken audiences cannot take its message seriously'. One might argue that, in the 1990s, when Wahome's plays were doing the rounds in different parts of the country, the advent of multi-party politics had, to a large extent, changed the political terrain, and so there was no longer any need to clamp down on such ventures. This conclusion, however, would likely be mistaken, given that, during this very period, a number of plays and theatre for development productions did not escape government censure. Indeed, reports abound of performances disrupted by the police, venues cancelled, and even of artists arrested while preparing to perform. Some were even interrupted in the middle of performances that were sponsored by such non-governmental organizations as the Legal Resources Foundation (LRF), the Kenya Human Rights Commission (KHRC), and organizations specifically dealing with civic education.

Ogova Ondego's declarative dismissal of Wahome's theatre as bar trivia and tribal drama is not merely intellectually dishonest; it also smacks of ignorance regarding the satirical genre. While it is tempting to disregard such critical impudence, it is important to examine the critique within the context of a society bedevilled by politicized ethnicities. The pub or bar-room should be viewed as the recuperated site of a repressed community's celebration and creation of identity, through discursive practice, performance and participation. In Kenya, the pub is the place where people meet to spend an evening, a weekend, or a lunch hour, but it is also regarded as the locale of more significant activity, giving rise to the commonly held belief that 'business deals are settled in the bar in Kenya'. In other words, the bar is not necessarily only about trivia.

It is through recuperating the bar-room that Wahome's plays venture to 'tell the truth laughingly', in the words of John Ruganda (1992). Expanding on this notion, Ruganda contends that, when the artist is caught 'between the demands of conformity to the authorities' ideology of dominance, and the dictates of his or her creative muse', which he must dissimulate. Ruganda further says that 'this seeming self-effacement helps the artists to appear conformist and dissentious at once, to be applauding when he is condemning' (Ruganda 1992: 3).

In exploring how an artist may creatively use the 'strategies of transparent concealment' or 'masking the truth transparently', Ruganda contends that 'the elements of the grotesque, the odd, the comic, and the absurd . . .

in eliciting our surprise or in violating our expectations, help us to demys-
tify ideology masquerading as truth' (Ruganda 1992: 23). Similar strategies
are used in Wahome's plays.

The first of Wahome's plays (co-written with W. Karengo) is *Mugaathe
Mubogothi*, which can be loosely translated from Gikuyu as 'his delirious
highness'. It makes satiric reference to 'his highness' (*mugaathe*), a preferred
form of address for the African 'big man'. *Mubogothi* makes reference to the
inevitable senility that attends the end of the lifelong dictatorial tenure of
most African presidents, and in this instance refers specifically to the end of
President Jomo Kenyatta's regime in Kenya. In this play, the main character is the president of the fictional country of Wiyumiririe ('persevere' or
'endure'). The character enters the stage carrying a toilet plunger as his
symbol of office – no doubt a parody of the flywhisk that Kenyatta used to
carry around as his insignia of office. President Mubogothi, like Kenyatta,
has ruled his country since it achieved independence. He has been conva-
lescent for most of his tenure as president, but no one outside his closest
associates knows about his poor state of health. Towards the end of the play,
his personal doctor makes a fatal blunder and gives him rat poison. His close
confidants expect that he will surely die. Imagine the dramatic effect and the
surprise, then, when he comes staggering back on stage, poised to rule
forever. The dramatic gaffe committed by the doctor – the most trusted of
confidantes – can be read two ways: as a calculated mistake committed in
order to advance the thickening plot within the play, or as a deliberate authorial intrusion, with the specific effect of parodying the oft-repeated statement by political sycophants in Kenya in the 1990s that KANU (the ruling
party) would rule for 100 years.

The second of Wahome's Mugaathe plays, co-written with Wakanyote
Njuguna, is *Mugaathe Ndotono*, which can be translated as 'his highness, the
Club', which makes reference to a knobkerrie that is meant to satirize the
club-like sceptre carried by President Daniel Arap Moi as his insignia of
office. In this play, the main character is, once again, the president. The club
he carries is larger than a human's head. Its purpose, both literally and
metaphorically, is to smash anyone who does not toe the president's line.
During the fictional Ndotono's tenure, which is meant to be reminiscent of
1980s Kenya, repression, political assassinations and arbitrary imprison-
ments reach unimaginable levels. The result is a popular uprising, civil
disobedience and public demonstrations.

Like President Moi, the fictional Ndotono is forced to introduce multi-
party politics and hold elections. His attempts at repression come a cropper
when, towards the end of the play, he is challenged for the presidency during
the elections by none other than his wife. He is shocked to discover that his
own wife would support the populace against him. In disbelief, and haunted
by his own inhuman treatment of his citizenry, he collapses, and the play ends.

In *Makaririra Kioro*, co-written with Ndungi Githuku, the character of the president suffers nightmares and hallucinations that take the audience into a series of plays within the play. The title can be translated as 'they will weep in the toilet'. This is a clear reference to one of the fictional president's nightmares, in which he and his inner cabinet are bundled out of office by an angry populace and end up holed up in a public toilet at the mercy of the mob, with only a street girl to help them. All their power and glory gone, they beg the girl to protect them from the murderous crowd that is baying for their blood.

Following Ruganda, the use of comic figures through which a playwright might 'speak the truth laughingly', relies on the classical clown, idiot or madman (Ruganda 1992: 10). Wahome does not use such classical comic figures, however. Instead, he brings out the comic from his main characters, a technique that may be called 'dramatic caricature'. Ruganda contends that 'political plays are deceptively un-Kenyan'. Writing of another celebrated Kenyan playwright, Francis Imbuga, Ruganda further elaborates: 'Imbuga has deliberately desisted from making direct parallels between the setting of his plays and the reality which surrounds them'. By contrast, Wahome's dramatic technique relies on direct signification. The distancing he employs distorts the real as we know it, without allowing the distortion to alienate either the characters or the set. In other words, Wahome's technique mirrors that of political caricature commonly employed in cartooning, wherein the distortion of particular features suffices to bring out the comic without recognitive alienation.

In using this technique of dramatic caricature, Wahome also introduces popular songs drawn from a variety of sources, from Gikuyu cultural pop music to political anthems to church hymns. The original, recognizable melodies are retained, but the lyrics are distorted to suit the themes of Wahome's scenes. This allows the audience to easily identify with the pop songs, heightening not only the entertainment quality of the production but also the satire and the biting humour in the reconstructed lyrics. By incorporating elements of dissimulation, the grotesque and the absurd, and by combining Ruganda's 'strategies of transparent concealment' with what I term the technique of dramatic caricature within theatrical performance, Wahome's work can be considered as a discourse on a historical identity that is consciously and perpetually being amended. In a very real sense, Wahome can be said to be writing a narrative of nationhood.

This narrative of nationhood is itself the consequence of a polity crippled by the paralysis of parliamentary democracy. What is ironic is that the paralysis is more apparent than ever now, even though Kenya finally enjoys multiparty politics. The liberalization of political activity in Kenya was largely seen as a way out of the political enigmas of single-party dictatorship, and as indicative of the identificatory problematics of harshly politicized ethnicities.

It is within this paradigm of politicized ethnicities that Ogova Ondego's criticism of Wahome Mutahi's theatre as tribal drama must be understood.

At the heart of Wahome's work there exists an awareness of a crisis of political and cultural representation. Femi Osofisan refers to this crisis as the 'rites of post-Negritude remembering' (Osofisan 1999). In distinguishing between postcolonialism and post-Negritude, Osofisan sees the postcolonial project as a continuation of the colonial legacy because postcolonialism 'continues to privilege the "centre" – by which is meant a former colonial country in Europe . . . thus all we do is prefigured as a continuous act of "writing back" to an "Empire"' (Osofisan 1999). He further notes:

> Postcolonialism is a return to the past, to the trenches of Negritude, whereas our identity crisis in Africa is of a different order entirely, relating to two urgent problems – first, the dilemma of creating a national identity out of our disparate ethnic communities; and secondly, that of creating committed, responsible, patriotic, and compassionate individuals out of our civil populations. (Osofisan 1999)

Ultimately, Osofisan sees post-Negritude's 'primary audience being the local public, which it wants to empower for moral and political action, against the negative forces of our societies'. While Negritude remembers, Osofisan contends, post-Negritude also remembers, and in doing so it recognizes the validity of our local languages without rejecting wholesale the inherited colonial language.

Kole Omotoso, in an article in the *New African* (July 2004), laments that Africa is lost without translation. He argues that the death of each language is the death of a whole world of knowledge. Indeed, he acknowledges that the use of local languages in Africa would translate to an expansion of cultural freedoms. He wonders, 'In what ways, subtle and blatant, did the use of English limit the aspirations for freedom?' In underscoring the importance of cross-translations, he concludes by urging that 'language activists must get to work, and mass language movements must come into being, insisting on mass literacy in African languages as well as English or French, as the case might be'. Yet this is the paradox of the crisis of representation. From a different perspective, Kimani Gecau (1972) asks whether ethnic languages divide the nation. Emmanuel Yewah (2001) offers a possible response:

> Ngugi's attempt to resurrect the Gikuyu language . . . may turn out to be a more subversive act than perhaps intended, in that it may lead to the rise of 'politically decentralised' but 'culturally united' societies or 'cultural nations', mini-nations, with the potential of undoing the whole structure, the imagined construct that we have come to know as Kenya.

Yewah does not seem to consider the undoing of the whole structure as a possibility of solving the myriad problems caused by this crisis of identity. Interestingly, current political trends are increasingly forcing the African to think more about reconstructing national boundaries – witness the situation in Ethiopia and Eritrea, or the peace negotiations of Sudan. Indeed, Wole Soyinka urged Nigerians to consider whether restructuring Nigeria might be the way to save the country from itself, by renegotiating 'the modalities of a productively harmonious co-existence' (Soyinka 2004).

Wahome's plays can easily be fitted within the milieu of a mass media that itself contributes to this debate about the cultural crisis of representation. Just like some readers would avidly follow his column on Sundays, so were there members of the public who never missed a chance to watch his plays every weekend. Wahome's plays had long runs – as much as a year of weekly performances on Friday, Saturday and Sunday – and appeared every weekend in a different venue. The mass appeal kept the productions going for as long as there was a sizeable house every time a play was put on. In every respect, Wahome's theatre was an extension of his Sunday newspaper humour column, in the same way that the technique he employed was similar to that of a political cartoon caricature. In short, just as he engaged mediatized techniques in popularizing his plays, so did these performances imbue the notions of mass media.

NOTES

1. I have borrowed this concept from John Ruganda who uses the idea of the 'dialectics of transparent concealment' to discuss the dramatic strategies that Francis Imbuga uses in his drama. Francis Imbuga is a leading Kenyan dramatist and professor of literature and drama.
2. Mwakenya was an underground socialist movement that operated in the 1980s in Kenya and which was committed to pressurizing the government to repeal repressive laws, stop the repression of political dissent, and release political prisoners. It was forced to operate as an underground pressure group since the government did not allow political organizations of any nature other than the ruling party. The government then terrorized perceived political dissenters by claiming they were members of the outlawed movement and summarily imprisoned them.
3. The travelling theatre movement is a movement that took root in university-based drama companies of most African universities. For details of the practice of the travelling theatre, see David Kerr's *African Popular Theatre* (1995).

REFERENCES

Gecau, Kimani (1972), 'Do Ethnic Languages Divide the Nation?' *African Perspectives* (2).

Kerr, David (1995), *African Popular Theatre*. London: James Carrey; Portsmouth, NH: Heinemann; Nairobi: EAEP.

Mungai, Mbugua wa (2003), 'The Big Man's Turn to Dance in Kenyan Bar-rooms: Wahome Mutahi's Parody of Power'. *Leeds African Studies Bulletin* (65).

Mutahi, Wahome and W. Karengo. *Mugaathe Mubogothi*. Unpublished manuscript.

— and N. Githuku. *Makaririra Kioro*. Unpublished manuscript.

— and W. Njuguna. *Mugaathe Ndotono*. Unpublished manuscript.

Ndigirigi, Gichingiri (1999), 'Kenyan Theatre after Kamiriithu'. *The Drama Review* 43(2).

Omotoso, Kole (2004), 'Africa Lost Without Translation'. *New African*, July issue.

Osofisan, Femi (1999), 'Theatre and the Rites of Post-Negritude Remembering'. *Research in African Literatures* 30 (1).

Ruganda, John (1992), *Telling the Truth Laughingly: The Politics of Francis Imbuga's Drama*. Nairobi: EAEP.

Soyinka, Wole (2004), 'How to Save Nigeria from Itself'. *Business in Africa*, July issue.

Yewah, Emannuel (2001), 'The Nation as a Constructed Construct'. *Research in African Literatures* 32 (3).

NAMES, CLOTH AND IDENTITY: A CASE FROM WEST AFRICA

To speak in proverbs, you hide the actual facts; you use words to conceal thoughts rather than to express them. Cloth is like a silent proverb, but with cloth you wear it.

Apagyahene, Abiriw-Akwapim (1988)

ADORNMENT AND VERBAL STRATEGIES

In the Akwapim kingdom of southeastern Ghana,[1] clothing is used as a form of communication to make statements about personhood and status; to conceal or reveal identity; to express desires and impulses. It may do so directly or indirectly, conventionally or rebelliously. Clothing is owned, bestowed and gives identity. The clothed body expresses the person of the wearer and society's image of that person. As a result, clothing absorbs the particular times in which it has been worn[2] and becomes like a relic of these past events.

In Akwapim certain kinds of cloth worn by both men and women in their daily lives have names that in a stylized and elliptical way communicate anger, hostility, lack of commitment, jealousy, sorrow and occasionally wry humour or sarcasm. Many of these names resemble the formulaic names once bestowed on pets, slaves and villages, and the proverbial responses (*tete nnyeso*) that a mother formerly gave to her child. In each of these genres, proverbs (or pithy expressions) are used to signal incidents concerning individual identity and emotions and to safely convey sentiments too sensitive or aggressive to express directly. Being impersonal, there is a degree of ambiguity and uncertainty in the conveyed meaning that allows for disavowal by the principal. Something is said without saying it; it is encoded in a highly structured and repetitive way.

Akropong, the Akwapim capital, was a dangerous place until the early twentieth century (Gilbert 1993a, 1994). Human sacrifice, if not frequent, was an ever-present and greatly feared reality. The swearing of oaths, at times excessively used, could bring financial ruin and reduce one to the level of a slave. Illness and drought could change a family's fortune. Witchcraft accusations were common. Factions and bitter divisions characterized the town and the state. Struggles for succession were frequent. The palace was viewed as a place of power and danger. This insecure past, while largely gone, is woven into the present-day imagination of Akwapim people. Times have changed. The names bestowed on slaves, pets and villages. and the responses that were 'scripted' for a child by a mother to immortalize the risks and tragedies of everyday life are now things of the past. Today, of the various genres discussed in this essay, it is only cloth with proverbial names that remains.

In the western Sahel, it is common to use a spokesperson or 'conversational intermediary' to relay a message even when the message source and the addressee are both physically present (Irvine 1990: 144–5). Among the Wolof, 'the *griot* is a repeater of messages from higher-ranking persons whose dignity precludes publicly expressing their own sentiments or arguing on their own behalf' (Irvine 1990: 144). In the forest region of Ghana, the Akan *ɔkyeame* plays a somewhat similar role as intermediary for both the chief and the public; a form of triadic communication commonly seen in formal gatherings – both royal and domestic. The indirect communication by the *griot* and *ɔkyeame* when they display ideas on behalf of another person is, I suggest, analogous to the communicative use of proverbial names in Akwapim for a child, pet, slave, village or cloth – though in these latter genres the audience (addressee) may be more ambiguously defined or may deny understanding and thereby refuse the message. These Akan 'verbal' strategies draw on the same thematic and linguistic materials; the discourses are overlapping, porous and sometimes parallel (cf. Barber 1991: 12–13 on Yoruba oral literary discourses).

In Akwapim, verbal eloquence is a highly valued art. To speak beautifully is a sign of high status and wisdom. Proverbs (*ɛbɛ*, pl. *mmɛ*) and allusive words are aesthetic and distancing devices for benign or malicious purposes; they appropriate the past and are powerful strategies for indirectly voicing controversial or offensive topics when direct expression might be taken as criticism or as too openly aggressive. They are a relatively risk-free strategy of communication, ascribed to an impersonal third and a neutral authoritative source (cf. Yankah 1995: 326; 1989). Proverbs allow Akwapim people to present a public face of 'cool' control when referring to delicate or forbidden matters. Palace speech was formerly suffused with proverbs. In everyday life there is an even wider range of possibilities, in the form of the proverbial responses that a mother demands of her child, and the names of pets, villages, slaves and cloth. These names and responses mix emotion and politics, but do so safely. They are personal, 'expressive' forms of communication that refer to past personal disasters; newly made rituals to reorder, tame, ward off or perhaps act as witness to the past. As they merge the specific and the general, such proverbial names are sufficiently vague as to be endlessly sensible.

In Akwapim towns, as in most other small and dense communities, people take care not to tread inadvertently upon the emotions of others; consensus and harmony are celebrated. Much dissension is expressed indirectly: the object of the criticism is aware of it but cannot take offence, and thus future alliances are left open. The concepts of *bo akutia* (to chide, scold or slander someone without mentioning his name) and *di nkasaguaa* (*kasa*: speech, *guaa*: to drive away; speech to move things aside) refer to speech that is meant to say something indirectly, although publicly, without mentioning the person's name – wanting him to know (Christaller 1933: 276). In other words, they want him to know but they also want him to be unable to respond. These are devices to control the potency and danger of the spoken word (Yankah 1995: 50–1), but they have implications for the 'truth' of the gossip or accusation. Lakoff and Johnson (1980) call this 'deniable' speech. The use of proverbs as names and responses is similar.

Akwapim cloth designs are named, but the name is 'visual', not verbal. The names of children, pets, slaves and villages are not visual, but spoken. I argue that the names of cloth and children's response names are fundamentally more similar than they are different; that these names and responses are concrete – like emblems or objects. Pets, slaves, villages, a mother's child – all are property and extensions of the person who bestowed the name. They are being used like a blank canvas to express dangerous ideas and emotions. I suggest, further, that even when the name or pithy expression is actually printed on the cloth, that this writing is being treated as an image. The names are forms of non-verbal communication – communication that is primarily hostile in nature. Pleasant communication, after all, need not be encoded.

In this essay I first describe different types of cloth and the various contexts of their use in Akwapim. I then show *how* Akwapim people communicate with one another by wearing judiciously chosen wax-print cloth whose named designs are the equivalent of verbal strategies. Finally, I address other categories of the Akwapim naming system that are extensions of the individual or corporate personality and show how similar proverbs bridge these various genres.

THE CLOTHED BODY

Inasmuch as adornment usually is also an object of considerable value, it is a synthesis of the individual's having and being . . .

Georg Simmel (1950)

In Akwapim, wearing cloth is associated with being civilized. Akropong people say that the first Omanhene of Akwapim, Fianko Betuafo (r. 1731–42) introduced cloth: before that people wore bark cloth to cover themselves.

Two hundred years later, influenced by the 'enlightenment' of Christianity, Ofori Kuma II (r. 1914–19 and 1932–41) is remembered for having introduced, despite great resistance, the so-called chemise or cover-shoulder law that stipulated women should wear, in addition to their wrapped skirts, a head scarf [*duku*] and a cloth to cover their breasts [*kabaa*]. An Akan proverb expresses the aesthetic pleasure of new cloth: *Opurow se ade foforo ye fɛ* ('The squirrel says new things are beautiful'). Akwapim people say that *opurow* (a species of small squirrel) gathers green leaves to make his nest look like cloth.

Akwapim people recognize three discrete categories of cloth. First, there is funeral cloth (*ayiase ntama*) which includes *adinkra* and indigenously dyed cloth – *kuntunkuni, ɔkɔben, birisi* – or any cloth that is dark in color, even with a design (for example, factory-produced wax-print) so long as it is new and presentable.[3] Secondly, there is cloth which is worn in the house (*ofie ntama*): ordinary cloth (generally wax-print) which can be poorer in quality or relatively worn out. And thirdly, there is festival cloth (*afa hyɛ ntama*) which is white or shiny and cannot be worn to a funeral: this includes hand-woven *kente*[4] and European imported velvet, eyelet, and so on. The latter is worn on special occasions by chiefs and the wealthy elite. Plain white calico is worn by a spirit medium (*ɔkɔmfo*), traditional priest (*ɔbosomfo*) or by a chief when he is in seclusion after being enstooled: it marks their liminal status.

Wax-print (wax batik) is factory-printed cotton cloth worn by most men and women in their everyday life. In the nineteenth and twentieth centuries it was printed in Switzerland, the Netherlands and in England for export to West Africa. In recent years it has is also been produced in Ghana and Côte d'Ivoire.[5] European wax-print is more prestigious than that made locally, or than non wax-print cloth. The patterns are named by the market women in Accra or by women in the villages who resell them. Although the relationship between a cloth's design and its proverb name is not necessarily obvious, they are easily 'read' by those who are familiar with textile rhetoric and who possess an awareness of local affairs. The significance of the colour of the cloth is more important than that of the name or message. Cloth that is designated as 'white' includes blue and is worn for celebrations; 'red' includes red, brown and green prints and is worn for funerals.

Cloth, beads, houses and land are the main traditional possessions of Akwapim people and they play a critical role in gift giving and exchange.[6] In the 1970s, men generally bought wax-print cloth for their girl friends or wives for the annual Odwira festival, for Christmas, or for the memorial service of a funeral. A woman, similarly, might give cloth to her husband at the annual festival. At the funeral of her husband's mother or father, she might publicly present him with as many as six pieces of cloth 'so that he won't feel so bad'. This is a statement about what the husband has and who he is: the gift shows his reputation as a man of means and honour. If the woman is a seller of cloth, she may present many pieces to outshine her co-wives and then, after the funeral is over, she may take them back.

When someone dies, cloth is always placed in the coffin for the deceased to use in Asaman, the land of the ancestors (conceived as a 'mirror' of the land of the living).[7] Even if the deceased was very poor, one cloth should be buried with him, apart from the shroud, which is of white cotton. An old man or chief might have five cloths added to the coffin to cover him – the number showing his importance. They are chosen from his own cloths: the pattern and colour do not matter. After the body is placed in the coffin, the cloths are laid on top of him, one on top of the other, with his hands placed on top. Some cloth is believed to be especially suitable: the cloth that a man wore to hospital when ill is generally buried with him because 'he seemed to like it'. This cloth is used to wrap his corpse when he is taken from hospital to the mortuary, from there to his home-town for the funeral, and then to wrap him for burial.

Other cloths (called *asiede*) are given to the deceased at his funeral by his wife, children and those with whom he had very close ties. A narrow strip is torn from these cloths for the giver, who ties it around his or her wrist or head, and the rest is put in the coffin.[8] Some of this cloth (called *funya* – *fun*: corpse; *nyaa*: have it) is publicly torn into narrow strips by close women relatives and shared with other close mourners who retrieve the pieces with their left hand (associated with the dead) from the ground where they are dropped. 'The deceased has given you something to show he has departed from you and therefore you must pick it [up] with your left hand.'

One cloth which belonged to the deceased is given to the women (two from the father's side and two from the mother's side) who wash and dress the corpse. This cloth, called *oguare tam* (washing cloth), is torn in narrow strips and tied around their wrist or head. Another cloth of the deceased is torn in half and tied around the drums at the funeral: *asokwafo funya*. Generally this is cloth which the deceased often wore, so everyone will recognize it. After the funeral, it is given to the drummer to makes culottes out of it.

The room in which the deceased's body is laid in state is also decorated with cloth. This is never wax-print, but hand-woven cloth (*nsaa*) from Mali or Niger,[9] or if there is not enough to cover the ceiling and walls, *kente* will be used. This cloth may be borrowed from anybody in town. For a chief, four to five layers of *nsaa* will be placed on the bed under his body. This is a reference to his power.

One year after the death, the family gathers, libation is poured, and the deceased's storage box is opened, whereupon his cloth and other possessions are shared among the children and successors. As a witch's *bayi* (power of witchcraft) may be transferred through her belongings, people may be wary of accepting beads or cloth from her. Similarly Christians may be reluctant to accept the smock (*batakari*) of a deceased priest (*obosomfo*) because of a vague fear that some of the deity's power controlled by the priest will continue to adhere to the cloth.[10] If someone dies a bad death, such as a pregnant woman, all her cloth will be buried with her, so that she will not come back to haunt the living, asking for her cloth.

Akwapim people sometimes wear cloth of a particular name and pattern to show group membership. A number of Akwapim people may wear the identical patterned cloth to show membership of a church fellowship, to show their relationship to the deceased at a funeral, or to express political support or indirect protest in local or national politics. Those who are dressed alike demonstrate a 'rhetoric of unity'; such a 'uniform' is a way to visibly extend oneself beyond one's bodily boundaries (Ferme 2001). This may be intensely personal or it may be a way safely to express sentiments concerning local or national politics. When Nana Addo Dankwa III, the present Akwapim Omanhene, was enstooled in 1975, his supporters flaunted their victory vis-à-vis the opposition by wearing a celebratory blue and white wax-print cloth on which was printed 'I told you so' (*meka kyerɛ wo*). In 1992 when Fl. Lt J. J. Rawlings was running for office as President of Ghana, he went to Kumase (where many Asante were opposed to him) and he was given an abrafo's *batakari*. Abrafo are the court executioners. Some thought he should have refused it because it is the duty of abrafo to kill people. The implication was 'he who wears the smock kills people'. Rawlings later went to Asante-Mampong, and the whole town appeared dressed in ɔkɔben (plain red funerary cloth). This was unexpected – after all, a visit of the head of state should be a happy occasion, so why should they mourn? The chief of the town said to him, 'Oh, we did not know you were coming, we are in mourning'. Left unspoken was the object of that mourning – General Afrifa, whom Rawlings had executed by firing squad, together with two other heads of state and five other generals, in June 1979.[11]

Some wax-prints with geometric or naturalistic patterns have simple descriptive names. These names may or may not have a direct relationship to the design. Some examples include: Christmas box (*Buronya adaka*); good woman (*ɔbaa pa*); Fatia's pen (a reference to Nkrumah's wife: the design looks like a pen or pencil); comb; corn and groundnuts; tomatoes; fan; Felicia (a woman's name); Ghana rice (written on it in English); cassava; the pole of an iron bed; mango leaf; sword (*afoa*); fish bones (*sire dompe*); guinea fowls; bamboo; knee; cows' eyes; eyebrow; bottom of a snail; *Nifa nifa* ('right-right': a reference to the change from left-hand to right-hand driving); yam leaves; Hausa writing (Arabic script); the back of a tortoise; cell-phone.

Other wax-prints commemorate topical events, such as the fiftieth anniversary of the Presbyterian Church of Ghana, a national political movement, or a funeral. Some of these cloths have photo-offset portraits as part

Figure 19.1   Wax-print cloths that bear proverbial names. Abiriw-Akwapim 1987

of their design. Some cloths, but not all, have printed messages in English or Twi as well as a portrait. One wax-print that depicts an elephant with two lions on its back (animals symbolic of royal power) has the message 'Be patient and you will see [what happens]' written on it in Twi, Ga and Ewe. Wearing cloth with commemorative patterns is not a recent practice. In 1957, when Nana Kwame Fori (r. 1944–52; 1958–74) was brought back as Omanhene after having been destooled, everyone in Akropong wore a cloth with his portrait printed on it during the annual Odwira festival to show their support.

THE METAPHOR OF CLOTH AS MEANING

Some wax-print cloths bear proverbial names, with or without the accompaniment of short written texts.[12] Not all of the metaphoric names of cloth are closely related to the design. And the names given to particular patterns in Akwapim are not always called the same elsewhere in Ghana. In northern Ghana, for example, cloth with a pattern of flying birds is called 'gossip flies'; in Akwapim the same cloth is named 'money flies'. According to Domowitz (1992: 87), cloth known as 'co-wife rivalry is like cow dung' in the Anyi region of Côte d'Ivoire is known as 'gramophone record' across the border in Ghana. Kwawu and Ga market women who sell cloth give it a name in order to attract customers. Old and new prints differ, but some popular ones are reprinted, with minor colour changes. Some designs are mostly for

Figure 19.2 Cloth with *Ntoboase ma nko nim* ('Be patient and you will know') written in Twi (and elsewhere on the cloth in two other languages: Ga and Ewe).

women, but not exclusively so. Certain prints from the colonial days, called *Otopa* and *Yaw Donkor*, both men's names, are mainly worn by men. Sometimes it is simply a matter of colour: women tend to like brighter, lighter colours. Most people are careful with their cloth and wear it for years. Occasionally, when a well-known wax-print is no longer available on the market, the same name may be given to a different design or even to a modern batik that it resembles.

Cloths with proverbial names are used strategically by both men and women in a form of oblique communication. The messages are taken seriously by the sender and receiver, but as they are indirect and non-verbal, they can be more polite – and therefore safer – than direct verbal confrontation. A woman, for example, may wear a cloth with a positive name to signal to a male admirer; or a co-wife may fight with her 'rival' by donning a cloth with a name expressing a veiled threat. Because the threat is indirect, she can state her opinion with impunity: if accused, she can reply: 'Is that directed at you? Did I say that?' Tensions often exist between co-wives (*akorafo*), as the name, which also means 'rival', suggests. A woman who thinks her co-wife hates her and no matter what kindness she shows her will never be satisfied, may buy a cloth to 'say' this, such as *ɔtan nnim akorɔkorɔ* ('Hatred does not mind pampering/does not know kindness'). A similar sentiment is expressed in the proverb named cloth *ɔtan nni aduru* ('There is no medicine for hatred'; i.e. if someone hates you, nothing will change his

Figure 19.3   *Okyeame* with linguist staff wearing cloth called 'If you are going to gossip ...' Akwamu 1987

opinion). Or she may wear one called *huhu huhu nyeme hu* ('You speak or gossip about someone in an undertone, a whisper, but your *huhu* (alarm, apprehension) doesn't frighten me').

An extremely old, blind and delightfully obstreperous senior woman (*aberewatia*) who was creating trouble for her whole lineage in Akropong once asked me to buy her a cloth called *Afe bi ye asiane* ('Some years are dangerous/risky/unfortunate'). I did. On another occasion I bought for myself a cloth with an over-all pattern of Akan stools called 'If you are going to gossip, pull up a stool' and wore it when I went to visit an elder I knew had been gossiping about me. I spoke about these metaphoric cloth names with the Apagyahene of the patrilineal town of Abiriw when he was disputing with the chiefs in his town and also litigating with his siblings – of whom there were fifty in number, as his father had been a very wealthy 'fetish' priest with many wives. Illustratively, he said,

Figure 19.4   Apagyahene of Abiriw wearing cloth called *Onyame Bekyere*.
Abiriw-Akwapim 1991

My father had many wives – too many wives. My brothers and sisters and I cannot agree on anything. There is always envy and jealousy. Everyone is looting the property to take to his mother's house. When I go to court [to litigate with my brothers] I will wear a cloth called *Wokɔ aware a bisa* ['If you are going to marry, ask].[13] It means 'Look at what my father's marriages have done. If you are going to marry, ask first, otherwise you will make a mistake to your eternal regret'. Or else, I will wear a cloth called *Nyame Bekyere* ['God will say/God determines everything'].[14] This will say to my brothers, 'You hate me and plan to kill me, but whatever you do, it is God who will decide'. On another day [in court] I will wear a cloth with a large floral print called *Ahene paa nka saa* ['Precious beads don't make noise']. Our women wear beads at their waist: those who wear good beads, valuable ones, when they walk the beads do not make sounds; but those beads made with mere glass, any movement and you can hear them. This means [metaphorically] that I need not say I am Asifu's son [i.e. that I am legitimate]. I need not say it. Anybody who knew my father will acknowledge it. I will not say it [a royal, *odehye*, need not brag; he should be humble and not show off.] But my brother [with whom I am litigating] is struggling! He is struggling to announce he is Asifu's son [and he is not].

He continued,

One day I want to buy a cloth called *Onipa nni aye* ['Ingratitude of man'].[15] I want to buy it because of the Alabiri people [the royal lineage of the town]. My father did so much for them, even buying a palanquin for the chief, and they have forgotten it and are now trying to expel me, Asifu's son, from the town. I shall buy this cloth and send it to the palace: I'll wear it to the palace. If they had it today at the market, I would have had it sewn up right there in the market and worn it.

Another cloth with a good name is *Okonkonsani bɛbrɛ* ['A betrayer will be tired'] which means a hypocrite or liar will suffer in life. If I were to wear this cloth, my [treacherous] cousin would know why. If that is not available, then I should like to buy one with a pattern of two gourds, one of which is open and one closed. It is called *Kata wo dɛɛ so* and indirectly suggests you conceal your secrets but expose mine.[16] This is because of those Asifu children [his paternal siblings]. They are slandering my name and yet they do worse [things]. If I wear this cloth to my village where they are saying bad things about me, they know they are saying it, it is no secret, and so I will be purposely wearing it to tease them. For outsiders [i.e. non-family members], it does not concern them; they don't care: the colour is nice, the pattern is too, so I wear it.

Some other examples include: (1) 'Marriage is not like corn' (*Aware nte se aburow*). This cloth depicts an ear of corn (maize). The implication is that if men were like corn, you could pull back the husk and examine the kernels before you bought it. Another cloth which expresses a similar sentiment has a design of peanuts (ground nuts) and is called 'Marriage is not like peanuts' (*Aware nte se nkate*). (2) 'Death's ladder' (*Owu antweri*). The name of this funeral cloth is an abbreviation of the expression 'one does not climb death's ladder alone'; the reference is to suffering and injustice. The pattern is abstract. (3) 'Cow dung' (*Nantwi bi*). The name implies that co-wife rivalry is like cow dung – the top is dry from the sun, the inside is sticky and moist. It means that you see your co-wife, a 'rival', and laugh and behave as if you like her, but deep down, you don't. (4) 'A royal does not cry' (*ɔdehye nsu*). This expression is commonly used to comfort someone, especially a man who is weeping.

Other names include 'Jealousy' (*ɔtan hunu*: i.e. hatred for nothing); 'Others are well off' (*Obi te yeye*) referring to the injustice of one's lot in life; 'Good living causes forgetfulness/makes people careless' (*Ntra yie ma awerefiri*); 'You've taken me like a snail' (*Wofa me nwaw*) alluding to the characteristics of a snail that cannot talk, so if your husband does not treat you well, you are like a snail; 'If a tree is alone in the forest, it will fall' (*Dua koro gye mframa a ebu*) suggesting that when there are family troubles, they will all come to you – if you are alone without your family to help, you will fall; and 'I am more beautiful than my rival' (*Me ho yɛ fɛ kyɛn me kora*).

Figure 19.5   Apagyahene of Abiriw wearing cloth called *Kata wo dee so*.
Akropong-Akwapim

OTHER GENRES: RESPONSES GIVEN BY A MOTHER TO HER CHILD

If you hear someone's name, you know where he comes from
Akropong elder, 1978

People's names show membership in particular social groups, and localize such membership in the individual. They are possessions, rights to which are bestowed on them by their guardians. Every Akropong person has a number of names that reflect the day of the week on which he or she was born, the group of patrifiliation, and so on. Soon after birth, a public naming rite (*abadinto*) is performed and the child becomes a social person.[17] The infant is given a *kra din* or 'soul' name, indicating the day on which he or she said goodbye to God. Stylized responses (*nnyeso*) are associated with this name, but are rarely used; and appellations (*mmran, mmrane* or *nsabrane*), though rarely heard, may be used to coax a child, flatter a loved one, cajole or admire. At the same naming ceremony, a family name (*din pa*: lit. 'good name') is given by the father, and the baby is bathed with herbs appropriate to his group of patrifiliation (*agyabosom*). Each *agyabosom* has a stock of names used only by its own members. Formalized praise-names (*mmran*) associated with the *din pa* are loosely mythico-historical and used to aggrandize and salute men (or less often women) and to enhance their reputation. Stylized responses for *din pa* follow greetings; as they require knowledge by the addressee of the greeter's social heritage, they reiterate the relationship between the greeter and greeted.[18]

In matrilineal Akropong in the early twentieth century, it was common for a mother troubled by a traumatic experience to demand of her young child that he or she respond to her every call by reciting a particular proverb (Gilbert 2006). The child was taught to reply in this way all her life. This stylized response (*tete nnyeso*) was a complex coded message that concretized the mother's emotion, named and thus exposed it, but did so in a safe way. Most of the responses alluded to an event or predicament – such as death, extreme poverty, hardship, envy, neighbourly spite. The response was given with no explanation, and the child was told to answer in this way to everybody, automatically. Few children knew the specific incident to which his/her response referred, but the general meaning could be understood by anyone. This suggests the meaning was of direct relevance to the mother as a means to deal (indirectly) with a disruptive event in her life.

The child was used as an instrument to voice what the mother wanted to voice but preferred not to voice. It was both a projection and a disavowal of the mother's anguished emotions. The mother, by using her child to remind her of an experience of 'unspeakable' anguish in her past, kept it alive at the same time. This proverbial response might also be a way to ward off something the mother feared or dreaded, a repetitive ritualized distancing mechanism to protect her or her matrilineal descendants. Examples include: *Ensa me yam*: 'It will never be finished' (*ensa*: exhausted, *yam*: womb); *Owu yɛ nya*: 'Death gets hold of you/death makes people ashamed';[19] *Owu agye me nim*: 'Death has seized my glory'; *Ye aboa yie*: 'Do good to an animal (they are more grateful than men)'; *Afisem*: 'Domestic issue'; *Se ebewie (Onyame na onim)*: 'How it will end, (god only knows)'; *Minni bi reba*: 'I have no one to come'; *ɛyɛ sɛ yɛ dɔ wo*: 'It seems they love you (but you should hear what they say about you)'. This form of response is no longer performed in Akropong

I suggest the use of named wax-print cloth fulfils much the same function as did these responses spoken by a child that safely recalled her mother's unsettled sentiments. These scripted responses, the named cloth, and the poetic names to be discussed below are not just aesthetic devices or literary representations. They are metaphors which enable an individual safely to comment upon or name the contradictions, unpredictability and loneliness of life, and the imagination of his or her incalculable fate. They are expressions of stories within stories and they place a person in the flux of history. Their art is to make narrative order out of confusion; to make sense out of a troubled or troublesome life. They are reactions to the disappointments, failures, greed, persecution and selfish search for power and pleasure encountered in everyday life. I turn now to these other categories of names that are extensions of individual or corporate personhood.

SLAVE, PET AND VILLAGE NAMES

The British outlawed the slave trade in 1807 but domestic slavery continued after this and informally some aspects continued until the late twentieth century. Slaves and war captives once comprised nearly half the population of Akropong, though they were gradually absorbed into the clans (*abusua*) of their owners. Akropong people distinguish between *odonko* (pl. *nnonkofo*, from *odo*: he has joined us, *nko*: not go back) and *ofie nipa* (house person). *Nnonko* were slaves who were purchased, mostly from northern Ghana. The children of *nnonko* were *ofie nipa*, as were the children of a union between an *odonko* and an *ofie nipa*. Such children take the *abusua* of the person they serve, their owner, and the *agyabosom* of their father or master; in greeting they use the reply of their master. Slaves from the north, in fact, would not have an *agyabosom*, but when they had lived in a house for many years, they would take the *agyabosom* of their owner, in the same way as a slave of the king would take the king's response. Children of a union between an *odonko* woman and a free male owner are non-inheritors.

An *odonko* was given a day name (*kra din*) corresponding to the day of the week on which he arrived in Akropong from the north because on that day he was symbolically reborn. Slaves from the north were not given a paternal name (*din pa*) but special proverbial names which reflected the feelings or experiences of the owner who bestowed the name. Examples of such names include *Pɛ mmɔne*: 'Wish evil' (i.e. someone wishes you ill); *Onyame asɛm*: '(What happened is) God's way'; *Maniasa*: 'They (trusted ones) are all gone'; *Obideɛ aba*: 'Someone's troubles have come'. Additional slave names include *Di asɛmpa*: 'Do good deeds'; *Ade yɛ onipa ya(w)*: 'Things are painful to people', i.e. people are jealous about other people's success; *Nyankwa ɛyɛ*: 'Receiving life is good', i.e. everyone is useful, no matter his faults; *Nna ɛba*: 'Days are coming', i.e. days are coming when a rich man will be poor, when a poor man will be rich, when a slave will be king, when a royal will be a slave; *Onipa pɛ nnɛ*: 'Man likes today (and forgets what will happen tomorrow)'.

If a woman's children all died before reaching one week of age, her next born formerly would be given a slave name and his face would be cicatrized like that of a northerner (i.e. a slave). In so doing, the mother metaphorically took away her child's identity; she 'killed' him, so that he would live. Here the 'name' was scarification at birth; no proper name (*din pa*) was given to the child or it was 'reserved' as a hidden name. The child was told to answer to a proverbial name, such as *Kwame Boame*: 'Help me' (Kwame: Saturday-born day name, *boa*: help, *me*: me); *ɔhyɛ brɛ*: 'Difficult to train' (*ohye*: force, *bre*: tired; i.e. you force repeatedly and it makes you tired, as in someone who is always being given instructions yet has no intelligence to follow them); *Suro onipa*: 'Fear people'; *Onyame bedi*: 'God will decide/deal with it'; *Ma wo ani nso ade*: 'Be humble/grateful', literally, let your eyes be pleased with something; *Kae dabi*: 'Remember that day'. For this last name, ingratitude is implied, as in 'Remember what my father/mother did for you'.

By bestowing a name on her child that refers to a social death, the mother refers to it in miniature and she gives what Frazer calls a 'mock calamity', a mock death, which is returned to her to remove the death from the child. The mother wards off something she fears by referring to it. I suggest that a mock calamity can be spoken and that these names are possessions, objects to be exchanged. The proverbial name is like an image, and words are being used as things.

In the past, pets such as pigs or cats were given similar kinds of names, with no humour implied. An elderly woman, unhappy because she did not have a child, named her pig *Fa ma Onyame* ('Give it to God'). An elderly man I knew named his cat *Efiɛ mu (asɛm dɔɔ so)* ('Matters in the house are many'), referring to domestic troubles. Naming pets in this way turns the animals into quasi-people. But pets, slaves and children are not complete persons and may all be considered 'objects' which are 'owned' and associated with ambiguous attitudes.

Finally, while all Akwapim towns have proverbial appellations (*mmran*) or praise poems with historical referents, in the early twentieth century during a time of factional turmoil, some farming villages became places of exile and were renamed to express protest against the opposition royal line. When Nana Kwasi Akuffo (r. 1895–1907) became king, those in the opposing faction withheld their support and stayed in their village rather than coming to Akropong. They named their village *Asɛmpanaɛyɛ* ('Good deeds are good'), implying that they stayed away from Akropong because of the king's bad behaviour. Later, after Nana Kwasi Akuffo was destooled and exiled to a town called Sansami, near Nsawam, his supporters renamed the town *Mogyabiyedom*: 'Some blood (matrikin) are enemies', i.e. some relatives are opponents. Those in the opposition faction continued to call the town Sansami.

CONCLUSION: DIFFERENT GENRES BRIDGED BY PROVERBS

Cloth in Akwapim is a valuable object that may be inherited or used in gift exchange; it is also an extension of the person who owns or wears it. The colour of the cloth designates the social self and indicates whether an event is happy or sad. But the names of wax-print cloth are multi-layered and may be used to express aspects of the wearer's inner or personal self. These names resemble the proverbial names given to pets, villages and slaves – also extensions of their owners and indeed owned and sometimes exchanged. These names also resemble the proverbial responses scripted for a child by a distressed mother. Cloth names thus are linked to the recognition of status and to change in status, but also have a subjective nature.

In all these genres a similar dynamic occurs, the key to which is repetition leading to healing or some form of catharsis. While Akropong people try to keep the conflicts, jealousies and treacheries of everyday life below the surface, one does not have to suffer passively. Names for cloth, pets, villages and children provide a medium for the sufferer to shift from passive to active, from one who is acted upon to one who does the acting, and they allow the actor to do it with impunity.

Cloth in Akwapim is worn by a 'silent actor' (Barber 1989)[20] to challenge, tease or make ambiguous statements about an 'other'. The proverbial responses scripted by a mother for her child twist back onto her, the originator of the response. While wax-print is meant to be 'read' and interpreted, the wearer cannot be certain of its reception: the viewer may – and indeed often does – deny that the message is understood. Similarly, the speaker of the response may not know the specific meaning of the words he repeats, but this does not deny the importance of the act for its creator, or for the relationship that is implied in the 'social drama'. The meaning of this silent conversation 'becomes clear through the structure of social relations in which it inheres and which it represents in dramatic form' (Barber 1989: 15). The distinction, simultaneously merged and distinguished, between self and speaker and between originator and receiver is critical.

NOTES

1. Research for this essay was done in the late 1970s and mid to late 1980s supported by the School of Oriental and African Studies of the University of London and by a Social Science Research Council grant. Some of the material was presented in 1988 at Stanford University, in 1995 in Cologne and in 1996 as 'Unspeakable events: Akwapim verbal strategies' at the XIIth Satterthwaite Colloquium on African Ritual and Religion. I am grateful to Gillian Gillison, Barbara Bianco, Susan Drucker-Brown and J. D.Y. Peel who helped me to clarify issues in these earlier versions. In Ghana I wish to thank Lydia Adi and the late B. E. Ofori in Akropong and Nana Asifu Yao Okoamankran, Apagyahene of Abiriw, for their help and friendship.

2. See Wendl 2001 on the link between photography and textile communication in Ghana.

3. *Adinkra* is hand-stamped cloth worn for funerals by men, not women. The meaning of the word is 'separation, to say goodbye'. It seems to have been introduced to Akwapim in the mid-nineteenth century from Asante. *Kuntunkuni* is dyed brown cloth or black with black *adinkra* stamps. *Birisi* is plain black cloth without design, and may be made by the Akosombo or Tema textile factory. *ɔkɔben* is red or ochre coloured cloth, dyed with red clay (*ntwoma*) and kola nut.

4. On *kente*, see Rattray 1927 and Ross 1998. Formerly among the Asante, certain patterns could be worn only by the king.

5. European textiles have been traded to West Africa since the twelfth century. See Nielsen (1979) for a good historical overview of European batik made for export to West Africa and for a description of the technical aspects of wax-print (in which the design is applied with hot wax on both sides of the cotton fabric) and non wax-print (roller print) cloth.

6. Gift exchange between people or for deities: in the 1980s at shrines in northern Ghana, – for example, Atongo in Tenzugu – a poor man from the south with little money might be asked to 'sacrifice' his cloth.

7. In the 1970s to 1990s, before a corpse was put in the coffin, the coffin was spread with mats (*mpa kɛtɛ*), a small blanket (*okuntu*) was placed on top and then a small white bed sheet and a pillow with pillow case. A sack of white calico was also included containing a comb, soap, sponge, towels, lime (deodorant) and pomade (*nku*) for the deceased to use on his journey.

8. A small strip of the cloth given to the deceased by his wife will be wrapped around his wrist.

9. The original use of these Fulani wool blankets (*khasa*), changes when they are brought to southern Ghana (see Gilbert 1993b).

10. Smocks are also worn by priests (*ɔbosomfoo*) and labourers. *Batakari* became almost a uniform during Nkrumah's time – they were associated with labourers (i.e. northerners).

11. Cf. Hess 2006: 22 on the wearing of cloth by the Asante to express political opposition to Nkrumah.

12. For names of wax-print cloth in Cote d'Ivoire and Ghana, see also Domowitz 1992; Toure 1985; Yankah 1989: 331–3, and 1995: 81–3; Wendl 2001.

13. The name of this cloth ('If you are going to marry, inquire first') refers to domestic strife. The idea is that you should look before you leap. The Apagyahene did wear this cloth to court – after consulting the medium (*ɔkɔmfo*) for the deity Nana Tongo. In the 1980s I knew a very poor Akropong woman who was around forty years old and the mother of seven daughters. Each of her three husbands had died or deserted her. When her eldest daughter became pregnant by the son of the Presbyterian pastor and the boy refused to acknowledge paternity, she bought this cloth in disgust and despair. She did not consider the pattern to be very beautiful, but it was an old design with a well-known name which provided a way to safely comment upon the unfortunate situation.

14. *Nyame bɛkyerɛ* is printed on the cloth. The implied meaning is consolation.

15. *Nnipa nni aye* is written on the cloth. It means literally, 'People are not good.' It suggests the ingratitude of man, or refers to someone who did something good and received no reward. The design shows someone drowning in the sea with a shark.

16. *Kata wo dee so* ('Open for me, closed for you'). The design shows open and closed calabashes and suggests that you gossip about me, but do not tell your own

secrets. This cloth name is taken from a popular song with the words 'Close yours, open mine; what about you? You are just like me' (*obi n'asɛm na aba, na woka no dɔkɔ dɔkɔ na woɛ, wonsu saa ara?*), 'Somebody's problem is now at stake and you discuss it sweetly. What about? (You are also just like that person)'.

17. The naming rite can be done at any time, even as much as three months after the birth. The 'out-dooring' rite (*tan fi*, from *tan tan* 'filthy thing'), on the other hand, must be on the eighth day after the child is born. At this time the infant is brought out from the room where he was secluded with the mother. The mother is given a fowl by her parents, if the infant's father is irresponsible and does not provide one: for a boy it is a cockerel, for a girl a hen.

18. Those born on the same day of the week are believed to share an affinity: they have the same *kra* (soul) and the same name, for example all Wednesday-born males are called Kwaku and all Wednesday-born females are Akua, and so on. Parts of the Akan naming system have been previously described (Field 1948; Opoku 1973; Akuffo 1950; Christaller 1933) but not the proverbial responses given by a mother to her child, nor the analogous names for slaves, pets and villages.

19. An Adenkum dance group in early twentieth-century Akropong had a song whose lyrics expressed a similar sentiment to this response: 'Granddaughter of one-who-has-none (*nnibi nana*) / Death has made people jeer at me / Death has made the enemy hear of me / Death has given me to the one who wants my downfall / Death has made me be alone'.

20. Barber explains that *oriki* are a way of re-experiencing the past and re-integrating it into the present in a 'very specific, intense and heightened form of dialogue, in which the silent partner is as crucial as the speaker' (1989: 14–15).

REFERENCES

Akuffo, B. S. (1950), *Tete Akorae*. Accra: n.p.

Barber, Karen (1989), 'Interpreting oriki as history and as literature'. In Karen Barber and P. F. de Moraes Farias (eds), *Discourse and its Disguises: The Interpretation of African Oral Texts*. Birmingham University Africa Studies Series I. Birmingham: Centre of West African Studies, pp. 13–23.

— (1991) 'Multiple Discourses in Yoruba Oral Literature'. In P. T. W. Baxter and Richard Fardon (eds), *Voice, Genre, Text: Anthropological Essays in Africa and Beyond*. Bulletin of the John Rylands University Library of Manchester, 73, no. 3, pp. 11–23.

Christaller, J. G. (1933), *Dictionary of the Asante and Fante Language Called Tshi (Twi)*. Second rev. edn. Basel: Basel Evangelical Missionary Society.

Domowitz, Susan (1992), 'Wearing Proverbs: Anyi Names for Printed Factory Cloth. *African Arts*, XXV, no. 3, pp. 82–7, 104.

Field, M. J. (1948), *Akim-Kotoku: An Oman of the Gold Coast*. London: The Crown Agents for the Colonies.

Ferme, Mariane C. (2001), *The Underneath of Things: Violence, History, and the Everyday in Sierra Leone*. Berkeley: University of California Press.

Gilbert, Michelle (1993a), 'The Cimmerian Darkness of Intrigue: Queen Mothers, Christianity, and Truth in Akuapem History'. *Journal of Religion in Africa*, 22, no. 1.

— (1993b), 'The Leopard Who Sleeps in a Basket: Akuapem Secrecy in Everyday Life and Royal Metaphor'. In Mary H. Nooter (ed.), *Secrecy: African Art That Conceals and Reveals*. New York: Museum for African Art, pp. 12–139.

— (1994), 'Aesthetic Strategies: The Politics of a Royal Ritual'. *Africa*, 64, no. 1, pp. 99–125.

— (2006), 'The Past Can Never Be Settled'. Paper delivered at the Sites of Memory colloquium at Harvard University, Cambridge.

Hess, Janet (2006), 'Spectacular Nation: Nkrumahist Art and Resistance Iconography in the Independence Era'. *African Arts*, 39, no. 1, pp. 16–25, 91.

Irvine, Judith T. (1990), 'Registering Affect: Heteroglossia in the Linguistic Expression of Emotion'. In Catherine A. Lutz and Lila Abu-Lughod (eds), *Language and the Politics of Emotion*. Cambridge: Cambridge University Press, pp. 126–60.

Lakoff, George and Mark Johnson (1980), *Metaphors We Live By*. Chicago: University of Chicago Press.

Nielsen, Ruth (1979), 'The History and Development of Wax-Printed Textiles Intended for West Africa and Zaire'. In Justine Cordwell and Ronald Schwartz (eds), *The Fabric of Culture: The Anthropology of Culture and Adornment*. The Hague: Mouton, pp. 467–494.

Opoku, A. A. (1973), *Obi Kyere*. Tema-Accra, Ghana: Ghana Publishing Corporation.

Rattray, R. S. (1927), *Religion and Art in Ashanti*. Oxford: Clarendon Press.

Ross, Doran (1998), *Wrapped in Pride: Ghanaian Kente and African American Identity*. Los Angeles: UCLA Fowler Museum of Cultural History.

Simmel, G. (1950), *The Sociology of Georg Simmel*. Trans. K. H. Wolf. New York: Free Press.

Touré, Abdou (1985), *Les Petits Métiers à Abidjan*. Paris: Karthala.

Wendl, Tobias (2001), 'Entangled Traditions: Photography and the History of Media in Southern Ghana'. *Res*, 39, pp. 78–101.

Yankah, Kwesi (1989), 'Proverbs: The Aesthetics of Traditional Communication'. *Research in African Literature* 20, no. 2, pp. 325–46.

— (1995), *Speaking for the Chief: Okyeame and the Politics of Akan Royal Oratory*. Bloomington and Indianapolis: Indiana University Press.

MUSEUMS IN AFRICA

The word 'museum' is derived from the Greek word *mouseion*. In ancient Greece, the *mouseion* was the temple of the muses, the goddesses of the arts and sciences, upon whom writers called for inspiration before beginning to work. Thus, as originally conceived, the *mouseion* implied an environment suited to creative inspiration. By about 300 BC, this word was used to designate a library and research area in Alexandria, Egypt. In other words, the earliest known museum in the modern sense of the term was actually built in Africa.

Modern museums also have their roots in the private collections amassed during the medieval era by European royalty and the church, and by rich merchants and noblemen. The Renaissance was a time in which interest in antiquities and in the natural worlds reached its peak, and collections tended to take the form of 'cabinets of curiosities' containing, for instance, paintings and sculptures, as well as natural specimens such as stuffed animals and seashells. Even today, many people still regard museums as places where rare or strange things are housed.

According to the International Council of Museums (ICOM), the modern museum is an institution which 'acquires, conserves, researches, communicates, and exhibits, for purposes of study, education, and enjoyment, material evidence of people and their environment' (cited in Pye 2001: 14). This definition implies that a museum has the dual responsibility of conserving the material objects in its custody and facilitating their use. The museum is also responsible for the preservation of the objects in its collections, and for communicating about those collections to the broader public through a variety of activities, ranging from static display to offering its patrons interactive access.

The terms 'preservation' and 'conservation' are generally used interchangeably, although some authorities (for example, Pye 2001) feel that the two terms are technically different. On the other hand, museum objects are studied by researchers, as well as by school children and college students.

Finally, according to Hooper-Greenhill (1994: 140), 'communication as a major museum function includes those activities that attract visitors to the museum (publicity and marketing), investigate their needs (research and education), and provide for their intellectual needs (education and entertainment)'. These three functions are linked together in an intricate relationship.

HISTORICAL DEVELOPMENT OF MUSEUMS IN AFRICA

The concept of a museum as a space where people can go for inspiration or where only a select few are permitted to enter is not new to Africa. As A. T. Adedze has pointed out:

> Family heads in various parts of Africa owned storehouses that contained the valuables of the ancestors, a focus point of respect and inspiration for the entire family. As their European counterparts, access to these valuables is restricted to acquaintances and connoisseurs. (1992: 167)

Jean-Baptiste Kiethega shares this viewpoint, adding:

> In Africa . . . we were able to observe that, in the period preceding colonization, collections of desacralized objects were constituted. Some kings had collections of diverse objects which, without being open to the public, were nevertheless museums. It was thus that King Ruwanika of Bweranyange in Tanzania held a collection of figurines of forged iron. The collection and safeguarding of objects of art and precious goods has been practised in traditional societies. (1992: 274)

However, the museums as we know them today were introduced in Africa as part of the colonial process. The first collections were assembled in schools and mission stations with the objective of ethnographic conservation, study and research from a strictly European perspective. The colonial administrations started looking for objects to present as part of large colonial and universal exhibitions.

In the Maghreb, modern museums were introduced in the nineteenth century in Algeria and Libya. The earliest were archaeological museums whose collections generally belonged to the classical era. Once established, these museums served a public consisting of scholars and enlightened amateurs. On the other hand, in Morocco, the earliest museums housed ethnographic collections which still form the major holdings of most museums in that country. The earliest of these institutions date back to 1915. The colonial government established the indigenous Arts Services in each region to take charge of the local museums. Each museum was charged with the responsibility of encouraging the development of crafts.

Writing of Morocco, A. Amahan has noted that 'the collected objects were exhibited essentially for two types of public: A professional public composed of the craftsmen and their instructors, and an exclusively foreign public of potential buyers' (1992: 281). It can be seen from this that, right from its creation, the museum in Morocco had the limited purpose of promoting handicrafts and encouraging foreign visitors to discover the country's antiquity. Thence, the institution was steadily directed towards a foreign public, that is, it catered for tourists from abroad and local expatriate settlers.

The principles guiding the selection and display of objects in the colonial museums were those in vogue in Europe. This was to be expected, since the people in charge of these museums knew nothing else. In fact, even the buildings constructed to house these collections imitated European palatial and monumental designs, thus embodying the munificence of the colonial governors. Furthermore, in a good number of cases, the museums were initially housed in government buildings.

Apart from cultural objects, colonialists, like their brethren at home, were also interested in natural history. Darwin's theory of evolution and the controversies that it generated had strongly affected natural history museums in Europe, and these were already experiencing rapid growth. This interest spread quite rapidly throughout the world in the nineteenth century, and natural history museums were established in many European cities, and in Canada, Australia, New Zealand, India, Sri Lanka, South America and South Africa (Pye 2001). Apart from South Africa, newly colonized countries in Africa with high European populations, for example, Kenya and Zimbabwe, also developed an interest in the establishment of natural history museums. Thus, in Kenya, the seeds for the current national museum in Nairobi were planted in 1909 by the East African Natural History Society. At their annual general meeting, the members agreed on the need for premises in which to store and exhibit their specimens, consisting of plants, insects, reptiles, mammals and cultural objects. In Zimbabwe, the Natural History Museum in Bulawayo was also founded on natural history specimens.

Starting from the second decade of the twentieth century, countries rich in paleontological and archaeological materials started adding these items to their museum collections. This was the case with Kenya, South Africa, Tanzania and Zambia. These materials also found their way into the local museums, because the professionals carrying out the investigations were associated with those institutions. The new collections were used for exhibits, as well as for strengthening the positions of the museums as centres of research and education. These roles became even more important in the immediate post-independence period, as the new nation states struggled to awaken people's interest in their own, unique cultural heritage and expand their traditional arts and crafts.

It is a truism that the material objects of a people are a manifestation of their way of life. By studying these objects, we gain insights into how a particular group of people interact with both their social and physical environments. In other words, a study of such objects enables us to understand why a particular community behaves the way it does. Unfortunately, however, throughout the colonial period, well-developed museums were of little value, significance or benefit to the local people. As Kiethega has vividly put it:

> In the colonies, museums were constructed in the capitals in order to present a cultural shortcut to different countries to foreigners, to tourists, and mostly to the administrative bourgeoisie and colonial businessmen. The colonial museum was a warehouse without any connection to its environment, which it ignored. (Kiethega 1992: 274)

In general, therefore, museums strove to be centres of excellence for foreigners. The locals were not involved in decisions regarding exhibitions or interpretations of the objects. There were no native scientists working in these museums, and no efforts were made to train the locals. The locals were only employed in subservient and non-professional positions, working as artisans or as mere collectors of scientific specimens. All these things combined to lead the local peoples to assume that museums were only meant for the benefit of foreigners.

CHANGES IN THE POSTCOLONIAL ERA

Fundamental political and social changes took place on the continent in the immediate postcolonial period. These changes brought about a fresh role for African museums, one which reflected the growing sense of cultural identity on the part of the continent's peoples and their desire to assemble and reconstruct a testimony of their indigenous civilizations. In Zimbabwe, for example, the regional museums developed a system of loaning materials to one another. This provided a great opportunity to people in the various parts of the country to see what might be available in their locality. By utilizing the collections in this way, the museums in Zimbabwe educated and wove the rope of history into the present, so that the past is well linked with the present for the benefit of present and future generations. In today's museums, this tradition lives on.

Most of the newly independent governments indigenized the management and administration of their museums, to make them more responsive to the national needs. However, in a few cases, the status quo was maintained. In such cases, the indigenous peoples were given only subordinate roles in the management and administration of museums. Kenya is a good example of this. It took almost twenty-seven years for the first indigenous person to be appointed the chief executive of the National Museums of Kenya. Unfortunately, this was to have disastrous consequences for the institution.

The newly independent governments also realized the need for new legislative and institutional frameworks to manage the heritage held in the museums. Existing laws were reviewed, although in many cases the new laws were, by and large, replicas of previous ones. In some cases, the laws set up museums with the mandate of caring for both the movable and immovable heritage. Examples here include Botswana, Kenya, Nigeria and Zimbabwe. In other cases, museums were only mandated to manage the movable heritage, whilst the immovable heritage was put in the hands of departments of antiquities. Malawi, Namibia, South Africa, Tanzania, Uganda and Zambia are some of the countries that followed this route. In most cases, the antiquities are under the control of government departments, which operate just like any other governmental departments.

The postcolonial period also led to the expansion of museums in many African countries. New museums were opened and some were constructed at the regional level. For example, the Malian government came up with the policy of establishing eight regional museums in 1976. Each museum was to focus on a specific theme of interest to the people of the region in which it is located. In Kenya, eight regional museums, all of which are linked to the National Museum headquarters in Nairobi, have been established since independence. These regional museums are tailored to the needs of the local communities.

However, by the 1980s, many museums in Africa had become irrelevant. One of the reasons for this state of affairs is that the well-established museums had continued to strive to be centres of excellence to the outside world. In many cases, for example, in Kenya, their excellent research facilities were being used more by expatriate and visiting scientists than by the local scientists. Local museum professionals had no funds with which to carry out research. On the other hand, small local museums operated on very meagre budgets, which prevented them from injecting new ideas into their programmes. This, in turn, made them irrelevant to the communities they were created to serve. It is also worth pointing out that many African museums operated with no mission statements and lacked properly trained human power. For example, between 1960 and 1980, the National Museum of Mali in Bamako went through a very difficult time because of inappropriate facilities, insufficient technical expertise, and lack of financial means (Keita 1992: 191).

THE PRESENT SITUATION

Museums in Africa have come a long way from their humble beginnings to what they are today. However, their development has not been uniform throughout the continent. It would appear that countries with better-developed economies also happen to have better-developed museum systems than those with less-developed or struggling economies. Thus, countries like Nigeria, Kenya, South Africa, Namibia, Tunisia, Morocco and

Egypt have better-developed museums than, for example, Malawi, Tanzania and the Democratic Republic of Congo. In some cases, museums and their development have, like any other aspect of national development, suffered from political instability. This has happened in countries like Somalia, Ethiopia, Democratic Republic of Congo, Angola, Mozambique, Rwanda and Burundi.

African museums are also faced with the problem of inadequately trained human resources. Many museums still have curators with no proper professional qualifications. In Kenya, for example, most museum curators were originally employed as non-graduate education officers. As Jean-Aime Rakotoarisoa argues, this situation results in a total lack of innovation in the evaluation and presentation of the collections (Rakotoarisoa 1992). In a recent study of Fort Jesus Museum in Mombasa, Kenya, Annely C. Imasiku found that the five major exhibitions had not fully taken advantage of contemporary exhibition techniques, nor had they included in their exhibitions new research findings or familiar objects that the visitors could easily identify with (2005: 6).

This use of untrained museum workers contributes greatly to the deplorable situation of some of these museums. Such staff lack the necessary professional knowledge to define the museum vision and mission statements correctly and the skills to interpret these statements. According to M. Luhila, this has led to 'poorly documented and uninventoried collections; congested, dusty, infested, and disorganized storerooms; poor, uneducative, and *very permanent* exhibitions' (1992: 121, emphasis in the original).

There is no doubt, however, that, regardless of its status, the African museum is now an important national tool for development. One of the roles of the modern museum in Africa is the protection of the continent's heritage. Museums are not just custodians of the continent's cultural heritage – the archaeological, historical and ethnographic materials – but also of its natural heritage. Both constitute a very important database for research on the existence and survival of humankind, as well as preservation of the environment. Archaeological and paleontological specimens held by museums in eastern and southern Africa have contributed greatly to our knowledge of the biological and cultural evolution of our species. It is these specimens that have enabled scientists to argue convincingly that Africa is the cradle of humankind.

Using botanical remains, a good number of museums in Africa have begun to appreciate the role of indigenous plants in enhancing food security and in the treatment of certain diseases using medicinal plants. In this way, museums contribute to the improvement of the health status of their nationals. In addition, the Entomology Department of the National Museums of Kenya, in Nairobi, contributes to pest control by advising farmers on which kind of pests are good or bad for their crops. This it does in collaboration with the International Centre of Insect Physiology (ICIPE), which is also based in Nairobi. In this case, the museum can be seen to be playing an important role in the dissemination of information to farmers, which then can be used in the improvement of the country's agricultural production.

Secondly, museums in Africa now play an important role as educational tools. Wherever they are located, museums serve as important resources in the teaching of the natural and social sciences. As M. M. Tchanile has aptly put it:

> The museum teaches by placing the student in direct contact with objects under investigation. It relieves the teacher of having to develop theoretical material, and allows him to engage in active experimental pedagogy, one fundamental principle of which is 'a lesson about things without things is a wasted lesson'. (1992: 353)

This educational role is not just restricted to school parties. The collections of objects on exhibition in museums are, in fact, invaluable educational resources for any museum visitor, regardless of age, class, intellectual ability, or any other social criterion. Thus, children, young people, adults, researchers and casual observers, both local and foreign, may consult such objects without experiencing any social or intellectual barriers. In educating school groups and other local parties, museums play a crucial role in the development of education on the continent.

The third developmental role played by African museums today is that of communicating with the public through visits to the communities. This is done through outreach programmes. For example, in an effort to take museum materials from Gaborone to as many rural areas as possible, the National Museum of Botswana started a mobile museum in 1976. This museum is popularly known as *Pitse Ya Naga* ('the Zebra'), after the logo of the National Museum. The mobile museum carries a set of artifacts, slides, films, power generators and projectors, and gives illustrated lectures to children and their parents on the environment and cultures of Botswana. This programme has enabled many rural Botswanans to see or learn something about the museum, a chance they would not have had, had the National Museum remained rooted in the capital city.

In some cases, museums in Africa also act as community spaces, that is, as platforms from which living communities can express their feelings and expectations. As George Abungu has observed:

> with the disappearance of many of their cultural and spiritual spaces, communities are beginning to regard museums as alternative spaces for cultural activities and community performances. Thus museums have become spaces for dialogue and free expression that also offer opportunities for re-creating the 'better past'. (2002: 41)

Fort Jesus Museum in Mombasa, Kenya, provides an example of this. Every year, this museum hosts 'Swahili Night', a special event which is aimed at promoting the local Swahili culture through dress, music and dance, poetry recitals, storytelling, and the preparation and consumption of Swahili dishes. Plays are also staged. The occasion provides an opportunity for people to enjoy themselves and make merry, while at the same time educating the young ones about their cultural heritage.

Museums in Africa are also contributing to their national economies through the sale of tourism services. It is not surprising, therefore, that museums in Africa are often placed under the aegis of the ministry of tourism as one of its departments. Like museums the world over, museums in Africa serve as repositories of a country's cultural and natural heritage. This heritage tends to attract tourists, both local and foreign, who pay entrance fees and buy souvenirs. In addition, foreign tourists have to pay for their transport and accommodation. It is important to point out, however, that the more developed museums, such as those of South Africa, Nigeria, Egypt, Morocco and Kenya, generate more cash from tourism than those located in less developed nations. In Kenya, the government has recently launched a programme aimed at promoting cultural tourism. Although the living cultures will undoubtedly be the focus of this venture, there is no doubt that the country's museums are also going to play a significant role in attracting tourists to different parts of the country.

Finally, museums in Africa contribute to the enhancement of unity, either at the national or local level. As Tchanile (1992) argues, a museum is essentially a place of cultural diversity which enables the people to gain an understanding of their ancestral richness, to view the objects around which one might construct the history of a family, of a village, a canton, a commune, a region, or a nation. Thus, a regional museum can be regarded as a mirror of the region from which it hails, for it reflects the various elements of the local cultural mosaic and sets up a dialogue between them. In a sense, when one visits a regional museum, one is able to identify oneself with some of the cultural objects on display. But at the same time, one is able to identify other people in the region through their objects. In this way, one is made to understand that, despite the cultural diversity presented by the objects, there is no fundamental difference between one's community and the other communities in the region.

FUTURE PERSPECTIVES

Although the modern museum in Africa was the creation of colonialism, there is no doubt that this institution, just like any other social institution, has evolved with the societies in which it is found, and has undergone changes in the process. Africa's museums have found themselves playing leading roles in complex socio-cultural and economic phenomena, such as globalization, sustainable development and tourism. These phenomena will increase in their complexity well into the twenty-first century. To meet these challenges, museums in Africa will have to become more responsive and innovative in all aspects of the development of their operations, functioning, programming and public outreach. So, what should the museums in Africa do in order to cope with the challenges of the twenty-first century and, thereby, remain relevant?

First, museums in Africa must become motors of the learning society. This can only be done by transforming these museums from static store-houses for artifacts into active learning environments for people (Hooper-Greenhill 1994). Thus, in addition to its traditional role of collection and preservation, the African museum, like the global museum, has to explicitly emphasize certain transformations. For instance, the museums must make their exhibits as interactive as possible. To do this, the museums must be rooted in the community, work with the local people to expand their data-bases, and encourage repeat visits. As J. M. Bradburne has argued, 'the visitor should have a real role to play: in being able to pose and answer their own questions in interacting/engaging intellectually with the material, by recognizing their expectations, competences, and fundamental activity in creating new understanding' (2002: 27). Second, museums in Africa must think seriously about the different types of public that need to access their facilities. Unlike the situation in the developed world, many museums in Africa have not made any provisions for the disabled to enjoy the same range of services offered by these institutions that is available to those who are not disabled. For example, in a recent study of Kisumu Museum in Kenya, D. O. Ouma (2005) found that physically handicapped school children were faced with many obstacles whenever they tried to access the facilities. The study found that the showcases were too high and that the landscape and roadways were not user-friendly for those in wheelchairs. They also found that, in the traditional homestead exhibit, the entrances were too narrow to allow easy access to the interiors for the wheelchair-bound.

Third, most museums in Africa have concentrated solely upon material objects of tangible heritage, to the almost complete exclusion of intangible heritage. Yet, it is the intangible heritage that is at the heart of the people, since this is what they relate to in their day-to-day contacts with the social and physical environment. In any case, the tangible heritage only makes sense when it is contextualized within the people's intangible cultural her-itage. Museums in Africa must therefore embark on the systematic collec-tion and preservation of oral traditions, local languages, ceremonies, beliefs, songs, poetry, stories, and so on. This will enhance their credibility with local communities and so sustain their relevance.

Fourth, museums in Africa must continue serving as centres of informal learning. Museums are unique spaces in this regard, because they are homes of the real – that is, real objects, real phenomena, real people. The objects are real because they exist and represent real phenomena as perceived by the people who made them. Their form is, therefore, a reflection of the people who made them. However, for the informal learning process to take place effectively, Africa's museums must stop aiming at merely satisfying casual visitors, such as foreign tourists, or focusing on the sole objective of increasing the number of visitors. They should, instead, focus on providing users with sufficient tools to make sense of the objects on display. This would encourage repeat visits and so contribute meaningfully to the sustainability of the institutions.

Fifth, museums in Africa are also likely to assume a more prominent role in the socio-economic development of their nations through tourism. Because of the current high levels of human/wildlife conflicts, those countries that rely heavily on wildlife as their main tourist attraction, such as Kenya, are now considering focusing their tourist development projects on cultural tourism. As leisure tourism catches up with the developing world, there is little doubt that many within the African middle class will soon participate. However, for this to happen, the museum will need to have highly trained and experienced professionals capable of designing museum exhibitions to the satisfaction of the public. Today, many museums lack this cadre of personnel, and instead rely on semi-skilled people.

Finally, as Bradburne (2002) has pointed out, we need to develop a new type of museum on the continent, to exhibit taboo objects and unpleasant things, narratives of the abuse of power, stories of intolerance, and expressions of grief and sorrow. Recently, Karega-Munene (2004) has argued for the establishment of a National Museum of Shame in Kenya, to act as a deterrent to human rights abuses in the country. According to him, such a museum should not be created for the purpose of tourists and curious citizens, but rather to serve as an instrument that will interact with the Kenyan community in a dynamic way. He argues that such a museum must be designed to serve the general public in four broad ways:

1. Educating them about their rights and obligations.
2. Educating them on the observance, promotion, and protection of those rights.
3. Educating them about the country's past trends in the observation of human rights.
4. Educating them on how to seek redress when their rights are violated (2004: 71).

As envisaged by Karega-Munene, a 'museum of shame' would be an historic as well as a political museum, documenting the history and politics of human rights in Kenya during the pre-colonial and postcolonial periods. These two periods have, of course, witnessed very many human rights abuses, sometimes resulting in great loss of life. This happened not only in Kenya, but also in Zimbabwe and South Africa during the struggle for independence. The postcolonial period has witnessed many civil wars leading to massacres of, sometimes, hundreds of thousands of people, for example, in Angola, Mozambique, Somalia, Ethiopia, Burundi, Democratic Republic of Congo, Uganda, Sierra Leone, Nigeria, Côte d'Ivoire, Liberia and Sudan. In some cases, these wars have led to genocide, for example, in Rwanda and Sierra Leone. These are the subjects that should be exhibited in national museums of shame. Rwanda has taken the lead in this, by constructing museums that house the skeletal remains of the hundreds of thousands that perished during the genocide.

National museums of shame could also conserve the buildings which housed the chambers of torture used during the colonial and postcolonial periods. South Africa already has Robben Island Museum, where Nelson Mandela and other nationalists were incarcerated by the apartheid regime. In addition, the Mayibuye Centre, at the University of the Cape in Cape Town, documents the history of apartheid, resistance, social life and culture in the country. In Kenya, Nyayo House and Nyati House in Nairobi, where opponents of the Daniel Arap Moi regime were confined and tortured, would be good examples of national museums of shame.

CONCLUSION

The modern museum in Africa, although a part of the colonial legacy, has evolved to be much more. It was originally meant to serve the interests of the colonial masters, serving as a place where they and their families would go to view the curiosities of the native peoples. However, the museums of today are an important resource to the nations of the continent. First, their collections communicate to us about our cultural, environmental and ecological heritage, either of the past or the present. The message is that although the exhibits might be from different communities within a given region or nation, the collections actually represent unity in diversity. Second, museums provide an opportunity for people to learn about themselves as well as about others. In this case, the role of the museum is to create an environment where visitors can explore the ways in which they can actively modify their relationship with culture, by enhancing their knowledge and piquing their critical judgment. Third, museums in Africa have collections which are used by researchers interested in both cultural and national heritage. In fact, at the moment, most of the information on the biological as well as cultural evolution of humankind can only be obtained from the study of paleontological and archaeological collections held by museums in Africa.

Museums can remain relevant to Africa as the twenty-first century progresses. However, for them to succeed in this, they must rethink the way in which they function. They have to abandon the top-down approach inherited from their colonial masters and become more user-friendly. To do this, they will require proper funding and professionally qualified personnel who

have been hired strictly on merit. It is also important to recognize that
national museums of shame are long overdue on the continent. Through displays and intentional messages, such museums could help heal the wounds
inflicted by colonial and civil wars, as well as the human rights abuses
committed by the postcolonial leaders.

REFERENCES

Abungu, G. H. O. (2002), 'Opening up New Frontiers: Museums of the 21st
    Century'. In Per-Uno Agren (ed.), *Museum 2000: Confirmation or Challenge*.
    ICOM Sweden and the Swedish Museum Association, pp. 37–43.
Adedze, A. T. (1992), 'Collection and Definition of Cultural Heritage in Togo'.
    Proceedings of the Encounters: What Museums for Africa? Heritage in the Future, 167–
    70.
Amahan, A. (1992), 'Museums and Tourism: The Example of Morocco'. *Proceedings
    of the Encounters: What Museums for Africa? Heritage in the Future*, 281–3.
Bradburne, J. M. (2002), Issues Facing the Museum in a Changing World'. In
    Per-Uno Agren (ed.), *Museum 2000: Confirmation or Challenge*. ICOM Sweden
    and the Swedish Museum Association, pp. 17–31.
Hooper-Greenhill, Eilean (1994), *Museums and their Visitors*. London: Routledge.
Imasiku, Annely C. (2005), *Museum Exhibitions as Educational Tools: A Case Study of
    Fort Jesus Museum, Mombasa, Kenya*. Postgraduate project paper, Institute of
    African Studies, University of Nairobi.
Karega-Munene (2004), 'Turning the Chapter: The Case for a National Museum of
    Shame as a Deterrent to Human Rights Abuses in Kenya'. *East African Journal
    of Human Rights and Democracy* 2 (1): 73–81.
Keita, F. B. (1992), 'Project for a Conservation Centre'. *Proceedings of the Encounters:
    What Museums for Africa? Heritage in the Future*. 191–5.
Kiethega, Jean-Baptiste (1992), 'Heritage and Contemporary Culture: Evolution of
    the Concept'. *Proceedings of the Encounters: What Museums for Africa? Heritage in
    the Future*, 273–7.
Konate, M. (1992), 'The Creation of Regional Museums in Mali'. *Proceedings of the
    Encounters: What Museums for Africa? Heritage in the Future*, 197–200.
Luhila, M. (1992), 'Training in the Museums of Sub-Saharan Africa'. *Proceedings of
    the Encounters: What Museums for Africa? Heritage in the Future*, 121–6.
Madondo, T. W. (1992), 'Travelling Exhibitions and the Use of National
    Languages'. *Proceedings of the Encounters: What Museums for Africa? Heritage in the
    Future*, 321–4.
Musonda, F. B. (1992), 'Museums and Tourism'. *Proceedings of the Encounters: What
    Museums for Africa? Heritage in the Future*, 324–8.
Nduku, Stella T. (1992), 'National Collections and Their Use in Regional Museums
    in Zimbabwe'. *Proceedings of the Encounters: What Museums for Africa? Heritage in
    the Future*, 201–3.
Ouma, D. O. (2005), *Problems Facing the Physically Handicapped School Children in
    Accessing Kisumu Museum, Kenya*. Unpublished project paper, Institute of African
    Studies, University of Nairobi.

Pye, Elizabeth (2001), *Caring for the Past: Issues in Conservation for Archaeology and Museums*. London: James and James.

Rakotoarisoa, Jean-Aime (1992), 'Notes on the Museum Network in Madagascar'. *Proceedings of the Encounters: What Museums for Africa? Heritage in the Future*, 79–83.

Tchanile, M. M. 'Regional Museums and Development Policy'. *Proceedings of the Encounters: What Museums for Africa? Heritage in the Future*, 351–3.

LITERARY PRIZES, BOOK PRIZES AND AFRICAN WRITING

Literary prizes and book prizes do not feature greatly in discussions about writing and publishing, perhaps because there are so few of them in Africa. When they do, the discussion tends to centre on the questions of who funds the few existing prizes, how the winners are selected, how the prizes are administered, and whether or not the administrators of the prizes are located within or outside of Africa.

LITERARY AND BOOK PRIZES IN AFRICA

There is a difference between a literary prize and a book prize. The former, as the name implies, is about works of literature – novels, short stories, poetry, drama, children's literature. On the other hand, a book prize deals with all kinds of books. For instance, the Caine Prize for African Writing is a literary prize, awarded to 'a work by an African writer published in English', which has as its focus 'the African story telling tradition'. Eligible works for this prize include 'a short story, a collection of short stories, a novella, or a narrative poem'. On the other hand, the Noma Award for Publishing in Africa is a book prize, established primarily to encourage African writers to have their books published in Africa, by indigenous publishing houses. African writers have historically believed it to be more prestigious to be published overseas, and this attitude still exists today to some extent. For writers in the former British colonies, the preference was to be published by a British or American publisher. For writers in former French, Spanish or Portuguese colonies, the preferred publishers were in Paris, Madrid or Lisbon, respectively. The situation has improved greatly in recent times, however, and many writers today make a point of being published in Africa by indigenous African publishing houses, even after they have received offers from European and American publishers. The Noma Award has encouraged this trend, focusing on 'any of the three categories: scholarly or academic, children's books, [and] creative writing'.

There are very few literary and book prizes in Africa, and in some countries there are none. Perhaps this is not surprising. In many countries the production of books other than textbooks is so low that it may not be feasible to run a literary or book prize. It could be argued that, if there is any book production at all, there ought to be a prize to encourage those authors and publishers who at least occasionally bring out prizeworthy books. That this is not the case suggests that, in most African countries, there is little or no recognition of the important place of literature in society, and hence little incentive to celebrate books and their creators.

Across the continent, there are differences in the way the organization of cultural industries is perceived. While there are no doubt many factors contributing to this situation, two reasons for the differences among African countries regarding book and literary productions come immediately to mind. Both of them have to do with colonial education and language policies, and the importance accorded the colonial language in postcolonial society.

COLONIAL LANGUAGE POLICIES AND THE CREATION OF AFRICAN LITERATURE

Colonial policies did not consider higher education for the colonized to be a priority. As a result, only a few Africans had access to education at the university level. In most countries, the first universities were established only after independence was attained. The few universities established during the colonial period were enclaves that sought to remove their African students as far as possible from their cultures of origin. The colonizers' languages and literatures were taught, and African values were systematically replaced by Western ones. After independence, nearly every black African country retained the language of its former colonizer as both its official and national language. (Tanzania is a special case which will be discussed separately.) The expansion of educational opportunities followed independence, but instead of reversing the trends established during the colonial era, the postcolonial educational system still favoured the colonial languages. Thus, educational institutions continued to stunt the development of literacy in African languages. In Tanzania, the situation was somewhat different: the use of English was socially discouraged and thus lost its mystique as language of the elite. Nonetheless, English was still used as the language of instruction in secondary and university education.

In light of these trends, it is not surprising that literature produced in most African countries is written in the languages of the colonizers: English, French, Portuguese and Spanish. In Tanzania, however, most writing is done in Swahili. This may be due to the anti-English sentiment that followed independence, but it may also be a reflection of Tanzania's ambiguous language policy, which makes it almost impossible for students to master the English language well enough to be able to enjoy reading or writing in it. Indeed, the same ambiguity may explain why there is less creative writing in Tanzania than in the rest of East Africa, because secondary and higher education – during which time developing writers come into their own – is given in English, in which students are poorly prepared at primary school.

African countries that continued in the literary and language-arts traditions of their former colonizers do appear to enjoy a comparatively high degree of literary creativity, particularly when their education systems nurture their students in the colonial language. In the case of Portuguese, a small *assimilado* group was so intensively steeped in Portuguese culture as to completely mirror Portuguese society. In East Africa, the experiences of Tanzania, Kenya and Uganda support this observation as well. In both Kenya and Uganda, the people demanded to be educated in English. A growing middle class with a Western orientation demanded – and produced – an African literature written in English. The rich literary productivity in Nigeria, Ghana, Zimbabwe, South Africa, Senegal and Côte d'Ivoire also supports this point. Further contributing to the flourishing of African literatures in colonial languages is the existence of a convertible currency (for instance, the CFA), which encourages indigenous publishing houses to offer the works of local writers to Western audiences as well. Thus, the Dakar-based Nouvelles Editions Africaines prints its books in France, and Longmans-Kenya is capable of distributing works by African writers in the United Kingdom.

Where a foreign language such as English dominates, it is clear that literature in other languages either will not be produced or will have limited appeal. The fact that higher education is offered only in a foreign language, and that employment and social mobility are contingent on proficiency in that foreign language, makes it inevitable that writing and publishing in indigenous languages will lag behind or simply not happen at all. However, English and French speaking graduates today are discovering that even language proficiency cannot guarantee that they will find jobs. They are finally realizing that their own languages may be more useful to them, if for no other reason than that they permit a closer connection with their fellow citizens.

LITERARY PRIZES AND THE LANGUAGE ISSUE

Literary prizes in Africa are really about rewarding writers whose works are written, for the most part, in one of the foreign languages. Even the Noma Award, which accepts works in all languages, has more often favoured works written in English and French than to those produced in indigenous African languages. Although the prize has been given to some works in Swahili, Arabic, Afrikaans and Gikuyu, the preference for books written in the languages of the former colonizers remains strong. Further reflecting this reality, 'Africa's 100 Best Books', a list that purports to represent the best works of African authors during the last century, were overwhelmingly in English.

But the fundamental question remains: what purpose can literary prizes and writing competitions serve? The simple fact of publication serves as a recognition that a work has value. It is often argued that the market is the best judge of a work, and that the author gains fame and fortune according to the level of sales. But it is also true that excellent books may not generate a large volume of sales for any number of reasons, not the least of which is the level of literary education and appreciation in a given society at a given time. And, of course, without marketing and publicity, even good books will not sell well.

Publishers organize writing competitions for a number of reasons. Announcing a competition, particularly if the prize includes a promise to publish the winning entries, is a good way to scout for new writers. Publishing houses also organize literary competitions and give prizes for the sake of generating publicity for themselves. Media coverage of the whole range of activities related to selection of the winner or winners and celebrations that follow is worth infinitely more than conventional advertisements in newspapers, and is often free. Radio stations also sponsor competitions and awards to encourage the writing of short stories and plays as a way to gain popularity and audience share. Book fairs also organize prizes connected to some aspect of the book industry. For instance, the Zimbabwe International Book Fair celebrated Zimbabwe's seventy-five best books, and also conferred an award upon Henry Chakava (of EAEP in Nairobi) for his many contributions to the development of the African publishing industry.

Literary prizes are also an important way of promoting and awarding literary creativity. For that reason alone, they deserve greater support than they are given in Africa. Authors are encouraged by winning prizes and, no doubt, the prizes provide them with the motivation to continue to write. As one award-winning author put it: 'The prize wasn't much, but it made me feel like a poet, and, instead of feeling that I was a housewife, I thought, "I am a poet".'

For authors, the prize can sometimes mean enough financial freedom to continue writing. African authors' incomes from royalties are generally modest. The limited book-buying public, the low cover price, and the relatively poorly developed marketing and distribution skills of publishers make it unlikely that most authors will realize large royalties. Winning a prestigious award presents an opportunity for an author's income to rise dramatically: prize-winning books often enjoy increased sales, and there is the additional possibility that they might be translated into other languages. The big multinational publishing houses usually buy up rights on the winning titles, which

they then market worldwide. A hitherto unknown author may thus be cata-
pulted onto the world stage, leading to lucrative contracts for future works,
opportunities for travel, and writing sabbaticals in luxurious settings.

There is a downside to all of this, however. It is often a struggling African
publisher who takes all the risks involved in publishing an unknown author's
first book. When that author is recognized through winning a prize, the big,
multinational publishing vultures descend on the writer, offering lucrative
contracts and snatching him or her from the original publisher. This does
not have to be the case, however. The simple adoption of proper author-
publisher contracts could protect the original publisher's investment by
requiring the author to give him first option on future manuscripts, and
giving the African publisher control of the rights, thus enabling him to participate in negotiating an equitable share of the income with the foreign publisher.

Unfortunately, authors tend to resist giving such powers to the originating publishers. Furthermore, the field of rights negotiations is very specialized, and not all African publishers are sufficiently versed in it to be able to
make favourable deals with the experienced foreign publishers, even if
opportunities do arise.

Every competition has its supporters and detractors, and it is not unusual
to discover attempts to influence the outcome. Advertisements in the press
on behalf of one or another of the competing works are not unusual, and
more subtle or more devious interventions are not unheard of. The integrity
of the award panel is therefore the single most important element in the
administration and awarding of a prize. Authors and publishers often submit
works for consideration for an award without properly reading the conditions
of entry, or they may even deliberately conceal potentially disqualifying information. In addition, a prize that is meant to represent a wide geographical
area can end up with a reputation for overwhelmingly favouring entries from
only one country or region. Such unevenness may end up discouraging other
authors and publishers from participating. The other side of this coin is the
possibility that 'political correctness' or other considerations of equity take
precedence over literary merit, so that a deserving winner is edged out in
favour of a less deserving one for reasons unrelated to the literary value of
the work.

EXISTING PRIZES AND AWARDS

There are many prizes and awards in the world for which African writers are
eligible, the most prestigious of all of them being the Nobel Prize for Literature. This was first won by an African, Wole Soyinka, in 1986. While there
was general satisfaction that African literature had been recognized and
honoured at last, there was also a lively debate about the award. A number

of critics expressed their dissatisfaction that the prize went to Soyinka, charging that his writing appeals more to Western sensibilities and does not speak to African audiences. This kind of debate can never be resolved, because it raises the unanswerable question of what most truly constitutes 'African' writing.

Also important is the Neustadt International Prize for Literature. This is based at the University of Oklahoma, where the highly respected quarterly *Journal of World Literature* is published. It is considered second only to the Nobel Prize in prestige and amount of prize money ($40,000). The Noma Award for Publishing in Africa is perhaps the most inclusive. It is open to all African countries, covering all literature (fiction, academic and children's) and all African languages. It establishes two important conditions, however. Works to be submitted must be written by African authors, and they must have been first published in Africa, by wholly-owned, indigenous African publishers. The aim of the Japanese philanthropist who endowed the prize, the late Shoichi Noma, was to support African writing through supporting African publishing. He believed, quite rightly, that supporting African publishing would be supporting African literature.

Soon after South African publishers became eligible (after the end of apartheid), the Noma Award had to deal with the overwhelming number of submissions from South Africa in comparison with the volume of work submitted by other countries. Several South African publishers were submitting as many as twenty books apiece, in the hope of improving their chances of sponsoring a winner. The jury decided to limit all publishers to a maximum of three submissions apiece. There are still many more entries from South Africa than from any other country, but the restriction on submissions by individual publishers has made the system somewhat fairer. The South African publishers introduced another possible inequity to the competition. In addition to the number of books submitted from South Africa, the quality of production from that country is also the highest on the continent. The award jury does consider quality of production, but it also takes into consideration the infrastructural conditions prevailing in each of the participating countries when making its judgements. On the whole, production quality of submitted books has generally been improving throughout the continent.

The British-based Booker Prize for Fiction is one of the most coveted awards, and excitement reaches a fever pitch on the night of the presentation. Fiction written in English from any country of the Commonwealth is eligible, and two African authors, Chinua Achebe and Ben Okri, have won the prize in the past. The Commonwealth Writers Prize is aimed at discovering new fiction-writing talents and making their work known more widely than just in the country in which it was first published. The Caine Prize for African Writing, which was established in 1999, has also had great success in launching new talent, mostly in the short story genre, although novellas and narrative poems are also eligible. The Caine Prize awards board also organizes writers' workshops for the short-listed authors, offering pleasant surroundings in which the writers may spend time discussing their work with one another.

Additional overseas-based prizes include the BBC's playwriting competition, the Arvon Foundation for International Poetry competition, the Cleveland State University Poetry Center Prize, the Iowa Poetry Prize, and the International IMPAC Dublin Literary Award for fiction. The Macmillan Writers Prize, launched in 2001 by Macmillan Education and Picador, is also prestigious. Based in the United Kingdom, Macmillan has a number of regional branches throughout Africa. The prize is awarded to children's fiction and adult fiction, and a special prize is awarded for the best new writer of children's books.

On the African continent there are only a few prizes offered outside South Africa and Nigeria, and most of them are limited to authors and publishers of a single nation. But there have been efforts to set up continent-wide prizes. These include the All Africa Okigbo Prize for literature, which is endowed by Wole Soyinka from his Nobel Prize money, and there is the possibility of an award to be offered by the Pan African Writers Association, in conjunction with the Organization for African Unity (OAU). The Jomo Kenyatta Literature Prize in Kenya has had mixed fortunes over the years, but it has recently become an important annual event in Kenya's publishing calendar. The Zimbabwe Book Publishers' Association has also been very active and, together with other institutions linked to the book trade (printers and booksellers), the association organizes several prizes for best novel in the three major languages of Zimbabwe (Shona, Ndebele and English). Genres eligible for the prize include poetry and children's books (in three age categories: four to seven, eight to ten, and eleven to fourteen).

South Africa has by far the largest number of prizes, and the best known, at the time of writing, are listed here:

The Sunday Times/Alan Paton Prize for Non-fiction
SANLAM/1820 Foundation and Tribute Magazine Prizes
MNet Book Prize
BookData South African Booksellers Book of the Year Prize
Natal Society Prize
The Bard Award for Zulu Language and Literature
The UCT Book of the Year Award
Federasie van Kultuurverenigings
The CAN Prize
HSBCA/SA PEN Literary Award (submissions from SADC member countries
   are accepted)
Mofolo-Plower Award.

Not long ago, the European Union set up an EU Award to encourage the distribution of South African writing in the EU countries. An interesting question being posed generally about the prizes in South Africa is the degree to which these prizes are still based on literary canons and rituals of the former colonial masters. It is unclear as yet whether they will evolve to become more truly South African in content and focus.

Nigeria is second to South Africa in the number of prizes offered. The following list enumerates the best known of these:

ANA (Association of Nigeria Authors) / NDDC (Nigeria Delta Development Commission or Niger Delta Development Corporation) Poetry Prize (in honour of Gabriel Okara)
ANA/NDDC Prose Prize (in honour of Ken Saro Wiwa)
ANA/NDDC Flora Nwapa Prize for Women's writing
ANA.NDDC Drama Prize (in honour of J. P. Clarke)
ANA Literary Journalist Prize
ANA/Atiku Abubakar Prize for Children's Books
ANA/Cadbury Prize for Poetry
NNLG (Nigerian Natural and Liquefied Gas) Literature Prize
Litramed Books Award
The Chief Victor Nwankwo Memorial Prize

It is laudable that nearly all Nigerian prizes are named in honour of deceased authors and publishers, offering recognition of the importance of writers and publishers and providing motivation to other writers and publishers to emulate those whose names the prizes bear. The active role of the Association of Nigerian Authors offers a good example for other African writers' associations. Other countries give prizes during their book fairs or book weeks, but these are more or less spontaneous activities, without high profiles or permanency. Nevertheless, they do serve to stimulate interest in literature and encourage the competitive spirit.

CONCLUSION

The fact that South Africa and Nigeria are the African countries with the highest number of literary and book prizes suggests that the more writing there is in a country, the more likely there will also be book prizes to honour it. Literary and book prizes no doubt play an important role in promoting writing and scholarship, but it is equally evident that they depend heavily upon universities to offer an excellent education in literature and the sciences; and government and other state institutions for the funding and organizational infrastructure to administer the awards. The alternative is to depend upon private institutions, such as banks, corporations and foundations, to provide support for the literary arts through the sponsorship of awards, sabbaticals, prizes, and the like.

Other factors heavily influence the likelihood of literary awards and book prizes. The state of a given country's economy, whether it has productive capacity to generate enough surplus to invest in art and literature, and whether there exists a class in that society with private wealth and an interest in patronizing art and literature, are also important in the discussion of literary and book prizes in Africa. The fact that the most of the well-known literary prizes are sponsored by philanthropists – even those who made their wealth from the sweat of black slaves or from colonial exploitation of Africa – is not surprising. Most African countries have been living the nightmare of poverty ever since they attained their independence. The wealth of South Africa, particularly of that section of society that was, and remains, materially and culturally Western, has been instrumental in setting up and maintaining that nation's many award programmes. In Nigeria, despite the successive military regimes that squandered its wealth, there are still first-class universities that produce probably the highest concentration of intel-lectuals in Africa and which are responsible for the country's high output of literary works and the support of the prizes.

An African renaissance, like its European predecessor, will produce great artistic and literary works. When this happens, one of the most urgent issues will be to determine how best to bestow recognition and legitimacy upon creators of artistic and literary works. Since the renaissance is as much about wealth creation as artistic creativity, resources will be found to endow prizes that are rooted in African culture and traditions. At that time, the debate about which African author deserves which of the foreign prizes will finally be put to rest. But even before then, the African Union ought to set up several continent-wide prizes, supervised by an African academy, in order to redeem the continent from dependence on foreign bodies to decide what is best of its intellectual and artistic productions. Likewise, all African states ought to set up more prizes, in order to discover, stimulate and nurture talent at the national level. This would be a particularly effective way of pro-moting writing and research using Africa languages, with the ultimate goal of restoring cultural pride.

INNOVATING 'ALTERNATIVE' IDENTITIES: NAIROBI *MATATU* CULTURE

This is an anecdote from my street notebook, circa 2000, when I was doing doctoral dissertation research:

> I am standing right inside the Old Nation roundabout, looking up along Tom Mboya Street. All round me there is a bustle of activity, as passengers dash from the roundabout into the circuit road . . . in the process, eliciting a stream of choice epithets and gestures from *matatu* driver crews. 'How utterly disorderly these *matatu* can be. No wonder they sport such fearsome names like Notorious and Nasty Boys!' exclaims a neatly dressed man standing next to me. Above the din of touts' voices calling for passengers, he has noticed the direction of my contemplative gaze that seems to indicate my somewhat alien position as an observer rather than a *matatu*-chasing, death-ducking, insulted commuter. I invent and mumble a quick reply, keen to proceed with my surveillance of these risky streets. However, I am left musing about the equation between *matatu* and chaos, an observation that takes on added meaning, given that no serious attention to order seems to have gone into planning this particular section of the city's roads. At the same time, I also notice how crews exploit such a paradox of planned disorder to achieve their own ends. My contemplation is interrupted by a loud thud; a *matatu* named Doggz, from whose interior issues a thousand watts of local rap, has rammed into the rear of another. In the ensuing altercation, a spontaneous crowd gathers and intrudes into my study – even my ethnographic exercise is not prepared for anything as intrusive and unmanageable as the data that this throng presents me. I flee the scene, feeling that I might be better off telling the analytical story of the data already collected.

As this entry illustrates, few objects command the centrality of place in Kenyan public life enjoyed by *matatu*, the privately owned vans and mini-buses that have been at the core of the country's public transport sector, moving people, goods and ideas for slightly over half a century. Yet the intensity of public hostility directed at these same objects of material culture might cause one to wonder why Kenyans have never staged public protests against them or, indeed, why the government has never considered banning altogether this mode of transportation. Setting aside questions of policy and the logistical intricacies of public transport in Kenya, it is worthwhile to interrogate the complex, multi-sensory, subcultural space that has sprung up around *matatu* since their first illegal entry into Kenyan public life in 1953 (Lee-Smith 1989). The phenomenon of *matatu* falls within a long history in which the car and other forms of transport have been used as expressive devices (Dillard 1976; Parrinder 1953; Miller 2001), in places as diverse as Pakistan, the United States, Nigeria, Sweden, Israel, Ghana and the Philippines. The imperative is to try to see how specific people in specific locations configure diverse meanings upon the site provided by this material object. *Matatu* culture here, then, provides an example of what might be called new sites of performance, where everyday acts have more valence than might otherwise be expected.

How are we to understand *matatu* culture? To many of my informants, it is 'just nonsense', to others, the practices of *matatu* folk are not admissible to critique and analysis as 'culture'. Some conceive *matatu* within a logic of order by which deviations from the norm are only understood as malignant disorders of the social body. Indeed, the Kenyan press, being one of the chief tools by which the discourse on *matatu* culture is constructed, is replete with this sort of observation (for instance, Mkangi 1986; Mbugguss 1992; Njoka 2001; Nyasani 2001; Mathiu 2002). Others single out inscriptions and other visual decorations that they find offensive, and declare the entire enterprise of vehicle adornment to be a form of 'vulgar graffiti'. Implicit in such objections are the concepts of high versus low culture. Fortunately, as Storey (2003) has shown, in the broad field of cultural theory, such patronizing perspectives are now no longer found useful.

Thus, in order to apprehend *matatu* cultural practice as meaningful performance, we need to ask how people make meanings with these forms. What do they seek to do with them? The insights we gain by asking such a question demonstrate some of the benefits of a serious examination of the sites of contemporary Kenyan popular culture, of which the *matatu* is a part. As the '*tatu*' ('three') suggests, this culture can be viewed as three dimensional. A little tilting of the object of analysis, complemented by an imaginative reading, will enable a perception of meanings that lie hidden from direct view.

In order to make analytical sense of it, *matatu* needs to be viewed as an aspect of performance within urban youth culture. Spectacular bodily presentation through imitation jewellery, fashion, local and American rap lyrics, aggressive humour, and abrasive idiom are some of the principal performative elements of this culture. These characteristics become the practitioners' means of specifying the interpretive codes by which *matatu* culture might be understood by Nairobi residents, most of whom participate directly, as travellers, or vicariously, as observers or fellow drivers on the road. Thus, this sub-culture might be apprehended quite literally as a compendium of moving texts.

Matatu culture can therefore be seen as an intersection of simultaneously competing and complementary interests upon which identity is dialogically and continually created, disseminated, reformulated and contested. It is, in essence, a performance characterized by slipperiness, a modality that makes meanings elusive, even as it enables multiple interpretations of the culture's intertextual and highly reflexive practices. For this reason, one must remain awake to the intriguing turns often taken by the sub-culture's tropes, for even as the sub-culture strikes an anti-mainstream pose, it simultaneously expresses a deep yearning for the symbols of the mainstream.

Consider, for instance, the dissonance created by the image of a mean-faced *konkodi* (conductor), whose foul language and mannerisms fit the general stereotype of an 'unpolished' body, and the aspirations expressed in his talk and symbols; huge, fancy cars; nice villas; and the occasional holiday on the beaches of Hawaii and Aruba that are readily transmitted via television. How are these apparent contradictions to be explained? And why does popular culture seem to be making so much sense to so many people?

At one level, the popular, everyday banalities of *matatu* culture provide an expressive space within which is encoded the politics of youth identity. A central concern in this project involves the expression of perceived marginality, that is, the feeling that they are denied the good things of life. This can be seen in the many *matatu* names that evoke the notion of exclusion. Consider, for example, the play on otherness and autochthony embedded in a name like AlterNative, apparently chosen in response to official regulations that require *matatu* operators to comply with strict rules or be ejected from the business. *Matatu* crews tend to feel that they are set apart from other natives (Kenyans); hence the proliferation of vehicle names that harp on the themes of marginalization and persecution. Such self-perceptions can be viewed against the official rhetoric of national unity so favoured by Kenyan politicians. By constituting an alternative sense of a marginalized community, the sub-culture calls into question the logic and narrative of a unified state, substituting for it one that celebrates diversity.

At another level, we can apprehend *matatu* culture within the terms of hybridity. Crews appropriate expressive symbols from other cultures and communicative media (for example, film, television, cyberspace, magazines and novels), in order to constitute an expressive channel into which they can then fuse local meanings. These meanings operate dialogically to speak to local concerns, even as they play at expressing the exotic. *Matatu* crews use the interstitial space thus created not merely to highlight their difference but, more significantly, to specify the local character of that difference. For instance, it is noticeable that local hip-hop artists such as Nazizi, Nameless, Nonini, Wahu and Redsan are increasingly contending for space on these vehicles, alongside foreign celebrities like R. Kelly, Beyonce and David Beckham. Nevertheless, this sub-culture does not seek to cast itself entirely out of mainstream society's frames of reference. This can be seen in the aspirations of *matatu* practitioners, particularly their desire to access consumer goods that symbolize modernity, such as nice cars, villas, flashy dress and jewellery ('bling').

In order to appreciate *matatu* as a medium of communication, it is necessary to examine some of its key characteristics, in order to see how, as a whole, it intersects with other media and ideas in the broader flows of Nairobi/Kenyan popular culture. One of the most conspicuous characteristics of *matatu* crews is their general proclivity to use obscene language. While it is true that some people find this language objectionable, it is also correct to state that a great many others find it, by their own admission, enjoyable. How might this ambivalence be explained, and what is the purpose of the use of obscenity? It is a profound mistake to displace the language of the crews from its context and attempt to analyze it within overdetermined frames (see Shorter and Onyancha 1997). Bakhtin (1984) cautions us that the vulgar practices of the carnivalesque need to be viewed on their own terms. Thus, if we accept that the modality of carnival as a basis of social critique (Stallybrass and White 1986), *matatu* culture's transgressions can be seen to have their own particular purposes, which cannot be explained by recourse to conventional frames of reference. The culture's vulgar banter is embedded in long traditions. For instance, there is an evident connection between *matatu* obscenities and the ribald speech associated with Gikuyu circumcision rituals. At any rate, for crews, verbal and gestural obscenity is a strategy for addressing the social body and the unequal power relations that obtain among its members.

One plausible way of apprehending *matatu* obscenity is to examine the wider logic within which it is formulated. In general, most Kenyan cultures evince a considerable degree of bias against women (see Ndungo 1998). These traditional perceptions of gender inevitably inform some contemporary attitudes about women, with sexism being one of the more prevalent ways in which men respond to women. Obscenity in *matatu* culture, which tends to formulate its metaphors around female bodies and carnality, might therefore be understood within a broader framework of a masculine discourse that is constructed upon traditional notions of gender relations. This language becomes especially useful for *matatu* men, who no longer command the authority of the traditionally defined male because they have no control over material wealth. Conversely, women increasingly have been able to gain access to property in their own right, and hence can be said to have entered 'male' space. The sight of female drivers is infuriating to many a *matatu* man, who may say that 'women have begun wearing trousers'. Regardless of legislation that has made it possible for women to join the ranks of *matatu* crews, the *matatu* discourse remains predominately masculine.

Whether by the use of sexist stickers or direct speech, *matatu* obscenity may be seen, then, as a manifestation of underlying tensions surrounding the changing definition and relevance of masculinity in contemporary Kenya. So long as society generally persists in its biases, it is to be expected that *matatu* crews will perpetuate the patriarchal modes of thought that form the basis of their obscenity. This might then explain why some male passengers, just as insecure about their manhood as the *matatu* crews, seem to enjoy and participate in some of these vulgar games.

LOCAL MUSIC

Perhaps nowhere are the tensions surrounding the issue of identity more pronounced and contested as in the field of contemporary local rap music, of which *matatu* forms a convenient and popular channel of dissemination. Indeed, some popular local rap tracks have been composed on the subject of *matatu*, and ably depict the intricate intersections and mutual interdependence of aspects of popular Nairobi youth culture. Initially, local rap was predominantly modelled along the styles of American rap; the 'dissing' and 'gangsta' talk associated with different strands of American hip-hop culture are still evident. Also, significant aspects of American rap are lewd, and this lewdness is graphically represented in Nairobi rap through the use of such technological advances as video recording. Nonini's 'We Kamu' and Joel and Circuit's 'Manyake' are apt cases in point.

However, while the vulgar language of local rappers can be explained along the lines of obscenity in *matatu* (youth) culture, rap presents a particularly intense form of engagement, precisely because of its raw sensory and emotional power. It is tempting to view this form of popular music according to Adorno's (1976) terms, as dulling the senses, or in Plato's terms, as corrupting accepted social norms. However, this can only be true if we ignore the role of agency in reception. Local rap, by speaking to the many desires and conflicts in the lives of Kenyan youth, heightens listeners' awareness of them. Whether they rap about male desire, female bodies or corrupt politicians, Kenyan rappers speak to the youth in a language style whose efficiency is unmatched by any other form of communication. As McClary (1994) has argued, whenever objections are heard about such radical music, it is a sign that something politically significant is at stake. *Matatu* crews, aware of the efficacy of this expressive modality, become key agents of its messages.

However, local youth music is not just about sexuality. Its very form might be understood as a generational clash of taste that is then used to stake claims to a particular identity. This is also seen when urban youth adopt the hip-hop style in costume, decor and attitude, as gestures of nonconformity. By so doing, they rob the mainstream of the authority to prescribe values.

The futility of remonstrations against such nonconformity becomes obvious if we consider that youth culture taps into and is aided by a wide field of mainstream forms, especially the increasingly popular FM radio stations and television, as well as music and sports magazines, which can be found in 'respectable' places.

IMAGES AND STICKERS: TRUNCATED NARRATIVES

The grotesque images posted on *matatu* – detached heads, mouths, flaring nostrils, ears, pointing fingers, arms and legs – are formulated as a symbolic commentary on society's preoccupation with finished bodies. The crews' unpolished bodies disrupt the mainstream's standards of taste. The macho character of crews' bodies might further be understood as expressing the notion of a wished-for masculinity, as a way of covering up for the diverse socioeconomic deficiencies (real or imagined) that undermine the traditional definition of manhood.

Thus the grotesque imagery on *matatu* may be understood as truncated visual clues that have been extrapolated from other, larger narratives, be they traditionally derived or rooted in the contemporary context of social struggle and survival. For instance, corrupt government officials are represented as ogres, police officers as hyenas, and the *matatu* crews themselves as hares or chameleons, all of which are readily recognizable characters in folklore from Africa and elsewhere. Stickers, which are conversational in nature, often encode texts from traditional sources: the Bible, for instance, or familiar sayings and proverbs drawn from both local and non-local traditions. A sticker's text evokes a context at the same time as it forms the basis of much heated discussion amongst commuters.

Nearly all *matatu* stickers evince an offensive aspect, an aggressive quality that will almost always provoke passenger reaction to its wording and meaning. In this way, ordinary, apparently banal forms aid in constituting a *matatu* ride as a social space comparable to the *leso* or *kanga*, a wrap-around cloth, popular amongst East African women, upon which are inscribed proverbs and sayings. Further, stickers can be seen as keeping alive traditional expressive forms (local proverbs and sayings) that were once transmitted from generation to generation. As a young informant stated to me, 'our urbanized parents rarely, if ever, tell us hare and hyena stories, [but] *matatu* culture helps us to reflect on some of these things from our heritage'.

SHENG

Sheng is a linguistic mode that is chiefly marked by code-shifting and code-switching. Most interesting is its capacity for evasion and its refusal to be constrained or apprehended by outsiders. It is an urban sociolect whose predominating invasion of the space occupied by accepted languages (such as English and Kiswahili) and the inversion of their hierarchies have drawn objections from educators, who feel that it has a deleterious effect on learners' performance in formal schooling. Whatever the merits of such arguments, it is the symbolic forms to which users put *sheng* as a cultural act that is important here. This can be productively explored through an emic understanding of youth culture.

Nairobi youth do not hide the fact that *sheng* is intended to be evasive. Their use of it clearly indicates a rejection of the linguistic codes already available. In *matatu* culture, this might be illustrated by looking at words used for the police: *ponyi* and *kopa*. Over time, these were changed, because they sounded too close to their English equivalents, 'police' and 'cop' (or 'copper'). Opaque names were adopted in their place: *mafisi* ('hyenas'), *miguu nyeusi* ('black feet'), *ahooi* ('beggars'), and *abatari* ('the needy'). By fragmenting language before reconstituting it in new ways, *sheng* becomes both an identity marker and a survival tactic. Continual innovations and semantic play are crucial to this process.

At another level, through *sheng*, *matatu* youths emphatically indicate their difference in order to express their displeasure with the rest of society, especially their displeasure with the inaccessibility of modernity's goods, since they lack high-paying jobs. By using *sheng* and ensuring the burgeoning of its vocabulary, *matatu* crews innovate and maintain a space of unintelligibility that complements their sub-culture's situatedness outside the strictures of regular surveillance, not merely as a heteroglossic act but also, principally, as an inherently subversive one. Simultaneously, this gives them the cultural capital by which they negotiate, especially with the *supuu*, but also with each other in evading the police, the de facto enforcers of the notions of conformity desired by mainstream society.

CONCLUSION

Matatu is, clearly, a medium of communication worthy of serious attention as a cultural site. The innovations that characterize its discourse make *matatu* a channel for both physical conveyance and, more significantly, for the traffic of cultural metaphors upon which a sub-cultural identity thrives. The interpretation of meanings in this discourse is necessarily tricky, and it is not incidental that some of the culture's major tropes, such as spider and hare, are constructed around the concept of ambivalence. In any case, in a situation wherein it is difficult, if not impossible, to define identity as a fixity, it seems appropriate that the everyday discourse of *matatu* culture be understood as an articulation of negotiations, whether or not the nature of the texts in these transactions can remain fixed.

REFERENCES

Adorno, T. W. (1976), *Introduction to the Sociology of Music*. New York: Continuum Press.

Bakhtin, M. (1984), *Rabelais and His World*, trans. H. Isawolsky. Bloomington: Indiana University Press.

Dillard, J. L. (1976), *Black Names*. The Hague and Paris: Mouton.

Gaitho, M. (2003), 'Is the *manyake* Culture Here to Stay?' *Daily Nation*, 3 August.

Lee-Smith, D. (1989), 'Urban Management in Nairobi: A Case Study of the *matatu* Mode of Transport'. In R. E. Stern and R. R. White (eds), *African Cities in Crisis*. Boulder, CO: Westview Press.

Mathiu, M. (2002), 'I Refuse to Let Go of the Manyanga'. *Sunday Nation*, 25 August.

Mbugguss, M. (1992), 'Discus on Wheels and Their Hidden Message'. *Lifestyle Magazine, Sunday Nation*, 8 September.

McClary, S. (1994), 'Same as It Ever Was'. In A. Ross and T. Rose (eds), *Microphone Fiends: Youth Music and Culture*. New York and London: Routledge.

Miller, D. (ed.) (2001), *Driven Societies Car Cultures*. Oxford: Berg.

Mkangi, K. (1986), '*Matatu* Graffiti: A Reflection of Our Society's Wrongs'. *The Standard*, 2 May.

Ndungo, C. M. (1998), *The Portrait of Women in African Oral Literature: The Case of Kikuyu and Kiswahili Proverbs*. PhD dissertation, Kenyatta University, Nairobi.

Njoka, A. (2001), 'The Coarse, the Crass, the Cranky'. *Daily Nation*, 27 April.

Nyasani, J. (2001), 'Get Rid of this *matatu* Idiocy Now'. *Daily Nation*, 11 July.

Parrinder, G. (1953), *Religion in an African City*. London: Hutchinson's University Library.

Shorter, A. and E. Onyancha (1997), *Secularism in Africa. A Case Study: Nairobi City*. Nairobi: St Paulines Publications Africa.

Stallybrass, P. and A. White (1986), *The Politics and Poetics of Transgression*. Ithaca, NY: Cornell University Press.

Stewart, S. (1987), '*Ceci Tuera Cela*: Graffiti as Crime and Art'. In J. Fekete (ed.), *Life after Postmodernism*. New York: St Martin's Press.

Storey, J. (2003), *Inventing Popular Culture*. Oxford: Blackwell Publishing.

Waihenya, W. (2002a), 'And More of Traffic Police's Impotence'. *East African Standard*, 23 October.

— (2002b), 'New Traffic Boss in Nairobi: Old Problems on the Road'. *East African Standard*, 10 December.

BRINGING CHANGE THROUGH LAUGHTER: CARTOONING IN KENYA

Popular culture can both entertain and contribute to social change. Cartoons and comics constitute a pop-cultural tool of visual communication that is gaining in popularity and use. The modern daily newspaper strip and political cartoon participates in what is, in fact, an ancient art form and mode of expression.

Cartoon images are generally impressionistic and economical, communicating through the visual invocation of experience shared by both the creator and the intended audience. The visual presentation constitutes a kind of shorthand, allowing the cartoonist to alternately raise questions, make statements, appeal and persuade. When done by an artist with strong social convictions and a deep understanding of the socio-political milieu, the cartoon can function as a catalyst for social and political change.

THE CARTOONIST'S TOOLKIT

Successful cartoonists employ solid psychological principles. They use their art to reflect back to the reader the challenges, concerns and experiences of everyday life. They rely heavily on satire, caricature and the juxtaposition of images and concepts. They can be highly effective in conveying their messages, because they are essentially visual, and employ broadly accessible images, concepts and subject matter. Thus, while an academic analysis of the political conditions prevailing in Kenya might be astute and engaging, its audience is restricted to the highly literate, whereas a political cartoonist might extract the major points of that analysis and make them universally available through presenting them in a well conceived satirical or allegorical drawing.

The toolkit of the cartoonist includes not only satire and allegory but also myth, pun and allusion. Conventions employed across the field of cartooning include signposting (labels identifying what would otherwise be a too generalized representation), balloon dialogue (requiring extreme brevity of

language) and exaggerated representations, particularly of well-known personages. A deft deployment of all these elements within a carefully created context is the key to creating powerful, socially relevant cartoons.

A BRIEF HISTORY OF POLITICAL CARTOONING

Political cartooning relies heavily on caricature, which can be originally attributed to Leonardo da Vinci, who famously explored grotesqueries in order to more fully understand the concept of ideal beauty. Da Vinci's art, in turn, influenced the development of portraiture as an art form, as artists exploited one or more dominant features of their subjects' visages to render their productions instantly recognizable. This trend, in turn, was further developed into the practice of full-blown caricature when it was determined that such exaggerated attention to one or a few prominent details or characteristics could achieve a humorous, instructive or even subversive end.

The editorializing potential of this kind of art eventually achieved broad usage – most notably during the Reformation era in Europe, when the development of printing expanded the production of books, pamphlets and other forms of mass communication. Such products were now far more broadly disseminated, the audience expanding from the prior, predominantly ecclesiastical and university-trained minority to the middle classes and even to the uneducated masses. A visual communicative technique that could get its message across to even an illiterate public, the cartoon soon achieved widespread use, for even a peasant could get the meaning behind a drawing satirizing the political elites of the time.

By the colonial era, the role of the political cartoonist in Europe, and beyond, was well established. The genre had been employed to expose governmental corruption, social hypocrisy and the abuse of power. The cartoonist had become accepted as a social and political commentator, at

A TYPICAL DAY ON GOVERNMENT STREET, NAIROBI...

least wherever the political regime permitted the expression of the dissenting voice.

Dr Robert Russell, Director of Cartoonists Relief Network, has observed that the editorial cartoonist in most developing countries continues to be an important and highly efficient point of national and policy debate. Commentary could even extend to issues more localized than national politics, as well. In Malawi, for instance, with the rise of the independent press, cartoonists did not spare their own newspaper when commenting on its foibles. A cartoonist contributing to the *Michiru Sun* satirized the host paper's tendency toward tabloid-style exploitation of scandal. One cartoon showed the character Takataka, driving an open sports car, viewing a street-corner news vendor displaying papers bearing screaming headlines, with Takataka commenting ' 'These Independent Newspapers are really doing a fine job in exposing official rot'. Malawian cartoonists attempted to expose and interpret ongoing political issues, at least during the mid to late 1990s, during a period of great political activity, but failed to sustain their momentum after the immediate election period, from which they drew the bulk of their subject matter, had passed.

CARTOONING IN KENYA

The growth of journalism and the growth of cartooning in Kenya are closely intertwined and mutually reinforcing. It is nearly impossible to tell the story

of cartooning without going back, even if only referentially, to that of journalism. While cartooning may be riding on the back of journalism today, it
can be argued that in Africa, the history of this art would simply dwarf that
of journalism if the former were documented, for caricaturing is much older
that journalism. The rocks of Africa are hosts to millions of images caricatured on them, literally across the continent. These go back in time about
12,000 years.

Newspapers in Kenya have used syndicated cartooning for a long time.
Indigenous cartoons began in the 1950s with *Juha Kalulu*, a Kiswahili, serialized cartoon by E. G. Kiragu in Kiswahili which ran in the daily *Taifa Leo*.
Juha Kalulu draws from two African languages. The word *juha* is Kiswahili
for a clown, and *kalulu* is Chinyanja (spoken in Malawi) for a hare. The strip,
which is still being published, features a man and his constant companion,
a dog. The main character roams the countryside, often undertaking mis-
sions that would befit a clown. The comic strip first appeared in *Tazama*,
then in *Baraza*, two Kiswahii newspapers. In 1960, the strip moved to *Taifa
Leo*. According to Gitau, the only other local cartoonist who was publishing
during this period was William Agutu – every other published cartoonist was
syndicated. This remained the state of the art until the emergence of
Terry Hirst, in the 1970s.

Terry Hirst, with Hilary Ng'weno, published *Joe*, the first political
cartoon in Kenya. Unlike characters in other cartoons, who were obviously
fictional, *Joe* gave the impression that he was your next-door neighbour. If
something affected ordinary people, *Joe* could be depended upon to speak

out about it, and chances were that his views would pretty much represent what you would have said. Although the magazine ran for only three years, *Joe* provided the inspiration for many cartoonists who followed. Besides serving as a role model, Hirst unlocked the potential of cartoons to discuss any issue (Katuni 2004). Power was demystified and sensitive private matters were brought to the public domain, laughingly.

The cartoonists who immediately followed *Joe* came from outside Kenya. Three were particularly influential: Tanzanian Philip Ndunguru, Ugandan James Tumisiime and Ghanaian Frank Odoi. Ndunguru joined the *Kenya Times* in 1983, when he introduced the character of Kazibure, who became very popular with readers as a social comic strip. His name literally meaning 'of no use', the main character of *Kazibure* spent time essentially living up to the title. James Tumisiime, an agricultural economist, joined the *Daily Nation* where, besides drawing political cartoons, he wrote humour columns. One of his most popular cartoon characters was 'Bogi Benda', who is probably best described as an African 'Andy Capp'. He enjoyed his beer, and was prone to offering commentary on the emerging middle class and its weaknesses, especially those weaknesses that centred around the groin. Ghanaian-born Frank Odoi started drawing political cartoons for the *Nation* in 1979. Odoi, who now produces a series of weekly comic strips, is one of the most socially and politically conscious cartoonists in the Kenyan scene. His characters tend to be much more mature and his themes are complex, reflective, and intended for adult readership. This is true particularly of the comic strips such as *The Mermaid of Motaba* and *Golgoti*. Like Hirst, Odoi, Tumisiime and Ndunguru have served as role models for later Kenyan

cartoonists, and have influenced the way in which they represent the reality around them.

Kenyan cartoonists started asserting themselves in the 1980s. At about that time, Odoi was working at the *Daily Nation*, and Paul Kelemba (Madd) did his first caricature of the then-President Moi. Other local cartoonists also began to make their presence felt. Koskei Kirui, who was first published in the *East African Standard,* has remained largely a commentator on social subjects. Madd was the first indigenous political cartoonist to reach national prominence. He joined the *Nation* in 1986 as the country's first full-time staff editorial cartoonist. Before that, he had been caricaturing for magazines and other publications in Mombasa on the Kenyan coast. At the *Nation*, Madd was primarily an op-ed cartoonist, focusing on political and social issues (Katuni 2004).

In the 1980s, when the first local editorial cartoons were printed in the local dailies, the prevailing political climate discouraged cartoonists from exploring sensitive subjects. For example, although one could caricature ministers and provincial commissioners, caricaturing the president was out of question, at least in the formal media. However, with the agitation for political change in the late 1980s and early 1990s, cartoonists became bolder. After Madd caricatured the then-president, Daniel Arap Moi, a

precedent for unmasking authority was set. The presidential caricature has since become commonplace in Kenyan cartoons, although in the 1980s it was revolutionary. When Madd moved to the *Standard*, Tanzanian Godfrey 'Gado' Mwampembwa replaced him at the *Nation*, and went on to become one of Africa's most internationally celebrated cartoonists. Gado's editorial cartoons remain extremely popular, due largely to their sharpness, brevity and succinctness.

The cartoonist's art has become institutionalized, with most newspapers now employing staff cartoonists. As newspapers recognized the important contribution cartoonists could make, more opportunities for cartoonists opened up. The advent of the multi-party democracy in the 1990s also contributed to the opening up of space for cartoonists and enabled them to be freer in their expressions. Today, most Kenyan dailies have more than one staff cartoonist. The editorial cartoon has become a permanent feature of editorial pages, and the popularity of the composite cartoon commentary pioneered by Paul Kelemba's *It's a Madd Madd World* is testimony to local cartoonists' talent as social and political commentators. Cartoonists have become bolder with time, and are even running satirical pieces in the public arena. But the rampant lampooning from 2003 onwards of Kenya's only publicly acclaimed First Lady, for instance, may not signify any active social or political agenda for cartoonists. Instead, it fundamentally functions as a marker of humour for the reader. Behind the apparent humour, however, there may be a subtle meaning, for instance, the contradictions that come with power.

BURYING THE HOPES OF KENYA

It is a matter of some concern that cartooning does not use local languages in Kenya. This is perhaps due to the limited available space in most newspapers, and the fact that most are published only in English. There are a few Kiswahili dailies that publish cartoons in local languages, and even fewer vernacular papers that would allow for the growth of more local-language cartoons, despite the need for diversity. A lack of recognizable women cartoonists in Kenya is equally worrying. This may be explained by the fact that cartooning is not taught in schools. The art of cartooning in Kenya is self-taught. This fact may limit opportunities for women to get into cartooning.

COMICS AS TOOLS OF SOCIAL CHANGE

Comics, including comic books, comic strips and animated films, are important and effective entertainment-education strategies to foster social change and the adoption of positive life values. Apart from being entertaining, comics are effective in addressing sensitive issues in a non-threatening way and without compromising cultural and social norms. They are also provocative, informative and attention-grabbing, capturing the attention of a wide cross-section of the public, policy makers and educators. Comics have the power to generate dialogue and discourse on these seemingly sensitive issues.

The challenges faced by development workers in effectively communicating messages to their target audiences has caused a great deal of frustration, not only in Kenya but throughout the developing world. The issues are myriad: how can people be taught new skills at a low cost? What would be a good way to deal with sensitive issues such as reproductive health? How can complicated new research, like in agriculture, be simplified so that ordinary people can benefit? The use of comics has often offered a good communi-

THE UNSEEN TSUNAMI

cation alternative. Comics employ visual storytelling, which must follow local perceptions and visual culture in order to be understood correctly. In order to achieve the desired results, these comics are created locally. Most importantly, locally created comics are made by people to reflect their own issues, in their own language. Local examples of cartooning used in this way include *Ushikwapo Shikamana*, *The Bridge*, *Pop- Ed* and *Maisha ya Nuru*.

The *Ushikwapo Shikamana* ('If Assisted, Assist Yourself') comic strip and comic books were created by Twaweza Communications in conjunction with the Africa office of Population Communications International (PCI). The comic strip first appeared in the Kiswahili daily *Taifa Leo* in 1999, and was published thrice a week for five consequent years. It was targeted at the general public, and was intended to strengthen the impact of the educational issues addressed in the popular radio drama *Ushikwapo Shikamana*, which was broadcast by the Kiswahili Kenya Broadcasting Corporation (KBC). Although it did not follow the radio soap opera episode by episode, its storyline and characters mirrored those of the serial drama, much like *Soul City's* serialized story, which was carried by eleven South African newspapers (Singhal and Rogers 2003).

The comic highlighted and educated the masses on issues that ranged from teenage sex, sexually transmitted infections, condom use and family planning, to safe motherhood and social responsibility issues such as environmental conservation. It also campaigned against social vices, such as wife battering, female genital cutting, drug abuse and rape. Also, it advocated for social responsibility and social justice. For instance, the character Tatu is a catalyst for positive HIV and AIDS messages in the comic strips. One of her students, Dimba, approaches her with what he thinks may be symptoms of HIV and AIDS. Tatu advises him to practise responsible sexual behaviour and to get tested for HIV. Dimba agrees, and the results show that he has a curable sexually transmitted infection. He is, however, strongly advised that, although he may have escaped HIV infection this time, he must act responsibly and use protection every time he has sex in the future. The comic book fulfils an extremely important role in communicating urgent social messages. It reaches out to a young audience facing the critical challenge of growing up in a world ravaged by HIV and AIDS (Singhal and Rogers 2003).

The Bridge was created by Africa Health and Development International (AHADI) for UNFPA, Uganda's Multi-media Programme on Reproductive Health. It targeted school-going youth aged between nine and thirteen years, offering information geared towards encouraging sexual abstinence and delayed onset of sexual encounters among adolescents and young people. These comic books rely heavily upon theories of social learning and recognize the critical role that identification plays in behaviour modification. Characters in the stories are modelled on positive, negative and transitional characters, all of whom are designed to appeal to the young mind while playfully highlighting serious issues related to adolescent sexuality, drug abuse and teenage pregnancy. In this way, these comics simultaneously entertain and educate their audiences.

Pop- Ed, a graphic narrative series by UNFPA, is another example of how comics can be used for entertainment-education. The narrative covers different subjects in its series, and is aimed at educating the widest possible readership. For example, Series 6 (published in 2003) focused on women. Here, different issues affecting women were highlighted, such as women in politics and leadership, retrogressive practices that denigrate women, such as female genital-cutting, reproductive health, gender-related violence, girl child education, and early marriages. On the other hand, Series 7, published in 2004, highlighted issues facing the family in general. These included sex education for adolescents, substance abuse, children's rights, reproductive health and media influence. These series also provided a chance for their readers to provide feedback.

The comic book *Maisha ya Nuru* was created by the Project for Appropriate Technology in Health (PATH), with the aim of encouraging intergenerational and interpersonal communication in Kenya. Due to the changing structure of families today, cross-generational communication has been neglected. People are unable to communicate to their children, and vice versa; women feel unable to talk to their brothers, partners, spouses and in-laws; and individual families have difficulty in communicating with their broader communities. Social etiquette makes it difficult in many communities to freely discuss important matters, particularly matters involving sexuality. At one time, sex and sexuality could be discussed, but such discussions took place in very specific settings and in very specific terms. Once the special forums that facilitated this communication were lost in the transition away from traditional society, a gap resulted. The comic opens a new, socially acceptable space in which this communication can take place.

CONCLUSION

Cartoons are able to capture in powerful images critical moments of life. In their playful commentary, they can persuade us to rethink our behaviour and attitudes about the world around us. Their brevity ensures that only the most important words are presented.

Behaviour modulation is key to social transformation and graphic artists are currently playing a central role among development workers. Cartoonists are reshaping the direction of politics and are making important commentary on sexual and reproductive health in Africa. These topics which are viewed as sensitive in communities have found a space through the pen and ink of the graphic artist.

The news media are a major instrument of social change. They make indispensable inputs to the psycho-political life of a transitional society via the minds and hearts of its people. Within that media, editorial cartooning has traditionally served as a visual means of protest. This tradition has been carried forward by Kenyan cartoonists beginning with Terry Hirst in the 1970s right down to the present. Cartoons in Kenyan newspapers are stories in their own right. They represent the issues or subject at hand in a humorous way and can be deeply critical in ways that written stories would generally not be. They convey subtle and hidden meaning. Cartoons are subject to different interpretation by the reader and therefore can vary with context, a situation that humorists tend to exploit. Though it is difficult to establish a link between Kenyan cartoonists' work and a particular political event, it is clear that cartoons have greatly influenced public attitudes towards political leaders. Kenyan cartoonists see the focus of their art as regulating the behaviour of political leaders and have largely succeeded in their goal of bringing them down to a level where they can be viewed as normal human beings who make mistakes. The public views cartoonists as fearless and objective, if not humorous commentators on the behaviour of hitherto untouchable politicians.

Comics have a tremendous ability in effectively passing information. This is because they are humorous and can be interpreted differently by different individuals. Therefore, they provide a unique way of passing on information in a non-threatening way. This ability has enabled many social scientists to use them to pass on developmental messages in their agenda of fuelling social change and development. As such, the power of comics and cartoons should be harnessed further for positive social programming.

REFERENCES

Chimombo, S. and M. Chimombo (1996), *The Culture of Democracy: Language, Literature, The Arts & Politics in Malawi, 1992–94*. Malawi: Wasi Publications.

Clough, J. (1982), *Cartoons 'N Comics: Communication to the Quick*. In *Media and Values*, USA.

Einser, W. (1985), *Comics and Sequential Art*. Florida: Poorhouse Press.

Katuni (2004), *Drawing the Line: The History and Impact of Political Cartooning in Kenya*. Nairobi: Friedrich Ebert Stiftung and Association of East African Cartoonists (KATUNI). Nairobi.

Singhal, A., and Rogers, E. M. (2003), *Combating AIDS: Communication Strategies in Action*. New Delhi: Sage Publications.

DEMONIC TRADITION: REPRESENTATIONS OF OATHING IN NEWSPAPER COVERAGE OF THE 1997 CRISIS IN COASTAL KENYA[1]

INTRODUCTION

During the last four months of 1997, the Coast Province of Kenya was under a state of national emergency. Collective and individual acts of violence occurred in both urban and rural areas, some of which were perpetrated by members of a loosely organized movement that did not have a consistent name or set of objectives. Throughout the following year, the investigations of the Kenya Human Rights Commission (KHRC) and the Judicial Commission of Inquiry led by Justus Akiwumi[2] convincingly showed that most of the initial collective acts of violence were planned and executed with the assistance of people loyal to Daniel Arap Moi, president of Kenya from 1978 to 2002, and the dominant political party, the Kenya African National Union (KANU). This political violence, organized to destabilize regions of the country in opposition to Moi and KANU, was an effort to influence the outcome of multi-party elections in December 1997.

Kenyan newspapers extensively covered the confusing events. They chronicled specific incidents and effects of the violence that included killings, arson, threats to residents, rapes, theft and the destruction of property. They followed the efforts of law enforcement units, the army and the General Service Unit and attempted to provide information on the membership of the movement. Some articles discussed the existence of oaths and rituals in the movement and speculated about their relationship to the culture of the Mijikenda, a dominant ethnic group in areas where the movement operated.

Many of the achievements in news reporting during this crisis (henceforth referred to here as the 1997 crisis) were the product of bitter post-independence struggles (Ochilo 1993; Ochieng 1992; Wanyande 1995). With increased freedom of the news media and the development of strong human rights organizations over the previous decade, a variety of perspectives on the crisis were available in major newspapers (Kadhi and Rutten

2001; Mazrui 2001). Within three days of the start of the violence, newspapers carried stories airing the views of prominent members of the opposition and the KHRC that implicated the government.[3] In the following months, newspapers provided information that showed cooperation among members of the police force, pro-government politicians and members of the movement. The Kenyan public had print media that could help them to critically conceptualize some of the events and observe the similarities between this episode of violence and other acts of state-sponsored violence years before.

I followed these events from the United States by reading online newspapers, conducting email and written correspondence with Kenyan friends living in Kenya, and engaging in discussions with friends and students from Kenya living in the United States. Having studied the dynamics of movements in the country for two decades, I was struck by the relative freedom of Kenyan newspapers to critically assess the roles of government officials and pro-Moi politicians. Familiar with discourses of colonial and postcolonial administrative officials concerning Mijikenda culture, I observed a tendency in some of the newspaper articles to confuse the practice of oathing with witchcraft, and to assume that anything having to do with oathing could be identified with Mijikenda culture.

In conversations and interviews with Kenyans in the US and Kenya, Kenyans who identified themselves ethnically as Mijikenda shared my perceptions. Many Kenyans who did not identify as Mijikenda seemed to be more interested in a different set of issues concerning the movement and maintained the general impression that oath administrators, witchcraft practitioners and Mijikenda religious authorities had supportive or overlapping roles and that these roles were grounded in Mijikenda culture. Some of them also indicated their ambivalence toward Mijikenda religious practices and authorities and said that the events of the 1997 crisis illustrated that Mijikenda people maintained a high degree of belief in outdated ideas such as witchcraft which had a detrimental effect on contemporary life.

Consistent with the perspective of the Kenya Human Rights Commission (1997, 1998), I viewed the conflation of Mijikenda cultural practices and the practices of the movement as an intentional part of the plan developed by pro-Moi architects of the movement. I was concerned by the responses of many of the people with whom I exchanged ideas, for it seemed that this state-sponsored political scheme, built on a series of well-worn ethnic stereotypes about cultural beliefs and backwardness, had succeeded in conveying the notion that Mijikenda was involved in oaths used by movement members, and that this was against the moral and political advancement of the county.

I wondered what role the news media might have had in reporting about the movement, the acts of violence, and the views and practices of coastal peoples that supported primitivizing ethnic stereotyping. Were the news media in Kenya sensitive to the difference between cultural views and practices, and the invented traditions of politics? Did representations of Mijikenda people as backward and absorbed in witchcraft, so common in administrative and Christian missionary discourses, continue to appear in the news media?

The present work attempts to establish a general understanding of the representational practices of the Kenyan news media concerning the subjects of oathing, witchcraft, Mijikenda culture, and violence in the 1997 crisis in coastal Kenya. It chooses oathing as its primary subject, and examines representations of oathing in newspaper articles written over a fourteen-month period in two of Kenya's most-read English-language newspapers, the *East African Standard* and the *Nation*. It assumes that the terms and framing devices used in these newspapers are illustrative of Kenya's English language news media in general, and does not make claims generalizable to media in other languages. Analysis relies on publications from Human Rights Watch, the Kenya Human Rights Commission, and the Akiwumi Commission Inquiry, and is informed by interviews I conducted from 1997 to 2004 in Kenya and the United States.

The first section of the paper provides an overview of the 1997 crisis and some of the central cultural institutions and practices of the Mijikenda.[4] The second section analyzes a selected group of newspaper articles that address the subject of oathing, in order to evaluate assumptions about the relationship between oathing on the one hand, and Mijikenda cultural institutions, authorities and practices on the other. It shows how newspaper representations of oathing practices in the 1997 crisis rely on framing devices that associate oathing with witchcraft, link oathing and witchcraft to danger and violence, and situate oathing and witchcraft in Mijikenda culture. It argues that these framing devices are guided by an umbrella theme, which I term 'the revelation of demonic tradition'. The representation of aspects of African cultural tradition as backward, dangerous, irrational, pathological and engaged with demonic or occult forces and beings has been well documented in a variety of colonial missionary, literary and social science texts. For some scholars, the persistence of these and related discursive traditions is of urgent concern to the future of African peoples and the continent of Africa (Mudimbe 1988, 1994). Of particular interest to this paper is the question of how the news media, influenced by these discursive traditions, develop framing techniques that shape the political imaginary. How do frames that conjure demonic tradition at the heart of cultural expression discourage the conceptualization of and support for forms of culturally inspired leadership in contemporary African political life?

STATE-SPONSORED VIOLENCE IN KENYA

Before Kenya returned to multi-party politics in 1991, the Moi regime worked to achieve success in elections through KANU's domination of local and regional political processes, and through the use of state repression that largely targeted individuals and organizations. Between 1992 and 1996, the Moi regime added to its repertoire the creation of large-scale acts of state-sponsored violence that led to the physical displacement of people and conditions of widespread insecurity in the Rift Valley and Western Provinces (KHRC 1998: 1). In 1997, coastal Kenya was added to the list of regions affected by what the KHRC (1997) regards as state repression under the guise of protecting citizens from ethnic violence. As in the Rift Valley, in 1997 in coastal Kenya there were formations of violence characterized by attacks or raids instigated by groups of people loyal to Moi and KANU, and styled to appear as long-standing ethnic conflicts or land conflicts. Another common feature of the violence in the Rift Valley and Coastal Kenya was that raiders wore clothing featuring symbols or design styles associated with particular ethnic groups, and carried weapons such as knives, spears, bows, and arrows that represent the material culture of pre-colonial warriors.

The official term given by the government of Kenya to these periods of violence was 'ethnic clashes' or 'tribal clashes'. President Moi and pro-Moi politicians blamed the violence in coastal Kenya on 'evil men' who were believers in 'small gods and ghosts',[5] implying that their beliefs were against monotheistic or Christian religions. They also claimed that the 'clashes' were fuelled by 'tribal sentiments' (KHRC 1998a: 59). Many newspaper reports and the government-sponsored Akiwumi Report (Government of Kenya 2001) similarly referred to the violence in 1997 coastal Kenya as 'tribal clashes'. Mazrui (2001) offered strong criticism of this position on the violence in coastal Kenya, preferring to characterize it as 'ethnicized violence'. Consistent with this and similar views of the KHRC (1997, 1998), the term '1997 crisis' used in this paper reflects an attempt to distinguish my perspective from one that conceptualizes ethnic conflict as the cause of violence.

According to the KHRC (1997, 1998a), programmes of state-sponsored violence conducted by the Moi regime have had wide-ranging harmful effects. They have intensified community conflict, further split community political interests, punished people with oppositional views, displaced those who were likely to vote for opposition candidates, and frightened people in ways that encouraged them to vote for the ruling party. It is possible to understand what Moi and KANU reasoned they would gain from widespread chaos in Coastal Kenya before the election: the displacement of large numbers of people from ethnic groups that were inclined to vote for opposition parties.[6] In addition, Moi, KANU and KANU-allied political candidates would gain votes from people who perceived the crisis to be resolved through government efforts, associated KANU with continuity and order, and considered KANU to be the most effective political organization to prevent continued political instability (KHRC 1998a).

The creation of theatres of violence in coastal Kenya in 1997 can be further understood as the Moi regime's attempt to counter the many pro-democracy movements that had rendered ineffective government efforts to thwart opposition parties. In the early and mid 1990s at the coast, the Moi government refused to register three major opposition parties: the Islamic Party of Kenya (IPK), the National Democratic Union (NADU), and the United Muslims of Africa (UMA). Some of these parties eventually allied with other registered parties whose support was based in central and western Kenya. Their potential ability to speak to popular sentiments against central government authority and political repression can be seen in a 1992 NADU federalist policy statement for the coast, which was explicitly positioned against 'internal colonization by upcountry groups' (KHRC 1998a). The growth of opposition parties and the potential for their alliance provided Moi and KANU with a formidable challenge.

POLITICAL AND CULTURAL DIFFERENCE IN COASTAL KENYA

The areas most affected by violence during the 1997 crisis were Mombasa Division (including Mombasa Island and Likoni) and Kwale District, located south of Mombasa. People who identify themselves as Mijikenda in 1997 composed approximately 80 per cent of the population in Mombasa Division and Kwale District, while the remaining 20 per cent identified themselves as Swahili, Kamba, Luo, Kikuyu or Luhya (KHRC 1997: 10). Mijikenda are also the dominant ethnic group in Kilifi District, another district adjacent to Mombasa.

In coastal Kenya, tensions between groups of people with different ethnic affiliations have often grown out of colonial economic, political and legal practices. Some of the polarizations manifested in the 1997 crisis were shaped in the late 1950s and early 1960s, when conditions of economic disparity and perceived inequalities in job opportunities contributed to conflicts between peoples with a long history of settlement on the coast (*wapwani*) and peoples from western and central Kenya who had migrated to the coast in the twentieth century (referred to as 'upcountry' people by many *wapwani* Kenyans, and 'people of the road', or *wabara*, by many Mijikenda).[7] In addition to ethnic differences between the more recent immigrants and *wapwani*, in some areas of the coast there were salient differences in the religious orientations of people from the two groups. In Likoni Division and Kwale District, administrative units that were the most affected by the 1997 crisis, the majority of *wapwani* were Muslim, and the majority of the more recent immigrants were Christian.

Perceived differences in economic opportunity structured by ethnicity and religion were exacerbated by a general economic decline on the coast and throughout the country beginning in the late 1980s. There were no consistent attempts on the part of the national or regional government to address the land problem: considerable portions of agricultural land on the coastal strip had not yet been registered or titled, and a large number of squatters and workers occupying crowded hostels lived near luxurious private beach homes and tourist hotels. Conditions of extreme economic disparity were intensified by what a Kenyan Human Rights Commission Report (1997: 17) refers to as 'localized despotism', a condition characterized by the coercive and tyrannical practices of police, chiefs and district officers, most of whom identified with immigrant groups. Mijikenda in urban and semi-urban areas spoke of animosity toward police, whom they believed unnecessarily harassed local Mijikenda (1997: 17). These differences worked to enforce the perception of opposition structured along the conceptual categories of 'local and coastal' versus 'exogenous and upcountry'.

FORMS OF VIOLENCE IN THE 1997 CRISIS

The 1997 crisis began on the night of 13 August when about twenty young men, some of whom identified themselves from the Digo sub-group of the Mijikenda, attacked and burned the Likoni Police Station, killed five police officers, released prisoners and took rifles and ammunition.[8] These men, later referred to in police and news reports as raiders, also destroyed Likoni police residences, the Likoni tourist booth, offices of the chief and district officer of Likoni, the Waa Chief's camp, the Ngombeni Administration Police Camp, and properties and businesses owned by more recent immigrants to the coast.[9] The Akiwumi Judicial Commission Report Government of Kenya (2001) shows that other police and military forces did not act to assist the Likoni police that night, and neither the Provincial police nor the Kenya navy (on the same side of the ferry) offered help.

After three days the violence had spread to other parts of Kwale District, Mombasa Division and Kilifi District. Leaflets circulated in Kwale that threatened '*wabara*' and urged them to return to 'ethnic homelands' (KHRC 1998a: 57), resulted in widespread panic. Schools closed and many people went to live with family in other parts of Kenya or sought refuge in churches and other sites on Mombasa Island. At the height of the crisis, between 4,000 and 5,000 Kikuyu, Luo and Luhya people camped in churches and schools, and women and children who were afraid to return to their homes stayed in overcrowded facilities for weeks and months (KHRC 1998a: 68).

In the first few weeks immediately following the Likoni attack, police and army units delayed investigating many of the areas known to be raider hide-outs, particularly the forests located in Kwale District. As has been noted in KHRC reports (1997, 1998), quickly capturing armed raiders might have ended some of the violence earlier and reduced the need for people to vacate their homes. A new wave of violence directed towards *wapwani* began three weeks after the first, which can be attributed to the actions of the Kenyan General Security Forces (GSU) who were stationed in Kwale District (KHRC 1998b). Digo and Duruma, two of the Mijikenda sub-groups, were the majority of people who fled their homes for fear of GSU searches, staying in other areas of the coast or in mosques and schools. Victims reported that members of the GSU stole possessions, raped women when they entered homes claiming to search for weapons, arrested and beat several hundred men, and fired on unarmed civilians. Most large-scale acts of violence con-cluded by the end of November 1997, but attacks on individual people and businesses were recorded until May 1998.[10]

THE MOVEMENT

The collectivity that planned acts of violence, organized the raiders, and par-ticipated in raids does not appear to have given itself a consistent name, although during interrogations some of the raiders caught by police referred to themselves as 'the force' (KHRC 1997: 23). Aside from the politicians and coastal administrators who were involved in planning and monitoring the raids, the raiders and their commanders were composed of two cate-gories of men,[11] the largest of which was from the coast and the majority of whom were young Mijikenda. A few were Kenyan ex-servicemen. The smaller group was composed of men with military experience from other areas of Kenya, a small number of men from Rwanda who may have been involved in the Rwandan genocide, and a few men from Uganda (KHRC 1998b: 61). The smaller group trained recruits and directed attacks. From the perspective of the KHRC reports and other analysts, it would appear that these men were identified and recruited by members of one of Moi's cliques or by KANU politicians. The Akiwumi Report estimated that over 6,963 youths from Kwale and Likoni were recruited for movement activi-ties, and approximately 800 servicemen and ex-servicemen trained them.[12] No women were ever reported to have been directly involved in the raids.

In addition to guns, raiders carried bows and arrows, knives and machetes.[13] The colour of many of the raider uniforms was black, and some had crossed stripes of red and white on the back of the shirt.[14] Black, red and white are the colours used in Mijikenda healing rituals, appearing in the clothing of Mijikenda healers who are members of spirit groups, on beaded armbands and necklaces worn by Mijikenda that carry protective medicines, and on strips of cloth tied to ancestor spirit posts placed near Mijikenda homes. The symbol of the cross used on some raider uniforms is possibly related to the cross design used for clothes worn by women undergoing treatment for spirit affliction, associated with possessory spirits bearing the names of ethnic groups with whom coastal peoples have had a long history of association, such as the spirits Mmassai and Nyari. Uniforms worn by raiders also included designs in the shape of a crescent and a star, which link them to Islam.

While it is clear that some members of the movement did rely on oaths to help form their organization, the exact connection to the cultural traditions and contemporary authorities of Mijikenda culture has not been well established in scholarly work.[15] It appears as though the architects of the movement attempted to identify movement members with symbols of Mijikenda culture, creating an invented tradition that many non-Mijikenda would classify as Mijikenda.

Within the first week of the crisis, newspapers reported that members of the movement had taken an oath. Although detailed reports of the oath were not published in newspapers, several articles described some of the items confiscated by police from places where oathing was alleged to have taken place, and at least one article reported information about the oath taken from men who were captured by police. During the first months of the crisis, it appeared that most of the oathing rituals took place in rural areas, particularly in forests associated with Mijikenda habitation. Some of these forests are known by the Mijikenda word *makaya*. Speculations on the identities of oath administrators continued throughout the crisis and in the investigations of the Akiwumi Judicial Commission the following year.

WHAT IS AN OATH?

An oath is a verbal request to divinity or a mystical power to judge the truth of what the oath taker says. A person who has taken an oath is then bound by the conditions stipulated in the pronouncement and subjected to punishment if the requirements of the oath are broken. Oaths can help to create and bind human relationships, identify and prevent moral transgressions, and resolve human conflicts. Taken by people inducted into restricted societies, they can help to create a sense of obligation to a group, instil devotion to courses of action, and prevent the disclosure of information to non-members.[16]

Most people in Kenya use the English word 'oathing' to refer to a ritual containing a verbal statement that commits a person to an action. It is also understood as a pledge of loyalty. These were also dominant understandings of oaths used in the Mau Mau movement.[17] Some similar understandings appear in the statements of government officials, police officers and movement informants to describe oathing practices concerning the movement involved in the 1997 crisis (KHRC 1998a: 61).

The term 'oath' in English does not have a direct translation in the Mijikenda language, but the closest term to it is *kiraho* (pl. *viraho*), which refers to a particular category of magic that offers protection to its users or to the virtuous in a dispute (Ciekawy 1997a, 1997b, 2009). One of the effects of a *kiraho* is to discourage potential transgressors who are afraid of its power to cause sickness or death. In order to recover, a transgressor must be treated by a *kiraho* specialist who removes the protective magic, an activity that is sometimes referred to as cleansing. Mijikenda distinguish this form of mystical harm from *utsai*, harmful magic that is directed at a particular person or group of people, and that is often referred to in English as witchcraft (Ciekawy 1998, 2001).

Some *viraho* are designed to directly protect the people and property of those who commission them, and others are administered as both oaths and ordeals in legal disputes. *Viraho* are also used to bind a person to a set of responsibilities and actions. In pre-colonial Mijikenda society, young men and women took a *kiraho* during initiation ceremonies, promising to contribute to the positive development of the members of their age set and to maintain the secrets associated with adulthood (Spear 1978; Brantley 1981). Ritual specialists gave *kiraho* and other forms of defensive magic to the members of warrior organizations before battle (Spear 1978).

The pre-colonial socio-political organization of peoples who are presently called Mijikenda rested on progressive advancement in the male age-set system and induction into restricted societies that sanctioned practices of giving *kiraho* (Spear 1978). Today *viraho* continue to be administered by members of these societies who are known as *azhere a kaya* (*kaya* elders). They are also administered by independent specialists who purchase the knowledge and skills, but *viraho* given by *kaya* elders are generally considered to be more powerful, for *kaya* elders have a particularly close relationship with the spirits of important deceased lineage elders who authorize Mijikenda *viraho* (Ciekawy 1997b, 2004).

OATHING AND THE CHALLENGE TO STATE POWER

Oathing procedures have been central to the organization of many resistance and revolutionary organizations throughout the colonial period in Africa. A *kiraho* was used in 1914 during the Giriama War by one group of Mijikenda, the Giriama, in their fight against British colonialism. Oaths in the Mau Mau war of liberation helped to established a code of moral behaviour and facilitated Gikuyu cooperation. The pronouncements and the accompanying ritual relied on the symbolism of older Gikuyu oaths adapted to address the problems posed by colonial rule and land dispossession.[18]

Colonists in Kenya, missionaries and British government officials actively engaged in a propaganda campaign to portray Mau Mau activities as uncivilized, irrational, pathological, coercive and amoral (Barnett and Njama 1966; Maloba 1998; Maughan-Brown 1985).

The colonial press presented sensationalistic details of oathing ceremonies, reinforcing existing colonial prejudices against African culture and the belief that African peoples were unable to establish forms of leadership appropriate for state governance. These responses to the Mau Mau were consistent with other representations that demonized African thought and culture. In Europe and the United States, the negative portrayal of the Mau Mau oath in colonial novels and in the international press served to create greater sympathy for the colonial government and undermine the legitimacy of African peoples' struggles (Maloba 1998; Maughan-Brown 1985).

Because of their power to influence collective action and support revolutionary organizations, many colonial governments in Africa regarded the oaths, oathing rituals and oathing organizations of colonized peoples as a threat to the administration of colonial law in local settings and to the control of state power. The colonial government in Kenya developed laws to limit collective gatherings, ban particular rituals and prohibit African peoples from taking or administering some oaths based on their religious traditions (Ciekawy 1997a).[19] Adopted by the independent government, many of the same laws are used today to suppress alternative political initiatives and support state institutions and the power of government office holders.

In the laws of Kenya, both giving and taking an oath are illegal (Mutungi 1977). 'Unlawful Oath' is the title of Section 59(b) of the Penal Code in the laws of Kenya; in the discourse of administrators in coastal Kenya, it is often called an 'illegal oath' (Ciekawy 1997a). Police are vested with the authority to arrest anyone on suspicion of engaging in oathing, which can be widely interpreted as any religious or healing ritual. In addition to the act of giving or taking an oath, an oath to commit an offence is also recognized in the laws of Kenya, as well as coercing someone into taking an oath (Mutungi 1997).[20]

KAYA AS A SYMBOL OF MIJIKENDA CONTINUITY

Until the mid-eighteenth century, ancestors of the Mijikenda occupied fortified enclosures located in forests along what is now the coast of Kenya. These enclosures and the immediate forest around them are known in the Mijikenda language as *makaya* (si. *kaya*). While serving as a settlement and ritual centres, *makaya* were also used for the purpose of defence against the raids of pastoralists and slave traders (Spear 1978; Willis 1993). Contemporary *kaya* elders who administer *viraho* are therefore seen as carriers of a protective tradition that supports some of the religious, legal, political and health institutions that are central to Mijikenda life.

There are extensive debates about claims to authoritative oathing practices of the *kaya* in many Mijikenda communities, although among Agiriama and Aravahi the continued maintenance of *kaya* institutions allows them to make clear distinctions between *kaya* elders and other men with knowledge of *kiraho* practices. As an inductee into a restricted society with set standards for education, men undergo training in oratorical skills and philosophical debate (Ciekawy 1997b). Like many other Mijikenda elders, they are experienced judges and arbiters in legal councils, but they have greater knowledge of Mijikenda philosophy and *desturi* (tradition). They singularly maintain the knowledge and skills to use certain forms of esoteric power, have their own institutional forms and membership requirements, and maintain the distinction of carrying staffs and wearing specific clothing (Ciekawy 1997b). They regularly meet to conduct collective rituals ensuring human and crop fertility, and to prevent large-scale epidemics.

For most Mijikenda, the knowledge and rituals of the *kaya*, the *kaya* forest and the *kaya* elders themselves are dominant symbols. According to Parkin (1991), both *kaya* elders and *kaya* forests are central to Mijikenda identity and are imagined in a variety of new ways that reflect the changing lifestyles of Mijikenda people. Regardless of the variety of other meanings it carries, most Mijikenda agree that the term *kaya* stands for Mijikenda tradition and continuity.

FRAMING THE 1997 CRISIS

The newspaper articles selected for analysis in this paper concern the topic of oathing. The two papers chosen for study were the *Daily Nation* and the *East African Standard* (both English-language newspapers) for the period 13 August 1997 to 31 December 1997. A total of twenty-eight articles mention oathing, mostly in the context of police and army battles with raiders, police and army search operations, and the capture of raiders in forests and cave hideouts. A smaller number, nine, address the administration of oaths, the arrest of people suspected of conducting oathing practices and witchcraft, and the uses of oathing by movement members. Framing devices used in five of these nine articles will be analyzed in this study.

Media frames organize information for journalists and readers. Goffman's work on frame analysis, on which many media analysts rely, points out that frames allow their users to 'locate, perceive, identify, and label a seemingly infinite number of concrete occurrences defined in its terms' (1974: 21). Gitlin defines frames as 'persistent patterns of cognition, interpretation, and presentation, of selection, emphasis, and exclusion, by which symbol handlers routinely organize discourse, whether verbal or

visual' (1980: 7). Framing devices work to select aspects of reality and position them in ways that shape users' orientation to a problem and facilitate a
particular interpretation or analysis of it.

Gitlin's best known work, applied to the study of movements,[21] identifies
three frames that are useful in the present analysis of newspaper articles on
oathing: marginalization (the act of portraying movement participants as
deviants), an over-emphasis on the perspectives and concerns of government officials (police, legal prosecutors and government officials), and
reliance on statements by government officials (Gitlin 1980: 27). I identify
two other frames in these articles. One is the emphasis on violent and sensationalistic aspects of oathing and witchcraft. This focus far exceeds contextual information about the cultural basis of oathing practices or the lives
of people suspected of participating in oathing activities. The other is the use
of description that presents people suspected of oathing and witchcraft as
backward, irrational, dangerous and amoral. The following analysis shows
that several of these frames are employed in each of the five articles selected
for this study.

THE CULTURE OF THE OATH

The article entitled 'Security Team Scours Hideouts', written three days
after the initial attack in Likoni, provides details on the conditions under
which the raiders were captured and cites sources that have information on
confessions taken from ten captured raiders.[22] It mentions the name of an
elderly oath administrator, Mzee Swaleh, who later becomes a notorious
figure in the reports of the KHRC and the Akiwumi Commission of
Inquiry.[23] It identifies Similani, Kaya Bombo and Kaya Waa as the wilder-
ness areas and forests in which raiders were trained.

This article is one of the first to provide the name *kinu* for the oath used
by the raiders and to speculate on its uses. *Kinu* in Kiswahili refers to a
wooden mortar used for pounding grain and crushing vegetable matter. At
the coast a *kinu* is used by ritual specialists to mix medicinal herbs that
afflicted or restricted society initiates apply to their bodies. The article states
that the oath 'is normally given to Mijikenda youth to invigorate them'. No
more information is available for readers to interpret how Mijikenda use the
oath, such as in a healing ritual or a rite of passage. The critical modifier in
the sentence is 'normally', which gives the impression that the oath is
commonly practised or is a customary aspect of Mijikenda culture. The
article also provides other information on events at the coast, including
the District Commissioner's plans to find raiders, raiders killed in Likoni,
an incident in which raiders kill residents in Timbwani Quarry, and
another in which raiders hit residents with a *panga* and shoot residents with
an arrow.

It is not possible to determine how the reporters obtained most of their information from the captured raiders. The article places the oath in Mijikenda culture, and does not instigate questions about how the oath could be an invented tradition of political strategy. Readers are likely to assume that the oathing activity and the location, an area populated by Mijikenda, mean that the oathing ritual is a Mijikenda one. Descriptions of violence in the remaining paragraphs serve to associate the oath with harmful consequences to human beings. The set of references to raiders, weapons, *kaya* forests, oaths and Mijikenda practices establishes a coherent story that enables an interpretation of movement subjects, actions, goals and places of operation. In the coming months the main components of this story would be re-represented in many other articles.

OFFICIAL VIEWS

In 'Eight Coast Raiders Killed', the author describes a raiders' camp, a police operation in Kaya Bombo that discovers a cache of weapons, and incidents where police killed raiders.[24] Seven of the fifteen paragraphs are devoted to the contents of a press release by the Coast Provincial Commissioner. The following is a quote from the article:

> The PC appealed to leaders to educate the people to abandon belief in witchcraft, which he said had been the motivating factor behind the raiders. He said that raiders still believe that when they wear the red band and bite their small finger they become invisible to the police and that no bullet can harm them.

The article also focuses on a special search conducted at a roadblock in Kwale for the purpose of finding movement youths who attempted to steal a police officer's rifle:

> Police in Kwale are also searching people for body marks which the raiders are believed to be having after taking traditional oaths to fight up-country people in Kikoni and Kwale areas. In the incident where two men attempted to snatch a rifle from the policeman who had stopped a Nissan matatu, the suspects were ordered to lift up their shirts to see if they had the marks.

In an article run the same day in a different newspaper, entitled 'Six More Kwale Raiders Killed', the author describes the same police search at the roadblock: 'Meanwhile, at the roadblock, all men were being asked to leave their vehicles and bare their chests for any witchcraft marks believed to be made during oathing'.[25] It devotes seven of its sixteen paragraphs to the PC's advice for community leaders and local people, presenting the following quote from the PC: 'I would call upon the raiders to surrender as they were fighting a losing battle as the witchcraft method they were using is not only primitive, but stupid and backward!' It goes on to report that 'local leaders were asked to organize education programmes for the local communities and discourage their belief in witchcraft'. PC is also said to have instructed the District Commissioner to 'Launch public barazas where people would be advised to root out this nonsense called witchcraft.' An additional comment finishes the piece: 'The oath is supposed to make the raiders believe they are immune to bullets. They also believe that by biting their small index finger and glaring at police officers, they become invisible.'

Both of these articles give half of their space to the positions and statements of the Provincial Commissioner. They offer his view that the lack of education among coastal people is a foundation for the raiders' irrational beliefs, which he in turn relates to coastal people's witchcraft beliefs. This dominant voice of the PC provides the logic behind police search operations. Both articles prominently feature the police roadblock and show that the police are guided by the assumption that oathing is related to witchcraft and that men who have engaged in oathing and witchcraft can be detected through bodily examination. A key detail that substantiates the assumption of continuity between raider beliefs and Mijikenda witchcraft rituals passes for ethnographic fact: that the raiders think that by biting their index finger they can effect invisibility. A portrait of movement of members' beliefs and motivations emerges as an irrational attachment to magical rituals guided by outdated traditions. The tone of mockery in the PC's voice, conveyed by the exclamation point, emphasizes the difference between the views of administrative and legal authorities and movement members' dependence on primitive means to address complex political problems.

THE DANGERS OF WITCHCRAFT AND OATHING

In two articles that report people arrested on suspicion of giving oaths, the word 'witchcraft' is used as a synonym for oathing. 'Witchdoctor on Oathing Charge' describes the arrest of three people who were charged with taking and administering oaths in Kaya Kambe 'binding them to kill when called upon to do so'.[26] The author appears to have been present when the suspects were charged in court. The three people are identified by name and described as a seventy-nine-year-old man and two youths. In the title the elder is referred to as a witchdoctor, without the qualifier 'suspected', shaping the authority of this representation even before the reader begins to learn more about the circumstances of arrest and the suspects' responses to the legal charge. The label 'witchdoctor' conveys antisocial and dangerous behaviour that is highly stigmatizing. Thus, in the first paragraph the reader is challenged to maintain empathy for the suspects and a critical attitude toward the reasons for their arrest.

The author has most likely relied on law enforcement personnel to guide the language used in the article. The acts of oathing and witchcraft are legal offences in Kenya, and in the English language spoken in Kenya they are often linked. It would be easy for readers who are not familiar with the suspects' ritual expertise to place both activities in the same category of illegality. The suspicions of legal enforcement officers and popular notions about oathing and witchcraft set the frame for the story and remain dominant throughout. As in all the other articles in this study, the absence of investigative reporting on the lives of those arrested provides few alternative interpretive avenues for the reader to follow.

It is nevertheless possible to speculate on the reasons why the men came to the attention of law officers, for in contrast to the other four articles, this reporter gives voice to one of the elder men who was arrested. The article says that the elder denied the charge and paraphrases the elder's statement that he was wrongfully arrested in the forest, where he had gone to perform routine rituals 'to please the gods'. Readers might assume that the elder is a *kaya* elder of Kambe, and that he might have gone to conduct a ritual to communicate with ancestor spirits or the supreme being. But because the first line of the article links the activity to an oath that binds takers to acts of killing, readers are inclined to think about the elder, his rituals and the *kaya* forest in harmful and dangerous terms.[27]

The article engages in an additional act that has the potential to prejudice readers against the suspected elder. For many readers, the use of the phrase 'to please the gods' positions the elder's religious orientation in opposition to monotheism. The reporter uses the word 'gods', not 'God'. It is likely that the reporter has little familiarity with Mijikenda religion and the Mijikenda language, and has used his/her own conceptualization or that of a non-Mijikenda police official to describe the elder's intended activity. The misrepresentation of Mijikenda monotheism and religious expression has been a persistent problem throughout the twentieth and twenty-first centuries. This article is likely to enforce a stereotype of Mijikenda religion as animistic and unchristian, and to diminish empathy for the elder.

The second article concerning oathing and witchcraft, entitled 'Police Arrest Two over Coast Oathing Reports', describes a man and a woman suspected of administering oaths to the perpetrators of violence.[28] The second sentence provides a striking and exoticizing qualification of their circumstance that most probably caught the attention of law officers: 'The two had a live monkey and feathers'. Although not narrating related events, the following sentence further connects the suspects and their unusual possessions to violence: 'And at Kaloleni township in Kilifi District, at least eight kiosks belonging to people from up-country were razed to the ground by raiders on Saturday night.'

The way this article is crafted, oathing is placed under the purview of witchcraft. It states, 'The oath the raiders are believed to have been taking to kill when called upon is administered by witchdoctors'. Here the author is careful to say that the raiders are believed to have taken an oath, but confidently asserts that the oath is given by witchdoctors. It appears that the author is trying to explain why the two people are suspected of oathing, and does so by assuming that they are witchdoctors. As in the previous article, it is likely that this reporter, as is common practice in the profession, encountered the suspects at a police station or a court. Most probably this reporter has taken a police officer's point of view, for reporters often speak with police and court officials in order to gather information for their stories. Partly because of the singularity of the event, and as a way of drawing attention to the article, the reporter mentions the monkey and the feathers two times. The overall effect is to portray the two suspects as deviant people who merit legal inquiry. As in many other articles written during the 1997 crisis, information concerning violence is included. This article concludes with a farmer's report of raiders in Likoni, police and GSU searches, and threats of an attack on the Msambweni District, further grafting the two suspects, their animal companion and their unusual possessions to violent acts and dangerous potentials.

CONCLUSIONS

Together, the framing devices identified in this study of newspaper representations of the 1997 crisis in coastal Kenya perform a particular kind of work. All of the articles examined in this paper rely on some frames that privilege the viewpoints of administrators and police. The articles demonstrate an absence of viewpoints held by many of the people subjected to investigation, a persistent problem identified in comprehensive studies of the news media in Kenya (Abugoa and Mutere 1988).

The content of the articles place movement oathing activities in the 1997 crisis within the cultural repertoire of the Mijikenda. The articles do not attempt to conceptually distinguish among violent acts, speculations on the beliefs of movement members, oathing and witchcraft practices, and contemporary Mijikenda cultural expressions. Two of the articles that attempt to provide information connecting oathing used in the movement to Mijikenda cultural practices perform major acts of misrepresentation.

Some of the framing devices act to portray oathing and Mijikenda cultural traditions as backward, irrational and dangerous. This is also accomplished by conflating oathing and witchcraft, and drawing from past mis-characterizations of Mijikenda religious practices and views. For national audiences, most of whom know little about coastal peoples and their cultural traditions, these articles facilitate a conceptualization of movement oathing beliefs and activities as part of an atavistic, irrational and dangerous Mijikenda tradition.

A narrative reminiscent of colonialist perspectives about the Mau Mau is also in play. The narrative goes something like this: mysterious traditional oathing practices bind members of a revolutionary organization who hide in forests; the mysterious traditional oaths and revolutionaries present a combined threat to the common people, the moral order, and state stability; and state agents must act to stop both the revolutionaries and the demonic tradition empowering revolutionary aims. While it is now clear that there is no comparison between the aims of the Mau Mau freedom fighter movement and the movement active in the 1997 crisis in coastal Kenya, a conceptual graft can be seen to shape some of the frames that presented the 1997 crisis. A portrait of the *kaya* forest and its cultural authorities as a centre of dangerous and disorderly power emerges from newspaper reports, one that is in contrast to the dominant notion Mijikenda hold. *Kaya* tradition as a site of moral reference, concentration of sacred power, and symbol of Mijikenda continuity does not achieve representation. What kind of effect does this create on the political imagination?

Hegemonic state interests were served by some of these newspaper reports, for Moi's continuation as president was at stake in the 1997 general election. The 1997 crisis was achieved through the manipulation of ethnic stereotypes and the use of violence structured by essentialized and polarized notions of ethnic identity. Some of the newspaper articles used to present and interpret the 1997 crisis supported these conceptualizations. Moreover, by speaking to fantasies of archaic and amoral oathing and witchcraft practices, framing devices presented in newspaper articles positioned Mijikenda tradition and cultural continuity in opposition to the political progress of the country. Well after the crisis, while the exact role of oathing in the movement remains unclear to most Kenyan people, it is still possible to suspect that power shaped by Mijikenda cultural authorities was somehow at the heart of the movement. Does this also imply that political advancement depends on the exorcism of particular cultural repertoires, along with the cultural authorities who animate them?

NOTES

1. I am grateful to Ousseina Alidou, Haley Duschinski, George Gathigi, Loisa Luiyana, Alamin Mazrui, V.Y. Mudimbe, Kimani Njogu, Peter Otiato and Ernest Waititu for comments on earlier versions of this paper, and thank Ernest Waititu for his research to identify newspaper articles used in this study.
2. The most comprehensive documents on the 1997 crisis are from the Kenyan Human Rights Commission (KHRC) and the Judicial Commission of Inquiry into the Tribal Clashes in Kenya, sponsored by the Government of Kenya and led by Justus Akiwumi. The Judicial Commission of Inquiry presented its findings as a report, which is referred to here as publication from the Government of Kenya. Dr Alamin Mazrui, who was in Mombasa at the time of the 1997 crisis, is the primary author of the 1997 and 1998 KHRC reports.
3. 'Kenyans Condemn Vicious Attack', *Daily Nation*, 16 August 1997.
4. The groups included in the Mijikenda are Digo, Duruma, Kambe, Chonyi, Rabai, Ribe, Giriama, Jibana and Kauma.

5. Cited in KHRC 1998b: 59, from 'Why Violence Erupted in Mombasa', *The Update*, no. 56, 30 September 1997.
6. The election results in 1997 were generally favourable to Moi and KANU. In Coast Province the percentage of votes for Moi (61.05) was only slightly lower than in 1992, but voter turnout was much lower (KHRC 1998a: 63). Detailed analyses of the results in coastal Kenya can be found in Grignon, Rutton and Mazrui (2001), KHRC (1998a, b), Mazrui (2001) and Throup and Hornsby (1998). Regardless of the election results, the KHRC argues that the technique of creating instability before elections has been a central feature of Moi's statecraft in the 1990s.
7. Before and after independence, Mijikenda strongly supported the Mijikenda politician R. G. Ngala, who was the leader of the Kenya African Democratic Union (KADU) party and a major advocate of regionalism (*majimboism*). Mijikenda often express to me their pride in Ngala's Mijikenda ancestry, emphasizing the importance of his leadership as the first interim president of Kenya and his contributions to political thought concerning regionalism. In the independence period, KADU and the Kenya African National Union (KANU) were the main competing political parties, and when KANU won, Ngala was pressured to formally end his participation in KADU and join KANU, a move that effected Kenya's transition to a one-party state. Most Mijikenda and many members of other small ethnic groups were allied with KADU, for it addressed their concern that people from the larger and more powerful ethnic groups would continue to dominate coastal economic and political life. Attracted to the regionalist (*majimboist*) political philosophy that explicitly addressed the problem of ethnic minorities, many Mijikenda considered its principles to be a way to ensure local or regional decision-making and control over resources, compared to the centralist orientation of KANU. Most Mijikenda welcomed the return to multi-party politics in the 1990s and the new conceptualization of majimboism as federalism.
8. This information is compiled from KHRC (1997: 19–21, 1998b: 56–9) and Muslims for Human Rights (2001).
9. Throughout Kwale District they damaged forty-three homes, 520 kiosks, thirteen shops, seventeen bars and restaurants, ten butcheries, and many vehicles (KHRC 1998b: 56–69).
10. Estimates are that a total of 100,000 people were displaced, and between 150 and 200 people were killed, most of whom were Kikuyu, Luo and Luhya (KHRC 1998b: 56).
11. With the exception of specific references, information in the paragraph is drawn from KHRC 1997, 1998b.
12. Government of Kenya 2001: 6.
13. 'Security Team Scours Hideouts', *Daily Nation*, 16 August 1997.
14. 'Six More Kwale Raiders Killed', *Daily Nation*, 3 November 1997.
15. Refer to Ciekawy (2004) for an analysis of the ways that movement leaders and its political supporters attempted to portray the oath givers as Mijikenda oathing authorities.
16. Refer to Kenyatta (1961), who considered oaths in pre-colonial Gikuyu society to encourage moral conduct and ensure justice. He argued that in Gikuyu court procedures, fear of the consequences of oaths discouraged people from giving false evidence, engaging in favouritism and taking bribes.
17. The many meanings of the oaths involved in the Mau Mau are addressed in Berman and Lonsdale (1992), Maloba (1998), and Maughan-Brown (1985).

18. The different kinds of Mau Mau oaths included the general one for the purpose of creating unity, the warrior oath or *Batuni* oath, and the more advanced oath that required the greatest commitment to the organization. The unity oath was administered widely for the purpose of developing political awareness among the population and encouraging their general support. The Batuni oath added to the general oath the promise to kill in support of the aims of the Mau Mau to recover lost land and act in raids against Europeans, loyalists and those who betrayed the Mau Mau organization (Berman and Lonsdale 1992; Maloba 1998).

19. Other laws specified that only oaths administered by state authorities were acceptable in state legal proceedings. The Oaths and Statutory Declarations Act of Kenya states that it is only in courts of law that persons can be lawfully examined, thereby distinguishing oaths under the statutes and oaths given in a customary or cultural setting (Mutungi 1977). Kenya's Criminal Procedure Code requires all witnesses in criminal cases to be examined under oaths administered by state officials.

20. In Kenyan history, oaths derived from cultural traditions also have been used in election campaigns. The Election Offences Act allows for the nullification of election results if there is proof that oaths were taken that required people to vote for a particular candidate (Mutungi 1977).

21. Gitlin's (1981) study focused on the Students for Democratic Society movement during the Vietnam War.

22. 'Security Team Scours Hideouts', *Daily Nation*, 16 August 1997.

23. Refer to Ciekawy (2004) for a discussion of the political patronage of oath administrators and the mythology surrounding Mzee Swaleh.

24. 'Eight Coast Raiders Killed', *Standard*, 3 November 1997.

25. 'Six More Kwale Raiders Killed', *Nation*, 3 November 1997.

26. 'Witchdoctor on Oathing Charge', *Daily Nation*, 3 October 1997.

27. In my conversations with *kaya* elders of Rabai held in 2000 and 2002, some *kaya* elders offered a critique of what they considered to be misrepresentations of their work in newspaper articles. Refer to Ciekawy (2004) for a discussion of some of these conversations.

28. 'Police Arrest Two over Coast Oathing Reports', *Standard*, 15 September 1997.

REFERENCES

Abugoa, J. B. and A. A. Mutere (1988), *The History of the Press in Kenya*. Nairobi: African Council on Communication Education.

Barnett, D. L. and K. Njama (1966), *Mau Mau from Within: An Analysis of Kenya's Peasant Revolt*. New York: Monthly Review Press.

Berman, B. and J. Lonsdale (1992), *Unhappy Valley: Conflict in Kenya and Africa*. Bks 1 and 2. London: James Curry.

Brantley, C. (1981), *The Giriama and Colonial Resistance in Kenya, 1800–1920*. Berkeley and Los Angeles: University of California Press.

Ciekawy, D. (1997a), 'Policing Religious Practice in Coastal Kenya'. *Political and Legal Anthropology Review* 20(1): 62–72.

— (1997b), 'Human Rights and State Power on the Kenya Coast: A Mijikenda Perspective on Universalism and Relativism'. *Humanity and Society* 21(2): 130–47.

— (1998), 'Witchcraft in Statecraft: Five Technologies of Power in Colonial and Postcolonial Coastal Kenya'. *African Studies Review* 42(2): 237–49.

— (2001), 'Utsai as Ethical Discourse: A Critique of Power from Mijikenda in Coastal Kenya'. In George C. Bond and Diane Ciekawy (eds), *Dialogues of Witchcraft: Anthropological and Philosophical Exchanges*. Athens: Ohio University Press, pp. 158–89.

— (2004), 'Oathing, Deoathing and Faux Oathing; The 1997 Crisis in Coastal Kenya'. Paper presented at the conference on Traditional Accountability and Modern Governance in Africa, Durham, UK, July 5–7.

— (2006), 'Party Politics and the Control of Harmful Magic: Moral Entrepreneurship during the Independence Era in Coastal Kenya'. In James Kiernan (ed.), *The Power of the Occult in Modern Africa: Continuity and Innovation in the Renewal of African Cosmologies*. Berlin: Lit, pp. 126–52.

— (2009), 'Oaths in African Societies'. In V. Y. Mudimbe (ed.), *Encyclopedia of Religion and Philosophy in Africa*. Rotterdam: Kluwer.

Gertzel, C. (1974), *The Politics of Independent Kenya, 1963–1968*. Nairobi: East African Publishing House.

Gitlin, T. (1981), *The Whole World Is Watching: Mass Media and the Making and Unmaking of the New Left*. Berkeley and Los Angeles: University of California Press.

Goffman, E. (1974), *Frame Analysis: An Essay on the Organization of Experience*. New York: Harper and Row.

Government of Kenya (2001), *Judicial Commission of Inquiry into Tribal Clashes in Kenya. Part II, Coastal Kenya*. Hon. Justice A. M. Akiwumi, Chairperson.

Grignon, F., M. Rutton and A. Mazrui (2001), 'Observing and Analyzing the 1997 General Elections: An Introduction In M. Rutten, A. Mazrui and F. Grignon (eds), *Out for the Count: The 1997 General Elections and Prospects for Democracy in Kenya*. Kampala: Fountain, pp. 242–73.

Kadhi, J. and M. Rutten (2001), 'The Kenyan Media in the 1997 General Elections: A Look at the Watchdogs'. In M. Rutten, A. Mazrui and F. Grignon (eds), *Out for the Count: The 1997 General Elections and Prospects for Democracy in Kenya* Kampala: Fountain, pp. 242–73.

Kenya Human Rights Commission (KHRC) (1997), *Kayas of Deprivation, Kayas of Blood: Violence, Ethnicity and the State in Coastal Kenya*.

— (1998), *Kayas Revisited: A Post-election Balance Sheet*.

— (1998a), *Killing the Vote: State Sponsored Violence and Flawed Elections in Kenya*.

Kenyatta, J. (1961), *Facing Mount Kenya: The Tribal Life of the Gikuyu*. London: Secker and Warburg.

Maloba, W. O. (1998), *Mau Mau and Kenya: An Analysis of Peasant Revolt*. Bloomington: Indiana University Press.

Maughan-Brown, D. (1985), *Land, Freedom and Fiction: History and Ideology in Kenya*. London: Zed Books.

Mazrui, A. (2001), 'Ethnic Voices and Trans-ethnic Voting: The 1997 Elections at the Kenya Coast'. In M. Rutten, A. Mazrui and F. Grignon (eds), *Out for the Count: The 1997 General Elections and Prospects for Democracy in Kenya* Kampala: Fountain, pp. 275–95.

Mudimbe, V. Y. (1988), *The Invention of Africa: Gnosis, Philosophy, and the Order of Knowledge*. Bloomington: Indiana University Press.

— (1994), *The Idea of Africa*. Bloomington: Indiana University Press.

Muslims for Human Rights (MUHURI) (2001), *Abandoned to Terror: Woman and Violence at the Kenyan Coast.* Published with the Kenya Human Rights Commission.

Mutungi, O. (1977), *The Legal Aspects of Witchcraft in East Africa.* Nairobi: East African Literature Bureau.

Ochieng, P. 1992. *I Accuse the Press: An Insider's View of the Media and Politics in Africa.* Nairobi: Initiatives.

Ochilo, P. J. O. (1993), 'Press Freedom and the Role of the Media in Kenya'. *Africa Media Review* 7(3): 19–33.

Parkin, D. (1972), *Palms, Wine, and Witnesses.* San Francisco: Chandler.

— (1991), *The Sacred Void: Spatial Images of Work and Ritual among the Giriama of Kenya.* Cambridge: Cambridge University Press.

Spear, T. (1978), *The Kaya Complex.* Nairobi: Kenya Literature Bureau.

Throup, D. and C. Hornsby (1998), *Multi-party Politics in Kenya.* Oxford: James Currey.

Wanyande, P. (1995), 'Mass Media State Relations in Kenya'. *Africa Media Review* 9:1–20.

Willis, J. (1993), *Mombasa, the Swahili, and the Making of the Mijikenda.* Oxford: Clarendon Press.

V.Y. Mudimbe

EPILOGUE: IN THE NAME OF SIMILITUDE

Ideo iuravi in ira mea, non introibunt in requiem meam.

Ps. 94

I

'I lie, I speak', such is the beginning of 'La pensée du dehors', by Michel Foucault, published in a 1966 issue of *Critique*. To apprehend the singularity of contemporary fiction, and to think of this fiction in its own right, instead of claiming to relate it to an absolute truth, the French philosopher invokes the old argument of Epimenides about a liar. Charles Manson, in interviews conducted by Neul Emmons and transcribed in *Manson in His Own Words* (1988), said: 'The more I speak, the more I lie; the less I speak, the less I lie.' Manson's rapport with Epimenides' liar (who expresses a truthful statement when stating it to be a lie) seems obvious. Its submission to the classical decoding elaborated by Foucault, on the speaking grammatical subject versus the object spoken about, also goes without saying.

What is less visible, at least immediately, is the deviation that the statement actualizes. In Epimenides as well as in Manson's self-judgement, the acting subject, who is also the cognitive subject, separates itself from the object of cognition, and makes any observer wonder whether the whole exercise might not be sheer fiction.

As a result, one no longer knows where to look for a credible, well trained, moral subject, and demurs at the suggestion of any responsible performer bearing witness to the truthfulness of an activity. One understands then how, deducing a lesson from Epimenides' paradox, Foucault could hypothesize that the speech of a speech leads us through literature, but perhaps also through other paths, to this outside where the speaking subject disappears.

In confronting the allegory of the African 'exodus' as is represented by the years since Nehru spoke in Bandung in 1955 and up to the present, I thought that I could emphasize its dramatic significance by rephrasing

Foucault's astonishment about the modernity of the Epimenides effect. In the 1950s and 1960s, contemporary with the Bandung project and often blinded by it, and judgemental of measures by an international economy that in the subsequent years would marginalize its alterity and folklorize it in a more efficient manner than during the colonial rule, the discourse of an African difference surges, combative and perplexing at the same time. From the outset, it is multiple, diversified in competing theories. Heterodox, these theories are often framed by reflectors and schools of thought which are generally mainstream, and whose intellectual and spiritual genealogies are stable, good mirrors of humanist assumptions and values. Self-referential, these theories are conceptualized and expressed frequently in foreign languages, and addressed primarily to a non-African audience. Insurrectionary, they are testimonies for the promotion of a human condition and its particular interpretations, but within the historicity they claim to challenge. From these qualities they derive their outsidedness. These theories for an African difference are an exegesis on an organism and its contrivances in a teleological history, its discursive procedures and the variety of its postulations.

There is, first, the process of temporalizing the organism as an object of knowledge in a retrojecting *parole* caught between an alienated present and its invented glorious antecedent achievements. The technique is well magnified in the fantastic constructions of Cheik Anta Diop, the Senegalese nuclear physicist who, in the 1950s, turned cultural anthropologist and historian of pharaonic Egypt.

There is, second, the demand of expressing one's own concrete existential experience and its humanity, and translating it into the language of a 'will to truth', expecting it to be a truthful discourse for oneself; and discovering that, by the logic of its own requirements, such a discourse, true or false, is also and necessarily a discourse for others. The best illustration of this might well be the indigenization of Marxism in the African socialisms of Léopold Sédar Senghor in Senegal and Julius Nyerere in Tanzania. In the same way, Anta Diop's Afrocentrist theory in what it negates or affirms about racial identity, automatically obligates its own validation or rejection in the intermediation of an *alter*. From its relation to the abstraction of an inclusive order, the Afrocentrist theory could be compared analogically to a unit of connectionist networks with learning abilities. The validity of Afrocentrist propositions may seem controversial, and its postulates criticized or disputed, but what they stimulate does not necessarily take to the streets against capitalism.

Finally, there is a third extasis, a most telling allegory about the subject and its potential multiplication. In a critical self-detachment, the subject cannot but identify with a tension between two polarities, the thinking subject (I) and the direct object of thought (me). Indeed, the veracity of this divided-self withstands the very limits of reason. The best of contemporary

African practices in philosophy bears witness to the rigour of such an exercise. In its proximity, one would readily integrate explorations in regional psychodynamics and the extraordinary patience of the work of Frantz Fanon. Somewhere in a gradually opposite direction and concerned with the fate of the city, the political discourse, faithful or treacherous, appears as a fold of something else: of the mute estrangement of millions of people who cannot assume their own subjugation as that which is first contained by their own polarities, a self and a for-others, and then empirically submitted to external determinations.

How is one to comment about that discourse without apprehending oneself as imprisoned in bad faith?

As students of a recent history of an unintentionally engineered major economic imbalance and its manifestations, probably an effect of a possibly widespread trained incapacity, we document it as a history of not-so-rational procedures determining the present conditions of the African presence in the world. The journey through decolonization is not a negation of the Western journey through economic time. Metaphorized on a scholastic table of logical relations, summarized and reduced to what they might analogically express, the African theories could stand, from the arrangement of the traditional square of opposed propositions, as universal or particular, affirmative or negative, and, depending on their reference, as contrary or subcontrary, subaltern or contradictory. Moreover, one could find thematics of conversion or obversion, contraposition or inversion. Conversion, in alterity theories, is generally understood as a simple interchange of the first concept, replacing the West and its virtues with a new historical subject, Africa. In this sense, conversion cannot be confused with its technical usage in logic. Obversion, the most commonly encountered thematic, administers the clearest operative value, closer to its canon in logic, namely the counterpart of a proposition obtained by exchanging its affirmative quality for the negative, or the negative for the affirmative, and then negating the predicate.

It is from this background that, situated vis-à-vis imperial power and its justifications in the colonial library, Aimé Césaire's *Discours sur le colonialisme* (1995), Kwame Nkrumah's *I Speak of Freedom* (1964) and *Towards Colonial Freedom* (1962), or Julius Nyerere's *Freedom and Unity* (1968) are said to have obverted the colonial ideology. Strictly speaking, conversion and obversion, as well as inversion (to which they are sometimes surreptitiously assimilated), function habitually as devices for restraining or tempering the quality of propositions. Their usage in African political discourse rarely qualifies as technical. They can also be perceived in roles of screening the convenience of statements – in titles for instance. Thus, to use the language of semioticians, along with other signals, they might unveil in a 'genetic ritual', the implicit train which, thanks to discreet marks, encodes the nature of a course to be pursued. A simple presentation of tables of contents from

two recent anthologies illustrates well how, through a simple thematic order-
ing and the authority of proper nouns, a genetic ritual proceeds in instruct-
ing theories of difference, and gives relatively clear glimpses about their
perspectives in fellowships of discourse.

A. *African Philosophy Reader* (P. H. Coetzee and A. P. J. Roux, eds, 2002)
  1. *Discourse on Africa* (Mogobe B. Ramose, Emevwo Biakolo, Kwasi
     Wiredu, F. Abiola Irele, Ngugi wa Thiong'o, H. Ocera Oruka, Tsenay
     Serequeberhan, Steve B. Biko, Issiaka P. Laleye)
  2. *Trends in African Philosophy* (Moya Deacon, F. Abiola Irele, H. Ocera
     Oruka, Paulin J. Hountondji, Lucius Outlaw)
  3. *Metaphysical Thinking in Africa* (Lebisa J. Teffo and Abraham P. J. Roux,
     Segun Gbadegesin, Godwin S. Sogolo, Olusegun Oladipo, Chukwudum B.
     Okolo)
  4. *Epistemology and the Tradition in Africa* (Didier N. Kaphagawani and
     Jeanette G. Malherbe, Mogobe B. Ramose, Kwasi Wiredu, Godwin G.
     Sogolo, Subairi B. Nasseem)
  5. *Morality in African Thought* (Pieter H. Coetzee, Kwasi Wiredu, Kwame
     Gyeke, Mogobe B. Ramose, Musambi Malongi Ya-Mona)
  6. *Race and Gender* (Jennifer R. Wilkinson, Gail M. Presbey, Kwame Anthony
     Appiah, Oyeronke Oyewumi, Uma Narayan, Emmanuel C. Eze)
  7. *Justice and Restitution in African and Political Thought* (Mogobe B. Ramose,
     Paulin J. Hountondji, Ibbo Mandaza, Eghosa E. Osaghae, Ali A. Mazrui)
  8. *Africa in the Global Context* (Pieter H. Coetzee, D. A. Masolo, M. F. Murobe,
     Howard McGary, Wole Soyinka, Mogobe B. Ramose)
B. *Postcolonialisms* (Gaurav Desai and Supriya Nair, eds, 2005)
  1. *Ideologies of Imperialism* (Christopher Columbus, Edmund Burke,
     Frederick Lugard)
  2. *The Critique of Colonial Discourse* (Aimé Césaire, Roberto Fernandez
     Retamar, Edward W. Said, Linda Tuhiwai Smith)
  3. *The Politics of Language and Literary Studies* (Thomas Babington Macaulay,
     Alexander Crummell, Ngugi wa Thiong'o, Carolyn Cooper)
  4. *Nationalisms and Nativisms* (Léopold Sédar Senghor, Chinweizu,
     Onwuchekwa Jemie, and Ihechukwu Madubuike, Frantz Fanon, Paul
     Gilroy)
  5. *Hybrid Identities* (Octave Mannoni, Derek Walcott, Homi Bhabha, Jean
     Bernabé, Patrick Chamoiseau and Raphael Confiant, Jana Sequoya)
  6. *Genders and Sexualities* (Leila Ahmed, Oyeronke Oyewumi, Gayatri
     Chakravorty Spivak, Timothy S. Chin)
  7. *Reading the Subaltern* (Ranajit Guha, David Lloyd, John Beverly, Nicholas
     Thomas)
  8. *Comparative (Post) colonialisms* (US Congress, Amy Kaplan, Pal Ahluwalia,
     David Chioni Moore)
  9. *Globalization and Postcoloniality* (Stuart Hall, Arif Dirlik, Rey Chow, Simon
     Gikandi)

The two lists of essay themes bring to light the *Weltanschaungen* they reflect
as explanations of differences in time and in space. Along with the dispositions suggested in the deviation between the language of philosophy and that
of the political, and the figures which, in the 1950s and 1960s, were facing

the two opposing models – of capitalism versus communism – I would like
to advance a number of hypotheses that might clarify this meditation and
suggest how we should revisit an alterity, the African, and what it means to
address it as an allegory of an exodus that I shall define as, simply a quest
for an exit from hell. Of course, the allegory of exodus has a biblical connection, as is evident from the Latin quotation from Psalm 94, which introduced this text. The verse refers to the biblical 'exodus'. It speaks of forty
years in the desert, the decimation of a whole generation, the act of a vin-
dictive deity: *Ideo turavi in ira mea, non introibunt in requiem meam*: 'In reality,
I did swear in my anger, they will not enter into my peace.' I should state that
in writing this paper, another arbitration was guiding the trail of my wan-
derings – Descartes' metaphor of the traveller lost in a forest.

II

The two tables of contents just presented bear witness to our time and our
questions about how we reflect on marginalized alterities. In what they
reproduce as histories and organize as knowledge, they also testify as
indefinite commentaries on an overused figure of our humanity, which says
it well, 'you give me your body and I shall inscribe on it the laws of our tribe'.
Further, they suscitate a number of specific paths for discerning a number
of lessons about a 'will to truth' and our condition in a shrinking world. A
way of summarizing some of the most important problems raised by the two
tables would be to outline a few of their boundaries.

Firstly, a critical awareness symbolized Nehru's 1955 non-alignment
principle and its validation in a critical autobiography, *Toward Freedom*
(1941). It identifies with an explicit statement, the sign of an ideal, and the
political measure of an intention. Since then, this book has been producing
rhetorics of routinized values. Nehru chose an uncomfortable position
between two forms of hubris, and rather than submit to what they represented as sovereignty in truth, he valorized a form of sublimation extolling
to the skies an exacting consciousness cognizant of its own suspension
between two conflicting mythologies of truth. The gesture did not secure all
the creative paths it projected, and somehow it still exceeds them. The will
to truthfulness in Nehru's testimony is signified in some exegeses whose
entries on the tables of contents connect chains of meanings about political
existence and human limits. They comment on the evidence of being an
inscribed entity, frequently using the metaphors of the machine and the
body, although the subject of the metaphor is always at cross-purposes with
the mechanical or the biological framework they inform. Within the determinations of these models, the whole of our condition seems regulated by
arrangements of control over historical distinctions which, as conceptuali-
ties, appear to be transcultural: false vs true, bad vs good, ugly vs beautiful.

From these distinctions, our heritages of different discursive economies translate in a variety of cultural experiences – ways of knowing, behaving, and seeing. On the other hand, a very simple reading of the historicities and their articulations presented in these readings divides us even more. Should we proceed with the task of interrogating and generalizing what, in his meditative reflection, Paul Ricoeur called *Le Conflit des interprétations* (1969)? Yet there is a dialogical intimation in evocations from today's interconnectedness that might unmask ways for going beyond our conflictual narratives of genesis and the interposition of their disciplinary axioms about our supposedly irreconcilable identity histories and politics. Duty might be a matter of individual liberty and choice on a course of moral response and behaviour. The problem was already well addressed by Kant, and inscribed in the connections existing between moral action, moral law and loving my neighbour, my enemy. For instance, in *The Black Image in the White Mind: Media and Race in America* (2000), Robert M. Entman and Andrew Rojecki unveil interacting forces in ordinary conversations as they are reclaimed in American mainstream culture, their influences in terms of needs and limitations, and how all this is related to evolving economics of media industries, themselves shaped by new technology, global market competition and government policy decisions. Thus, against any dream of authenticity in assertions of 'I ought', one faces the objective fascinations of the communication industry as well as the exigencies for personal growth in conflict with economic expectations as orchestrated through media content, both news and entertainment. The whole issue of a structured alienation within the atmosphere created by the present global economy and culture topologizes a racial figure in 'black and white' as a palimpsest. This work confines to a political awareness an unstable creation supposedly unaffected by properties invested on it in a history of inequalities. In the movement, the operation transforms the process into its worst traumatic fear about diversity. In effect, beyond the legibility of traces given to a 'racial' consciousness, the operating act might obliterate what it makes visible – the confusing anxiety of knowing that a denial possibly covers the evidence, namely that the constructed figure in 'black and white' is just a simple entry to the infinite ways of existing in the complexity of the world today.

Second, it is certain that such a perspective on alterities and differences transliterates our beings as lack, defining our anxieties and motivating them through regional definitions expounded by reality, and processing them into neurotic and moral narratives of our defence mechanisms. What better perspective to refer to, and in which to collapse both the mechanical and the biological models about the machine or the organism we are supposed to be?

Anyway, despite Nehru's suspension of the usefulness of what we have inherited from Marx as a lesson about the dialectic of the infrastructure and superstructures, how could one ignore the correlations between processes of production and social relations; organization of power, political discourse, and social classes; and how they operate diversely in different societies, in different periods? From contemporary prodigality and an extravagant diffuseness of conjectures, no third-world intellectual can choose to ignore deductions about our common future-oriented present as they are clinically interrogated by Antonio Negri and Michael Hardt in *Multitude* (2004), and Gayatri Chakravorty Spivak's work on alienation, particularly her recent *Critique of Post-Colonial Reason: Toward a History of the Vanishing Present* (1999). Would it be useless to consider the intellectual pertinence of this orientation, insofar as its warnings might allow a way of transcending, at least theoretically, the contradictions of an argument, political liberalism fails qua global theory, and help to formulate the real quandary of any organism defined as an abstraction by the rules of contemporary transactions which contain it in over mystified systems of productivity?

Third, on the procedures exercised on the organism, normalizing principles and terminology lists conceived and stretched in the name of a diversity, the major issue appears to be about an abstract and constrictive 'law' articulating criteria for distinguishing the 'normal' from the 'pathological' and the 'developed' versus the 'underdeveloped'. (These days, 'underdeveloped' is relabelled 'developing', as a way of silencing the implicitly negative moral value of the original term.) If one agrees that the normal rationally takes precedence over its negation, genealogically it is the other way around, the normal always succeeding what it has normed, thus one admits the anteriority of the unexpected as what defines normalcy as a reference. Georges Canguilhem demonstrated in *Le Normal et le pathologique* (1966) how these constrictive figures establish the decrees of each other. Michel Foucault expanded the debate, and generalized a suspicion about the experience of axiomatic systems of classification, as well as the history of their privileges and their culturally derivative procedures for organizing systematology and systematics, or sciences of systems of knowledge and their constitution. For the study of 'differences' as 'alterities' or vice versa, his regulatory principles allowed him to qualify new objectives that could handle reversals, discontinuities and specificities in their own right. Now let us face the astonishment created in 1975 by the publication of an anthology that included contributions from renowned naturalists: *Ants, Indians, and Little Dinosaurs: A Celebration of Man and Nature for the 75th Anniversary of Natural History Magazine*. The collection celebrated a pluralization of knowledge and commendation of respect for all beings and things as comprising individually their own systems, with their own regulations and norms. It offered itself as a testimony on the diversity of the world and the richness of that diversity. In the conclusion of the book, significantly titled '*Vive la Différence*', Marston Bates, then a professor of zoology at the University of Michigan, dwells on the excesses of both the politics of uniformity and the politics of diversity. He echoes a collective preoccupation well signified in our shared experience of cultural aloneness and relatedness. Policies of diversity and normalization might be contributing to an excellent encyclopedia of ethnographic curiosities that itemizes domesticated habits as well as folklorized customs. Thus, for instance, among many from the anthology, there is a discussion of the 'missionary symptom', a manifestation of normalized sexuality of third-world converts to Christianity, and an exploration of the American fascination with 'the British skill in stashing peas in the mash potatoes on the back of the fork, held always in their left hand'. This paradox should bring us back to Kant's advice which, in its simplicity, might consign the highest criterion for solidarity and tolerance between dissimilar histories and cultures, that commonsense is what unites them, and 'madness', is that which prevents a necessary dialogue. But, as Bates observes: 'Commonsense. But whose, yours or mine? We can't all think alike – that would be uniformity instead of diversity. So let's argue – but let's not kill each other in the process.'

One way out of the paradox might be a return to the practicality of notions such as conversion, obversion and inversion, and their instrumentalization as operative images in transcultural solidarity dialogues. They can serve as connective concepts in allegories for reading differences and, against prejudice, from one region to another, accord possibilities of comparisons in illusions of identities. In their everyday acceptance within any 'we-community', it is certainly meaningful to invoke and designate the implications of their less technical understandings. Thus, conversion embodies, beyond a logical operation of permutation of terms, the complex mechanism through which repressed ideas, values or conflicts are expressed by a healthy organism in order to suscitate a change. On the other hand, obversion, or alteration of an appearance and its transformation into one of its alternatives, may be the closest figure to Hume's image of identity as flux. Finally, inversion has determinations that convey emulation-values in taking the roles of the opposite. The process permits anyone to be occasionally the minority to someone else's majority. In so doing, inversion combines and arranges into reassuring metaphors possible figuration activities of mutual toleration in what Will Kymlicka has dubbed a *Multicultural Citizenship* (1995).

III

I have invoked the power of Nehru's initiative in awakening consciousness. One could also refer to the compelling alternative of the so-called Asian 'miracle' in the global economy. The countries participating in that miracle symbolize vivid metaphors of fecund organisms and dedication against mechanically instituted cultures of delinquency. What they enunciate is also a principle at the time of action in the Third World, as the other side of

a consciousness inscribed in its own history of an alterity assumed and negotiated with other histories and cultures. From what such a horizon outlines,
the phrase Third World can productively substitute East Asia in this quotation from the philosopher Kok-Chor Tan's *Toleration, Diversity, and Global
Justice.*

> But while the student of international relations ignores issues of power, domina-
> tion, and nation-interests at his or her own peril, it is just as distorting and mis-
> leading to squeeze entire debates into a 'West against the Rest' framework, as
> many defenders of the East Asian position tend to do. This realist paradigm does
> not do justice to the complexity of international relations; it fails to see that foreign
> policies are motivated by different competing realist considerations as well as ide-
> alist (normative) ones. A constructive cross-cultural human rights dialogue can
> commence only if both parties set aside 'absolutist' frameworks – the West as
> imperialistic, the East as socially unprogressive – that have tended to poison the
> dialogue to date. And in this regard, to counter this (not entirely baseless) per-
> ception of liberalism, liberals have much work to do toward demonstrating the
> sincerity of their commitments to a better world. (Tan 2001: 145)

The quotation can be transmuted into a lesson about a competent usage of
statements in what, since Kant, it is customary to call a legal order of peace.
The enigma of any individuality reflecting itself to itself in an embodiment
of multiple histories (of family, community, people, and culture) unfolds in
what should be for everyone the burden of responsibility and freedom. Categorically, any individual should be acknowledged as unique: an *a priori*
alterity, which is simultaneously, *sui generis a posteriori*, an unabsorbable
person in the order of things. Yet what such an enigmatic alterity might
signify because it is an incommensurable experience in the world seems, in
the aesthetics and ethics of the media, almost always reducible to crisis-
capsules of today's global culture. In her *Compassion Fatigue*, Susan D.
Moeller remembers:

> Reporters love the word 'crisis', said Bernard Gwertzman, now editor of *The Times*
> on the web. But what makes a crisis? 'I don't have a definition', Gwertzman said,
> 'some things feel like a crisis and others don't. Stories traditionally are published
> or fronted or aired depending on the answers to a range of questions. *Timeless*:
> Did the event just happen? *Proximity*: How close is the event, physically and psy-
> chologically? *Prominence*: How many people have some knowledge or interest in
> the subject? *Significance*: How many people will (potentially) be affected by the
> event? *Controversy*: Is there conflict or drama? *Novelty*: Is the event unusual?
> *Currency*: Is the event part of an ongoing issue? If not, should people know?
> *Emotional appeal*: Is there humor, sadness, or a thrill? And when the medium is
> television, a final question looms: How good are the pictures? (Moeller 1995: 17)

The questions, in their specificity, are indicative of media procedures for
inventing beings and contexts of crisis. These should be empirically mar-
ketable. This means that the crisis phenomenon, whatever it is, should obey
very precise requirements. These would include consumers' preferences as

tabulated by market analyses; as well as the market value – an objective price at which it can be bought or sold. As a matter of fact, a media product (an advertisement, for instance, or coverage of an assassination, a natural disaster, or the New York celebration of New Year's Eve) has a market share, or the specific percentage of its sale during a particular time frame. The title of a book by Todd Gitlin, a New York University professor of sociology, captures well the spirit of this universe: *Media Unlimited: How the Torrent of Images and Sounds Overwhelms our Lives* (2001). Everything in the order of this culture can be equated to a product value in the marketplace, from basic commodities such as clothing and food to ideals of human brotherhood and interspecies cooperation. Among the items popularized recently, for instance, one might list: anger management in Scandinavian countries, laughter training in East Asia, sampling church services in the United States, virginity testing in South Africa, and assisted-death rituals in a number of countries. Contrary to what most of us might believe, however, capitalist market makers have an ethical grid of reference whose fundamentals were theoretically epitomized in an ill-known 1759 treatise of Adam Smith: *The Theory of Moral Sentiments* (2000). This thinker who, in his 1776 *The Wealth of Nations*, expounded the free market basics, was also a moralist preoccupied by connections between economic self-interest in the pursuit of happiness and a morally virtuous life. He saw a solution in a self-referential and individualistic conception, and put it clearly at the beginning of his ethics book:

> Every faculty in one man is the measure by which he judges of the like faculty in another. I judge of your sight by my sight, of your ear by my ear, of your reason by my reason, of your resentment by my resentment, of your love by my love. I neither have, nor can have, any other way of judging about them. (Smith 2000: 18)

The formula functions effectively in the contemporary normative economy. It can be coupled with the inequality and exploitation outputs predicated by its systemic application, thus lead to a necessary distinction between evils it produces. If one agrees that human dignity is, in principle at least, an evidential value-index in all cultures, to degrade or negate it qualifies as evil. And, in good method, one would then have to dissociate domains: the domain of a pre-moral evil that comprises inescapable limits as represented by natural catastrophes, disease, or death; the domain of a human engineered evil that is the result of an activity or a volition that diminishes human quality and value without a sufficient reason test, and, indeed, the intersecting area of the two domains. Surely, in today's global world, hunger, lack of education and poverty, for example, would not inevitably belong to the strict field of pre-moral evils.

IV

In 1976, inspired by Thomas Kuhn's *The Structure of Scientific Revolutions* (1962), Marilyn Ferguson published *The Aquarian Conspiracy: Personal and Social Transformation in Our Time* (1976). In it she affirmed the fact of a major alteration in the general configuration of contemporary individual lives and collective work – a major shift in organizational principles. The rupture, she wrote, could be characterized by some of its effects: confusion, dislocation, and uncertainty. A decade later, two businessmen, Don Tapscott and Art Caston, overtaxed the concept in *Paradigm Shift: The New Promise of Information Technology* (1993), using the term 'paradigm' to 'define a broad model, a framework, a way of thinking, or a scheme for understanding reality'. From the double awareness of an interdependency of nations and that which creates it, 'global telecommunications networks [that] energize the metabolism of world commerce and move us inexorably toward Marshall McLuhan's global village', they concentrated on four open paradigm shifts that would circumscribe a new global geography: (1) a geopolitical order, for a volatile multipolar world; (2) a networked information-based enterprise organization; (3) a business environment that is a qualified, competitive, and a dynamic marketplace; (4) a new technology conceived as user-centred, that is a network computing system with new goals for information technology.

Because media are businesses structured by agents, work organization and information frames, they are coherent elements of the new space. Through an economic necessity, these shifts would integrate all the countries of today's world into a global trading market. In consequence, their engineering policies, as well as technical performance, are dependent on a number of factors in an action-oriented architecture whose principles deduce specific rules. Among these are 'diversity', or the promotion of the most adapted types of information technology for a given purpose; 'interchangeability', or a way for maximizing performance; 'workstation orientation', or the best system for activating and delivering functionality; and finally, a 'network orientation' which, relying on the precedent principles, develops useful linkages for production. The whole machinery operates thanks to the efficient conjunction of determining rules-sets that I am rephrasing here while maintaining their definition from *Paradigm Shift* (1993). These include:

   (a) key-drivers of the new environment: productivity of knowledge, quality of
        service programmes, competent responsiveness, a twenty-four-hour global-
        ization activity, outsourcing of key areas for value-added capability, partner-
        ing, social responsibility;
   (b) an innovative computing network of information technology that Tapscott and
        Caston describe through eight 'critical shifts' from outmoded models: (1)

from traditional semiconductors to microprocessor-based systems; (2) from host-based to network-based systems; (3) from proprietary software to open software standards; (4) from single media forms to multimedia combining data, text, voice, and image; (5) from account-control to computerized vendor-customer partnerships based on free will; (6) from craft to factory in software development; (7) from alphanumeric interfaces to graphical, multi-form user-interfaces; (8) from stand-alone to integrated software applications;

(c) the principal condition for a successful implementation of this paradigm shift would reside in an original new type of leader. The new leaders should be managers of 'work-groups environments' and 'responsive organizational structures' who, instead of figuring themselves as 'information technology executives', view themselves as 'business executives'. This concept requires leaders to be managers of customers' expectations who are concurrently managers of enthusiasm, and focused on business results all the while.

This analysis of what the paradigm shift brings about reveals structurations of mechanisms and the general horizon of a globally oriented activity. They surely distinguish it from the recent past, and should one have to characterize such a deviation, one might consider testing some of the effects defining the new political economy as John Naisbitt, a specialist of mega trends, was projecting them in 1994 in his *Global Paradox*. One may quote the four main paradoxes he foresaw:

(a) the world's trends point overwhelmingly toward political independence and self-rule on the one hand, and the formation of economic alliances on the other
(b) the bigger the world economy, the more powerful its smallest players, and all the big players are getting smaller
(c) the study of the smallest economic player, the entrepreneur, is merging with the study of how the global economy works.
(d) Big companies are breaking up and becoming confederations of small, entrepreneurial companies in order to survive. (Naisbitt 1994: 56)

This presentation encompasses a number of problems related to the dialogical approach suggested by Kok-Chor Tan. It also suggests the intricate topographies deducible from our two anthologies' tables of contents. But how is one to exhaust significant topographies vis-à-vis the transformation described by Don Tapscott and Art Caston, and what might their model ignore, delay or repress? Before everything else, there is a demand: an interrogation about the meaning conveyed, which requires a hermeneutics of suspicion that could search for idols and strip away masks of a fabled reality.

Let me pinpoint, as clearly as possible, three accessible entries to such a debate. First, the abstract integrated environment of the new economic paradigm shift is a text on rational choice strategies for organizing a global economy in which interactions of capital, technology, work, and skills are strictly aimed at productivity. The product to be sold by the machinery does not really matter. It can incorporate any commodity, including news, knowledge, pestilence, even intelligence. Productivity depends on the machine's functions, inclusive of its internal capabilities for potential expansions through enterprise partnering, cross-licensing mechanisms, interchangeable standards, and so on. In brief, efficiency summons productivity and, thus, profits. But for whom, and corresponding to what needs? In any case, the new promise born of the synchronization of information technologies, in its explicit intention and policy, does not spell out its own complement, or the supplement of its self-preserving megalomanic productivity objectives. They can possibly prove to be a disservice to the interests of the subject.

Secondly, the paradigm-shift theory brings the other of modernity as a simple opportunity agent in its own mechanical structure of surplus-value productivity. The text of the paradigm defines its own normativity in terms of the efficiency of its functions, rules and significance; and thus, from this background, orders of all other collective experiences are to be subsumed as modalities in its exteriority and fused in the master narrative. A number of things should be noted here. They concern the self-referentiality of the topography. The arguments for adhering to the paradigmatic economy – say, third-world territories blending into the newly affirmed totality – are not negotiated, since these arguments supposedly coincide with the evidence of better conditions of existence. Subsequently, in integrable orders, enabling appropriate guidelines might provide concrete procedures for effective incorporation in the regulatory scheme, such as time management grids, computer-based learning tools, job diagnosis evaluation indices, well-tabulated resources for high performance, and the like. An overvaluation frames this new order, prescribing it to be the most advanced achievement of humankind. Its will to knowledge and to power came to be identified with both the will to truth and with an unconditional truth itself. Thus, most visibly during the last six centuries, the history of its anterior statements has been doubling the authority of the emergence of truth and all its possible relations to human experience. In this context, the convergence idea asserts the sovereignty of a model from widening data and the sciences, and legitimates the thesis of a correlation between economic determinations, their systems of values and a total history. Since the nineteenth century, this concern has expressed itself in the conjunction of a search for civilization's origins, its historical necessity and the primacy of its continuum. Such a hypothesis, translated into a justification, outlines convergence paradoxes and their multiple semantic lines of discussion. In one, pragmatists and realists have been debating whether the truth can be defined in terms of intersections, or in those of successive inter-approximating approaches. In another, theorists talk of a coordination in transformations that can accent compatibility between members of a variety of classes; giving rise to the concept of assimilation in evolution theories; or to social engineering, as in the case of French colonial doctrine, which attempted to colonize meaning in order to erase the differences and promote a core conformity. A third approach, found in political economy, is offered by the work of Jan Tinbergen and, in a special manner,

John Kenneth Galbraith, in his volume *The New Industrial State* (1967). These thinkers have been associated with economic convergence theory because of their belief in an intrinsic validity of capitalism over socialist models, and their demonstrations of the unifying effects of liberalism. From the constructed interference of disparate, often conflictual imports, no method in convergence theories has succeeded in answering George Cantor's question: what is the identifying nature of continuity that makes thinkable the convergence hypothesis? However, one should note that the same genealogical and structural characteristics, series and schemata validating the convergence hypothesis can objectively support the authority and verification of discrimination policies, including class and racial platforms. The relation to a cumulative combinatory table allows, in effect, inclusion or exclusion on the basis of value judgments bestowed on types of filiations.

Thirdly, and finally, the concepts of diversity and differentiation, with their several prongs, designate a host of strategies in the global economy's styles of expansion. Among them, one might distinguish internationalization programmes of a multinational company from the organization of global-scale activities of another company; or the planning capabilities for world-wide adapted interventions of a third one. Whether or not it makes sense, one would demark diversity in its most popular understanding, that is the quality of being different, from the strategic abilities to adapt, manage and exploit the knowledge and policies of an institution in international large-scale operations. On account of both its technical legitimacy and cultural imperatives, the diversity problem was taken up in *Managing Across Borders: The Transnational Solution* (1998), a comprehensive study by the Harvard business administration professor Christopher A. Bartlett, and the London Business School director of the Strategic Leadership Programme, Sumantra Ghoshal. For them, the reliability of the diversity concept can be related to both economic logic and cultural grammar, through three thematic mediations. First, a theoretical cadre analyzes the transnational in its specificity as an emerging model that transcends differences in a worldwide integrated reason; accordingly, this could be apprehended in the transnational's capability, challenge, and administrative heritage. Second, a discussion on the nature of the transnational would present its structural dispositions for building integrated networks, processes for multiple innovations and flexible roles. Finally, for the triumph of the transnational, a diversity symbol, the authors describe its capacity for varying flexible junctions, perspectives, character-qualities, cultural dynamic tasks; in sum, write Bartlett and Ghoshal, one could conjure up a biological analogy:

> Formal structure defines an organization's basic anatomy; systems and information flows shape its physiology; and culture and value represent its psychology. Change strategies that work through only one of these elements are less effective than those that address all three. (1998: 286)

This is the closest I have come to recognize, in a contending interpretation, the symbolic efficacy of a dynamic organism for imaging the life capacity of a socioeconomic ensemble. The metaphor might well duplicate the organic constitution of vital functions of the transnational as a body, yet without accosting what, in his book *Ética de la liberación en la edad de la globalización y la exclusión*, Enrique Dussel calls the 'material principle of a liberation ethics'. This refers to concrete rules for surviving and existing as a worthy human being in this newly organized global economy. Moreover, this material moment has a co-determining formal principle of 'truth' and 'validity' in an intersubjective community of dialogue. In any case, the beauty of the biological analogy in the 'transnational solution' could be affixed to another figure used by Don Tapscott and Art Caston in *Paradigm Shift*: 'software as art', and how a programme might become a 'symphony':

> We estimate, for example, that somewhere upward of 150 billion lines of code are written in an era I language called COBOL. Like a musical score for a symphony, a single mistake (one note in the second cello part) could mess up the entire program. Finding the mistake and fixing it is typically a major challenge, and (unlike a symphony) by changing the cello part you're likely to have a ripple effect that messes up the tuba. Moreover, the size of these intricate programs means that they take a long time to create. Like a symphony, the era I software composer could labour for years creating the work of art. Unfortunately, many software works are never completed – leaving many later-day Schuberts with at least one unfinished symphony to their credit. (1993: 167)

Art or not, the new international political economy articulates its textual reflexive systems within a history and, at the same time, formulates implicitly their rival methods, aims and objects. Nonetheless, the rationality of other, possibly divergent arguments, such as those designated in the entries of our two anthologies' tables of contents, belongs also to this same history? All these undertakings equally witness identical conditions of possibility. Yet in the contradictions diffused by all these text, (global liberal theories, and anthologized cultural statements), and echoed in multimedia, critical voices surge sometimes from what must be moral anxieties. From *In the Name of Humanity, Reflections on the Twentieth Century* (2001), here is the banality of a nineteenth-century lesson that still runs beneath efficiency and productivity paradigms, as it is rephrased by the French philosopher Alain Finkielkrut: 'for Marx, in effect, nothing is natural in either man or nature. Evil and suffering are socially constructed. They are not intrinsic to the human condition. Things are not things: they are social facts' (2000: 27). The conclusive statement at the end of Finkielkraut's reflections addresses the very heart of this meditation on Africa in theories of difference.

> Have we reconciled ourselves? In the name of diversity, worldwide webs are building a global society. Angelic, busy, and vigilant, their apostles believe they embody resistance to all acts of inhumanity. But to exchange old demons for new networks

of communication is to make a mistake. Beneath the edifying appearance of a primordial combat, information technology obscures the fact that friendship has disappeared into sentimentality, and mass tourism has erased traditional distinctions between near and far. This, in the end, is the worldwide victory of those who have succeeded in bringing together the same with the same over those seeking to build a common world with a shared idea of humanity, based on gratitude. Life goes on, things happen, but nothing seems exciting enough to change modern man. Feelings reign freely, and ideology is defeated – at least for the time being – but the new age has not conquered the empire of resentment. Has the twentieth century therefore been useless? (2000: 112)

To this powerful interrogation of our contemporary mythologies, why not add a word from John Kenneth Galbraith's *Journey Through Economic Time* (1984: 164): 'The sale of indulgences did not end with the church reform.' It is true, Galbraith was depicting a Third-World case of trained incapacity. Only?

V

With competing orders of difference in the interdependent political economies we are inhabiting today, basic commonsense might still be the most decent and reasonable option, despite its precariousness. The media have an immense responsibility here for accenting our trained capacity or incapacity. Indeed, alterity and difference, as well as the theories they suscitate, have become a business in the ordinary sense of the word. Their relation to human dignity seems to depend, more and more, on calculations of actual or symbolic investments. As a consequence, why not, in the name of good faith, suspend judgements and, independently from normative grids of political economy and the validity of their inferences, simply acknowledge human challenges as they are signified in our conflictual conversations and allegories? Demonstrations of absolute and definitive rulings, in terms of truth and falsity, are probably always relative to something else. I personally choose not to qualify any affirmation or negation made in good faith as an error, a failure or a sin; but instead, each time, as an unexpected response on a progressive quest, approximating not a truth, but a more truthful expression of a need.

REFERENCES

Bartlett, Christopher A. and Sumantra Ghoshal (1998), *Managing Across Borders: The Transnational Solution*. Boston, MA: Harvard Business School Press.

Bates, Marston (1975), '*Vive la Différence*'. In *Ants, Indians, and Little Dinosaurs: A Celebration of Man and Nature for the 75th Anniversary of Natural History Magazine*. New York: Scribners.

Canguilhem, Georges (1966), *Le Normal et le pathologique*. Dordrecht, Holland: D. Reidel, Publishing.

Césaire, Aimé (1950), *Discours sur la colonialism*. Paris: Reclame.

Coetzee, P. H., and A. P. J. Roux (eds) (2002), *An African Philosophy Reader*. London: Routledge.

Desai, Gaurav and Supriya Nair (eds) (2005), *Postcolonialisms: An Anthology of Cultural Theory and Criticism*. New Brunswick, NJ: Rutgers University Press.

Dussel, E. (1998), *Ética de la liberación en la edad de la globalización y la exclusión*. Madrid: Editorial Trotta.

Emmons, Nuel (1988), *Manson In His Own Words*. New York: Grove.

Entman, Robert M. and Andrew Rojecki (2000), *The Black Image in the White Mind: Media and Race in America*. Chicago: Chicago University Press.

Ferguson, Marilyn (1976), *The Aquarian Conspiracy: Personal and Social Transformation in Our Time*. New York: St Martins Press.

Finkielkraut, Alain (2000), *In the Name of Humanity: Reflections on the Twentieth Century*. New York: Columbia University Press.

Foucault, Michel (1966), 'La pensée du dehors'. *Critique* no. 229.

Gitlin, Todd (2001), *Media Unlimited: How the Torrent of Images and Sounds Overwhelms Our Lives*. New York: Metropolitan Books.

Galbraith, John Kenneth (1967), *The New Industrial State*. Boston: Houghton Mifflin.

— (1984), *A Journey Through Economic Time*. Boston: Houghton Mifflin.

Kuhn, Thomas (1962), *The Structure of Scientific Revolutions*. Chicago: Chicago University Press.

Kymlicka, Will (1995), *Multicultural Citizenship*. Oxford: Clarendon Press.

Moeller, Susan D. (1995), *Compassion Fatigue*. London: Routledge.

Naisbitt, John (1994), *Global Paradox*. New York: W. Morrow.

Negri, Antonio and Michael Hardt (2004), *Multitude*. New York: Penguin.

Nehru, Jawaharlal (1941), *Toward Freedom*. New York: John Day.

Nkrumah, Kwame (1962), *Towards Colonial Freedom*. London: Panaf.

— (1964), *I Speak of Freedom*. New York: Praeger.

Nyerere, Julius (1968), *Freedom and Unity*. London: Oxford University Press.

Ricoeur, Paul (1969), *Le Conflit des Interprétations*. Paris: Editions de Seuil.

Smith, Adam (2000), *The Theory of Moral Sentiments*. Amherst, NY: Prometheus.

Spivak, Gayatri Chakravorty (1999), *Critique of Post-Colonial Reason: Toward a History of the Vanishing Present*. Boston, MA: Harvard University Press.

Tan, Kok-Chor (2001), *Toleration, Diversity, and Global Justice*. University Park, PA: Pennsylvania State University.

Tapscott, Don and Art Caston (1993), *Paradigm Shift: The New Promise of Information Technology*. McGraw Hill.

INDEX